PREACHING CHRIST FROM ECCLESIASTES

PREACHING CHRIST FROM ECCLESIASTES

Foundations for Expository Sermons

SIDNEY GREIDANUS

WILLIAM B. EERDMANS PUBLISHING COMPANY

GRAND RAPIDS, MICHIGAN / CAMBRIDGE, U.K.

Published 2010 by
Wm. B. Eerdmans Publishing Co.
2140 Oak Industrial Drive N.E., Grand Rapids, Michigan 49505 /
P.O. Box 163, Cambridge CB3 9PU U.K.
www.eerdmans.com

Printed in the United States of America

16 15 14 13 12 11 10   7 6 5 4 3 2 1

Library of Congress Cataloging-in-Publication Data

Greidanus, Sidney, 1935-
Preaching Christ from Ecclesiastes: foundations for expository sermons /
Sidney Greidanus.
p.   cm.
Includes bibliographical references and indexes.
ISBN 978-0-8028-6535-9 (pbk.: alk. paper)
1. Bible. O.T. Ecclesiastes — Sermons — Outlines, syllabi, etc.
2. Bible. O.T. Ecclesiastes — Criticism, interpretation, etc.
3. Jesus Christ.   I. Title.

BS1475.54.G74   2010

223′.8077 — dc22

2010006437

To our grandchildren:
Jeremy & Julie, Jeffrey, Cara & Peter, and Caitlin
Zachari, Anna, and Jessica, and
Mikayla, Solomon, and Katherine

May the "goads and nails" (Ecclesiastes 12:11)
of the Teacher's wisdom
provide direction, stability, and security for your lives.

Contents

Contents

Contents

Preface

In 1976, while a pastor in Delta, British Columbia, I preached a series of sermons on Ecclesiastes. After hearing one of these theocentric sermons, a retired pastor approached me and said, "I appreciated your sermon, Sid, but could a rabbi have preached your sermon in a synagogue?" I was dumbfounded by the question, but it set me to thinking about the issue of Christocentric preaching. Of course, a rabbi and I have the Old Testament in common. Moreover, since wisdom is a reflection on "customary 'orders' in the world" (see Chapter 1), the message of wisdom literature would be the same for the church as for the synagogue. So yes, a rabbi could have preached that sermon in a synagogue without causing offense. But if that was the case, had I preached an "Old Testament sermon" instead of a "Christian sermon"?[1] Should not my sermons on Old Testament passages reflect that these passages now function in the context of the New Testament? Should not the sermons of Christian preachers be distinctively Christian?

Some twenty years later I had the opportunity to research this question in depth. The result was the book *Preaching Christ from the Old Testament: A Contemporary Hermeneutical Method.* I concluded that sermons based on Old Testament passages cannot merely be theocentric sermons but must be Christocentric. The Church Fathers knew this well but unfortunately adopted allegorical interpretation to accomplish the Christocentric focus. For example,

---

1. This is Edmund Clowney's profound distinction: "The Christian proclamation of an Old Testament text is not the preaching of an Old Testament sermon." *Preaching and Biblical Theology* (Grand Rapids: Eerdmans, 1961), 75. Cf. Graeme Goldsworthy, *Preaching the Whole Bible as Christian Scripture: The Application of Biblical Theology to Expository Preaching* (Grand Rapids: Eerdmans, 1988), 195: "The ultimate concern of the preacher should be to preach the meaning of the text in relation to the goal of all biblical revelation, the person and work of Christ. Can I maintain my integrity as a Christian preacher if I preach a part of the Bible as if Jesus had not come?"

they preached the frequent refrain in Ecclesiastes to enjoy eating and drinking as partaking of the Lord's body and blood in the Eucharist. And Ambrose, preaching on "a threefold cord is not quickly broken" (Eccl 4:12), linked it to the Trinity.[2] Today we can no longer with integrity use allegorical interpretation to obtain Christocentric interpretation. Applied to genres other than allegory, allegorical interpretation is arbitrary and subjective; it subverts the intention of the biblical author.

But how, then, does one preach Christ from wisdom literature which does not contain a promise of the coming Messiah and only rarely a type of Christ? Especially with wisdom literature in mind, I broadened the definition of preaching Christ. The common definition is to preach the person and/or work of Christ. Since the work of Christ is frequently restricted to the atonement, I broadened the definition of preaching Christ by adding the category of the *teaching* of Christ. Jesus himself highlighted the importance of his teaching when he said, "If you continue in my word [teaching], you are truly my disciples" (John 8:31). He underscored the significance of his teaching when he sent out his followers with the mandate: "Go . . . make disciples of all nations, baptizing them . . . , and teaching them to obey everything that I have commanded you" (Matt 28:19-20). Subsequently, John writes, "Everyone who does not abide in the teaching of Christ, but goes beyond it, does not have God; whoever abides in the teaching has both the Father and the Son" (2 John 9). Hence I defined "preaching Christ" as "preaching sermons which authentically integrate the message of the text with the climax of God's revelation in the person, work, and/or teaching of Jesus Christ as revealed in the New Testament."[3]

Based on my study of the New Testament and church history, I concluded that there are seven legitimate ways to move from an Old Testament message to

---

2. Longman, *Book of Ecclesiastes*, 30-31. Svend Holm-Nielsen, "On the Interpretation of Qoheleth in Early Christianity," *VT* 24/2 (1974) 175, states: "Hieronymus' understanding of Qohelet is based on the same principles as his interpretation of Biblical texts . . . in the Old Testament . . . , the *interpretatio literalis* and the *interpretatio spiritualis*. But it should be remembered that the *spiritualis* . . . is equal to a Christological interpretation." Even today preachers are tempted to use allegorical interpretation to preach Christ from Ecclesiastes. For example, Parsons, "Guidelines," *BSac* 160 (2003) 300, mentions a wedding sermon where the threefold cord of Ecclesiastes 4:12 was preached as the bride, the groom, and Christ. Cf. Matthew Henry and Thomas Scott, *Commentary on the Holy Bible*, Vol. 3 (Grand Rapids: Baker, 1960 reprint), p. 413: "Two together are a three-fold cord; where two are closely joined in holy love and fellowship, Christ will by his Spirit come to them, and make the third, as he joined himself to the two disciples going to Emmaus; then there is a threefold cord that can never be broken." Preachers have also preached the passage about sending out your bread upon the waters (Eccl 11:1) as sending out Christ, the Bread of Life, upon the waters (see Percy P. Stoute, "Bread upon the Waters," *BSac* 107 [1950] 223).

3. Greidanus, *Preaching Christ from the Old Testament*, 10.

Jesus Christ in the New Testament. They are redemptive-historical progression, promise-fulfillment, typology, analogy, longitudinal themes, New Testament references, and contrast. Depending on the text, preachers can use one or more of these ways to preach Christ.

I have written this book primarily for preachers, seminary students, and Bible teachers. My aim is to encourage and help busy preachers and teachers proclaim the messages of Ecclesiastes. This book will enable them to uncover rather quickly the important building-blocks for producing sermons and lessons from Ecclesiastes: the literary unit which is the preaching text; the message for Israel (the textual theme); the response sought from Israel and by analogy from the church today (the goal); the various ways of linking the textual theme to Jesus Christ in the New Testament; the sermon theme and goal; and relevant biblical exposition of all verses in the passage.

Preachers may wish to use this book to preach a series of sermons on Ecclesiastes. I suggest a series of seven sermons on the first half of Ecclesiastes (1:1–6:9) to be followed later by a series of seven sermons on the second half (6:10–12:8) plus one on the Epilogue (12:9-14). Or one can opt for three series of five sermons each. Bible teachers may wish to work their way through Ecclesiastes in fifteen lessons, assigning to their students only the reading of the "Sermon Exposition" section of each chapter.

Readers will notice that I follow the same basic pattern for each passage. This pattern is based on the ten steps from text to sermon I developed for first-year seminary students (see Appendix 1). The resulting repetition in each chapter is intended to inculcate a basic hermeneutical-homiletical approach to the biblical text. First we seek to identify the boundaries of the literary unit and check its context. Next we analyze important literary features that help us sketch the structure (flow) of the text. After noting where and how the text speaks of God, we seek to formulate the textual theme and goal. With this theme in mind, we can brainstorm how each of the seven roads could possibly lead from this text's message to Jesus Christ in the New Testament. At that point we are ready to formulate the sermon theme, goal, and need addressed (the problem, the target) and consider the sermon form. I conclude each chapter with a major section on "Sermon Exposition."

In this "Sermon Exposition" section I seek to provide a model for the sermon by using oral style[4] as much as possible and giving the verse reference *be-*

---

4. Oral style is marked, among other characteristics, by short sentences, active voice, short but vivid words, strong nouns and verbs, concrete language, narration in the present tense, verse references before the quotation, use of questions to involve the hearers, use of gender-inclusive language without distracting the hearers, and use of repetition and parallelism. See Mark Galli and Craig Brian Larson, *Preaching That Connects: Using the Techniques of Journalists to Add Impact to Your Sermons* (Grand Rapids: Zondervan, 2004).

fore the quotation so that the congregation can read along (comprehension is much better when the congregation not only hears but also sees the words). To keep the sermon exposition moving, I have relegated most quotations, complex arguments, and technical details to the footnotes. Although I comment on every verse in the text, in preparing sermons preachers may have to be more selective in order to avoid information overload. I have indicated where in the exposition and how I might make the move(s) to Christ in the New Testament. These moves are intended only as suggestions; while writing the actual sermon, preachers may be guided by the Spirit to better ways and places in the sermon to move to Christ. Finally, related to the goal and the need addressed, I make brief suggestions for application. In actual sermons, these applications will need to be fleshed out with illustrations and concrete suggestions appropriate to the situation of the congregation being addressed. In the appendixes I have included an expository sermon model, a meditation on Ecclesiastes 3:1-15, and a sermon on Ecclesiastes 9:1-12.

Unless otherwise noted, the Bible version quoted is the NRSV (it follows the Hebrew more closely than the TNIV does). In these quotations I have occasionally emphasized words by italicizing them. Without notation, every reader will understand that these are *my* emphases since they are neither in the original Hebrew nor in the NRSV. The various transliterations of Hebrew words have been standardized as indicated on the chart on p. xvii. In quoting other authors I have also regularized the different transliterations of the Hebrew name "Qohelet" but have kept the author's preferences in the titles of their books and articles.

I have kept references in the footnotes to a minimum: full references can be found in the Bibliography. When a book or article is not included in the Select Bibliography, complete information is found in the footnote.

I send out this book like "bread upon the waters" (Eccl 11:1), with the hope and prayer that it may stimulate many preachers to preach on the frequently neglected book of Ecclesiastes in order to help people live their daily lives wisely and joyfully to the glory of God.

Grand Rapids, Michigan   SIDNEY GREIDANUS

Acknowledgments

First of all I would like to thank all the authors of the books and articles listed in the bibliography. Even though they arrived at widely divergent results, without their struggles to understand Ecclesiastes and publishing their findings, this book on preaching Ecclesiastes would not have seen the light of day. Next I need to thank my proofreaders for their excellent work. They are my brother, the Rev. Morris Greidanus, retired pastor of the First Christian Reformed Church, Grand Rapids, MI, and my former students, the Rev. Ryan Faber of Pella, IA, and the Rev. Joel Schroers of Denver, CO. All three carefully read the manuscript and offered many helpful suggestions for improving its contents and clarity. I also appreciate the work of the staff of the Calvin College and Calvin Theological Seminary library in providing the books and articles needed for this research. I thank also the staff of Eerdmans Publishing Company for competently preparing this book for publication, especially the copy editor of my last three books, Milton Essenburg. Once again I thank my wife, Marie, for her encouragement and for creating a peaceful home and quiet atmosphere where I could fully concentrate on this project. Above all, I am grateful to the Lord for providing daily joy in working on this book and for providing health and strength to see this project through to completion.

Abbreviations

AUSS	*Andrews University Seminary Studies*
BBR	*Bulletin for Biblical Research*
Bib	*Biblica*
BSac	*Bibliotheca Sacra*
BTB	*Biblical Theology Bulletin*
CBQ	*Catholic Biblical Quarterly*
CTJ	*Calvin Theological Journal*
CQ	*The Congregational Quarterly*
ETL	*Ephemerides Theologicae Lovanienses*
EvRT	*Evangelical Review of Theology*
EvQ	*Evangelical Quarterly*
Int	*Interpretation*
JBL	*Journal of Biblical Literature*
JETS	*Journal of the Evangelical Theological Society*
JHS	*Journal of Hebrew Scriptures*
JPS	Jewish Publication Society
JQR	*Jewish Quarterly Review*
JSOT	*Journal for the Study of the Old Testament*
JSS	*Journal of Semitic Studies*
n(n).	footnote(s)
NASB	New American Standard Bible
NEB	New English Bible
NRSV	New Revised Standard Version
NICOT	New International Commentary on the Old Testament
NIDOTT&E	*New International Dictionary of Old Testament Theology and Exegesis*
p(p).	page(s)

par.   parallels
PSBul   *Princeton Seminary Bulletin*
RB   *Revue Biblique*
rpt.   reprint
TDOT   *Theological Dictionary of the Old Testament*
TNIV   Today's New International Version
TSFBul   *Theological Students Fellowship Bulletin*
TynBul   *Tyndale Bulletin*
v. (vv.)   verse(s)
VT   *Vetus Testamentum*
VTSup   *Vetus Testamentum Supplements*

Transliterations

Hebrew

א = ʾ	ו = w	כ, ך = k	ע = ʿ	שׂ = ś
ב = b	ז = z	ל = l	פ, ף = p	שׁ = š
ג = g	ח = ḥ	מ, ם = m	צ = ṣ	ת = t
ד = d	ט = ṭ	נ, ן = n	ק = q	
ה = h	י = y	ס = s	ר = r	

No distinction is made between the *bgdkpt* with or without the dagesh lene.
Compare: תּוֹרָה = *tôrâ*   הַתּוֹרָה = *hattôrâ*   תּוֹרָתוֹ = *tôrātô*

Vowels

הָ = *â*	ֶ = *e*	וֹ = *ô*
ָ = *ā*	ְ = *ĕ* (if vocal)	ֹ = *ō*
ַ = *a*	ֱ = *ĕ*	ָ = *o*
ֲ = *ă*	ִ = *i*	ָ = *ŏ*
ֵ = *ē*	ִי = *î*	וּ = *û*
ֵי = *ê*		ֻ = *u*

CHAPTER 1

Preaching Ecclesiastes

Vanity of vanities, says the Teacher,
vanity of vanities! All is vanity.

(Eccl 1:2)

Ecclesiastes may be the most difficult biblical book to interpret and preach. A major reason for this difficulty is that Old Testament scholars are not agreed on key issues: the number of authors involved in writing this book; the identity of the main author; when, where, and why the book was written; the quality of the Hebrew style; which sections are poetry and which are prose;[1] the book's structure, or lack thereof; and whether its message is pessimistic or positive.[2] Duane Garrett adds, "Perhaps an even greater hindrance to preaching Wisdom is the suspicion many have that it contains no gospel."[3] Small wonder that many preachers consider it the better part of wisdom to omit Ecclesiastes from their preaching schedule. In fact, the *Revised Common Lectionary* assigns readings from Ecclesiastes for only two worship services: for New Year's Eve (Years ABC), Ecclesiastes 3:1-13; and for the Sunday closest to August 3 (Year C), as an alternative to Hosea 11:1-11, Ecclesiastes 1:12-14 and 2:(1-7, 11) 18-23.[4] Unfortu-

---

1. See Whybray, *Ecclesiastes,* 16.

2. "There is scarcely one aspect of the book, whether of date, authorship or interpretation, that has not been the subject of wide difference of opinion." Gordis, *Poets, Prophets, and Sages* (Bloomington: Indiana University Press, 1971), 326.

3. Garrett, "Preaching Wisdom," 108.

4. Compare this minimal use of Ecclesiastes with the practice of some Jewish communities of reading all of Ecclesiastes during the annual feast of Sukkot (Tabernacles). Some of the reasons suggested for reading Ecclesiastes during this feast are: "Qohelet recommends rejoicing, which is the mood of Sukkot; . . . he declares the transience of human life, which is well symbol-

1

nately, omitting Ecclesiastes from one's preaching schedule is a major loss for the church.

The Value of Preaching Ecclesiastes

Ecclesiastes offers a unique perspective on human life — a perspective that is extremely relevant for the church today.[5] Iain Provan observes, "In focusing our attention on this life rather than the next, indeed, this book contributes to the correction of an all-too-frequent imbalance throughout the ages in Christian thinking, which has sometimes presented Christianity as if it were more a matter of waiting for something than a matter of living."[6] Sandy and Giese state, "The Book of Ecclesiastes is one of the most important possessions of the Christian church, since it compels us to continually evaluate and correct our understanding of God and our teaching about God in the light of the whole of biblical revelation. . . . The reflections of the sage in Ecclesiastes unmask the myth of human autonomy and self-sufficiency and drive us in all our frailty and inability to find meaning in a crooked world in the Creator-creature relationship — the ultimate polarity."[7]

Moreover, Ecclesiastes is relevant especially for our culture because it tackles many of the temptations posed by secularism. Leland Ryken calls Ecclesiastes "the most contemporary book in the Bible. Ecclesiastes is a satiric attack on an acquisitive, hedonistic, and materialistic society. It exposes the mad quest to find satisfaction in knowledge, wealth, pleasure, work, fame, and sex."[8]

Before preachers can preach Ecclesiastes with integrity, however, they will

---

ized by a temporary booth; and . . . autumn is the season evocative of mortality." Michael Fox, *Ecclesiastes*, xv.

5. According to Ellen Davis, *Proverbs, Ecclesiastes, Song of Songs*, 160, "Martin Luther said we should read 'this noble little book' every day, precisely because it so firmly rejects sentimental religiosity!"

6. Provan, *Ecclesiastes*, 42. Cf. Brown, *Ecclesiastes*, 21, "Contrary to what is commonly preached, life is not simply a journey of edifying experiences, a pilgrimage of glee. It is about confronting inevitable despair, disillusionment, and, yes, death face to face, the via negativa. Ecclesiastes, in short, covers the gamut of life down under, that is, 'under the sun' and under God. His is a theology from below, not for liberation's sake but for navigating the turbulent waters of the living of these days in reverence to God. Qohelet is a teacher for preachers who has lived to tell about it all . . . barely."

7. D. Brent Sandy and Ronald L. Giese, *Cracking Old Testament Codes: A Guide to Interpreting the Literary Genres of the Old Testament* (Nashville: Broadman and Holman, 1995), 271.

8. Ryken, "Ecclesiastes," 274. Cf. Garrett, "Preaching Wisdom," 119: "Ecclesiastes . . . strips away the ideologies and false hopes by which men and women live and loosens the grip that the quest for wealth, power, and education hold over people. In so doing, Ecclesiastes eloquently turns the reader toward God, the only hope of eternal meaning and life."

have to gain some clarity on the difficulties with which commentators have struggled for more than two thousand years.[9] We shall first explore difficulties in interpreting Ecclesiastes and next difficulties in preaching this book.

Difficulties in Interpreting Ecclesiastes

We shall discuss in turn five major issues in interpreting Ecclesiastes: the nature of wisdom literature, the historical setting of Ecclesiastes, its genre and forms, its structure, and its overall message.

The Nature of Wisdom Literature

One cannot rightly interpret and preach a text until one has taken into account its specific genre. Wisdom literature, like Hebrew narrative, Psalms, prophecy, and apocalyptic literature, is a specific literary genre. Therefore a key question is, What is the nature of wisdom literature? Elizabeth Achtemeier responds, "Wisdom is the result of practical experience and the careful observation of both the natural and human worlds. Out of all of the chaos of experience, Wisdom finds customary 'orders' in the world — ways in which human beings and natural phenomena ordinarily behave. Its aim, then, is to teach men and women these 'orders,' so they may know how to act in harmony with the world around them."[10] J. A. Loader observes similarly, "Wisdom is concerned with the correct ordering of life. Wise action is that which integrates people harmoniously into the order God has created. The rules of life that prescribe how human beings must integrate themselves into that order are the precepts of wisdom."[11]

The Relation of Wisdom to Redemptive History

In contrast to other biblical genres, wisdom literature does not deal with the mighty acts of God. Graeme Goldsworthy observes that this does not mean that wisdom is "a self-contained and alternative way of looking at God and reality." Wisdom, he states, "complements the perspective of salvation history. Indeed,

---

9. See the extensive historical review by Craig Bartholomew in his *Reading Ecclesiastes: Old Testament Exegesis and Hermeneutical Theory*, 31-205.

10. Achtemeier, *Preaching from the Old Testament* (Louisville: Westminster/John Knox, 1989), 166. Cf. von Rad, *Wisdom in Israel*, 92-95; and Bernhard W. Anderson, *Contours of Old Testament Theology* (Minneapolis: Fortress, 1999), 264-67.

11. Loader, *Ecclesiastes*, 4.

we should go further than that and say that wisdom is a theology of the redeemed man living in the world under God's rule. It is thus as much an aspect of kingdom theology as salvation history is."[12]

There are also clear connections between Ecclesiastes and the beginning of redemptive history as recounted in the early chapters of Genesis. As Genesis 1 teaches that God is the sovereign Creator, so Ecclesiastes proclaims the sovereignty of God (3:14; 8:17). As Genesis teaches that God in the beginning set the times (day and night, 1:3-5) and upholds the seasons (8:22), so Ecclesiastes teaches that God has set the times (3:1-8) and "made everything suitable for its time" (3:11). As Genesis teaches that God created this world good (*tôb*, 7 times), so Ecclesiastes acknowledges that there is still good to be found in this world (*tôb*, e.g., 2:24; 3:12-13; 5:18). As Genesis teaches that God created human beings upright, so does Ecclesiastes (7:29). As Genesis (1:27; 2:15) teaches that human beings were created for fellowship with God, so does Ecclesiastes (12:13). Genesis further relates that human beings broke this relationship by rebelling against God (3:6), subsequently hiding from God (3:10), being driven out of the Garden of God (3:24), and suffering the penalty of living in a God-cursed creation (3:17) where meaningful work (2:15) would become toil (3:17-19) and where life would inevitably end in death (3:19, "You are dust, and to dust you shall return"). Ecclesiastes similarly speaks of our present distance from God (5:2), God's curse on the earth (1:15; 7:13), the burden of human toil (1:3; 2:22), and the tragedy of death (3:20; 12:7: "The dust returns to the earth as it was"). Moreover, Genesis reveals that evil resides in the human heart (6:5) and that sin unchecked (4:7) leads to murder — the first victim appropriately named Abel (4:8, *Hebel* = vanity). Ecclesiastes, similarly, shows that evil dwells in human hearts (7:20, 29; 8:11; 9:3) — one of the reasons for its repeated declaration that "all is vanity" (*hebel*, 1:2; 12:8).[13]

In spite of these connections with Genesis and the beginnings of redemptive history, Ecclesiastes does not focus on God's redemptive acts. Duane Garrett formulates the contrast this way: "Genesis tells the story of how humans — originally in a state of life, paradise, and innocence — fell into guilt, toil, and mortality. Ecclesiastes tells how persons now made weak and mortal should live."[14] William Brown observes, "Most conspicuous about the wisdom literature is its 'ahistorical' character. Strikingly absent among Proverbs, Job,

12. Goldsworthy, *Gospel and Kingdom,* 142.

13. See Charles G. Forman, "Qohelet's Use of Genesis," *JSS* 5 (1960) 256-63; Robert Johnson, "Confessions of a Workaholic," *CBQ* 38 (1976) 22; Roger Whybray, "Qoheleth as a Theologian," 247-48; Walter Kaiser, *Ecclesiastes,* 36-37; Arian Verheij, "Paradise Retried: On Qohelet 2:4-6," *JSOT* 50 (1991) 113-15; and David Clements, "The Law of Sin and Death: Ecclesiastes and Genesis 1-3," *Themelios* 19/3 (1994) 5-8.

14. Garrett, *Proverbs, Ecclesiastes, Song of Songs,* 279.

and Ecclesiastes are the great themes of biblical history, such as the exodus, covenant, and conquest of the land. God's role as deliverer and lawgiver, in turn, is scarcely mentioned in the wisdom traditions. Rather, emphasis is placed upon creation and humanity's place in it."[15]

This does not mean, however, that God is absent from Ecclesiastes. God is the great Creator (12:1) who made and still "makes everything" (11:5). God set the times and "has made everything suitable for its time" (3:11). God gave human beings their breath (12:7) and made them "straightforward [upright], but they have devised many schemes" (7:29). God made "the day of prosperity" as well as "the day of adversity" (7:14). God gives us "the days of life" (5:18; 8:15), "wealth and possessions," and the ability "to enjoy them" and to "find enjoyment [even] in toil" (5:19; 6:2). God gives "wisdom and knowledge and joy" (2:26), as well as "the collected sayings" of wisdom (12:11). God wants people to enjoy life, "for God has long ago approved what you do" (9:7). God tests people (3:18), "has no pleasure in fools" (5:4), and can become angry (5:6). God holds people accountable for their actions and "will judge the righteous and the wicked" (3:16; 11:9; 12:14). Therefore people should "rejoice" in all their years (11:9), remember their "Creator" (12:1), "fear God" (3:14; 5:7; 7:18; 8:12), and "keep his commandments" (12:13).

Goldsworthy notes that wisdom, like salvation history, "finds its goal and fulfilment in Christ. . . . Three aspects of wisdom confront us in the New Testament. First, the Gospel narratives portray Jesus as the wise man who, in the form and content of many of his sayings, follows in the traditions of Israel's wisdom teachers. Secondly, Jesus goes beyond this actually to claim to be the wisdom of God. Thirdly, certain New Testament writers . . . understand the meaning of Christ's person and work in the light of certain wisdom ideas."[16]

Contradictions

Several commentators have faulted Ecclesiastes for its contradictions. Compare, for example, the Teacher's assertions, "I thought the dead, who have already died, more fortunate than the living, who are still alive" (4:2), and, "Whoever is joined with all the living has hope, for a living dog is better than a dead lion" (9:4). Or consider the contradiction within a single passage: "I know it will be well with those who fear God, because they stand in fear of him, but it will not be well with the wicked" (8:12-13), and, "There are righteous people who are treated according to the conduct of the wicked, and there are wicked people who are treated according to the conduct of the righteous" (8:14).

---

15. Brown, *Ecclesiastes*, 11-12.
16. Goldsworthy, *Gospel and Kingdom*, 149.

Contradictions, however, are natural in wisdom literature because life is complex.[17] One of the clearest examples of contradictory advice is found in Proverbs 26:4-5,

> Do not answer fools according to their folly,
>   or you will be a fool yourself.
> Answer fools according to their folly,
>   or they will be wise in their own eyes.

Sometimes it is wise not to answer fools; at other times it is wise to answer them.[18] Instead of faulting Ecclesiastes for its contradictions, one ought to utilize them in seeking to understand the message of the author[19] (see pp. 17-18 below, "Juxtapositions"). As Raymond Van Leeuwen puts it, "Rather than forcing us to erase or 'harmonize' the ambiguities and 'contradictions,' biblical wisdom invites us to ponder the nuances and complexities of life; it invites us to become wise."[20]

The Historical Setting of Ecclesiastes

Since wisdom teaches "customary 'orders' in the world,"[21] identifying the historical setting of the author and his recipients is not as crucial as it is for other genres of biblical literature. Nevertheless, having some sense of the historical setting in which Ecclesiastes was written will help preachers better understand

---

17. Some scholars seek to explain the contradictions in terms of changing thoughts over a lifetime or changing circumstances. Crenshaw, *Ecclesiastes*, 49, states, "I believe the tensions of the book represent for the most part the fruit of a lifetime's research. Changing circumstances evoke different responses to conventional wisdom and to one's own former thoughts. Differences in societal concerns also dictate a variety of expressions. . . . But the contradictions suggest more than the result of time's passage. They express the ambiguities of daily existence and the absurdity of human efforts to understand it." Other scholars use the contradictions to argue for multiple authorship (see p. 7 below).

18. Similar "contradictions" are found among English proverbs: sometimes we have to say, "The early bird catches the worm," but at other times "Better late than never" is more suitable; sometimes we need to say, "He who hesitates is lost," but at other times "Look before you leap" or "Haste makes waste" is more fitting.

19. Cf. Fox, *A Time to Tear Down*, 3, "The contradictions in the book of Qohelet are real and intended. We must interpret them, not eliminate them." See this whole section "On Reading Contradictions," ibid., pp. 1-26. See also his *Qohelet and His Contradictions*, and his "The Inner Structure of Qohelet's Thought."

20. Raymond C. Van Leeuwen, "Proverbs," in *A Complete Literary Guide to the Bible*, eds. Leland Ryken and Tremper Longman (Grand Rapids: Zondervan, 1993), 266.

21. See p. 3 above.

the message and discern its original relevance. The questions which we must seek to answer are: Who wrote this book? To whom? When? Where? And why?

The Author(s)

Traditionally biblical scholars identified King Solomon as the author of Ecclesiastes. But Luther already began to question this simple identification.[22] If Solomon were the author, why did he not directly identify himself as he does in Proverbs 1:1, "The proverbs of *Solomon* son of David, king of Israel"? Instead we read in Ecclesiastes 1:1, "The words of *the Teacher,* the son of David, king in Jerusalem." The author is identified as "the Teacher," *Qohelet.*[23] If Solomon were the author, why would he and his editor conceal his name? Instead of Solomon's using a pen name, Tremper Longman argues, "It is much more likely that the nickname Qohelet was adopted by the actual writer to associate himself with Solomon, while retaining his distance from the actual person. It is a way of indicating that the Solomonic persona is being adopted for literary and communicative purposes. In brief, the wise man who adopts the nickname Qohelet pretends to be Solomon while he explores avenues of meaning in the world."[24]

After Luther rejected Solomon as the single author of Ecclesiastes, the floodgates of speculation opened. Because of the book's contradictions and swift changes in perspective, "at one time there were scholars ready to suggest that two, or three, or even as many as nine different minds had been at work on the book."[25] If all these different minds had been working on this book at cross-purposes, then discerning the specific message of a preaching text would be practically impossible. What would be the context for determining the message of the text?

22. "Martin Luther was probably the first to deny the Solomonic authorship. He regarded the Book as 'a sort of Talmud, compiled from many books, probably from the library of King Ptolemy Euergetes of Egypt.'" J. Stafford Wright, "Interpretation of Ecclesiastes," *EvQ* 18/1 (1946) 19.

23. The Septuagint translated *Qohelet* as *Ekklēsiastēs.* "In classical Greek *ekklēsiastēs* means 'one who sits or speaks in the *ekklēsia,*' that is, an assembly of local citizens. The Hebrew term *qohelet* — which occurs only in this book — is almost certainly a participle of the verb *qhl,* 'to assemble,' which is in turn related to the noun *qāhāl,* 'an assembly' (often rendered as *ekklēsia* in the Septuagint)." Whybray, *Ecclesiastes,* 2.

24. Longman, *Book of Ecclesiastes,* 4-5. A few commentators still defend Solomonic authorship (e.g., Kaiser, *Ecclesiastes* [1979], 25-29, and Garrett, *Proverbs, Ecclesiastes, Song of Songs* [1993], 264, 266). For arguments against Solomonic authorship, see, e.g., Young, *Introduction to the Old Testament,* 347-48; Kidner, *Wisdom of Proverbs, Job, and Ecclesiastes,* 105; and Longman, *Book of Ecclesiastes,* 4-8.

25. Kidner, *Time to Mourn,* 14. The nine authors were suggested by D. C. Siegfried, "Prediger und Hohelied," in W. Nowack, *Handkommentar zum Alten Testament* (Göttingen, 1898).

Fortunately for preachers today, a consensus is emerging for a single author,[26] possibly with one or two editors who wrote the Epilogue of 12:8-14 or 12:9-14 and perhaps the Prologue of 1:1; 1:1-2; 1:1-3;[27] or 1:1-11[28] (the Prologue and the Epilogue are written in the third person instead of the first person in the body of Ecclesiastes). The key question now becomes whether the final editor, as some scholars propose, critically evaluates (and undermines) the message of the Teacher. The position one takes on this question determines to a large extent how one will interpret the Teacher's message. For example, Longman argues that a so-called "frame-narrator" critically evaluates the teachings of the Teacher.[29] Jerry Shepherd adopts Longman's "frame theory" but expands on it by comparing preaching the wisdom of the Teacher to preaching the speeches of the friends of Job: "The long autobiographical speech of Qohelet in Ecclesiastes is not the word of God but is contained in a book that is God's Word."[30] With the stroke of a pen twelve chapters of the Teacher's wisdom are disqualified by two verses (12:11-12) which are understood to be critical of the Teacher — and the Teacher can no longer get a fair hearing.[31] Iain Provan rightly argues that it is not "generally plausible that Qohelet's voluminous words would be cited in full just so that the author of 12:8-12 could append a few comments allegedly doubting and criticizing them (and even then not

---

26. "There is near universal agreement [in historical critical readings of Ecclesiastes] that Solomon was not the author and that the book was written in the third century BC or thereabouts. Throughout the twentieth century there has been a growing commitment to the basic unity of Ecclesiastes with the exception of the epilogue." Bartholomew, *Reading Ecclesiastes,* 81. Cf. p. 104.

27. See Whybray, *Ecclesiastes,* 35-36, for the commentators who hold these different positions.

28. So Longman, *Book of Ecclesiastes,* 7-9, 20-21, 37, 57-59.

29. See ibid., 38, "The epilogue begins with the second wise man's summary of the teaching of Qohelet. By quoting the now familiar 'meaningless' refrain, the frame narrator indicates what he considers Qohelet's ultimate conclusion: 'Everything is meaningless.' From this point, he proceeds with his evaluation, which begins with praise and then moves to doubt and finally to criticism." See also ibid., 281 on 12:12, "In essence he says to his son, 'Qohelet's thinking is dangerous material — be careful." Cf. Longman, "Comparative Methods in Old Testament Studies: Ecclesiastes Reconsidered," *TSF Bul* 7 (1984) 5-9, esp. 8-9; and Dillard and Longman, *Introduction to the Old Testament,* 252-54.

30. Shepherd, "Ecclesiastes," 269.

31. See, e.g., Shepherd's depiction of the Teacher: "He is not to be considered, as it were, a pre-NT apologist for the Christian faith, or for that matter the faith of the OT; rather, he represents in this book the very thing against which the prophets preached and against which Christ and the apostles warned — a syncretistic fusion of skeptical, pessimistic wisdom philosophy derived from empirical investigation, with a faith that is only minimally orthodox, lifeless, and colorless, without any real devotion." Ibid., 327.

managing to do so clearly)."[32] Along with most commentators we shall assume that the Teacher and his editor speak with one voice.[33]

For interpreters this still leaves another crucial question about the author. Several commentators assume that the Teacher is critical of and opposes traditional biblical wisdom. For example, Loader writes, "We have to conclude . . . that the Preacher's opposition to the generally optimistic teachers of wisdom never relaxes."[34] Seow even claims that the Teacher at a certain point "employs the rhetoric of subversion."[35] Again the Teacher has been put in a box which precludes a fair hearing of his wisdom. The fact is that we do not know for sure which proverbs the Teacher quotes from traditional wisdom and which are his own compositions. Michael Fox presents a more open-minded position for hearing the Teacher. The Teacher, he asserts, "does not oppose or present antitheses to the doctrines of traditional wisdom. It is not even clear that he recognizes a difference. He is not 'using traditional wisdom against itself.' He is just using it."[36]

The Original Recipients

Internal evidence offers some clues regarding the intended readers of this book. Garrett argues that "the book was not written for the ordinary Israelite. To the contrary, members of its original audience had access to the king (8:3), devoted themselves to the pursuit of wisdom (1:12-18), and either had or were in pursuit of wealth (5:10-17). In short, the first readers were members of the aristocracy."[37] Whybray adds: "Qohelet was . . . a Jewish theologian-teacher whose

32. Provan, *Ecclesiastes*, 33, n. 13. Cf. Eaton, *Ecclesiastes*, 40, "It is quite conceivable that an editor sent out Ecclesiastes with a commendatory note, but it is scarcely likely that anyone would do this if he were unhappy with the content of the work." See further p. 300 below.

33. Cf. Garrett, *Proverbs, Ecclesiastes, Song of Songs,* 263, "The frame-narrator, wisdom, and the Teacher are all masks behind which we hear the one voice of the author."

34. Loader, *Ecclesiastes,* 82. See also R. Gordis, "Quotations in Wisdom Literature," *JQR* 30/2 (1939) 123-47, esp. pp. 132-39. Cf. Seow, *Ecclesiastes,* 40-41. For detailed references, see Scott C. Jones, "Qohelet's Courtly Wisdom: Ecclesiastes 8:1-9," *CBQ* 68 (2006) 211-12, n. 2. Fox, "Inner Structure of Qohelet's Thought," 226, counters: "Currently the prevalent approach is to identify certain statements as words that Qohelet quotes in order to dispute or modify them. But this is too facile. . . . Quoted or not, words an author speaks in his own voice are an expression of his own ideas, unless he shows us otherwise." See further below, pp. 157-58 and 201.

35. Seow, *Ecclesiastes,* 244.

36. Fox, *A Time to Tear Down,* 275. Cf. ibid., 250, "The weakness of this approach is its arbitrariness in separating out traditional wisdom from Qohelet's. And it sometimes involves projecting a notion of traditional wisdom from Qohelet's words which is not actually found in 'traditional wisdom.'"

37. Garrett, "Preaching Wisdom," 117. Cf. Huwiler, "Ecclesiastes," 177: The implied readers

purpose was, out of a genuine religious faith, to show a young but adult male audience how to maintain their faith in circumstances that militated powerfully against this."[38] These people must have been living in the proximity of Jerusalem and the temple, as we can surmise from the exhortation: "Guard your steps when you go to the house of God" (5:1).

Internal evidence suggests further that the original recipients were preoccupied with money. Many of the words used in this book are from the world of commerce.[39] Seow concludes that the Teacher's "'congregants' were apparently preoccupied with all sorts of social and economic issues — the volatility of the economy, the possibility of wealth, inheritance, social status, the fragility of life, and the ever-present shadow of death. Qohelet drew on these concerns and employed idioms that were familiar to his audience in order to subvert their preoccupations."[40]

The book also gives us a good idea of the worldview of its intended readers. The Teacher addresses people "whose view is bounded by the horizons of this world; he meets them on their own ground, and proceeds to convict them of its inherent vanity. This is further borne out by his characteristic expression 'under the sun.'"[41]

The Date of Composition

If this book were written by Solomon in the glory days of Israel's existence as a nation, it would be difficult to account for its pessimistic tone. The conservative scholar Edward Young states, "Solomonic authorship is not widely held, and is rejected by most orthodox Protestant scholars." One of the major reasons for this rejection is that "the background of the book does not fit the age of Solomon. It was a time of misery and vanity (1:2-11); the splendour of Solomon's age was gone (1:12–2:26); a time of death had begun for Israel (3:1-15); injustice and violence were present (4:1-3); there was heathen tyranny (5:7, 9-

---

are "young Israelite men who are living at better than subsistence level, probably in or near Jerusalem. They might include government officials, businessmen, and farm owners. . . . Junior members of the bureaucracy may be the principal audience."

38. Whybray, "Qoheleth as Theologian," 245.

39. "Besides general terms like *kesep* 'money,' *'ōšer* 'riches,' *'āšîr* 'rich,' *sĕgullâ* 'private property,' *śākār* 'salary, reward, compensation,' *naḥălâ* 'inheritance,' and *kišrôn* 'success,' one finds a concentration of terms that suggest a lively commercial environment: *yitrôn* 'net gain, surplus,' *ḥesrôn* 'deficit,' *ḥešbôn* 'account,' *nĕkāsîm* 'assets,' *tĕbû'â* 'yield,' *hămôn* 'wealth,' *'inyān* 'business,' *'āmāl* 'toil, fruit of toil,' *'ôkēl* 'consumer,' *'ôbēd* 'employee,' *ḥēleq* 'portion.'" Seow, "The Socioeconomic Context of 'The Preacher's' Hermeneutic," *PSBul* 17/2 (1996) 173-74.

40. Ibid., 195.

41. Hendry, "Ecclesiastes," 570. For further discussion on the phrase "under the sun," see below, p. 17, n. 67 and pp. 35-36 and 43.

19); death was preferred to life (7:1); 'one man ruled over other men to their hurt' (8:9)."[42]

A postexilic date fits the evidence much better. Whybray states, "The book was written many centuries after Solomon, most probably in the third century B.C. The main reasons for this dating are three: the character of the Hebrew in which it is written, its mood and style of argument, and its place in the history of thought. Each of these considerations would be sufficient in itself to prove that it is one of the latest compositions in the Old Testament."[43] Whybray suggests that the book was probably written "when Palestine was ruled from Egypt by the Ptolemaic dynasty." It was a period of "intense economic development . . . , expansion of international trade . . . , opportunities for great fortunes to be made by entrepreneurs. Money as a means of exchange assumed an importance which it had never had before. These developments help to explain Qohelet's preoccupation with money and profit."[44] Brown remarks, "Qohelet reflects the anxiety and hopes that such an emerging economy inspired among the general populace of Judah (e.g., 5:10-12; 7:12; 10:19). Indeed, the sage cuts to the chase in his opening reflections about the human condition by posing the question of economic gain in 1:3: 'What do people gain from all the toil at which they toil under the sun?' (see also 3:9; 5:16)."[45]

In addition to Israel's socioeconomic background, we should also take into account its changed religious perspective. Loader writes, "Since the deportation of Israel in the sixth century B.C., by which the nation was forced into exile, profound changes had occurred in the people's religious outlook. They still worshiped the same God their fathers worshiped, but their God-concept became more impersonal."[46]

The Place of Composition

Where did the Teacher write this book? Although some have argued for a place of composition outside Palestine, the book itself alludes to Palestine. "The ref-

---

42. Young, *Introduction to the Old Testament*, 347-48, with credit to Hengstenberg.

43. Whybray, *Ecclesiastes*, 4. Kidner, *Wisdom of Proverbs, Job, and Ecclesiastes*, suggests a date between 350 and 250 B.C., while Crenshaw *Ecclesiastes*, 50, suggests a date between 250 and 225 BC, and Towner, "Book of Ecclesiastes," 351, opts for "the middle of the third century B.C.E., perhaps around 250."

44. Ibid., 9-10.

45. Brown, *Ecclesiastes*, 9. Cf. Seow, "The Socioeconomic Context of 'The Preacher's' Hermeneutic," *PSBul* 17/2 (1996) 171-89; his "Theology When Everything Is out of Control," *Int* 55/3 (2001) 238-43; and his *Ecclesiastes*, 35-36. For preaching purposes it makes little difference whether the date of composition was the fifth century B.C. (Seow, Brown) or the third century B.C. (Whybray, Crenshaw) as long as one is aware of a background of economic upheavals and temptations.

46. Loader, *Ecclesiastes*, 11.

erences to climatic conditions such as the unpredictability of the weather, dependence on rainfall . . . and to successions of rainstorms (12:2) . . . reflect those of Palestine. . . . Among local customs mentioned by Qohelet we find several which are characteristic of Palestine but improbable in Egypt, such as the hewing of wood (10:9) and the use of cisterns (12:6). . . . Equally decisive for a Palestinian locale are the references to the Temple [5:1-7; 8:10; 9:2]."[47]

The Purpose of Ecclesiastes

Why did the Teacher write this book? Since the Teacher himself does not explicitly mention his purpose, we shall have to look more into the content and structure of the book (see below) before we can give a definitive answer. But we can give a provisional answer here by seeing his reflections as a response to the situation in which the original recipients found themselves. We have seen that these recipients had lost their theological moorings: their God was distant as they lived their lives only at the horizontal, secular level, that is, "under the sun." The Teacher's purpose, then, was to show these readers the deficiency of this secular wordview. From this perspective he proclaims, "All is vanity" (the inclusio, 1:2; 12:8). Hendry, therefore, calls Ecclesiastes "a major work of apologetic" and "a critique of secularism and of secularized religion."[48] Bartholomew adds, "Ecclesiastes is crafted by a wisdom teacher as an ironical exposure of such an empiricistic epistemology [Greek Epicurean] which seeks wisdom through personal experience and analysis without the 'glasses' of the fear of God. . . . Ecclesiastes exhorts Israelites struggling with the nature of life's meaning and God's purposes to pursue genuine wisdom by allowing their thinking to be shaped integrally by a recognition of God as Creator so that they can enjoy God's good gifts and obey his laws amidst the enigma of his purposes."[49]

The Genre and Forms of Ecclesiastes

Before we can understand *what* Ecclesiastes means, we need to know *how* it means, that is to say, what genre, forms, and language (literal or figurative) it uses to convey its message. The broad genre of Ecclesiastes is wisdom literature (discussed above). Commentators have tried to specify the genre of Ecclesiastes more precisely, such as "framed wisdom autobiography"[50] and "autobiographi-

---

47. Whybray, *Ecclesiastes*, 13.

48. Hendry, "Ecclesiastes," 570. Cf. Eaton, *Ecclesiastes*, 44, "What, then, is the purpose of Ecclesiastes? It is an essay in apologetics. It defends the life of faith in a generous God by pointing to the grimness of the alternative."

49. Bartholomew, *Reading Ecclesiastes*, 263.

50. Longman, *Book of Ecclesiastes*, 17.

cal treatise."[51] Roland Murphy states, "One may say that no single genre, even diatribe, is adequate as a characterization of Qohelet's book. This seems due to the fact that it is the publication of his teachings, which would have embraced many different genres [forms] of writing."[52]

For interpreting Ecclesiastes, therefore, we must keep in mind that it is wisdom literature and pay special attention to its subgenres, that is, its forms. We shall enumerate the most common types.

Reflection

Reflection is a characteristic form in Ecclesiastes. It contemplates the deepest questions of life and is usually marked by first-person verbs such as "I applied my mind," "I said to myself," "I have seen (saw, observed)." Reflection "has a loose structure; it begins with some kind of observation, which is then considered from one or more points of view, leading to a conclusion. Within it one may find sayings or proverbs [or anecdotes], employed to develop or round out the thought (e.g., 1:12-18)."[53]

Proverb

Proverbs are found throughout Ecclesiastes but especially in chapters 7, 10, and 11. "A proverb is a pithy, highly stylized statement of a truth about life."[54] For example, Ecclesiastes 10:12 says,

> Words spoken by the wise bring them favor,
>   but the lips of fools consume them.

A proverb states a general truth but does not cover every situation. Thomas Long explains, "A proverb is larger than one case, but not large enough to embrace all cases. The presence of contradictory proverbs within the same collection . . . indicates that proverbs have an 'upper limit' to their applicability. As wisdom, they transcend a single situation, but they do not have indiscriminate force to be applied anywhere and at all times."[55]

Proverbs can be subdivided into "true" proverbs (e.g., 1:14, "All is vanity and a chasing after wind"); "better than" proverbs (e.g., 4:9, "Two are better

---

51. Brown, *Ecclesiastes*, 17.
52. Murphy, *Wisdom Literature*, 131.
53. Murphy, *Ecclesiastes*, xxxii.
54. Longman, *Book of Ecclesiastes*, 20.
55. Thomas G. Long, *Preaching and the Literary Forms of the Bible* (Philadelphia: Fortress, 1988), 55.

than one"; cf. 7:1-3, 5, 8); and "as . . . so" proverbs (e.g., 11:5, "Just as you do not know how the breath comes to the bones in the mother's womb, so you do not know the work of God").[56]

Instruction

"An instruction is a teaching in which the author seeks to persuade his reader toward or away from a certain course of behavior or thought."[57] The form of instruction is usually marked by one or more imperatives, frequently supported by "motivations" — reasons for obeying the command. For example, Ecclesiastes 5:1-2 is an instruction supported by motivations:

> Guard your steps when you go to the house of God; to draw near to listen is better than the sacrifice offered by fools; for they do not know how to keep from doing evil. Never be rash with your mouth, nor let your heart be quick to utter a word before God, for God is in heaven, and you upon earth; therefore let your words be few.

Autobiographical Narrative

Autobiographical narrative is "a first-person description of a personal experience, real or imagined . . . or stylized as a literary fiction (i.e., a description of a personal experience created by the biblical writer or editor for literary, and/or theological, and/or didactic reasons)."[58] Examples of autobiographical narrative are Ecclesiastes 1:12–2:16 and 7:23-29.

Anecdote

An anecdote (sometimes called a parable) is a third-person "short story told in order to illustrate a principle or truth of interest to the author."[59] For example, Ecclesiastes 9:13-15 begins as a reflection on wisdom and illustrates it with an anecdote:

> I have also seen this example of wisdom under the sun, and it seemed great to me. There was a little city with few people in it. A great king came against it and besieged it, building great siegeworks against it. Now there was

56. See Loader, *Ecclesiastes*, 5-6.
57. Longman, *Book of Ecclesiastes*, 20.
58. Andrew E. Hill, "Non-Proverbial Wisdom," in *Cracking Old Testament Codes: A Guide to Interpreting the Literary Genres of the Old Testament*, eds. D. Brent Sandy and Ronald L. Giese (Nashville: Broadman and Holman, 1995), 265-66.
59. Longman, *Book of Ecclesiastes*, 20.

found in it a poor wise man, and he by his wisdom delivered the city. Yet no one remembered that poor man.

Metaphor

A metaphor is "a figure of speech in which a word or phrase literally denoting one kind of object or idea is used in place of another by way of suggesting a likeness or analogy between them."[60] For example, Ecclesiastes 12:6 piles up four metaphors for a person's death: "the silver cord is snapped, and the golden bowl is broken, and the pitcher is broken at the fountain, and the wheel broken at the cistern." The most repeated metaphor in Ecclesiastes is "vanity," literally "vapor" or "breath." What does the Teacher mean when he compares human life to "vapor"? Is he suggesting that life is short-lived, ephemeral, or is he saying that life is without substance or futile, or is he implying that life is absurd or meaningless? The context will have to decide the specific nuance.[61]

Allegory

An allegory is an extended metaphor. See, for example, Ecclesiastes 12:3-4, where an elderly person is described in terms of a house and its occupants:

> The guards of the house tremble, and the strong men are bent, and the women who grind cease working because they are few, and those who look through the windows see dimly; when the doors on the street are shut.

Allegory, of course, requires allegorical interpretation. Although it may be tempting to preach Christ by using allegorical interpretation for other texts, this kind of interpretation should be restricted to the literary form of allegory.[62]

The Structure of Ecclesiastes

Identifying the overall structure of Ecclesiastes is important since one can rightly understand a text only in its literary context. The familiar ancient story

60. *Webster's New Collegiate Dictionary.*

61. James Kugel, *Great Poems of the Bible,* 310, suggests that the Teacher "frequently uses this word to describe something in life that seems to him futile and useless (Eccl 2:1, 11, 17, 20, 23, and frequently thereafter); at other times *hebel* seems to mean something that is just baffling (Eccl 5:9; 7:15); at still other times it is used to mean something unfair, unjust (Eccl 2:26; 4:7; 6:2; 8:10, 14). And [in Eccl 12:8] . . . it is breathlike, evanescent: 'So fleeting.'"

62. For examples of allegorical interpretation applied to nonallegorical texts in Ecclesiastes, see the Preface above, pp. x-xi, and below, pp. 73-74, 111, 243, 264.

of a blind man touching an elephant illustrates this important principle of biblical hermeneutics. When the blind man touched the side of the animal, he concluded that he had bumped into a wall. Moving along "the wall," he felt a leg and inferred that there was a large tree growing next to the wall. Moving further, he touched the trunk of the elephant and concluded that there was a snake in the tree. If only the blind man had known about the whole, that he was touching an elephant, he would have been able to identify the parts correctly.

Similarly, for correct interpretation, the parts of Ecclesiastes have to be understood in the context of the whole book. Unfortunately, determining the overall structure of Ecclesiastes has proved to be notoriously difficult. Longman states, "Close study shows that Qohelet's thought rambles, repeats, and occasionally contradicts itself."[63] Franz Delitzsch predicted in 1891, "All attempts to show, in the whole, not only oneness of spirit, but also a genetic progress, an all-embracing plan, and an organic connection, have hitherto failed, and must fail."[64] But such skepticism regarding discovering an overall structure has not stopped commentators from trying.[65] No detailed proposals, however, have met with general favor. What are preachers to do when scholars are gridlocked on the structure of Ecclesiastes?

Literary Patterns

A good way for preachers to respond to the scholarly gridlock is not to get caught up in complex literary structures, but to examine the book for a more modest overall structure that will help in understanding the parts. It is clear that Ecclesiastes shows its unified structure with an inclusio: "Vanity of vanities, says the Teacher, vanity of vanities! All is vanity" (1:2; 12:8). The inclusio is reinforced by an opening poem on the lack of gain from human toil (1:3-11) and a concluding poem encouraging its readers to remember their Creator before old age and death (12:1-7). Between these two "bookends" the Teacher searches for the meaning of life. His opening, "All is vanity," is repeated some

---

63. Longman, *Book of Ecclesiastes*, 22, with references to 1:12-18 and 2:11-16; 4:1-3 and 5:7-8 (Eng. 5:8-9); and 4.4-12 and 3:9 6:9 (Eng 5:10-6:9).

64. Delitzsch, *Commentary on the Song of Songs and Ecclesiastes* (1891; rpt. Grand Rapids: Eerdmans, 1982), 188. For commentators in general agreement with Delitzsch, see Wright, "Riddle of the Sphinx," *CBQ* 30 (1968) 314, n. 3.

65. For an overview of the various proposals of Norbert Lohfink, J. A. Loader, Addison G. Wright, A. Glasser, François Rousseau, Michael V. Fox, Hans-Peter Muller, H. W. Hertzberg, Robert Gordis, and others, see Crenshaw, *Ecclesiastes*, 38-48, and Bartholomew, *Reading Ecclesiastes*, 69-81, 118-205. See also Murphy's overview in his *Ecclesiastes*, xxxv-xli, and Wright's in "Riddle of the Sphinx," *CBQ* 30 (1968) 315-16, nn. 4-6. Crenshaw concludes his overview as follows (p. 47), "This discussion of Qohelet's structure has failed to resolve a single issue, but it demonstrates the complexity of the problem."

thirty-eight times but is balanced by his frequent use of the word "good/good-ness" (fifty-one times) and his sixfold encouragement to fear God (3:14; 5:7; 7:18; 8:12-13 [3 x]). This leads to an editor's final summary of the quest for meaning: "The end of the matter; all has been heard. Fear God, and keep his commandments; for that is the whole duty of everyone" (12:13). Through many stops and starts to find meaning in life, the pattern in Ecclesiastes progresses to this final, seventh, exhortation, "Fear God," elucidated by, "and keep his commandments."[66]

We should also note an alternating pattern of horizontal and vertical strands in Ecclesiastes. The horizontal strands describe life "under the sun," while the vertical strands point to God. We can compare the book to a woven cloth in which vertical threads intersect horizontal threads to bind the whole together. The horizontal threads describe life from a secular perspective: life "under the sun" is life without God.[67] "Vanity of vanities! All is vanity. What do people gain from all the toil at which they toil *under the sun?*" (1:2-3). The answer is, Nothing, absolutely nothing! There is more to life, however, than a world without God. Thirty-nine times the Teacher mentions God. When he speaks of God, "the 'under-the-sun' terminology falls into the background or lapses altogether (2:24-26; 11:1–12:14); instead he refers to the 'hand of God' (2:24), the joy of man (2:25; 3:12; 5:18, 20; 9:7; 11:7-9), and the generosity of God (2:26; 3:13; 5:19). . . . On twelve occasions God is said to 'give.' On seven occasions mankind is said to have a joyful 'portion' from God."[68] The Teacher speaks of God giving "wisdom and knowledge and joy" (2:26), food and drink and pleasure in toil (3:13), "wealth and possessions" and the ability to enjoy them (5:19; 6:2), and God's desire that people enjoy his gifts (9:7). The Teacher also warns that God "has no pleasure in fools" (5:4), and "will judge the righteous and the wicked" (3:17; 11:9). Therefore people should "fear God" (3:14; 5:7; 7:18; 8:12-13; 12:13).

Juxtapositions

The pattern of vertical strands intersecting horizontal strands partly explains the contradictions in Ecclesiastes. The Teacher places himself in the position of

66. Cf. Fox, *Ecclesiastes*, xvi, "The book begins with a general principle (1:3), continues with a thematic prelude, introduces the persona and his background, describes his task, previews his results, and then proceeds with his investigation. The last unit, 12:1-7, is climactic and could stand nowhere else."

67. "The phrase 'under the sun' is a trademark of Qohelet and is closely related to the concept of futility. It occurs twenty-nine times and projects the perspective of man alone, using his own wisdom and senses in the realm of 'this world' alone." Reitman, "The Structure and Unity of Ecclesiastes," *BSac* 154 (1997) 301, n. 17.

68. Eaton, *Ecclesiastes*, 45.

a person who lives without God, and from that secular perspective he concludes, "All is vanity." But if one has eyes for the reality of God, all is not vanity; there is meaning in life, even though from the Teacher's perspective it is restricted because of the finality of death. To describe this polarity in Ecclesiastes, some scholars speak of a "polar structure,"[69] or "juxtaposition";[70] still others characterize the book as a "diatribe,"[71] "dialogical,"[72] or "dialectical."[73] The common element in these varied descriptions is that they refer to this tension in Ecclesiastes between a secular[74] and a God-centered perspective.

The juxtapositions are purposeful. The book is like a Rembrandt painting where the dark background and figures draw one's eyes to the figures in the light. The Teacher's dark background of vanity and death seeks to draw the reader to the elements in the light: enjoy; it is God's gift; "fear God, and keep his commandments." The light is the focal point of the Teacher's message, but only in contrast to the darkness of life without God. The homiletical significance of observing this polarity between the negative and the positive is that one cannot isolate a negative section of Ecclesiastes and preach it as the Teacher's message. Every preaching text must be understood in its broader literary context.

The Overall Structure

Several commentators have sought to utilize the Teacher's sevenfold *carpe diem* ("seize the day").[75] In 2:24 the Teacher enjoins, "There is nothing better for mortals than to eat and drink, and find enjoyment in their toil." He repeats this advice to enjoy life in 3:12-13; 3:22; 5:18-20; 8:15; 9:7-10; and 11:7-10. Although one should certainly pay attention to this important repetition to enjoy each day, as can be seen from the large gaps between them, it does not function adequately as the Teacher's structure of Ecclesiastes.

69. Loader, *Ecclesiastes*, 11. See also his *Polar Structures in the Book of Qohelet* (Berlin and New York: de Gruyter, 1979).

70. Bartholomew, *Reading Ecclesiastes*, 238-54, with references to Sternberg's *The Poetics of Biblical Narrative*.

71. Norbert Lohfink, *Kohelet* (Stuttgart, 1980).

72. T. Anthony Perry, *Dialogues with Qohelet: The Book of Ecclesiastes* (Philadelphia: Pennsylvania State University, 1993).

73. Ryken, "Ecclesiastes," 269, speaks of "the dialectical structure of the book": "Contrast, not sequence, is the organizing principle. The book itself presents a fluid movement back and forth, without transition, between the two types of material, one negative, the other positive."

74. "The shafts of light that we have noticed are signals to the reader that the author's own position and conclusions are very different from those of the secularist, in whose shoes he is standing for the purpose of his thesis." Kidner, *Wisdom of Proverbs, Job, and Ecclesiastes*, 93.

75. See, e.g., Kaiser, *Ecclesiastes*, 17-24; and Perdue, *Wisdom Literature*, 190-91.

Of all the proposals,[76] Addison Wright has probably produced the most compelling detailed literary structure of Ecclesiastes.[77] His analysis is based on the author's "simple technique of concluding related sections with the same word or phrase." On the basis of these repetitions Wright concluded "that the body of the book consists of two halves, 1:12–6:9 and 6:10–11:6. In the first half Qohelet examines 'what is good for man to do' (2:4) and expresses his own experiential observations in two introductory statements of purpose (1:12-18) and six expository sections (2:1–6:9) each of which ends with '(all is vanity and) a striving after wind' (a line that never again occurs in the book after 6:9). . . . In the second half of the book (6:10–11:6) Qohelet begins by asking two questions: Who knows what is good for man, and who knows the future (6:10-12)? He develops the first question in four sections (7:1–8:17). . . . Each of these sections ends with *l' mṣ'* ('not find out'), and the last section with a triple *lō' yûkal hā'ādām limṣō' . . . wĕlō' yimṣa' . . . lō' yûkal limṣō'* ['no one can find out . . . they will not find it out . . . they cannot find it out'] (8:17). He develops the second question in six sections [later reduced to four sections][78] (9:1–11:6) in which he illustrates man's inability to know the future. Each of these sections ends with *l' yd'* ('do you know') and the last section with a triple *'ênĕkā yōdēa' . . . lō' tēda' . . . 'ênĕkā yōdēa'* ['you do not know . . . you do not know . . . you do not know'] (11:5-6)."[79]

Wright's second study confirmed his earlier conclusions and buttressed them with interesting numerical details.[80] Although several commentators are critical of his method and its results,[81] I include his proposed structure (see

76. See n. 16, n. 65 above.

77. Wright, "The Riddle of the Sphinx: The Structure of the Book of Qohelet," *CBQ* 30 (1968) 313-34, and "The Riddle of the Sphinx Revisited: Numerical Patterns in the Book of Qohelet," *CBQ* 42 (1980) 38-51.

78. See Wright, "Riddle of the Sphinx Revisited," *CBQ* 42 (1980) 42, n. 15e.

79. Wright as summarized in his second study, "The Riddle of the Sphinx Revisited," *CBQ* 42 (1980) 38-39.

80. 111 verses from 1:1–6:9 and 111 verses from 6:10–12:14; 216 verses from 1:1–12:8, the numerical value of *hbl hblym hkl hbl* (1:2; 12:8); in 1:2, "*hbl* (= 37) occurs three times in the singular for a total numerical value of 111 (37 x 3) — the number of verses in the first half of the book (1:1–6:9)"; and "the probable total of 37 occurrences of *hbl* in the book equals the numerical value of the word *hbl* itself." Ibid., 43-44.

81. E.g., Fox, *Ecclesiastes*, xvi, argues: "Wright's hypothesis faces a number of objections: the criteria for unit division are not well-defined phrases; the key phrases are not always at the *end* of the unit, where they 'should' be; the units are of very different size and character; and the plan does not match the content." Cf. Fox, *A Time to Tear Down*, 148-49; Crenshaw, *Ecclesiastes*, 41-42; Longman, *Book of Ecclesiastes*, 21, n. 76; and Seow, *Ecclesiastes*, 44-46. Other commentators follow the structure proposed by Wright: e.g., Murphy, *Ecclesiastes*, xxxix, who mentions also J. S. M. Mulder and R. Rendtorff; Stephen Brown, "The Structure of Ecclesiastes," *EvRT* 14/3 (1990) 195-205, generally agrees with Wright's analysis but seeks to develop the patterns in more detail.

the opposite page)[82] because he seems to have caught most divisions intended by the author of Ecclesiastes. Although Wright's formal categories do not reflect the contents of Ecclesiastes — and as such do not offer much help for understanding the individual units — his analysis should prove helpful in determining the boundaries of intended literary units which can serve as preaching texts.

The Overall Message of Ecclesiastes

Since commentators are not agreed on the structure of Ecclesiastes, they also are not agreed on the overall message of Ecclesiastes. Opinions range from "all is vanity"[83] to "enjoy your life."[84] Some scholars opt for several themes. Brown states, "Finding a uniform, determinate meaning in Ecclesiastes is as elusive as securing enduring gain was for the sage behind the book. Nevertheless certain themes do stand out, particularly the fragility of human existence, the inability of human beings to secure themselves, the inscrutable will of God, and the call to *carpe diem,* to 'seize the day' before the sun sets, as it were."[85] These themes can be legitimately preached when the preaching texts make these points.

Given the fact that the Teacher expounds a variety of themes, is there a way to formulate a single overarching theme? If we had to preach one sermon on the whole book of Ecclesiastes, what would be its theme?[86] We have already

82. Wright, "Riddle of the Sphinx Revisited," *CBQ* 42 (1980) 49 (I have changed his use of "man" and "he" to "one"). See also his "Additional Numerical Patterns in Qohelet," *CBQ* 45 (1983) 32-43.

83. Loader, *Ecclesiastes,* 14, "We will have to acknowledge, then, that there is but one fundamental idea in the book: the declaration of meaninglessness, an idea that is clarified and illustrated from a number of viewpoints."

84. "The seven passages where he recommends the whole-hearted pursuit of enjoyment . . . are arranged in such a way as to state their theme with steadily increasing emphasis and solemnity." Whybray, "Qoheleth, Preacher of Joy," *JSOT* 23 (1982) 87. See also Kaiser, *Ecclesiastes,* 42, "The mood of Ecclesiastes is one of delight, with the prospect of living and enjoying all the goods of life once man has come to fear God and keep his commandments."

85. Brown, *Ecclesiastes,* 12. Crenshaw, "Wisdom Literature," 379, suggests several themes that run through the entire book: "Vanity of vanities, all is vanity," and "He cannot find it out," that is, God has imposed limits on human knowledge. In addition, he lists "several other formulas": "These include the concluding summary that encouraged the enjoyment of life during youthful vigor, the 'contemplative' observations that referred to self-examination and the resulting personal action, and the allusions to chasing after the wind, toil, and lot."

86. It is not advisable, of course, to preach a single sermon on all of Ecclesiastes, unless it is to introduce a series of sermons on this book. Our concern for an overarching theme at this stage is to gain an idea of the whole in order to better understand the parts.

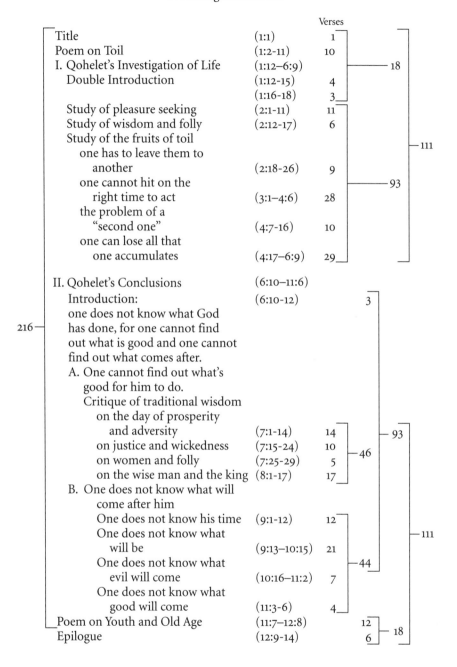

Verses

Title (1:1) 1
Poem on Toil (1:2-11) 10
I. Qohelet's Investigation of Life (1:12–6:9)
  Double Introduction (1:12-15) 4 — 18
  (1:16-18) 3
  Study of pleasure seeking (2:1-11) 11 — 111
  Study of wisdom and folly (2:12-17) 6
  Study of the fruits of toil
    one has to leave them to
      another (2:18-26) 9
    one cannot hit on the — 93
      right time to act (3:1–4:6) 28
    the problem of a
      "second one" (4:7-16) 10
    one can lose all that
      one accumulates (4:17–6:9) 29

II. Qohelet's Conclusions (6:10–11:6)
  Introduction: (6:10-12) 3
  one does not know what God
216 — has done, for one cannot find
  out what is good and one cannot
  find out what comes after.
  A. One cannot find out what's
    good for him to do.
    Critique of traditional wisdom
      on the day of prosperity
        and adversity (7:1-14) 14 — 93
      on justice and wickedness (7:15-24) 10 — 46
      on women and folly (7:25-29) 5
      on the wise man and the king (8:1-17) 17
  B. One does not know what will
    come after him
    One does not know his time (9:1-12) 12 — 111
    One does not know what
      will be (9:13–10:15) 21
    One does not know what — 44
      evil will come (10:16–11:2) 7
    One does not know what
      good will come (11:3-6) 4
Poem on Youth and Old Age (11:7–12:8) 12 — 18
Epilogue (12:9-14) 6

noted the Teacher's emphasis with his inclusio and constant repetition that "all is vanity." But we have also noted his refrain, "Enjoy God's gifts." In addition, we have seen his repeated emphasis on "Fear God," which is further highlighted in the conclusion, "The end of the matter; all has been heard. Fear God, and keep his commandments; for that is the whole duty of everyone" (12:13). Can we cover these major themes with an overarching theme? One might consider the following as an overall theme: Fear God in order to turn a vain, empty life into a meaningful life which will enjoy God's gifts.[87]

Given this overarching theme, the Teacher's overall purpose (goal) would be to encourage his readers to reject the secular worldview and to make God the focal point of their lives. As Eaton puts it, "The fear of God which he [the Teacher] recommends (3:14; 5:7; 8:12; 12:13) is not only the beginning of wisdom; it is also the beginning of joy, of contentment and of an energetic and purposeful life. The Preacher wishes to deliver us from a rosy-coloured, self-confident godless life, with its inevitable cynicism and bitterness, and from trusting in wisdom, pleasure, wealth, and human justice or integrity. He wishes to drive us to see that God is there, that he is good and generous, and that only such an outlook makes life coherent and fulfilling."[88] Within this overall framework, preachers will need to determine more specific goals with each preaching text.

Difficulties in Preaching Ecclesiastes

Not only do preachers have to come to terms with difficulties in interpreting Ecclesiastes, but they are also faced with specific difficulties in preaching this book. We shall highlight three difficulties: first, selecting a proper preaching text; second, formulating a single theme; and third, preaching Christ from Ecclesiastes.

---

87. Cf. Young's suggestion: "The grand theme of the book [is that] life apart from God can have no meaning, for God alone can give life meaning." *Introduction*, 351. Cf. Ryken, "Ecclesiastes," 269: "The theme of the book, far from being a problem, is a virtual summary of the biblical worldview: life lived by purely earthly and human standards is futile, but the God-centered life is an antidote." Cf. Fox, "The Inner Structure of Qohelet's Thought," 225: "My basic thesis is that the central concern of the book of Qohelet is *meaning* — not transience, not work, not values, not mortality. These themes are there, but they are all ways of approaching the more fundamental issue, the meaning of life."

88. Eaton, *Ecclesiastes*, 48. Cf. Garrett, *Proverbs, Ecclesiastes, Song of Songs*, 278: the Teacher seeks to urge his readers "to recognize that they are mortal. They must abandon all illusions of self-importance, face death and life squarely, and accept with fear and trembling their dependence on God."

Selecting a Proper Preaching Text

In order to do justice to the thought of the biblical author, a preaching text should be a literary unit — not a fragment of a unit or a verse.[89] With biblical narratives, the units are fairly easy to spot, but this is not the case with Ecclesiastes. W. Sibley Towner states, "It is more difficult to identify most of the individual pericopes in Ecclesiastes than in any other book of the Hebrew Bible, except perhaps the book of Proverbs."[90]

Commentators generally agree that Ecclesiastes 1:1-11 and 1:12–2:26 are literary units, but they fail to agree on those that follow. Since the meaning of a text can change with a change in the dimensions of a text, it will be all-important to select proper preaching texts from Ecclesiastes. If the chosen text is not a literary unit, it will derail the sermon from the start.

Fortunately, the Teacher does provide some help in determining major and minor literary units with opening constructions for his reflections such as "I saw/have seen/observed" (e.g., 3:16; 4:1, 7; 5:18; 7:15; 8:9; 9:11, 13) and closing markers such as "All is vanity and a chasing after wind" (1:14, 17; 2:11, 17, 26; 4:4, 6, 16; 6:9).[91] Addison Wright's literary analysis (see above, p. 21) will also be helpful in confirming our choices of proper preaching texts. As he correctly observes, "Ecclesiastes is a difficult book in that it can be made to say many different things depending on how one divides the material into sections. . . . Consequently if the author has indicated in any way how he divided the material, those indications will be of the utmost importance for valid exegesis."[92]

Preachers, of course, are free to choose smaller units than those identified as preaching texts in this book, but for valid interpretation these subunits[93] still have to be understood in the context of the larger unit. Two indexes in the back of this book, "Targets for Sermons" and "Topics for Sermons," may also spark ideas for occasional sermons on Ecclesiastes.

Formulating a Single Theme

Modern sermons require a single theme for the sake of their unity and movement.[94] But the Teacher frequently seeks to make his point in stereo sound by juxtaposing a negative pole with a positive one or presenting two positive poles such as, "Rejoice while you are young!" and "Remember your creator in the

89. See my *Modern Preacher*, 126-28.
90. Towner, "The Book of Ecclesiastes," 265.
91. Cf. Reitman, "The Structure and Unity of Ecclesiastes," *BSac* 154 (1997) 308-9.
92. Wright, "Riddle of the Sphinx Revisited," *CBQ* 42 (1980) 50.
93. For some of these subunits, see below, pp. 48-49, 70, 88-89, 107-9, 138, 224, 228, 240.
94. See my *Modern Preacher*, 131-36.

days of your youth!" (11:9; 12:1). When the preaching text contains two messages, it will be a challenge to formulate a single theme while doing justice to both poles. We will have to consider whether one of the two themes is dominant so that we can subsume one under the other, or whether we can formulate an overarching theme that encompasses both.

Preaching Christ from Ecclesiastes

Preachers cannot simply proclaim Old Testament wisdom as "gospel" in the Christian church. Just as Old Testament law (think of circumcision, sabbath, unclean foods) has to be validated by the New Testament before it can be proclaimed as "gospel' (in the sense of good news also for the church), so Old Testament wisdom has to be confirmed by the New Testament before it can be proclaimed as "gospel." The core of New Testament wisdom is Jesus Christ, who not only personified the "wisdom of God" (1 Cor 1:24, 30) but who taught people wisdom "as one having authority" (Matt 7:29). Jesus said to the Jews, "You search the scriptures because you think that in them you have eternal life; and it is they that testify on my behalf. Yet you refuse to come to me to have *life*" (John 5:39-40). We should not just preach the Old Testament scriptures but link them to Christ so that people can have life.

As mentioned in the Preface, after preaching a sermon in a series on Ecclesiastes some thirty years ago, I was asked by a retired pastor if a rabbi could have preached my sermon in a synagogue. I had to admit that a rabbi could probably have done so. But this meant that I had preached an "Old Testament sermon" instead of a "Christian sermon."[95] Further study convinced me that the Church Fathers were right in insisting that a Christian sermon must preach Christ. But how? Ecclesiastes contains not even one "messianic text";[96] there is no promise of the coming Messiah. How does one preach Christ from a book that has no messianic texts?

Unfortunately, for much of the church's history allegorical interpretation became the method of choice for preaching Christ from the Old Testament.[97] But allegorical interpretation is a form of eisegesis: it reads the New Testament Jesus back into the Old Testament. Today we face another dangerous trend for preaching Christ. Brown writes, "The temptation looms large among Christian interpreters to treat Qohelet merely as a foil for the Gospel message, a deficient

---

95. Clowney's terms. See the Preface above, n. 1.

96. Ronald Knox, *Waiting for Christ* (New York: Sheed and Ward, 1960), 279-82, lists 150 "messianic texts" in the Old Testament, but not one of them is from Ecclesiastes.

97. See my *Preaching Christ from the Old Testament*, 69-176.

and dangerous perspective in dire need of rehabilitation."[98] Although contrast with the message of Ecclesiastes may sometimes be the way to preach Christ, there are many more options to consider. A study of the New Testament and church history discloses at least seven legitimate ways of preaching Christ from the Old Testament. Investigating which of these ways leads from the message of the text to Christ in the New Testament is a form of brainstorming that usually leads to several possibilities. In the sermon one should not use all these ways, of course, but select the most compelling way, perhaps supported by one or two of the others. We shall briefly review each of these seven ways.[99]

Redemptive-Historical Progression

When a colleague saw the title of this manuscript, *Preaching Christ from Ecclesiastes,* he quipped, "You are trying to find Christ under every rock, aren't you?" On the spur of the moment I responded, "You are confusing me with Paul" (see 1 Cor 10:4). Reflecting on this impromptu exchange later, I concluded that I gave the wrong response. I should have said, "It's not a matter of trying to find Christ under every rock but it's a matter of connecting the dots" — the dots that run from the periphery of the Old Testament to the center of God's revelation in Jesus Christ.

Redemptive-historical progression is the basic, foundational way of connecting the dots. Because redemptive history progresses from its earliest beginnings after the Fall into sin (Gen 3:15), through God's dealings with Israel, to the incarnation of Christ, his life, death, resurrection, and ascension, and finally to his Second Coming, Christian preachers must understand an Old Testament passage in the light of this progression in redemptive history.[100]

For example, the Teacher does not know about a resurrection from the

---

98. Brown, *Ecclesiastes,* 121. As an example, Brown mentions the commentary of Tremper Longman, *Book of Ecclesiastes.* See p. 8 above. Jerry Shepherd's "Ecclesiastes" of 2008 also follows this approach (see p. 8 above). James Steward, "Ecclesiastes and the Christian Preacher: An Exercise in Sermon-Preparation," *CQ* 29 (1951) 120-27, called Ecclesiastes "essentially a negative book" which "contains nothing or little that is inspiring or edifying in a positive way" (p. 120). Hence the preacher's "task is to reveal the imperfections of the characters depicted and, when that is done, to set beside these old portraits a likeness of the one Man in Whom full and satisfying life is to be found" (p. 122).

99. For a more detailed explanation, see my *Preaching Christ from the Old Testament,* 227-77.

100. Progression in redemptive history is closely related to progression in revelation. As redemptive history progresses, so does God's revelation. Progression in redemptive history is basic for the ways of promise — fulfillment, typology, and contrast, while progression in revelation comes to expression particularly in the way of longitudinal themes. The way of analogy reflects the overall continuity that exists even as redemptive history and the history of revelation unfold.

dead. Although he hints that there may be a final judgment (3:17; 8:12-13; 11:9), his main assumption is the finality of death.[101] He writes,

> The fate of humans and the fate of animals is the same; as one dies, so dies the other. They all have the same breath, and humans have no advantage over the animals; for all is vanity. All go to one place; all are from the dust, and all turn to dust again. Who knows whether the human spirit goes upward and the spirit of animals goes downward to the earth? (3:19-21; cf. 2:15-16; 9:5)

But this assumption of the finality of death changes drastically as redemptive history moves forward to the resurrection of Jesus. Death is not the end. Jesus conquered death. Jesus himself teaches his followers, "I am the resurrection and the life. Those who believe in me, even though they die, will live, and everyone who lives and believes in me will never die" (John 11:25-26). The progression in redemptive history to Jesus' resurrection casts the Teacher's message in a whole new light.[102]

Promise-Fulfillment

The Old Testament contains many promises of the coming Messiah. From such a promise one can move directly to its fulfillment in the coming of Jesus. But we cannot use the way of promise–fulfillment with Ecclesiastes because it contains no messianic promises.

Typology

Typology is another way to move from an Old Testament text to Christ in the New Testament. Old Testament redemptive events, persons, or institutions can function as types which foreshadow the great Antitype, the person and/or work of Jesus Christ. However, because Ecclesiastes is wisdom teaching, one should not expect a type of Christ in this book. Two possible exceptions are the figure of "Solomon" in Ecclesiastes 1:12–2:26 and the "one shepherd" of 12;11 (see pp. 56 and 301-2 below). Further, one could possibly argue that the wise Teacher himself in teaching wisdom is a type of the wise rabbi Jesus who also taught in *māšāl* (proverbs/parables).[103] But this kind of typology is not

---

101. See Antoon Schoors, "Koheleth: A Perspective of Life after Death?" *ETL* 61/4 (1985) 295-303.

102. Cf. Hertzberg's comment that because of Qohelet's comprehensive verdict of vanity, "the book of Qohelet, standing at the end of the Old Testament, is the most striking messianic prophecy the Old Testament has to offer." *Der Prediger*, 237-38, cited by Kidner, *The Wisdom of Proverbs, Job and Ecclesiastes*, 114.

103. Some of the Church Fathers (Didymus, Origen, and Gregory of Nyssa) did indeed see

necessary since we will cover these parallels in teaching under the category of analogy.

Analogy

Another way to move from the Old Testament to Christ in the New Testament is the way of analogy. Applied to Ecclesiastes, analogy looks for parallels between the teachings of the Old Testament Teacher and the teachings of Jesus. These analogies exist because Jesus was the supreme wise Teacher. Paul claims that in Christ "are hidden all the treasures of wisdom and knowledge" (Col 2:3). Consequently he can speak of Jesus as "wisdom from God" (1 Cor 1:24, 30). With respect to wisdom Jesus himself claimed to be "greater than Solomon" (Luke 11:31; cf. 2:52; 7:35). It is no surprise, therefore, that his contemporaries assessed Jesus as a wise Teacher (Mark 1:22) and that he taught primarily in the wisdom forms of proverbs[104] and parables.[105]

We can, therefore, look for analogies between the teachings of the Teacher of Ecclesiastes and those of Jesus. For example, the Teacher warns against working hard to obtain wealth: "I hated all my toil in which I had toiled under the sun, seeing that I must leave it to those who come after me — and who knows whether they will be wise or foolish? Yet they will be master of all for which I toiled and used my wisdom under the sun. This also is vanity" (2:18-19; cf. vv. 20-23). Jesus warns similarly: "Do not store up for yourselves treasures on earth, where moth and rust consume and where thieves break in and steal . . ." (Matt 6:19). In fact, Jesus tells a parable about a rich *fool.* The fool built larger barns to store all his goods and said, "'Soul, you have ample goods laid up for many years; relax, eat, drink, be merry.' But God said to him, 'You fool! This very night your life is being demanded of you. And the things you have prepared, whose will they be?' So it is with those who store up treasures for themselves but are not rich toward God" (Luke 12:19-21).

"the Preacher," understood to be Solomon, as a type of Christ. See Robert Wright, *Proverbs, Ecclesiastes, Song of Solomon,* 190.

104. See Alyce M. McKenzie, "All Who Exalt Themselves Will Be Humbled: Jesus' Subversive Sayings," in her book *Preaching Proverbs: Wisdom for the Pulpit* (Louisville: Westminster John Knox, 1996), 59-78.

105. Jesus' "predominant teaching form was the parable (*parabolē,* in Hebrew *māšāl* [also translated 'proverb']), a wisdom form." Dillard and Longman, *Introduction to the Old Testament,* 245. Cf. Ben Witherington III, *Jesus the Sage: The Pilgrimage of Wisdom* (Minneapolis: Fortress, 1994), 155-56, "By even a conservative estimate, at least 70% of the Jesus tradition is in the form of some sort of Wisdom utterance such as an aphorism, riddle, or parable."

Longitudinal Themes

Longitudinal themes provide another way from an Old Testament text to Christ in the New Testament. "Longitudinal themes" is a technical term in the discipline of Biblical Theology. It refers to themes that can be traced through the Scriptures from the Old Testament to the New. We can utilize this concept of longitudinal themes for preaching Christ because every major Old Testament theme leads to Christ. For example, we have seen that one of the major themes in Ecclesiastes is to fear God.[106] This theme of God's people's obligation to revere God goes back to the beginning of Israel's history (see Gen 22:12; Exod 14:31) and can be traced from there to God's later commands with the refrain, "You shall fear your God: I am the LORD" (Lev 19:14, 32; 25:17, 36, 43), to the Psalms (e.g., 34:9), to wisdom literature (e.g., Prov 1:7; 9:10; 15:33; Job 28:28), to Nehemiah after Israel's exile (Neh 5:9), to Ecclesiastes (3:14; 5:7; 7:18; 8:12-13; 12:13), to Jesus' teaching in the New Testament: "Do not fear those who kill the body but cannot kill the soul; rather fear him who can destroy both soul and body in hell" (Matt 10:28).

New Testament References

A sixth road from an Old Testament passage to Christ in the New Testament is that of New Testament references. Although the most direct references for preaching Christ are quotations from the teachings of Jesus in the Gospels, one can also utilize the New Testament letters when they link their teachings to Christ. Unfortunately, the New Testament seldom quotes Ecclesiastes directly and quotes or alludes to Ecclesiastes only twelve times.[107] For New Testament teachings similar to those of Ecclesiastes, one can check concordances, cross-reference Bibles, commentaries, and *The Treasury of Scripture Knowledge* on *Libronix* or the *PC Study Bible*. It is best, however, not to use New Testament references as the single road to Christ but to use them to support one of the other ways to Christ (for examples, see the New Testament references above under redemptive-historical progression, analogy, and longitudinal themes, and below under contrast).

Contrast

A final road from the Old Testament to Christ is the way of contrast. Because of the progression in redemptive history and in revelation the message for the

106. See above, pp. 17, 22, and below, p. 127, n. 18.
107. See the appendix in Nestle-Aland's *Novum Testamentum Graece* (1993 ed.).

contemporary church may be quite different from the Teacher's original message for Israel. Thus one can use contrast to preach Christ by moving from the Teacher's message for Israel to Christ's message for the church. For example, the Teacher stresses that "all is vanity." He asks (1:3), "What do people gain from all the toil at which they toil under the sun?" The expected answer is, We gain absolutely nothing from all our toil. If we do gain any wealth, we have to leave it to others when we die (2:18). So all our hard work is in vain. After Paul met the living Lord on the road to Damascus, he acquired quite a different perspective. He concludes his powerful chapter on the resurrection of Christ with these words, "Therefore, my beloved, be steadfast, immovable, always excelling in the work of the Lord, because you know that *in the Lord your labor is not in vain*" (1 Cor 15:58).

*   *   *

Investigating which of these ways lead from the message of the preaching text to Christ in the New Testament is a focused method of understanding the text in the context of the whole Christian canon. It may bring out a contrast with the Old Testament message, but often it will confirm and enrich that message in the light of the person, work, and/or teaching of Jesus Christ who fully revealed God the Father (Matt 11:27; John 1:18).

CHAPTER 2

No Gain from All Our Toil

Ecclesiastes 1:1-11

What do people gain from all the toil
at which they toil under the sun?

(Eccl 1:3)

This first passage from Ecclesiastes is a great text for focusing on the contemporary issue of materialism: the human drive to work for and find security in material wealth and possessions. The major challenge for preachers will be to understand and explain correctly the meaning of several ambiguous words and
phrases. Take, for example, the oft-repeated keyword *hebel*. The NRSV translates it as "vanity,"[1] the TNIV as "meaningless," the Anchor Bible as "vapor,"
and the New JPS Bible as "futility" or seven other words, depending on the context.[2] Other scholars suggest several nuances: "temporal ('ephemerality') and

---

1. Jerome was the first to translate the Hebrew *hebel* into the Latin *vanitas*. From there English versions used "vanity." But in modern English, "vanity" does not cover all the connotations of *hebel*. According to Webster's dictionary, "vanity" is "that which is vain or empty, idle,
or useless." It fails to cover that which is short-lived, ephemeral, or transitory. Although preachers should usually follow the pew Bible in preaching, they can certainly make the case for a different translation, preferably by quoting another Bible version.

2. See Fox, "The Meaning of *Hebel* for Qohelet," *JBL* 105/3 (1986) 413. Cf. Whybray,
"Qoheleth as a Theologian," 263-64, "Qohelet uses the term with respect to a bewildering variety of matters: of wealth and the love of wealth (5:9; 6:2); of the fact that wisdom confers no advantage over folly when death occurs (2:15; cf. 3:19); of the deceptiveness of pleasure (2:1) and of
the inane laughter of fools (7:6); and, more generally, of life itself (7:15; 9:9) and in particular of
youth (11:10); of toil (2:11; 4:4, 8); of human ignorance of the future (2:19) and the inequitable
distribution of rewards and punishments (2:26; 8:10, 14); of the need to relinquish one's possessions at death (2:19-21); of the uncertainties of political power (4:13-16); and finally of 'all that is
done under the sun' (1:14; 2:17)."

30

existential ('futility' or 'absurdity'),"[3] mainly "futility" but sometimes "brevity,"[4] "senseless" or "absurd,"[5] and "the notion that life is enigmatic, and mysterious; that there are many unanswered and unanswerable questions."[6] Other words and phrases in this passage, such as "all" (v. 2), "gain," and "under the sun" (v. 3) are equally ambiguous.[7] Another challenge is to preach Christ from a passage that does not even mention God. In fact, it seems that the author deliberately bypasses God in order to focus his attention exclusively on this earth — life "under the sun" (vv. 3 and 9).

Text and Context

Selecting the textual unit is not difficult with this opening passage. It begins with Ecclesiastes 1:1, obviously, and it ends with verse 11, since verse 12 begins a new unit with the autobiographical narrative, "I, the Teacher. . . ." Hence there is general agreement that Ecclesiastes 1:1-11 is a literary unit.

As to the context, it is important to note that verse 2, "Vanity of vanities, says the Teacher, vanity of vanities! All is vanity," is repeated in shortened form in chapter 12:8, thus forming an inclusio encompassing the entire book. Verse 2, therefore, can be understood as a basic theme underlying the entire book — a theme that will subsequently be developed in various ways, witness the repetition of the word "vanity" some thirty-eight times in Ecclesiastes. Moreover, the opening poem on the futile cycles in nature (vv. 4-7) is matched by the closing poem on aging and death (12:2-7). These two poems "envelop the book in a shroud-like fashion,"[8] setting a realistic, if not pessimistic, undertone.

Verse 3, as can be seen from the subsequent poem, appears to be the heart of this particular passage. It raises the rhetorical question, "What do people gain from all the toil at which they toil under the sun?" This question plays a key role in the remainder of the book. The word "gain" *(yitrôn)* will be repeated eight more times (see, e.g., 2:11, 3:9, and 5:16). The word "toil" *('ămāl)* will be re-

---

3. Crenshaw, *Ecclesiastes*, 57-58.

4. Whybray, *Ecclesiastes*, 36.

5. Fox, *Ecclesiastes*, 3.

6. Ogden, *Qoheleth*, 22. James Kugel, *Great Poems of the Bible*, 310, suggests that the Teacher "frequently uses this word to describe something in life that seems to him futile and useless (Eccl 2:1, 11, 17, 20, 23, and frequently thereafter); at other times *hebel* seems to mean something that is just baffling (Eccl 5:9; 7:15); at still other times it is used to mean something unfair, unjust (Eccl 2:26; 4:7; 6:2; 8:10, 14). And [in Eccl 12:8] . . . it is breathlike, evanescent: 'So fleeting.'"

7. See Lindsay Wilson, "Artful Ambiguity in Ecclesiastes 1:1-11: A Wisdom Technique?" in *Qohelet in the Context of Wisdom,* ed. Antoon Schoors (Leuven: Peeters, Leuven University, 1998), 357-65.

8. Salyer, *Vain Rhetoric*, 264.

peated twenty-two more times. And the phrase "under the sun" *(taḥat haššāmeś),* which appears only in Ecclesiastes, is found twice in this passage (1:3, 9) and will be repeated a total of twenty-nine times.

Literary Features

Noting the literary features of this text will help us determine its structure, which, in turn, will aid us in discerning the theme of the passage as well as the outline for an expository sermon.

Literary Forms

Verse 1 is a superscription which identifies the primary author of this work as the Teacher. Verse 2 consists of only eight words, five of them "vanity" *(hebel)* and four of these in the heightened form, "vanity of vanities" (cf. "holy of holies"). As noted, this verse forms an inclusio with 12:8, thus signaling that "all is vanity" is an underlying theme of this book.

Verses 3-11 are presented in the form of a reflection about human toil.[9] It begins with the rhetorical question: "What do people gain from all the toil at which they toil under the sun?" (v. 3). "Gain" is literally "profit" in business. Does it merely stand for economic profit or is it to be understood in a broader sense? Toiling "under the sun" is clear in its literal sense, but what does it stand for? Merely this earth? Or the earth to the exclusion of the world of the dead and the heavens? Or a secular perspective that fails to take God into account?

The expected answer to the rhetorical question — no gain from all our toil — is illustrated by the poem about the endless cycles in nature which gain nothing (vv. 4-8). Verse 9 restates the theme of "no gain" in terms of "nothing new." Verse 10 raises and answers a possible objection, while the concluding verse states that there is no remembrance of people who lived in the past — another form of "no gain."

Parallelism in the Poem

Since the distinctive feature of Hebrew poetry is parallelism, it may be helpful to quickly review the various kinds of parallelism. We can diagram the different rhetorical patterns as follows:

9. Murphy, *Ecclesiastes,* 133.

A — B   regular parallelism,
                either synonymous, synthetic, or antithetic[10]
A′ — B′   (either affirming, advancing, or opposing)[11]

A ⤬ B   inverted parallelism,
B′   A′   either synonymous, synthetic, or antithetic

A   B   a chiasm,[12] also called "concentric structure" and "introversion";
   C   there can be fewer or more elements on either side of the center
B′   A′   of a chiasm, e.g., A B **C** B A, or A B C **D** C′ B′ A′, or even a dual
                center such as A B C **D D′** C′ B′ A′.

A — A′   inclusio, also called "ballast lines," "ring structure," "envelope
                structure," and "bookends"

In this poem we find antithetic parallelism in verse 4, synthetic parallelism in verses 5 and 6, and synonymous parallelism in verse 7. Verse 8 concludes, "All things are wearisome," followed by three parallel statements which read literally:[13]

A man	is not able	to speak
An eye	is not satisfied	with seeing
An ear	is not filled	with hearing

Textual Structure

For understanding the thrust of this passage we need to outline the logical progression of ideas in the text. Again, commentators are not agreed. Fox probably comes closest to presenting a simple but valid outline:[14]

10. For more discussion of the different forms of parallelism, references, and examples, see my *Modern Preacher,* 60-62, 246-47, 293-94.

11. New nomenclature introduced by Gerald H. Wilson, *Psalms: Volume 1* (Grand Rapids: Zondervan, 2002), 40-48.

12. "Although most commentators use the term "chiasm" for inverted parallelism, since the main characteristic of Hebrew poetry is parallelism, it would be well to distinguish clearly between inverted parallelism and chiasm. In distinction from inverted parallelism, a chiasm — from the Greek *chiazein,* 'to mark with a *chi* (X)' — forms an X around a central component. Cf. John Breck, "Biblical Chiasmus: Exploring Structure for Meaning," *BTB* 17/2 (1987) 71, "The uniqueness of the chiastic structure lies in its focus on a pivotal theme, about which the other propositions of the literary unit are developed." For more discussion on chiastic structures, examples, and references, see my *Modern Preacher,* 62-63, 209-11, 249-50, 280-82, 292-93, and 320-21.

13. Ogden, *Qoheleth,* 32.

14. Fox, *A Time to Tear Down,* 164. Murphy, *Wisdom Literature,* 133, posits an inclusio of

A. 1:3. Thesis
B. 1:4-7. Arguments by analogy
C. 1:8. Reaction to observations in B
D. 1:9. Conclusion abstracted from B and justifying A
E. 1:10-11. Prose addendum, reinforcing A.

Adding the contents of each heading and more details is helpful for developing the sermon later. I therefore propose the following structural outline:

I. Introduction
   A. Superscription identifying the author as "the Teacher" (v. 1)
   B. Underlying theme of the book: "All is vanity" (v. 2)
II. Reflection on the theme: People gain nothing from their toil (v. 3)
   A. Theme illustrated by analogies of futile activity in nature (vv. 4-7)
      1. Generations go and come, but the earth remains (v. 4)
      2. The sun rises, goes down, and hurries back (v. 5)
      3. The wind goes round and round, and returns on its circuits (v. 6)
      4. Streams keep running to the sea but do *not fill* it (v. 7)
   B. Conclusion: All things are wearisome (v. 8a)
      1. A man is not able to speak (v. 8b)
      2. An eye is not satisfied with seeing (v. 8c)
      3. An ear is *not filled* with hearing (v. 8d)
III. Restatement of theme: Nothing new under the sun — no gain (v. 9)
   A. Objection: See, this is new (v. 10a)
   B. Response: It has already been (v. 10b)
   C. There is no remembrance of people — no gain (v. 11)

---

hōlēk ("goes") in vv. 4 and 6, and another of *mālēʾ/timmālēʾ* ("fill") in vv. 7 and 8. Consequently he holds together vv. 4-6 and 7-8, resulting in the following outline:

A. Thesis: there is no profit in man's toil	3
B. Thesis illustrated	4-8
1. An endless round of events	4-6
a. Generation	4
b. Sun	5
c. Wind	6
2. Failure of creation to be filled	7-8
a. Sea	7
b. Man	8

Of course, not every repetition functions as an inclusio. An author may simply repeat a word because there is no other word available or to establish a connection between one statement and another (such as "filled" in vv. 7 and 8). In any event, the *contents* of these verses trump any questionable inclusios.

Theocentric Interpretation

What does the Teacher say about God? The answer is, Nothing. In contrast to Genesis 1–3, Psalm 104, and Job 38–41, the Teacher manages to speak of creation without reference to God. William Brown writes, "The world according to Qohelet is an empty cosmos running perpetually like clockwork in its wearying courses. . . . The constant rhythms of day and night are not praised for their salutary roles in sustaining and ordering life (cf. Ps 104:19-23); they are rather disparaged for their incessant repetitions. According to the psalmist, the gushing streams provide for life, including the 'birds of the air' (vv. 10-12). For Qohelet, they flow for nothing. Qohelet's world reflects neither God's transcendent glory nor God's immanent presence. Whereas Psalm 104 vividly describes a *creatio continuata,* creation sustained and directed in all of its manifold forms, Qohelet dolefully describes perpetual uniformity, a monotony of the spheres."[15] But the Teacher did forewarn us that he was going to reflect on the world on the horizontal level, the world without God. He describes life "under the sun" (vv. 3, 9).[16] He describes life from a secular perspective.

Textual Theme and Goal

The outline of the text (above) helps us discover the textual theme. The Teacher states two themes: "All is vanity" (v. 2) and "People gain nothing from all their toil" (v. 3). "All is vanity" functions as the underlying theme of the book. In this passage the Teacher will give one argument for this theme, and that is that people gain nothing from their toil. The specific textual theme is therefore, "People gain nothing from all their toil."[17] But his key question is, "What do people gain from all the toil at which they toil *under the sun?*" "Under the sun" is a major

---

15. Brown, *Ecclesiastes,* 24.

16. "Under the sun" is "the seen world, interpreted in terms of itself." Eaton, *Ecclesiastes,* 63. Cf. Reitman, "The Structure and Unity of Ecclesiastes," *BSac* 154 (1997) 301, n. 17. "The phrase 'under the sun' is a trademark of Qohelet and is closely related to the concept of futility. It occurs twenty-nine times and projects the perspective of man alone, using his own wisdom and senses in the realm of 'this world' alone." Cf. Seow, *Ecclesiastes,* 105. "Qohelet clearly knows the more common expression 'under the heavens' and uses it, but his preference is for 'under the sun.' . . . Whereas 'under the heavens' refers to the universality of human experiences everywhere in the world (i.e., it is a spatial designation), 'under the sun' refers to the temporal universe of the living (cf. 8:9, where 'under the sun' is defined temporally: 'a time when . . .'). . . . The this-worldliness of the expression 'under the sun' explains its recurrence in Ecclesiastes."

17. Cf. Fox, *A Time to Tear Down,* 164, and Seow, *Ecclesiastes,* 111.

qualifier. The Teacher is looking at human life apart from God. He sets up his argument from a secular perspective. Since this particular perspective is of crucial importance for understanding the message he brings, we have to include it in the theme. The textual theme, therefore, becomes, "People gain nothing from all their toil under the sun."

However, the phrase "under the sun" is not immediately clear. Since this phrase implies a horizontal, secular perspective, we can clarify the theme by formulating it as follows, "From a secular perspective, people gain nothing from all their toil." But this formulation may still be puzzling to people. The challenge is to formulate the theme in such a way that it is brief, yet clear at first hearing. Probably the clearest and shortest formulation will be, *Apart from God, people gain nothing from all their toil.*

The next question is, Why did the Teacher wish to send this message to Israel? What was his goal? As we saw above (pp. 9-10), the Teacher addresses Israelites who were "preoccupied with all sorts of social and economic issues — the volatility of the economy, the possibility of wealth, inheritance, social status, the fragility of life, and the ever-present shadow of death."[18] They lived far from God but close to the marketplace with its concern for "profit." "To all those who try to 'gain' from life, whatever it is they claim to be doing, Qohelet presents stark reality — reality that does not change simply because we wish it to, but remains fundamentally as it is in spite of all that comes under the heading 'progress.' The more things change, the more they stay the same. The universe is not designed to enable 'gain' to happen."[19] The goal of the Teacher, then, is *to warn Israel that, apart from God, they will not gain anything from all their toil.*

Ways to Preach Christ[20]

Of the seven ways of moving from an Old Testament message to Christ in the New Testament, we have seen that promise-fulfillment and typology (with two possible exceptions) are not applicable to the book of Ecclesiastes. This leaves five

18. Seow, "The Socioeconomic Context of 'The Preacher's' Hermeneutic," *PSBul* 17/2 (1996) 195.

19. Provan, *Ecclesiastes*, 63.

20. In this and the following chapters, we use the sections "Ways to Christ" to list all the possible legitimate moves from the text to Christ in the New Testament. In writing the sermon we can subsequently select from this collection the best way(s) to focus the sermon on Christ. In their own research for sermons, preachers need not go into as much detail as in these presentations, which are intended to demonstrate more fully how one can move to Christ along each of the eligible ways.

possible ways: redemptive-historical progression, analogy, longitudinal themes, New Testament references, and contrast. We shall check each way in turn.

Redemptive-Historical Progression

Given the theme, "Apart from God, people gain nothing from all their toil," does redemptive-historical progression provide a way to Christ in the New Testament? Notice in verse 9 that the Teacher restates his theme with different images: "What has been is what will be, and what has been done is what will be done; there is nothing new under the sun." If there is nothing new, there is nothing gained. But as redemptive history moves forward, there is indeed a radically new event: Jesus, the Son of God, enters this world. Jesus says to the Jews, "You are from below, I am from above; you are of this world, I am not of this world" (John 8:23). Jesus gives a new word, "If you continue in my word, you are truly my disciples; and you will know the truth, and the truth will make you free" (John 8:31-32). Jesus also offers a new birth for entering the kingdom of God (John 3:3), establishes a new covenant (Luke 22:20), and, most significantly, conquers death (Matt 28:5-6). In fact, because of the new age Jesus ushered in, John sees a new heaven and a new earth and hears God's promise, "See, I am making all things new" (Rev 21:1, 5). As redemptive history progresses, therefore, there are new events, new realities, and new hopes that God will make all things new. Although people gain nothing from all their toil apart from God, through Jesus Christ there is much to be gained from our toil. Paul writes, "In the Lord [i.e., in Christ] your labor is not in vain" (1 Cor 15:58).

Analogy

As Ecclesiastes claims that we gain nothing from all our toil apart from God, so Jesus claims that we gain nothing in working for earthly possessions. Jesus asks, "What will it *profit* them if they gain the whole world but forfeit their life? Or what will they give in return for their life?" (Matt 16:26). In fact, Jesus tells the parable of the rich fool who lost everything and concludes, "So it is with those who store up treasures for themselves but are not rich toward *God*" (Luke 12:16-20). Therefore Jesus encourages us, "Do not store up for yourselves treasures on earth, where moth and rust consume and where thieves break in and steal; but store up for yourselves treasures in heaven, where neither moth nor rust consumes and where thieves do not break in and steal. For where your treasure is, there your heart will be also. . . . No one can serve two masters; for a slave will either hate the one and love the other, or be devoted to the one and despise the other. You cannot serve God and wealth" (Matt 6:19-24). Elsewhere Jesus says, "Do not work for the food that perishes, but for the food that endures for eternal life, which the Son of Man will give you. For it is on him that God the Father has set his seal" (John 6:27).

Longitudinal Themes

One can trace the biblical-theological theme of toiling for nothing from the Fall into sin, when meaningful work becomes "toil" and a lifetime of toil ends in human beings returning to the dust of the earth (Gen 3:17-18) — no gain. The theme of toil ending in death runs through the Old Testament from generation to generation (cf. the repeated, "and he died," in Gen 5) and seemingly on into the New Testament. Saints and sinners die, and "the people of long ago are not remembered" (Eccl 1:11). Jesus proclaims, however, "I am the resurrection and the life. Those who believe in me, even though they die, will live, and everyone who lives and believes in me will never die" (John 11:25-26).

New Testament References

Aside from the New Testament references used to support the three ways above and contrast below, one may also consider Romans 8, where Paul uses the same Greek word, *mataiotēs*, which the Septuagint uses for the Hebrew *hebel*: "for the creation was subjected to *futility*."[21] But because Christ has come, Paul can move beyond Ecclesiastes: "for the creation was subjected to futility, not of its own will but by the will of the one who subjected it [i.e., God; see Gen 3:17], in hope that the creation itself will be set free from its bondage to decay and will obtain the freedom of the glory of the children of God" (Rom 8:20-21).

James also comes close to using the imagery of Ecclesiastes that "all is vanity," literally, "all is vapor, breath," when he writes, "You are a mist that appears for a little while and then vanishes" (Jas 4:14). But James does not link his observation directly to Christ.

Contrast

Because of the coming of Jesus Christ and his resurrection, contrast also provides a strong bridge to Christ in the New Testament. Paul concludes his chap-

---

21. See the reference in the appendix to Nestle-Aland's *Novum Testamentum Graece.*

ter on Jesus' resurrection with these profound words, "Therefore, my beloved, be steadfast, immovable, always excelling in the work of the Lord, because you know that in the Lord your labor is *not in vain*" (1 Cor 15:58). Ecclesiastes implied that people gain nothing from their toil (1:3). Paul states that people gain from their "work in the Lord": "in the Lord your labor is not in vain." Paul himself lived out of this perspective. He writes the Philippians: "For to me, living is Christ and dying is *gain*" (Phil 1:21). Paul also contradicts Ecclesiastes' statement that there is nothing new. He writes, "So if anyone is in Christ, there is a new creation: everything old has passed away; see, everything has become new!" (2 Cor 5:17).

Jesus himself affirms that our work can bear fruit: "I am the vine, you are the branches. Those who abide in me and I in them bear *much fruit,* because apart from me you can do nothing" (John 15:5). Jesus even says that we will gain a reward from our work: "Whoever welcomes a prophet in the name of a prophet will receive a prophet's reward; and whoever welcomes a righteous person in the name of a righteous person will receive the reward of the righteous; and whoever gives even a cup of cold water to one of these little ones in the name of a disciple — truly I tell you, none of these will lose their reward" (Matt 10:41).

Sermon Theme and Goal

We formulated the textual theme as, "Apart from God, people gain nothing from all their toil." We now need to decide whether in the sermon we'll put the emphasis in our move(s) to Jesus in the New Testament on analogy or contrast. If we emphasize the *contrast* between the message of Ecclesiastes and that of Jesus, we'll have to change the textual theme almost into its opposite to arrive at a sermon theme. Then we might consider for a sermon theme Paul's words, "In the Lord your labor is not in vain." Or, reflecting Jesus' words, we might consider, "Whoever abides in Jesus will bear much fruit." But the unfortunate result is that our preaching text no longer supports the sermon theme. In order to do justice to an Old Testament text, it is usually advisable to stick as closely as possible to the textual theme, that is, to focus on the *continuity* with the New Testament rather than the discontinuity.[22] In our sermon exposition, therefore, we shall focus primarily on the analogies. This means that our sermon theme can be the same as the textual theme, *Apart from God, people gain nothing from all their toil.*

The goal of the Teacher for Israel we formulated as, "to warn Israel that,

22. For further discussion on this issue, see pp. 96-97 below, "Sermon Theme and Goal."

apart from God, they will not gain anything from all their toil." Our goal in preaching this sermon should be similar to the Teacher's goal and match the sermon theme. We can accomplish this by making a slight change in the sermon goal: *to warn the hearers that, apart from God, they will not gain anything from all their toil.*

This goal indicates that the need addressed by this sermon, the problem targeted, is broadly the rampant materialism in our culture that affects also our hearers. The need is the danger that the hearers will buy into the American dream that with our toil we can gain something important: we can become prosperous, self-made men and women.

The Sermon Form

Since the Teacher's "reflection" is a didactic form, the sermon can best follow the didactic form. Moreover, he states his theme early on (v. 3) and then argues for his theme (vv. 4-11). In other words, he uses deductive development. An expository sermon can follow suit by using deductive development.

The sermon introduction is an important part of the sermon. Although it ought to create interest and "lead into" *(intro ducere)* the topic of the sermon, it can do much more. The introduction can show the relevance of the sermon by disclosing its target (why the sermon is preached and why people should listen); it can set the tension that will keep the hearers listening for the resolution; it can create a hunger to hear the word of the Lord. Therefore I suggest that preachers usually begin with an illustration of the need addressed by the sermon; next connect this illustration pastorally to the need of the hearers; then show that this need is similar to Israel's need at that time (the question behind the text) and (with deductive development) state the textual theme.[23]

Sermon Exposition[24]

For this sermon the introduction can illustrate the common desire to accumulate wealth. Our society offers countless illustrations of this desire: the increas-

---

23. See Appendixes 1 and 2 below (pp. 311-14).

24. In this and the following chapters, the sections of "Sermon Exposition" seek to expose the meaning of practically every verse in the preaching text. Since including all this information in an actual sermon will lead to information overload, one will have to select from this material what is pertinent to the point made and add illustrations and applications that focus the sermon on one's specific congregation.

ing gambling addictions, millions of people buying lottery tickets in the hope of hitting the jackpot, people on television risking a sure $200,000 for a chance at a million; the drive for ever higher wages, ever bigger cars, ever bigger boats, ever larger houses. Instead of listing all these and more examples, it is more engaging to tell the story of a person who fell into this trap of seeking to accumulate wealth. Then carefully link this illustration to our desire for ever more wealth: Could it be that we are not immune to the rampant materialism in our culture? Could it be that we, too, have bought into the "bigger-is-better" syndrome of our society?

The Teacher of Ecclesiastes is addressing Israelites for whom a new day had dawned. They no longer lived their quiet, agricultural existence — depending on the LORD to provide their daily bread. They lived at the crossroads of a new, booming international trade between Egypt and Asia/Europe. Fortunes could be made, and lost, overnight. The Israelites were scrambling to get rich. But the Teacher begins his book by warning them: "Apart from God, people gain nothing from all their toil."

He begins his message in verse 2,[25] "Vanity of vanities, says the Teacher, vanity of vanities! All is vanity." The word translated here as "vanity" is literally "vapor" or "breath." "All is vanity" is literally "all is vapor," "all is breath." Stand outside on a cold winter morning and breath out. What do we see? We see our breath as a vapor. What else do we see? The vapor is there for a second and then disappears. All things in this world are like our breath, the Teacher says. It's here one moment and then it's gone. The Psalmist also cries out.

> You have made my days a few handbreadths,
> and my lifetime is as nothing in your sight.
> Surely everyone stands as a mere breath *(hebel).*[26]

In the New Testament, James uses a similar image. He writes, "You are a mist that appears for a little while and then vanishes" (Jas 4:14). Ask older people about their life and, even when they are ninety years old, they will agree that their life was like "a mist that appears for a little while and then vanishes." Here today, gone tomorrow. That is what the Teacher is after, to teach Israel and us that our life on this earth is extremely brief; it's like our breath on a cold winter morning: we see it for a moment, and then it's gone.[27]

---

25. We need not deal with verse 1, concerning the author, in this sermon. This topic will arise in the next section starting at Ecclesiastes 1:12.

26. Psalms 39:5. Cf. Psalm 144:4.

27. Provan, *Ecclesiastes,* 52, rightly questions the TNIV translation of "meaningless": "It makes little sense for Qohelet to advise a young person to be happy while living reverently before God only then to remind him that 'youth and vigor are meaningless' (11:10)! It makes great

But there is more to this image than brevity. Breath out on a cold winter morning and try to grab the vapor. There is nothing to hold on to. Not only does it disappear quickly, but even during its short life span there seems to be no substance to it; it is elusive. Our life is transitory and elusive. It makes no sense; it all seems so pointless, so futile.[28]

"Vanity of vanities, says the Teacher, vanity of vanities! All is vanity." "Vanity of vanities" is a way of expressing the superlative. The "holy of holies" is the most holy place in the temple. The "heaven of heavens" is the highest heaven. "Vanity of vanities" is utter vanity.[29] The Teacher repeats it again to make sure we get the point: "vanity of vanities": human life is utter vanity.

He concludes by saying that "*All* is vanity." Everything we see on this earth is short-lived and lacks substance. The clothes we wear will soon wear out and we have to buy new ones. The car we buy will soon go to the scrap yard and we have to get another one. The house we live in lasts longer but will eventually be torn down and replaced by a new building. "All is vanity." To prove his point that "all is vanity," the Teacher in this book will look at life from different angles.

In this passage he is going to look at life from the angle of what we *gain* from life with our work. In verse 3 he raises the question, "What do people gain from all the toil at which they toil under the sun?" The expected answer to this question is, Nothing. People gain nothing from all the toil at which they toil under the sun!

The word "gain" (*yitrôn*) appears nine times in Ecclesiastes[30] and nowhere else in the Old Testament. The word comes from a verb "to be left over," "to remain" — as when one invests in a business, paying expenses and receiving income, and at the end of the year one checks what is left over. So "gain" can also

---

sense for him, however, to offer this advice in the context of the *brevity* of youth. . . . The summarizing conclusion that follows the graphic description of aging and death in 12:1-7 as well as all of Qohelet's words (12:8) most naturally refers likewise to the fleeting nature of all things, not to their meaninglessness. If 12:8 has this meaning for *hebel,* then 1:2 most likely does as well."

28. Commentators understandably want clarity and therefore seek to pinpoint a single meaning for a metaphor that may have several depth dimensions. But the author may well have intended more than a single meaning. As we are to hear two meanings together in synonymous parallelism, like stereophonic sound, so we may be intended to hear more than one meaning in a metaphor, like surround sound. Certainly ambiguity can lead to various connected depth dimensions. In this case, because all things are transitory, they are insubstantial; in fact, they may be futile. The context will have to decide which is the dominant tone.

29. Kidner, *A Time to Mourn,* 22. Cf. Seow, *Ecclesiastes,* 101, "*Qoh. Rabb.* takes the word to be 'like the steam from the oven' and the superlative is taken to mean that humanity is even less substantial than steam."

30. Ecclesiastes 1:3; 2:11, 13; 3:9; 5:9, 16 (Hebrew 5:8, 15); 7:12; 10:10, 11.

be translated as "profit."[31] "What do people profit from all the toil at which they toil under the sun?"

"Under the sun" is also a typical expression found only in Ecclesiastes. The Teacher uses it twenty-nine times.[32] "Under the sun" refers to living in this world without taking God into account. "The scene in mind is exclusively the world we can observe, and . . . our observation point is at ground level."[33] "What do people gain from all the toil at which they toil under the sun?" The answer is, Nothing. From a secular perspective, apart from God, people gain nothing from all their toil. In the New Testament Jesus raises a similar question: "What will it *profit* [people] if they gain the whole world but forfeit their life?" (Matt 16:26). If they forfeit their life, their soul, the essence of their being, they have nothing left.

The Teacher will prove his point with a carefully constructed argument. He compares the futility of human life with the cycles we can observe in nature. Verse 4, "A generation goes, and a generation comes, but the earth remains forever." "A generation goes, and a generation comes," seems to point to the brevity of human life.[34] But in reality this verse supports the idea that there is no gain. Normally one would say, "A generation comes, and a generation goes." But the Teacher has reversed the order: "A generation goes, and a generation comes." "The word order in verse 4 actually places the emphasis on the replacement of one generation by another (the generation that *goes* is replaced by the one that *comes*), a process like that of the other phenomena described."[35] In spite of constant changes, in reality nothing changes. There is no gain. Verse 4 is similar to verse 7, "All streams run to the sea, but the sea is not full." In spite of all this water pouring into the sea, it is not full. There is no change. So here, "A generation goes, and a generation comes, but the earth[36] remains forever." The earth remains the same, like the sea. Nothing changes. There is no gain.

---

31. See Provan, *Ecclesiastes*, 54. Perdue, *Wisdom Literature*, 192, suggests, "Qohelet desires to find something that endures beyond the limited life span of a human being, something that would enable one to live beyond the grave, at least in human memory." See also p. 63 below.

32. Ecclesiastes 1:3, 9, 14; 2:11, 17, 18, 19, 20, 22; 3:16; 4:1, 3, 7, 15; 5:13, 18 (Hebrew 5:12, 17); 6:1, 12; 8:9, 15 (2x), 17; 9:3, 6, 9 (2x), 11, 13; 10:5.

33. Kidner, *A Time to Mourn*, 23.

34. See, e.g., Murphy, *Ecclesiastes*, 7, "This verse affirms the ephemeral character of humankind, against the background of the ever-lasting earth." This interpretation would support verse 2, "All is vanity." But the Teacher here seeks to support verse 3, which says that there is no gain.

35. Fox, *Ecclesiastes*, 5.

36. Fox argues that "the earth" *(hā'āreṣ)* "here does not mean the physical earth, but humanity as a whole — 'le monde' rather than 'la terre." "Qohelet 1:4," *JSOT* 40 (1988) 109. Cf. his *Ecclesiastes*, 5. But there is no need to change the translation from "earth" to the much rarer "humanity." When one takes the word to mean the physical earth — the sun, wind, and sea are physical — the argument still holds: generations go and generations come on the earth, but it remains the same.

From the earth, the Teacher moves to the sun, and here too he observes cycles that do not change anything. "The sun rises and the sun goes down, and hurries to the place where it rises." This description of the sun is quite different from the Psalmist's glowing description: "In the heavens he has set a tent for the sun, which comes out like a bridegroom from his wedding canopy, and like a *strong* man runs its course with *joy*" (Ps 19:4-5). In Ecclesiastes "the sun rises and the sun goes down, and [literally] *pants*[37] to the place where it rises." It struggles back to the place where it rises. "The sun gasps for breath from its enervating circuits."[38] Meanwhile, "it does not attain anything by going around and around. It is mere toil, for following its daily journey there is no opportunity for rest to make itself ready for the repeat performance. It is all pauseless, breathless treadmill-like repetition."[39] And there is no gain.

From the earth and the sun the Teacher turns to the wind. Verse 6, "The wind blows to the south, and goes around to the north; round and round goes the wind, and on its circuits the wind returns." While the sun (from our perception) always moves from east to west, the wind goes to the south and goes around to the north. But unlike the sun, which is trapped in its constant cycle from east to west, the wind seems entirely free. The Teacher calls attention to "the rapid and repeated movements: . . . literally 'going . . . turning around . . . turning around, turning around, going."[40] The wind is free to blow where it wills. But the upshot of all this turning around is: "on its circuits the wind returns." Even the wind is "caught in a rut."[41] Even the wind follows a fixed path and nothing is gained.[42]

From the earth, the sun, and the wind, the Teacher finally turns to the sea. Verse 7, "All streams run to the sea, but the sea is not full; to the place where the streams flow, there they continue to flow." The Teacher may well have thought of the Dead Sea — at 1380 feet (420 meters) below sea level the deepest sea on earth and therefore without outlet. While the Jordan River and

37. "The word *hurry* (*šāʾap*) is literally 'pant.' Commentators have rightly pointed out that the OT uses it in a positive as well as a negative sense. Positively, the word means to pant with eagerness or desire (for God's commandments in Ps 119:131), negatively, to pant with exhaustion (like a woman in childbirth in Isa 42:14)." Longman, *Book of Ecclesiastes*, 69. In the context of Ecclesiastes, Longman opts for the negative meaning, finding support also in the Septuagint translation *helkei*, "drags," and Targum *štyp*, "crawls."

38. Brown, *Ecclesiastes*, 24.

39. Loader, *Ecclesiastes*, 20.

40. Seow, *Ecclesiastes*, 108.

41. Crenshaw, *Ecclesiastes*, 64, "This sense of being caught in a rut reaches its peak in three successive participles *sōbēb sōbēb hōlēk* just before the subject *hārûaḥ* is introduced."

42. Seow, *Ecclesiastes*, 115, "The wind moves about a lot, but even the unpredictable wind returns because of its rounds. There is a lot of movement, but ultimately nothing new happens. No advantage is gained, despite all the busy-ness."

many wadis empty into the Dead Sea, it does not overflow. The same is true for the Mediterranean Sea and the oceans. "All streams run to the sea, but the sea is not full. To the place where the streams flow [i.e., the sea], there they continue to flow."[43] We know, of course, that the sea is not full because the water evaporates and the clouds bring the rain back to the land — another cycle.[44] But that is not the point of this verse. The point is rather that the streams continue to flow into the sea, yet the sea is not full. All that activity shows no results. There is no gain.

"The whole world is a scene of incessant movement and activity. But is it purposeful? . . . For all the constant motion that characterizes the cosmos, one would think that something is being accomplished. But no. Even as the millennia come and go, any semblance of progress is only a mirage. Activity abounds; everything is in perpetual motion, like a hamster in a wheel, but no destination is reached. This display of endless cosmic exertion is all for naught."[45] The earth remains the same; the sun seems always to toil in the same orbit; the wind returns on its circuits, and the sea does not fill up. Earth, fire, air, and water are all caught in a rut. If the basic elements for the ancient world gain nothing from all their toil, then surely human beings gain nothing from all their toil.[46]

The Teacher sums it all up in verse 8, "All things are wearisome; more than one can express; the eye is not satisfied with seeing, or the ear filled with hearing." "All things"[47] refers to the foregoing cycles in nature. Contemplating all these things is wearisome. "More than one can express" is the first of three parallel statements which read literally:

A man	is not able	to speak
An eye	is not satisfied	with seeing
An ear	is not filled	with hearing

43. The TNIV translates verse 7b as completing the circle, "To the place the streams come from, there they return again." Garrett, *Proverbs, Ecclesiastes, Song of Songs* 285, comments, "The last phrase does not refer to the cycle of evaporation and rainfall as implied in the NIV translation. Gordis [*Koheleth*, 207] correctly calls such an interpretation 'linguistically forced.' It should read, 'To the place where the rivers go, there they continually go.' The implication here is not cyclic motion but futile activity."

44. Whybray, *Ecclesiastes*, 42-43, argues for the cyclical movement.

45. Brown, *Ecclesiastes*, 23.

46. Jerome, quoted by Crenshaw, *Ecclesiastes*, 63, remarked, "What is more vain than this vanity: that the earth, which was made for humans, stays — but humans themselves, the lords of the earth, suddenly dissolve into dust?"

47. Contrary to many commentators who translate *kol-haddĕbārîm* as "all words," in the context "all things" is a better translation, as is "a thing" for *dābār* in 1:10. See, e.g., Whybray, *Ecclesiastes*, 44, and Crenshaw, *Ecclesiastes*, 66.

"Each phrase offers a concrete illustration, this time from human life, of the continuous operation of mouth, eye . . . and ear."[48] The mouth cannot say enough about the wearisome repetition of futile cycles in nature. "No one can speak meaningfully . . . about the world; that is, no one can explain, influence, or control it."[49] The eye also "never reaches the point that it cannot take in more, nor does the ear become so filled with sound that it cannot accept any more impulses from the outside world."[50] The ceaseless activity of the generations, the sun, wind, and streams is mirrored in human life. As all this activity in nature gains nothing, so all human activity of speaking, seeing, and hearing gains absolutely nothing.

In verse 9 the Teacher approaches his point about the lack of gain from a different angle. "What has been is what will be, and what has been done is what will be done; there is nothing new under the sun." "What has been is what will be" seems to hark back to the futile cycles displayed in nature.[51] The generations will keep going and coming, as will the sun, the wind, and the streams. "What has been is what will be." Nothing new. No gain.

But then the Teacher switches to human history: "and what has been done is what will be done." In human history, too, he says, we see frantic activity but it is not going anywhere. All we see is futile repetition. "What has been done is what will be done." And he concludes, "there is nothing new under the sun." Nothing new! Human history also shows that there is no gain. If there is no gain in human history, then there certainly is no gain for individuals. There is nothing new!

In verse 10 the Teacher anticipates an objection to his radical claim that there is nothing new under the sun. "Is there a thing of which it is said, 'See, this is new'?" His answer to the objection is short and abrupt, "It has already been, in the ages before us." A new baby is born. People say, "See, this is new." The Teacher responds, "It has already been." Babies were born also in the past. A war starts. People say, "See, this is new." The Teacher responds, "It has already been." Wars started in the past too.[52] "In light of the repetitive nature of history, any allegedly new thing is simply a variation of something from the past."[53]

---

48. Ogden, *Qoheleth*, 32.

49. Garrett, *Proverbs, Ecclesiastes, Song of Songs*, 287.

50. Ogden, *Qoheleth*, 32.

51. Whybray, *Ecclesiastes*, 45.

52. "As Augustine [*City of God*, 12.13] observed when arguing against the theory of cyclical time, Qohelet is speaking of recurrence of *types* of beings and events. . . . Archetypal events (including deeds, seen as events) — birth, death, war, embracing, and so on — come to realization in specific manifestations: the birth of particular individuals, particular acts of embracing, the outbreak of particular wars, etc." Fox, *Qohelet and His Contradictions*, 172.

53. Brown, *Ecclesiastes*, 27. Longman, *Book of Ecclesiastes*, 75, adds, "Even if it is granted that new discoveries are made, people remain the same."

The Teacher concludes this passage with verse 11, "The people of long ago are not remembered, nor will there be any remembrance of people yet to come by those who come after them." Here he expands on a point made in verse 4, "A generation goes, and a generation comes, but the earth remains forever." Even though the going and coming of generations makes no difference to the earth, is it possible for a generation of people or for individuals to stand out somehow and show some gain? Is it possible for people to make such an impact on history that they will be remembered and at least gain *recognition?* His pessimistic answer is, No, "the people of long ago are not remembered." Human memory is too short.

The Teacher "is not so much claiming that human beings are utterly oblivious to the past as he is undercutting their deepest and vainglorious aspirations to secure some permanent place or 'remembrance' in history. A life oriented toward ensuring its legacy for posterity only pursues the wind. The future cannot be controlled any more than the past can be fully remembered."[54] People have had mountains named after them, but a following generation changes the names. People have had their names etched into buildings, but in time the buildings will be demolished and the names forgotten. People write books to be remembered by posterity, but in time the books will be replaced by other books and the authors will be forgotten. "It makes no difference what one has accomplished or who one may be (see 2:16). When death comes, all hopes perish, and no one is better off than others. . . . Death dashes all hopes of immortality, including the 'immortality' of being remembered forever."[55]

The Teacher has clearly made his point that people gain nothing from all the toil at which they toil under the sun; that is, they gain nothing from the toil at which they toil apart from God. He will reinforce this point later with other images. In chapter 2:18-19 he writes, "I hated all my toil in which I had toiled under the sun, seeing that I must leave it to those who come after me — and who knows whether they will be wise or foolish? Yet they will be master of all for which I toiled and used my wisdom under the sun. This also is vanity." And in chapter 5:16 he writes, "This also is a grievous ill: just as they came [naked from their mother's womb], so shall they go; and what gain do they have from toiling for the wind?"

In the New Testament Jesus makes the same point. Jesus asks, "For what will it *profit* [people] if they gain the whole world but forfeit their life?" (Matt 16:26). When people forfeit their life, they have gained nothing — no profit. Jesus makes the same point as Ecclesiastes with a simple story, a parable: "The land of a rich man produced abundantly. And he thought to himself, 'What

54. Brown, ibid., 28.
55. Seow, *Ecclesiastes*, 117.

should I do, for I have no place to store my crops?' Then he said, 'I will do this: I will pull down my barns and build larger ones, and there I will store all my grain and my goods. And I will say to my soul, 'Soul, you have ample goods laid up for many years; relax, eat, drink, be merry.' But God said to him, 'You fool! This very night your life [literally, your soul] is being demanded of you. And the things you have prepared, whose will they be?'" When the rich man died, he had gained nothing from all his toil. There was nothing left over: no profit. Jesus concludes this parable, "So it is with those who store up treasures for themselves but are not rich toward *God*" (Luke 12:16-20). Apart from God, people gain nothing from all their toil.

Is there then nothing to be gained from our life on earth? Nothing left over when we die? No profit? Yes, Jesus says, there can be a profit, but then we ought not to store up treasures for ourselves but be rich toward God. Therefore Jesus encourages us, "Do not store up for yourselves treasures on earth, where moth and rust consume and where thieves break in and steal; but store up for yourselves treasures in heaven, where neither moth nor rust consumes and where thieves do not break in and steal. For where your treasure is, there your heart will be also" (Matt 6:19-21).[56] Elsewhere, Jesus admonishes, "Do not work for the food that perishes, but for the food that endures for eternal life, which the Son of Man [i.e., Jesus] will give you" (John 6:27).

Jesus' message is clear: We gain nothing if we store up treasures on earth. We gain nothing if we toil apart from God. But our lives can have a profit if we are, in Jesus' words, "rich toward God," if we "store up treasures in heaven," if we "serve God." Paul confirms Jesus' words. He writes, "Therefore, my beloved, be steadfast, immovable, always excelling in the work of the Lord, because you know that *in the Lord your labor is not in vain*" (1 Cor 15:58).

But if our labor is not "in the Lord," if our work is apart from God, we gain nothing. Therefore Jesus warns us, "Do not store up for yourselves treasures on earth . . . ; but store up for yourselves treasures in heaven" (Matt 6:19-20).

---

56. Jesus continues in Matthew 6:24, "No one can serve two masters; for a slave will either hate the one and love the other, or be devoted to the one and despise the other. You cannot serve God and wealth."

CHAPTER 3

The Teacher's Search for Meaning

Ecclesiastes 1:12–2:26

> *I, the Teacher, when king over Israel in Jerusalem,*
> *applied my mind to seek and to search out by wisdom*
> *all that is done under heaven;*
> *it is an unhappy business that God has given*
> *to human beings to be busy with.*
>
> (Eccl 1:12-13)

This is an ideal passage for exploring the contemporary concern for the meaning of life. Since Ecclesiastes 1:12–2:26 is the longest preaching text in this book, a major challenge will be to do justice to its many elements in a single sermon and still keep it unified and moving. Another challenge is to formulate a single theme that encompasses both the negative results of the search for meaning ("vanity and a chasing after wind") and the final positive advice ("There is nothing better for mortals than to eat and drink, and find enjoyment in their toil").

Text and Context

It is clear that a new literary unit begins in Ecclesiastes 1:12-13, "I, the Teacher, when king over Israel in Jerusalem, applied my mind to seek and to search out by wisdom all that is done under heaven." The conclusion of this unit, however, is not so evident. Some commentators end the unit at 1:18, others at 2:11, others at 2:23,[1] still others at 2:26, and still others at 3:15.[2] While 1:12-18 is certainly a

1. See Murphy, *Wisdom Literature*, 136.
2. See Seow, *Ecclesiastes*, 142.

subunit, the Teacher continues his search for meaning in 2:1, "I said to my-self. . . ."[3] Again, 2:1-11 is certainly a subunit, but the Teacher continues his search in 2:12, "So I turned to consider wisdom. . . ." Again, 2:12-23 is a subunit, but the whole unit is not complete until the final conclusion of the Teacher's search in 2:24-26, "There is nothing better for mortals than to eat and drink, and find enjoyment in their toil. This also, I saw, is from the hand of God. . . ."[4] 3:1 begins a new unit, "For everything there is a season. . . ." Our textual unit, therefore, is Ecclesiastes 1:12–2:26.[5]

As to the context, the Teacher further explores in this passage the key question raised earlier, "What do people *gain* from all the toil at which they toil under the sun?" (1:3). He comes to the same conclusion, "I considered all that my hands had done and the toil I had spent in doing it, and again, all was vanity and a chasing after wind, and there was nothing to be *gained* under the sun" (2:11). Many words and phrases in the former passage are repeated here — "toil," "vanity," "under the sun," "remembrance" — and will be repeated again in later passages. The final advice after the Teacher's lengthy search, "There is nothing better for mortals than to eat and drink, and find enjoyment in their toil" (2:24), will be repeated six more times in Ecclesiastes (3:12-13, 22; 5:18-20; 8:15; 9:7-10; 11:8-10) "with steadily increasing emphasis and solemnity."[6]

Literary Features

In this section, the Teacher makes use of several literary forms (subgenres). The whole unit is cast in the form of an autobiographical narrative. Ecclesiastes 1:12-15, beginning with "I applied my mind," is a reflection on the vanity of using wisdom, as is 1:16-18, beginning with "I said to myself." Each of these two introductory reflections ends with a proverb (1:15 and 18). 2:1-11, beginning with, "I said to myself," is a reflection on pursuing pleasure. 2:12-17, beginning with, "I turned to consider," is reflection on the benefits of wisdom over folly. This reflection also includes a confirming proverb (2:14). Finally, 2:18-26 is a reflection focusing specifically on

---

3. See ibid., 142-43, for the inclusio "under heaven" in 1:13 and 2:3, and "many continuities between 1:13-18 and 2:1-3.

4. In 2:24-26 "the author returns to the themes raised in the introductory section (1:13–2:3): God, the giving of a preoccupation, the place of wisdom, knowledge, joy, and seeing good. One may argue, then, that 2:24-26 constitutes the concluding section of the entire literary unit, forming with the introduction in 1:13–2:3 a theological framework within which to interpret the whole." Ibid., 143.

5. Cf. Dorsey, *Literary Structure*, 193, "The book's second unit begins with shifts of person (from third-person to first-person) and genre (from poetry to prose autobiography). This autobiographical account continues through 2:26, at which point the author shifts back to poetry."

6. See Whybray, "Qoheleth, Preacher of Joy," *JSOT* 23 (1982) 87-98.

the results of human toil (possessions), concluding with the admonition that human beings should "eat and drink, and find enjoyment in their toil" (2:24-26).[7]

The Teacher again uses repetitions to emphasize important points. In this passage he repeats twice the common term "under heaven" (1:13; 2:3) but seven times his specific term for life "under the sun" (1:14; 2:11, 17, 18, 19, 20, 22) — that is, life considered from a horizontal, secular perspective; life without taking God into account.[8] He repeats eight times "all is vanity" (1:14; 2:1, 11, 17, 19, 21, 23, 26), combining this phrase four times with "a chasing after wind" (1:14; 2:11, 17, 26) and once "a chasing after wind" by itself (1:17). He repeats fifteen times in this passage the keyword "toil" of 1:3, "What do people gain from all the toil at which they toil under the sun?" He usually refers to the vanity of "toil," but twice he combines pleasure with toil (2:10, "my heart found pleasure in all my toil," and 2:24, "find enjoyment in their toil"). And three times he refers to God (1:13 and 2:24, 26), forming a possible inclusio for this literary unit.

The Teacher uses synonymous parallelism in the first two proverbs (1:15, 18) and antithetic parallelism in the third proverb (2:14). He also uses many metaphors in this passage, such as "vapor," "chasing after wind," "under the sun," "my heart," "hand of God," "darkness," and possibly "eat and drink."[9]

Textual Structure

The reflections highlighted under "Literary Features" above provide the main divisions in this passage: 1:12-18; 2:1-11; 2:12-17; 2:18-23; and 2:24-26. These divisions are confirmed by the closing of each section with a proverb or the declaration of "vanity." We can outline the complex flow of the Teacher's argument as follows:

I. Introduction: the Teacher searches out by wisdom (1:12-13a)
   A. All that is done under heaven (1:13b)
      1. Conclusion: God has given humans an unhappy business (1:13c)
         a. Reason: all deeds done under the sun are vanity (1:14)
            i. Confirmed by a proverb:

               One cannot make straight what is crooked
               One cannot count what is lacking (1:15)

---

7. See Murphy, *Wisdom Literature*, 134-36.

8. "Under the sun" is "the seen world, interpreted in terms of itself." Eaton, *Ecclesiastes*, 63. See also Chapter 2, p. 35, n. 16 above.

9. Cf. Seow, *Ecclesiastes*, 157, "He is not referring here to specific activities of eating and drinking, but to a general attitude toward life."

    B. He searches out how to distinguish wisdom from folly (1:16-17a)

        1. Conclusion: distinguishing wisdom from folly is chasing after wind (1:17b)

            a. Confirmed by a proverb:

                In much wisdom is much vexation

                    Those who increase knowledge increase sorrow (1:18)

II. The Teacher tests what is gained by pleasure (2:1a)

    A. Enjoy yourself (2:1b)

    B. Conclusion: this also is vanity (2:1c)

    C. Reasons:

        1. Laughter is mad (2:2a)

        2. Pleasure is of no use (2:2b)

    D. Objects tested:

        1. Wine (2:3)

        2. Various possessions (2:4-8a)

        3. Art (2:8b)

        4. Sex (2:8c)

    E. Results:

        1. I became great (2:9)

        2. My heart found pleasure in my toil (2:10)

    F. Conclusion:

        1. My toil was vanity (2:11a)

        2. Nothing gained under the sun (2:11b)

III. The Teacher tests the benefits of wisdom over folly (2:12)

    A. Thesis: Wisdom excels folly as light excels darkness (2:13)[10]

        1. Confirmed by a proverb: "the wise see/but fools walk in darkness" (2:14)

    B. Problems:

        1. The same fate befalls both the wise and fools (2:14c-15)

        2. No enduring remembrance of the wise or of fools (2:16)

    C. Result: I hated life (2:17a)

    D. Conclusion: All is vanity (2:17b)

IV. The Teacher tests the gain of toiling for possessions[11]

    A. Statement: I hated my toil under the sun (2:18a)

    B. Reasons:

        1. I must leave my possessions to those coming after me (2:18b)

        2. I don't know whether they will be wise or foolish (2:19a)

---

10. Whybray, *Ecclesiastes*, 57, calls vv. 13-17 "the first example in the book of the so-called 'broken aphorism.'"

11. Note the parallel statements A, B, C, A', B', C'.

C. Conclusion: this also is vanity (2:19b)

A′. Statement: I gave my heart up to despair concerning my toil (2:20)

B′. Reason: I must leave my possessions for another to enjoy (2:21)

C′. Conclusion: humans gain nothing from all their toil (2:22)

    1. Their days are full of pain (2:23a)

    2. At night their minds do not rest (2:23b)

    3. This also is vanity (2:23c)

V. The Teacher's final advice

  A. There is nothing better than to eat, drink, and find enjoyment in toil (2:24a)

  B. Reasons:

    1. This also is from the hand of God (2:24b)

    2. Apart from God we cannot eat and have enjoyment (2:25)

    3. God gives wisdom and joy to those who please him (2:26a)

    4. To the sinner God gives the work of gathering, only to give the fruit to those who please him (2:26b)

      a. Conclusion: This also is vanity and a chasing after wind (2:26c)

Theocentric Interpretation

The references to God in this passage are few and far between. The Teacher mentions God in his introduction, "It is an unhappy business that God has given to human beings to be busy with" (1:13b). God then disappears as the Teacher explores "all the deeds that are done *under the sun*" (1:14). But in the conclusion God reappears in a powerful way: God enables human beings "to eat and drink, and find enjoyment in their toil" (2:24). In fact, "God gives wisdom and knowledge and joy" to the one who pleases him, even taking from the sinner and giving to the one who pleases him (2:26).

Textual Theme and Goal

In formulating a single theme for this passage we need to weigh its two major themes. Most of the text is taken up with the theme that all human endeavors are vanity, while only three verses are devoted to the theme, "eat and drink, and find enjoyment in your toil." But these three verses form the important conclusion to the Teacher's search for the meaning of life. He has searched for gain in life in many different directions and has come up empty. But finally he does arrive at an answer: "There is nothing better for mortals than to eat and drink, and find enjoyment in their toil" (2:24). It is no coincidence that in this conclusion the Teacher names God as the giver of this joy. Against the backdrop of the vanity of human endeavors "under the sun," the Teacher's message for Israel is to eat, drink, and find enjoyment in their toil. We can do justice to both of these themes by subordinating the theme of "vanity" to the theme of "enjoy." The textual theme, then, can be formulated as follows, "Since all human endeavors 'under the sun' are vanity, find enjoyment in God's daily gifts of food, drink, and toil." For the sake of clarity, we will have to find a more lucid word to replace the phrase "under the sun." This phrase, we have seen, is the Teacher's view of the world from a horizontal, a secular perspective. For "endeavors 'under the sun,'" therefore, we can substitute "apart from God" or "worldly endeavors." We should also clarify the word "vanity," which in this context is connected with "no gain" (see 2:11, 22-23). Which of the various connotations of "vapor" would express the sense of "no gain"? The best options are "futile" or "empty." These considerations lead to the following theme formulation: *Since all worldly endeavors are futile, find enjoyment in God's daily gifts of food, drink, and toil.*

Why would the Teacher encourage Israel to enjoy their food, drink, and toil? Against the backdrop of Israelites looking for the meaning of life in working hard, making a fortune, and enjoying life later, the Teacher wishes to encourage them not to postpone enjoyment to some future time but to savor God-given joy in the present moment of eating and drinking and working. The Teacher's goal, then, is *to encourage Israel to find enjoyment in God's daily gifts of food, drink, and toil.*

Ways to Preach Christ

How can we move from the theme, "Since all worldly endeavors are futile, find enjoyment in God's daily gifts of food, drink, and toil," to Jesus Christ in the New Testament? There is no promise of Christ, thus eliminating the way of promise-fulfillment. This leaves six possible roads to Christ in the New Testament. Because redemptive-historical progression and longitudinal themes are intertwined[12] we shall combine them in this analysis.

Redemptive-Historical Progression/Longitudinal Themes

One can trace through redemptive history and the Scriptures the theme of finding enjoyment in God's daily gifts of food, drink, and work. In Paradise

12. For the reason why these are often intertwined, see p. 25, n. 100 above.

God provided Adam and Eve with meaningful work ("to till and keep" the garden [2:15]) and with good food ("You may freely eat of every tree in the garden" [Gen 2:16]). The Fall into sin destroyed God's good design: "Cursed is the ground because of you; in toil you shall eat of it all the days of your life. . . . By the sweat of your face you shall eat bread" (Gen 3:17, 19). Work became toil without much joy. But toil was not entirely futile: it still provided food to eat. God commanded Israel, "Six days you shall labor and do all your work" (Exod 20:9). And God could still make toil enjoyable. Israel prayed,

> Satisfy us in the morning with your steadfast love,
> so that we may rejoice and be glad all our days. . . .
> Let the favor of the LORD our God be upon us,
> and prosper for us the work of our hands. (Ps 90:14, 17)

Psalm 128:1-2 declares,

> Happy is everyone who fears the LORD,
> who walks in his ways.
> You shall eat the fruit of the labor of your hands;
> you shall be happy, and it shall go well with you.

Thus the Teacher in Ecclesiastes 2:24 can also advocate, "There is nothing better for mortals than to eat and drink, and find enjoyment in their toil. This also, I saw, is from the hand of God."

Still, in this fallen world toil leaves much to be desired. Isaiah (65:21-23) looks forward to the new earth where

> They shall build houses and inhabit them;
> they shall plant vineyards and eat their fruit.
> They shall not build and another inhabit;
> they shall not plant and another eat; . . .
> My chosen shall long enjoy the work of their hands.
> They shall not labor in vain . . . (cf. 1 Cor 15:58).

When Jesus comes to this earth, he works — first as a carpenter (Mark 6:3), then as a teacher (Mark 6:2, 6) and miracle worker: feeding people (Mark 6:30-44) and healing the sick (Mark 6:53-56). Jesus sends out his disciples to preach the gospel and says, "The laborer deserves to be paid" (Luke 10:1-7). Jesus also teaches us not to worry about food, drink, or clothing but to focus our lives on the kingdom of God, "and all these things will be given to you as well" (Matt 6:33). In fact, Jesus promises gain, the kingdom of God, to those who have done their work well: "Come, you that are blessed by my Father, inherit the kingdom prepared for you from the foundation of the world; for I was hungry and you gave me food, I was thirsty and you gave me something to drink. . . . 'Truly I tell you, just as you did it to one of the least of these who are members of my family, you did it to me'" (Matt 25:34-40). Through Jesus Christ our work has been redeemed and can again provide meaning, joy, and even gain. Consequently Paul can command us, "Rejoice in the Lord always; again I will say, Rejoice" (Phil 4:4).

Typology

This is one of only two[13] passages in Ecclesiastes where we can possibly make use of typology. The Teacher seeks to give added weight to his message by casting it in the experiences and words of the great king Solomon. King Solomon, of course, was widely known for his wisdom and his great works. Even the queen of Sheba heard of his fame, traveled many miles to hear him, and praised the LORD: "Blessed be the LORD your God, who has delighted in you and set you on the throne of Israel! Because the LORD loved Israel forever, he has made you king to execute justice and righteousness" (1 Kings 10:9).

Solomon *(šālôm)*, the king of peace, ruled wisely in the city of peace (Jerusalem). King Solomon is a type of the great King of peace; he prefigures Jesus Christ. When some people asked Jesus for a sign to prove that he was special, Jesus responded, "The queen of the South will rise up at the judgment with this generation and condemn it, because she came from the ends of the earth to listen to the wisdom of Solomon, and see, something greater than Solomon is here!" (Matt 12:42). Jesus is another Solomon, the great and wise king; but Jesus is much greater than Solomon.

Analogy

The Teacher's message is to find enjoyment in God's daily gifts of eating, drinking, and toil. Jesus teaches us to pray to our Father in heaven, "Give us this day our daily bread" (Matt 6:11). Our daily bread is God's gift to us. Jesus also tells us, "Do not worry about your life, what you will eat or what you will drink. . . . Look at the birds of the air; they neither sow nor reap nor gather into barns, and yet your heavenly Father feeds them. Are you not of more value than they? . . . And why do you worry about clothing? Consider the lilies of the field, how they grow; they neither toil nor spin, yet I tell you, even *Solomon* in all his glory was not

---

13. The other possibility is the mention of the "one shepherd" in 12:11 (see below, pp. 301-2).

clothed like one of these. But if God so clothes the grass of the field, which is alive today and tomorrow is thrown into the oven, will he not much more clothe you — you of little faith? Therefore do not worry, saying, 'What will we eat?' or 'What will we drink?' or 'What will we wear?' For it is the Gentiles who strive for all these things; and indeed your heavenly Father knows that you need all these things. But strive first for the kingdom of God and his righteousness, and all these things will be *given* to you as well" (Matt 6:25-33). Our heavenly Father will give us whatever we need. So we can be content and daily enjoy his gifts.

New Testament References

Aside from the New Testament references mentioned above, there are a few others that can possibly be used as bridges to Christ in the New Testament. Paul encourages the early Christians to live their lives with gratitude for God's gifts: "Let the word of Christ dwell in you richly; teach and admonish one another in all wisdom; and with gratitude in your hearts sing psalms, hymns, and spiritual songs to God. And whatever you do, in word or deed, do everything in the name of the Lord Jesus, giving thanks to God the Father through him" (Col 3:16-17). Elsewhere Paul writes, "Whether you eat or drink, or whatever you do, do everything for the glory of God" (1 Cor 10:31).

Reflecting the Teacher's view of the vanity of riches and the importance of living content with God's daily gifts, Paul writes, "Of course, there is great gain in godliness combined with contentment; for we brought nothing into the world, so that we can take nothing out of it; but if we have food and clothing, we will be content with these. But those who want to be rich fall into temptation and are trapped by many senseless and harmful desires that plunge people into ruin and destruction. For the love of money is a root of all kinds of evil, and in their eagerness to be rich some have wandered away from the faith and pierced themselves with many pains" (1 Tim 6:6-10). If one were to use this passage, one would have to connect it to Jesus Christ by referring to the context, "Whoever teaches otherwise and does not agree with the sound words of our Lord Jesus Christ . . ." (1 Tim 6:3), or perhaps by linking it to Jesus' parable of the rich fool (Luke 12:13-21) or his parable of the rich man and Lazarus (Luke 16:19-31).

Contrast

In contrast to the Teacher's positive message to find enjoyment on this earth, Paul also looks *beyond* this earth: "For to me, living is Christ and dying is gain.

If I am to live in the flesh, that means fruitful labor for me; and I do not know which I prefer. I am hard pressed between the two: my desire is to depart and be with Christ, for that is far better" (Phil 1:21-23).

Sermon Theme and Goal

We summarized the Teacher's message for Israel in the theme, "Since all worldly endeavors are futile, find enjoyment in God's daily gifts of food, drink, and toil." Although the New Testament moves far beyond this idea (see "Contrast" above), it does not contradict the theme of finding enjoyment in God's daily gifts. Therefore the sermon theme can keep the same focus as the textual theme: *Since all worldly endeavors are futile, find enjoyment in God's daily gifts of food, drink, and toil.*

Against the backdrop of the Israelites looking for the meaning of life in working hard, making a fortune, and enjoying life later, the Teacher's goal was "to encourage Israel to find enjoyment in God's daily gifts of food, drink, and toil." People today face the same temptations of materialism and consumerism as Israel did. We can therefore maintain the Teacher's goal as the sermon goal: *to encourage people to find enjoyment in God's daily gifts of food, drink, and toil.* This goal exposes the need addressed in this sermon: people look for the meaning of life and joy in the wrong places and time (the future).

Sermon Form

The Teacher presents his overall argument inductively, that is to say, he discloses his main theme only at the end. Modern preachers can follow this method and develop the sermon inductively. In fact, the Teacher uses a classic sermon (speech) form sometimes called "the chase technique": "Not this, nor this, nor this, nor this, but this."[14] The Teacher declares: Not wisdom, nor pleasure, nor the benefits of wisdom over folly, nor possessions, but daily enjoyment An expository sermon can follow suit by exposing not only the meaning but also the structure of the text.

The sermon introduction can focus on the need addressed. For example, one can begin with the impact of materialism and consumerism on the hearers. Countless people believe the advertisements that promise happiness through buying and consuming products. Bigger is better: bigger cars, bigger houses, and of course bigger paychecks. But does consumerism really lead to greater joy?

14. Fred B. Craddock, *Preaching* (Nashville: Abingdon, 1985), 177.

Or one can begin more simply by asking how many people look forward to their retirement. At that time, many think, they can begin to enjoy life. Meanwhile they slave away to save enough money for that great day. Many hate their work; they call it a rat race, but they put up with it because, in the future, retirement beckons. Transition to Israel, which long ago was caught up in the same rat race.[15]

Sermon Exposition

In this passage the Teacher speaks as if he were Solomon, the wise and wealthy king of Israel. In chapter 1:1 he identifies himself as "*the Teacher,* the son of David, king in Jerusalem." The Teacher wrote this book probably some six hundred years after King Solomon (see pp. 10-11 above). But in this passage he pretends to be Solomon in order to give his important message greater impact.[16] So he begins in verse 12, "I, the Teacher, when king over Israel in Jerusalem, applied my mind to seek and to search out by wisdom all that is done under heaven." In verse 16 he adds, "I said to myself, 'I have acquired great wisdom, surpassing all who were over Jerusalem before me.'" Though he still does not say that he is Solomon, we are to hear this passage as if it were written by Solomon himself, for none had greater wisdom than this wise king.

"Solomon," then, says that he applied his mind "to seek and to search out by wisdom[17] all that is done under heaven." After the earlier conclusion that people gain nothing "from all the toil at which they toil under the sun" (1:3), the Teacher as "Solomon" is going to use his great wisdom to try several experiments to see if all is indeed vanity, futile, or if somewhere there is something more substantial.

His first test is to use his wisdom to seek to understand "all that is done under heaven." But he immediately comes to the conclusion that this searching by

15. The Teacher "shows the inherent absurdity of a 'total-work' culture. Although he is speaking to Hellenistic Jews on-the-rise, his expose is perfectly suited to modern professional America, where many of us have learned to value ourselves chiefly in terms of how hard we work. In this culture, it is admirable to be continually pressed for time." Davis, *Proverbs, Ecclesiastes, Song of Songs,* 181.

16. "The choice of Solomon for this 'royal fiction' was made not only because he was the archetypal wise king but equally in view of his reputation for great wealth: if even Solomon, who possessed everything which a man can possess, nevertheless found all his efforts to achieve happiness and contentment profoundly unsatisfactory, how much more would lesser persons be likely to fail in that attempt!" Whybray, *Ecclesiastes,* 48.

17. "*Hokmâ* itself refers to practical knowledge, skill, cleverness, guile, insight, general intelligence, and wisdom." Crenshaw, *Ecclesiastes,* 72.

wisdom "is an unhappy business[18] that God[19] has given to human beings to be busy with." Why is searching out by wisdom an unhappy business? He answers in verse 14, "I saw all the deeds that are done under the sun; and see, all is vanity and a chasing after wind." Observing all this activity "under the sun," all this worldly striving,[20] the Teacher concludes that it is futile and empty. It turns out that "the consummate wise king (Solomon) is engaged in . . . windy pursuits."[21] Literally he says, "All is vapor and herding[22] the wind." Trying to capture vapor is futile and herding the wind leaves one with empty hands. In other words, the searching out by wisdom is futile and results in nothing.

The Teacher confirms his conclusion with a proverb, verse 15,

> What is crooked cannot be made straight,
>   and what is lacking cannot be counted.

One cannot change the world as given. "What is crooked cannot be made straight." Wisdom cannot make straight what is crooked. Later in his book the Teacher writes: "Consider the work of God; who can make straight what he has made crooked?" (Eccl 7:13).[23] After the Fall, God cursed the ground, giving rise to thorns and thistles (Gen 3:17-18), tornadoes and hurricanes, influenza and cancer. Paul speaks of the groaning of creation. He says that "the creation was subjected to futility, to vanity" (Rom 8:20). This vanity raises many questions for

18. The referent of "unhappy business" is ambiguous: it can refer back to v. 13, the searching out by wisdom, or it can refer to v. 14, "all the deeds that are done under the sun." The parallel structure of vv. 12-15 and 16-18 would argue for searching out "by wisdom" since wisdom is also the focus of v. 17. I, therefore, agree with Fox, who, contrary to many commentators, writes that "unhappy business" refers "to the search for understanding. Qohelet sees this search as a hopeless, frustrating task, even when undertaken in wisdom and by the wise (1:12, 16; 8:16-17), of whom the Solomonic Qohelet is the foremost example." *Ecclesiastes*, 9. So also Whybray, *Ecclesiastes*, 49, with references to Lauha and Lohfink. Cf. Eaton, *Ecclesiastes*, 63.

19. This is the first mention of God. "Here, as in thirty-nine other instances in the book, God is called by the generic name, 'ĕlōhîm, the name preferred in the wisdom tradition over YHWH. The preference may have to do with wisdom tradition's interest in universal truths, rather than the relation of a particular deity to a particular people. YHWH is the name for the God of the covenant, the God of Israel, whereas 'ĕlōhîm, is the universal term for the deity, the God of the universe and of every person. This God described by Qohelet is very present and very active in the cosmos, always giving . . . and doing/making. . . . It is a transcendent and inscrutable God of whom Qohelet speaks." Seow, *Ecclesiastes*, 146. Cf. Murphy, *Ecclesiastes*, lxviii-lxix.

20. See p. 51, n. 8 above.

21. Seow, *Ecclesiastes*, 146.

22. "*Rĕʿût rûaḥ* . . . suggests the shepherd attempting to herd the wind as he would herd the sheep and goats." Ogden, *Qoheleth*, 35.

23. Cf. Jesus' words in Matthew 6:27: "Can any of you by worrying add a single hour to your span of life?"

us that we cannot answer. We cannot understand these crooked things: why do tornadoes destroy homes on one side of the street while leaving those across from them untouched? Why does cancer strike some people and not others? We cannot make straight what is crooked. We can only hope with Paul that some day "the creation itself will be set free from its bondage to decay" (Rom 8:20-21).

The proverb continues, "And what is lacking cannot be counted." Politicians may wish to give a positive spin to a deficit, but the simple truth is that "what is lacking cannot be counted." A similar proverb in English would be, "You cannot count your chickens before they hatch." If we don't have it, we cannot count it as profit. So it is with wisdom that seeks to search out "all that is done under heaven." There is nothing to add up; it is a futile and empty pursuit. The whole search is "vanity and a chasing after wind."

Next the Teacher takes a slightly different tack. From the search of all things *by* wisdom he moves to examining wisdom itself. He writes in verse 16, "I said to myself, 'I have acquired great wisdom, surpassing all who were over Jerusalem before me; and my mind has had great experience of wisdom and knowledge.' And I applied my mind to know wisdom and to know madness and folly." In these two verses he uses the word "wisdom" three times. He wants to know precisely how wisdom is different from folly.[24] But this search, too, is futile: "I perceived that this also is but a chasing after wind." Seeking to understand wisdom itself is also a chasing after wind — a pursuit that leaves one empty-handed.

Again the Teacher confirms his conclusion with a proverb, verse 18:

> For in much wisdom is much vexation,
>   and those who increase knowledge increase sorrow.

Much wisdom brings with it much frustration because the world does not seem to make sense.[25] Also, wisdom increases sorrow because one becomes more aware of the pain and suffering in this world.

Having failed to find meaning in searching out by wisdom all that is done, the Teacher decides, secondly, to experiment with the pursuit of pleasure. Chapter 2:1, "I said to myself, 'Come now, I will make a test of pleasure; enjoy

---

24. "Perhaps it is possible through concentrated intellectual effort to distinguish these things more accurately — to refine one's understanding of the world — and thus to escape from the trap set by life for the ordinary person." Provan, *Ecclesiastes*, 70.

25. Cf. Ecclesiastes 8:16-17, "When I applied my mind to know wisdom, and to see the business that is done on earth, how one's eyes see sleep neither day nor night, then I saw all the work of God, that no one can find out what is happening under the sun. However much they may toil in seeking, they will not find it out; even though those who are wise claim to know, they cannot find it out."

yourself.'" Now we should understand that in Ecclesiastes pleasure is not evil. In fact, in this very passage, 2:26, the Teacher calls it a gift of God: "God gives wisdom and knowledge and *joy*."[26] And later in his book he encourages his readers, "Go, eat your bread with *enjoyment,* and drink your wine with a merry heart; for God has long ago approved what you do" (9:7). The pursuit of pleasure itself is not wrong. The problem is that the Teacher seeks to find meaning in pleasure "under the sun." He writes at the end of this section, 2:11, that "there was nothing to be gained *under the sun.*" In other words, he sought pleasure apart from God, without taking God into account.[27]

Again he quickly comes to the conclusion that the pursuit of pleasure apart from God is futile. In verse 2 he reports, "I said of laughter, 'It is mad,' and of pleasure, 'What use is it?'" And he goes on to describe his various experiments that made him conclude that pleasure is futile. He tested successively the pleasure of wine, of great works, art, and sex. He begins with wine. Verse 3, "I searched with my mind how to cheer my body with wine — my mind still guiding me with wisdom — and how to lay hold on folly, until I might see what was good for mortals to do under heaven during the few days of their life." The Teacher did not want to become drunk. He just wanted to cheer himself with wine while his mind could still guide him with wisdom. Would this give him insight into what is good for people during their brief stay on earth?

Apparently not, for he moves quickly to building great works. The description of the great works here comes close to what we know about the works of the real king Solomon (see 1 Kings 7; 10:21). But notice how selfish this pursuit of pleasure is: "I built myself . . . planted myself . . . made myself . . . made myself . . . there were to me . . . there were to me . . . I also amassed for myself . . . I acquired for myself. . . ." Michael Fox aptly describes this effort as "a sort of intense consumerism."[28] Verse 4, "I made great works; I built houses and planted vineyards for myself; I made myself gardens and parks, and planted in them all kinds of fruit trees. I made myself pools from which to water the forest of growing trees." "Solomon" created for himself another Paradise[29] on earth. Surely in Paradise he would find meaning.

---

26. "This noun (*śimḥā*) occurs eight times in Ecclesiastes, and the RSV translates it in various different ways according to the contexts in which it occurs: pleasure, joy, mirth, enjoyment." Whybray, *Ecclesiastes,* 52.

27. "It is because 'Solomon' has determined to seek it independently for himself that he discovers that, like his corresponding attempt to rely on his own wisdom and knowledge (1:13, 17), it proves totally unsatisfactory." Ibid.

28. Fox, *A Time to Tear Down,* 176.

29. "Vineyards were planted, gardens and parklands established (*pardes,* 'park,' is a Persian loan-word, which in Greek becomes *paradeisos,* 'paradise') and in them various fruit trees were planted reminiscent of the Edenic Garden in Genesis 2." Ogden, *Qoheleth,* 40. For this associa-

Verse 7 continues, "I bought male and female slaves, and had slaves who were born in my house; I also had great possessions of herds and flocks, more than any who had been before me in Jerusalem. I also gathered for myself silver and gold and the treasure of kings and of the provinces." In addition to all these possessions, "Solomon" added the pleasure of art: verse 8b, "I got singers, both men and women," and the pleasure of sex: "and delights of the flesh, and many concubines."

He concludes in verses 9-11, "So I became great and surpassed all who were before me in Jerusalem; also my wisdom remained with me. Whatever my eyes desired I did not keep from them; I kept my heart from no pleasure, for my heart found pleasure in all my toil, and this was my reward for all my toil. Then I considered all that my hands had done and the toil I had spent in doing it, and again, all was vanity and a chasing after wind, and there was nothing to be *gained* under the sun." Here explicitly is the answer to the rhetorical question raised in chapter 1:3, "What do people *gain* from all the toil at which they toil under the sun?" The answer is, Absolutely nothing. Even the great king "Solomon," after trying to build another Paradise on earth, comes to the conclusion that "there was nothing to be gained under the sun." In fact, he deduces, "All was vanity [futility] and a chasing after wind [leaving him empty-handed], and there was nothing to be gained under the sun [no profit[30]]." "All the Preacher's key terms combine at this point: *toil, vanity, striving after wind, no profit, under the sun.* The pileup of terms conveys bitter disillusionment. . . . Secular man is being shown the failure of his life-style, *on its own premises.*"[31] Materialism and consumerism fail to provide human life with meaning.

The Teacher has struck out first with wisdom and now also with pleasure. So he devises a third test. He will investigate whether the use of wisdom offers benefits over the use of folly. He writes in verse 12, "So I turned to consider wisdom[32] and madness and folly; for what can the one do who comes after the

---

tion with the Garden of Eden by way of the sevenfold rhythmic pattern in this passage ("The sevenfold pattern evokes the seven days of creation, which are also recounted in rhythmic style"), see Davis, *Proverbs, Ecclesiastes, Song of Songs,* 178. For this association by way of the combined recurrence here of Hebrew words found in Genesis 1 and 2 (to plant, garden, tree/all/ fruit, to drench, to sprout, to work, make), see Arian Verheij, "Paradise Retried: On Qohelet 2:4-6," *JSOT* 50 (1991) 113-15.

30. "His achievements, unprecedented though they be, shrink to nothing when judged against the criterion of 'gain' (*yitrôn*). Economically, 'gain' marks the bottom line, the profit margin of every human endeavor. More broadly, it marks the material legacy that provides last-ing benefit for the achiever, the 'rate of return' against which all things are measured." Brown, "'Whatever Your Hand Finds to Do,'" *Int* 55/3 (2001) 277. See also p. 43, n. 31 above.

31. Eaton, *Ecclesiastes,* 68 (his emphases).

32. "The words 'wisdom,' 'wise,' and 'be wise' together occur six times in 2:12-17. This is matched by six occurrences of the words 'folly' and 'fool.'" Seow, *Ecclesiastes,* 152.

king? Only what has already been done." "Solomon," the wisest king on earth, is really going to get to the bottom of this issue. Because he is the wisest king that ever lived, his successor can never improve on his experiment and its results.[33]

Immediately the Teacher discerns a major difference between a wise person and a fool. Verse 13, "Then I saw that wisdom excels folly as light excels darkness." He confirms his observation with a proverb in verse 14,

> The wise have eyes in their head,
>   but fools walk in darkness.

"Darkness here is a metaphor for (spiritual) blindness. The fool is like a blind man who stumbles as he walks (cf. Prov 3:23; 4:18-19); the wise man, on the other hand, has eyes in his head: he can see, and is therefore able to avoid disaster."[34] What a tremendous advantage the wise have over fools!

But then the Teacher observes, "Yet I perceived that the same fate befalls all of them." Both the wise and fools die. In verse 15 he despairs, "Then I said to myself, 'What happens to the fool will happen to me also; why then have I been so very wise?' And I said to myself that this also is vanity." Death, in his view, is the end; game over.[35] What is the point of being so wise? If the wise as well as fools end up dead, there is no gain in being wise.

Or is there some gain? We may die, but our reputation can live on in the memory of those who come after us. Fools may be quickly forgotten, but is it possible that wise people will be remembered? The Teacher's glimmer of hope is soon extinguished. Verse 16, "For there is no enduring remembrance of the wise or of fools, seeing that in the days to come *all* will have been long forgotten" (cf. 1:11). Agonizingly he asks, "How can the wise die just like fools?" And he confesses, "So I hated[36] life, because what is done under the sun was grievous to me; for all is vanity and a chasing after wind." Life is futile and without substance. "All is vanity and a chasing after wind." At the end of life, even the wise have nothing to show for having lived wisely. They also die and will soon be forgotten.

Having failed to find some "gain" in life in using wisdom, in pursuing pleasure, and in looking for the benefits of wisdom over folly, the Teacher conducts a final test. There is something left when we die. Our possessions do not die

---

33. The Teacher "in this way asserts the universal applicability of his experiment. He sets himself up as the king and concludes that, if the king cannot find meaning, then no one else will be able to do so." Longman, *Book of Ecclesiastes,* 96.

34. Whybray, *Ecclesiastes,* 58.

35. See Murphy, *Ecclesiastes,* lxvii-lxviii.

36. "Because wise and foolish, good and evil, experience the same fate, death, there is no point in striving for wisdom and goodness. This awareness evokes in Qohelet hatred of life, which is futile and chasing wind." Crenshaw, *Ecclesiastes,* 70.

with us. Those who die leave an inheritance behind. Are these possessions a "profit," a "gain," from a lifetime of toil?

The Teacher quickly closes this door to some possible meaning in life. He cries out in verse 18, "I hated all my toil[37] in which I had toiled under the sun, seeing that I must leave it to those who come after me — and who knows whether they will be wise or foolish? Yet they will be master of all for which I toiled and used my wisdom under the sun. This also is vanity." All his toiling with wisdom is futile. For at death he will have to leave his possessions behind, and even a fool might inherit it.

He continues in verse 20, "So I turned and gave my heart up to despair concerning all the toil of my labors under the sun, because sometimes one who has toiled with wisdom and knowledge and skill must leave all to be enjoyed by another who did not toil for it." And again he exclaims, "This also is vanity and a great evil." All his toiling with wisdom turns out to be futile because he has to leave it to "another who did not toil for it."

Again he raises the question, verse 22, "What do mortals get from all the toil and strain with which they toil under the sun?" The answer is, Nothing! Indeed, it is less than nothing for a workaholic — a person who, "like 'Solomon' himself, is possessed by a restless ambition to achieve something — whatever it may be — for himself, and who puts this 'business' . . . before everything else."[38] The gain is less than nothing because, as he observes in verse 23, "All their days are full of pain, and their work is a vexation; even at night their minds do not rest." And for the third time in this section, the Teacher exclaims, "This also is vanity." Human life and work is futile, useless!

What then? The Teacher has failed with four experiments. He found no meaning in seeking to understand life by wisdom, no lasting value in pursuing pleasure, no advantage in being wise in contrast to being a fool, and no lasting benefit from gathering possessions. All our worldly endeavors are futile and empty. What then? Is there no benefit at all to living on this earth?

Yes, there is. The Teacher concludes in verse 24, "There is nothing better[39]

---

37. "This passage is built around the notion of *'āmāl*, understood both as the fruit of one's toil and as the toiling itself. As a noun or as a verb, it occurs no less that eleven times in this short section." Murphy, *Ecclesiastes*, 27.

38. Whybray, *Ecclesiastes*, 62.

39. Though a few commentators, e.g., Leupold and Kaiser, follow the original Hebrew reading, "It is not a good thing [inherent] in man . . . ," most think that the letter *m* has been inadvertently dropped (Delitzsch, *Commentary*, 251, calls it "above all doubt") and that the phrase should be read, "There is nothing better," as in 3:12, 22 and 8:15. Note also that "the closing verses of chapter 2 contain four occurrences of *ṭôb* ['good'] . . . in parallel to the four occurrences of *hebel*, 'pointlessness,' that refer to the life of the person pursuing the wind in verses 17-23." Provan, *Ecclesiastes*, 76.

for mortals than to eat and drink, and find enjoyment in their toil." This is not an entirely new thought. When he was investigating pleasure he made an interesting discovery. When he was toiling away building houses and planting vineyards, he writes in 2:10, "My heart found *pleasure* in all my toil, and this was my reward for [literally, my portion from][40] all my toil." Even though he describes all his toil as "vanity and a chasing after wind" (2:11), it did carry an unexpected side benefit. He received pleasure from all his toil.

When God created human beings, he put them in a garden with the mandate "to till it and keep it" (Gen 2:15). Work would give people a sense of accomplishment and pleasure. Now the Teacher discovered that even though all his toil was futile, it still did carry with it this sense of pleasure. And so, coming to the end of his experiments and finding no lasting meaning in life "under the sun" — life apart from God — he advises us to at least experience the pleasure of the present moment: eat and drink[41] and find enjoyment in your toil. Don't look for enjoyment in the future but find enjoyment in your everyday activities: eating and drinking and your daily work. With ever increasing force, the Teacher will repeat this advice seven times, climaxing in chapter 11:9, "*Rejoice, young man, while you are young, and let your heart cheer you in the days of your youth.*" "Enjoyment has the power to redeem the notion of toil amid (rather than over and against) the vicissitudes of life, the elusiveness of gain, and the ravaging power of death."[42]

Should we, then, pursue pleasure after all? That would be to misunderstand the Teacher. For after advising us to eat, drink, and find enjoyment in our toil, he continues in verse 24b, "This [enjoyment] also, I saw, is from the hand of God; for apart from him who can eat or who can have enjoyment?" Enjoyment is God's gift to us. Pursue it on your own for yourself ("under the sun"), and it will vanish like the wind — as the Teacher discovered (2:1-2).[43] Instead, we are to receive enjoyment as God's gift to us.

The Teacher concludes in verse 26, "For to the one who pleases him God gives wisdom and knowledge and joy; but to the sinner he gives the work of gathering and heaping, only to give to one who pleases God. This also is vanity

---

40. See Brown, *Ecclesiastes*, 33.

41. Eat and drink "is to be taken literally, though probably — as elsewhere in the Old Testament and in ancient Near Eastern literature — as standing for the enjoyment of the material things of life in general" Whybray, *Ecclesiastes*, 63. Cf. Seow, *Ecclesiastes*, 157, "He is not referring here to specific activities of eating and drinking, but to a general attitude toward life."

42. Brown, "'Whatever Your Hand Finds to Do,'" *Int* 55/3 (2001) 279.

43. "Enjoyment is not an end to be sought. Joy is not something to be pursued. Indeed, nowhere does Qohelet call on people to seek pleasure. Rather, enjoyment is presented as a divine gift (2:26; 3:12-13, 22; 5:19; cf. 9:7)." Seow, "Theology When Everything Is out of Control," *Int* 55/3 (2001) 244.

and a chasing after wind." "To the one who pleases him God gives[44] wisdom and knowledge and joy." Those who please God are those who acknowledge the sovereign God: those who receive enjoyment from their toil as a gift from God; those who honor God by being grateful for God's gifts. On those who please God, God showers his good gifts: not only joy but also wisdom and knowledge.

"But to the sinner he gives the work of gathering and heaping, only to give to one who pleases God." "The sinner" is literally "the one who misses the mark." In the Teacher's vocabulary, "the word designates someone who, though not wicked, has missed the point of the life that God has given."[45] In this context the sinner is the person who seeks the goal of life in himself and the goods he can acquire "under the sun." To such a one God gives "the work of gathering and heaping." There is no letup. This is a true workaholic. His whole life is focused on "gathering and heaping." And what is the result? Instead of ending up with riches, God gives it to the one who pleases him.[46]

Jesus' parable of the ten pounds carries a similar message: the master took the pound of the servant who had missed the mark of doing business with the master's pound and gave it to the one who had gained ten more pounds. When people complained that this was not fair, the master said, "I tell you, to all those who have, more will be given; but from those who have nothing, even what they have will be taken away" (Luke 19:26). Those who miss the mark in life end up with nothing. "This also is vanity and a chasing after wind."[47]

The Teacher's message, then, is that since all our worldly endeavors are futile, since all our striving apart from God is futile, we ought to find enjoyment in the gifts God gives us every day. We ought to savor the moment and find enjoyment in our present eating, drinking, and work because these are God's gifts to us.

---

44. "The verb 'give' occurs twenty-eight times in this short book, in fifteen instances referring to a divine act." Davis, *Proverbs, Ecclesiastes, Song of Songs*, 161.

45. Ibid., 181.

46. "Elsewhere we find the principle, 'The sinner's wealth is laid up for the righteous' (Prov 13:22; cf. 28:8). Occasional incidents (Mordecai receiving Haman's signet ring, the Canaanites' 'great and goodly cities' falling into Israel's hands) give a glimpse of what the Preacher has in mind." Eaton, *Ecclesiastes*, 76.

47. Crenshaw, *Ecclesiastes*, 91, states, "The final comment, 'this also is futile and striving after wind,' sums up the whole business that Qohelet has endeavored to assess rather than issuing a judgment about God's unpredictable treatment of humans." Cf. Longman, *Book of Ecclesiastes*, 110, "The typically ambiguous *This* [in "This also is vanity"] likely refers to more than v. 26, but certainly includes it." It is unlikely, however, that the Teacher would recommend "enjoyment" in vv. 25-26 if he considered it vanity. Also, in all his following recommendations to enjoy (3:12-13; 3:22; 5:18-20; 8:15; 9:7-10; and 11:8-9), he does not conclude with the evaluation of vanity. I think, therefore, that the "vanity and a chasing after wind" in v. 26 refers specifically to the gathering and heaping of the person who misses the mark in life and subsequently loses all his goods.

Unfortunately, many people postpone enjoyment to a time in the future. Many people today hate their work. Instead of thanking God for their work, they say, "Thank God, it is Friday!" They call work a rat race, but they don't know how to escape. Many buy lottery tickets in the hope of winning a million dollars so they can quit their jobs. But few escape work. People look forward to retirement; that's when they will begin to enjoy life. But retirement may never come. Even Christians often complain about living in this "vale of tears." And they look forward to the future joy of heaven. But the Teacher, like much of the Old Testament, enjoins us to find joy in this life here and now. "There is nothing better . . . than to eat and drink, and find enjoyment in . . . [your] toil."

The New Testament continues the same emphasis. To be sure, the New Testament also knows of life beyond death, and a future new heaven and earth where "mourning and crying and pain will be no more" (Rev 21:4). But Jesus also teaches us to savor God's gifts in the here and now. He teaches us to be content with our lives and to receive our food and drink as God's gifts to us: "Do not worry about your life, what you will eat or what you will drink," he says. "Look at the birds of the air; they neither sow nor reap nor gather into barns, and yet *your heavenly Father* feeds them. Are you not of more value than they? . . . Do not worry, saying, 'What will we eat?' or 'What will we drink?' or 'What will we wear?' For it is the *Gentiles* who strive for all these things; and indeed your heavenly Father knows that you need all these things. But strive first for the kingdom of God and his righteousness, and all these things will be *given* to you as well" (Matt 6:25-33). The Gentiles miss the mark of life. Jesus' followers know the mark: Seek first the kingdom of God, and God will give you food, drink, and clothing.

Paul also encourages Christians to live their lives grateful for God's gifts. He writes, "Let the word of Christ dwell in you richly; teach and admonish one another in all wisdom; and with gratitude in your hearts sing psalms, hymns, and spiritual songs to God. And *whatever you do,* in word or deed, do everything in the name of the Lord Jesus, giving thanks to God the Father through him" (Col 3:16-17). "Whatever you do" includes our eating and drinking and work. We ought to thank God every day for his wonderful gifts. And we ought to enjoy his gifts every day. If we do *not* enjoy God's gifts, we snub God the Giver. But if we *enjoy* our food and drink and work, God will be pleased. Enjoy God's gifts every day!

CHAPTER 4

God Set the Times

<hr>

Ecclesiastes 3:1-15

I know that whatever God does endures forever;
nothing can be added to it, nor anything taken from it;
God has done this,
so that all should stand in awe before him.

(Eccl 3:14)

Of all the passages in Ecclesiastes, this one about the times is probably the best known and most frequently preached.[1] It is a wonderful passage to help people reflect on the greatness of our God. A major challenge will be to arrive at a correct understanding, for commentators propose a variety of different interpretations. For example, verse 5 states that there is "a time to throw away stones." But what does this mean? Some commentators understand this as a time of war when one would throw stones on the fields of the enemy; others read this as an economic time for distributing wealth (precious stones);[2] and, surprisingly, several modern interpreters understand this as a time for sexual intercourse (see below). Verse 11 says that God has put *hāʿōlām* in the human heart. But what is *hāʿōlām*? Crenshaw states, "Among many possible answers, the most likely are: (1) the world; (2) eternity; (3) darkness."[3] Verse 15b reads literally, "God seeks out what is pursued" (NRSV footnote). The question is, What does God seek out?

<hr>

1. This is the only passage from Ecclesiastes that the *Revised Common Lectionary* assigns for Years ABC.

2. Provan, *Ecclesiastes*, 88, writes, "It seems more likely . . . that this line in 3:5 concerns the accumulation and distribution of wealth and that the image of the gathering of stones is used to refer to the practice of accumulation. The Hebrew *ʾeben* (stone) can indeed be used of precious stones."

3. Crenshaw, *Ecclesiastes*, 97.

"Several answers have been offered: (1) the persecuted; (2) the events of the past; (3) the same; and (4) what God sought previously."[4] Another challenge is to link this message from Ecclesiastes to Jesus Christ in the New Testament.

Text and Context

It is clear that Ecclesiastes 3:1 begins a new literary unit: the style changes from prose to poetry and the topic changes from God giving wisdom and joy to God setting a time for everything. But it is not so clear where this unit ends. On the basis of the recurrence of the phrase "vanity and a chasing after wind" in 4:4, 6, Addison Wright proposes a unit from 3:1 to 4:6 under the heading "one cannot hit on the right time to act."[5] Since this section is much too large to be covered in a single sermon, we need to look for a smaller subunit.

The *Revised Common Lectionary* assigns Ecclesiastes 3:1-13 for New Year's Eve. However, this is not a complete literary unit since verse 14 (repeating the "I know" of v. 12) continues the conclusion of the Teacher's reflection. Our options for a preaching text are either 3:1-15 or 3:1-22. Provan, in seeking to justify his selection of 3:1-22, writes, "Verses 16-17 pick up and develop the theme of divine control of 'the times,' using it to address the question of injustice in the world. . . . Verses 16-17 are clearly related to verses 1-15 both thematically and syntactically ('I saw something *else*,' Heb. *'ôd*)."[6] Although the two sections are clearly related, it is equally clear that verses 16-22 move to other topics, namely the wickedness in this world and humans dying like animals. Whybray rightly states, "Verses 1-15 must be considered as a single section. Verse 16 probably marks the beginning of a new section, although — as is the case elsewhere in the book — there is no absolute thematic break."[7] We shall, therefore, select Ecclesiastes 3:1-15 as our preaching text.

This text, of course, must be understood in its broader context. There is a significant connection between the poem about the times (3:2-8) and the earlier poem about the cycles in nature (1:4-9). The poem about nature begins

---

4. Ibid., 100.

5. Wright, "Riddle of the Sphinx Revisited," *CBQ* 42 (1980) 49. See his diagram on p. 21 above. Murphy, *Ecclesiastes*, 28-39, suggests the same unit under the heading, "A Reflection upon Time and Toil." Along with other commentators, Murphy, ibid., 31, subdivides this unit "from the point of view of content" into four parts: 3:1-15; 3:16-22; 4:1-3; 4:4-6.

6. Provan, *Ecclesiastes*, 91, 92. To be sure, one can handle a larger unit in a commentary than in a sermon which requires a single focus.

7. Whybray, *Ecclesiastes*, 65. Cf. Ogden, *Qoheleth*, 51, "This section has a distinctive theme — time — which separates it from the previous chapter. Its terminal point we are able to fix at 3:15 on the grounds that vv. 16-22 address a different topic."

with the rhetorical question, "What do people gain from all the toil at which they toil under the sun?" (1:3), while this poem concludes with a similar rhetorical question, "What gain do the workers have from their toil?" (3:9). Further, "the earth remains forever" (1:4) is similar to "whatever God does endures forever" (3:14). "To the endlessly repeated cyclical movement of the sun, the wind and the waters correspond events in the life of the individual and of humanity."[8] A prose commentary follows each of the poems (1:10-11; 3:10-15). "The conclusions are similar in both cases, as well: whatever happened happens again. In other words, what goes around comes around (1:9; 3:15)."[9]

The Teacher will come back to the question of "time" in 3:17; 7:17; 8:5-6, 9; 9:11-12; and 10:17. His advice to enjoy God's daily gifts (3:12-13), given earlier in 2:24-25, he will give again in 3:22; 5:18-20; 8:15; 9:7-9; and 11:8-9. He will also revisit his point that "all should stand in awe before" God (lit. "should fear him"; 3:14) in 5:7; 7:18, and 8:12, while an editor will sum up the book, "The end of the matter; all has been heard. Fear God, and keep his commandments; for that is the whole duty of everyone" (12:13).

Literary Features

A detailed analysis of various literary features will help us not only in discerning the textual structure but also in arriving at a correct interpretation of this frequently misunderstood passage. We shall first note the literary forms, then examine the parallelism of the poem, and finally discuss whether (parts of) the poem should be understood literally or figuratively.

The Literary Forms

This passage contains various literary forms. After an introductory thesis statement (3:1), the Teacher presents a poem on the times (3:2-8). This is followed by the rhetorical question, "What gain have the workers from their toil?" (3:9). With his "I have seen," the Teacher begins a reflection on the poem (3:10-11), which is followed by two conclusions, each beginning with "I know" (3:12 and 14). The second conclusion contains a proverb, "Nothing can be added to it, nor anything taken from it" (3:14).[10]

8. Joseph Blenkinsopp, "Ecclesiastes 3:1-15: Another Interpretation," *JSOT* 66 (1995) 63.

9. Seow, *Ecclesiastes*, 169.

10. "As a proverb, we are not surprised to find similar statements with nearly identical vocabulary elsewhere (Deut 4:2; 13:1 [Eng. 12:32]; and in part in Prov 30:6." Longman, *Book of Ecclesiastes*, 123.

Parallelism in the Poem

Repetition shows up particularly in the parallel constructions in the poem. The poem consists of fourteen lines, each line constructed in the form of antithetic parallelism. For example,

> a time to be born, and a time to die [A — B].

Most verses of two lines are constructed in the form of regular parallelism (either synonymous or synthetic).[11] For example:

> a time to be born,   and a time to die;   [A — B]
> a time to plant,   and a time to pluck up what is planted [A′ — B′]

Verse 8, by contrast, has inverted parallelism:

> a time to love,   and a time to hate;   [A ⤫ B]
> a time for war,   and a time for peace   [B′ ⤫ A′].[12]

The poem begins with birth and death and ends with war and peace. Crenshaw suggests that "this gives the poem a ring pattern, a closed structure."[13] If this is indeed an inclusio, it is rather weak. It would be better to say that the poem indicates its conclusion with the unusual (for this poem) inverted parallelism which makes "peace" the final word in line fourteen.

The poem uses the word "time" 28 times (4×7), distributed over 14 lines (2×7). Since 7 is the number of completeness (think of the seven days of creation), the author, without naming all possible times, intends to depict the complete number of different times humans may encounter in their lifetime. This is also evident from the first pair, birth and death, which "marks the extreme limits of human existence itself and so by anticipation defines the scope of the whole list."[14] While the poem is dominated by "time" (*ʿēt*), this concept "is significantly contrasted with *ʿōlām*, 'duration,' in v. 11, a word that is also used to characterize the divine activity in v. 14."[15]

---

11. For a quick review of these different kinds of parallelism, see p. 33 above. For an example of synthetic parallelism, see verse 4 in "Sermon Exposition" below.

12. For a concrete example of how awareness of parallelism can help in interpretation, see n. 36 below.

13. Crenshaw, *Ecclesiastes*, 93.

14. Whybray, *Ecclesiastes*, 68. This poetic device is called "merismus."

15. Murphy, *Ecclesiastes*, 31. Loader, *Ecclesiastes*, 33-38, presents a more elaborate pattern for the poem based on what he considers favorable and unfavorable times. But his decisions on what is favorable are sometimes speculative and force a specific interpretation on the text (e.g., v. 5a). For a critique of Loader's pattern, see Whybray, *Ecclesiastes*, 69, and Seow, *Ecclesiastes*, 170-71.

A few other repetitions should be noted. God "has given" three things: "the business for everyone to be busy with" (v. 10), "a sense of past and future" (v. 11) and the ability to "eat and drink and take pleasure in all their toil" (v. 13). Further, in his conclusion the Teacher twice repeats the confident, "I know" (vv. 12, 14).

Literal or Figurative Language

A final literary feature we should discuss is the presence or absence of figurative language. Many commentators abandon the relative safety of literal interpretation in order to step out on the slippery slope of figurative interpretation. This is frequently done on the basis of ancient interpretations or the usage of these terms in other parts of Scripture. For example, Leupold holds that the activities mentioned in verses 2-8 are not about "purely human relationships" but about God's "control and . . . governance of the *church*."[16] Thus "a time to be born" (v. 2) would speak of "seasons when God grants His church the ability to bring forth children." "A time to die" refers to "seasons of death for the church when God chastises her because of her sins," and so on.[17]

Walter Kaiser rightly objects, "The result is a travesty of the meaning intended by the author."[18] Preachers should resist spiritualizing and allegorizing when the literal meaning makes perfectly good sense and when the author does not signal that his words should be understood figuratively. Why would one interpret "a time to plant, and a time to pluck up what is planted" (v. 2b) as "metaphors for life/death"[19] when this has already been stated literally in the foregoing line? If these phrases are metaphors, then one can hardly object when another commentator puts a different spin on their meaning: "In life generally there are times of 'planting' and putting down roots and times of 'uprooting' and disruption."[20]

---

16. Leupold, *Exposition of Ecclesiastes*, 81 (his emphasis). Leupold justifies his allegorical interpretation as follows: "For thus, Jerome indicates, this passage was from the days of old interpreted by the Jews in the Targum . . . as referring to Israel. . . . It can also be demonstrated that all these activities for which it is said that there is a special time are elsewhere in the Scriptures spoken of as forms of activity which God at some time or another has engaged in either for the correction or for the deliverance of the church." Ibid., 81-82.

17. Ibid., 84.

18. Kaiser, *Ecclesiastes*, 63.

19. Murphy, *Ecclesiastes*, 33. Cf. Seow, *Ecclesiastes*, 160, "The literal meaning is adequate, although it is also possible that this line continues the subject matter of v. 2a, as many scholars suggest. That is, 'planting' may be a metaphor for coming to life and 'uprooting' may be a metaphor for death."

20. Provan, *Ecclesiastes*, 88.

Similarly, "a time to break down, and a time to build up" (v. 3b) makes perfectly good sense when understood literally. Why would one understand it figuratively: "In the Old Testament the words for tearing down and building up are often used with reference to the destruction and building up of a human life"?[21]

The most outrageous allegorical interpretation is that of verse 5a, "a time to throw away stones, and a time to gather stones together." Murphy writes, "Many commentators propose the view found in *Midrash Rabbah* that interprets the actions as sexual intercourse; thus a certain parallelism with v. 5b is obtained. But the peculiar nature of the metaphor remains unexplained."[22] I have been unable to find any evidence that "throwing away stones" ever meant sexual intercourse[23] — except for such identification in ancient Jewish and Christian sources.[24] But surely allegorical interpretation in ancient sources, when allegorical interpretation was in vogue, is not to be followed by us today. Allegorical interpretation can be used legitimately only when the author clearly presents an allegory, such as Ecclesiastes 12:3-4a. But in this passage, the author gives no hint that he intended his words to be understood metaphorically while a literal interpretation throughout makes good sense. In fact, in its context a literal interpretation of this disputed phrase brings out a striking parallel. The seventh line states, "A time to throw away stones" on enemy fields in a time of war, and "a time to gather stones together" so that one can plant again in a time of peace. Compare this with the fourteenth line (2×7): "A time for war, and a time for peace."

Textual Structure

We have seen that the Teacher begins with a thesis statement (3:1), and follows it with a poem on the times (3:2-8). Next he raises the rhetorical question, "What gain have the workers from their toil?" (3:9). With his "I have seen," he next begins a reflection on the poem (3:10-11), which leads to two conclusions, each be-

---

21. Loader, *Ecclesiastes*, 36. Loader's reason for this interpretation is that it supports his assumed overall pattern: "The first line in verse 3 is expanded by the second."

22. Murphy, *Ecclesiastes*, 33. Murphy continues: "K. Galling, who points out that metaphor is otherwise absent in vv. 2-8, suggests that these are stones for counting, used in commercial transaction. H. Hertzberg refers to the actions of a farmer working his field."

23. For details, see Seow, *Ecclesiastes*, 161.

24. See J. Robert Wright, *Proverbs, Ecclesiastes*, 223-25. For example, Wright quotes from Augustine's *The Excellence of Widowhood* 8.11, "As for you, you both have children and live in that end of the world when the time has already come not 'to scatter stones but to gather; not to embrace but to refrain embraces." [This is a time] when the apostle cries out, 'But this I say, brethren, the time is short; it remains that those who have wives be as if they had none.'"

ginning with "I know" (3:12 and 14). These forms help us in outlining the textual structure:

I. Thesis statement: For everything there is a season . . . , a time (3:1)
   A. Poem with fourteen (2 × 7) pairs of times, one canceling out the other (3:2-8)
   B. Conclusion: workers have no gain from their toil (3:9; cf. 1:3; 2:11)
II. Reflection on the business God has given us to be busy with (3:10)
   A. God made everything suitable for its time (3:11a)
   B. God put a sense of past and future into our minds (3:11b)
   C. Yet we cannot find out what God has done from beginning to end (3:11c)
   D. Conclusion: Therefore, nothing better than to enjoy God's gifts (3:12-13)
III. Whatever God does (presumably the setting of the times) endures forever (3:14a)
   A. Supported by a proverb:

> Nothing can be added to it,
> nor anything taken away from it (3:14b)

   B. Purpose: God has done this, so that all should stand in awe of him (3:14c)
   D. Conclusion: there is nothing new (cf. 1:9); God seeks out what has gone by (3:15)

Theocentric Interpretation

As mentioned, the *Revised Common Lectionary* assigns this passage about the times for New Year's Eve. Unfortunately, this placement on New Year's Eve may entice preachers to speak about our New Year's resolutions and how we ought to act at the appropriate time. As Seow points out, "The poem is popularly understood to mean that there are appropriate moments for people to act and, at the proper moment, even an ordinarily objectionable situation can be 'beautiful in its own way.'"[25] If we were to develop the sermon in this direction of people acting at the right time, we would end up with a human-centered sermon and miss the author's intention. That is why it is important before for-

---

25. Seow, *Ecclesiastes*, 169. Seow continues, "Placed properly in its present context, however, it becomes clear that the poem is not about human determination of events or even human discernment of times and seasons. It is about God's activity and the appropriate human response to it." Ibid.

mulating the textual theme to raise the question, What does this passage say about God?

William Brown writes, "Even though humanity is the grammatical subject of the various infinitives — *people* plant and pluck up, mourn and dance — the human subject is by no means the determiner of such events. Qohelet makes clear that God alone is the one who determines; God is the primary, albeit implicit, actor on the temporal scene. The ever-constant swings of time's pendulum are suspended and held firmly by God."[26]

Even though God is not mentioned in the opening thesis statement and the poem about the times (vv. 2-8), the sequel makes clear that it is God who set the times. God also has given "business . . . to everyone to be busy with" (v. 10). Moreover, he has given us food and drink and pleasure in our toil (v. 13). God has made "everything suitable for its time" (v. 11a) and put "a sense of past and future" into our minds (v. 11b). God acts "from the beginning to the end" (v. 11c), and seeks out "what has gone by" (v. 15c). Whatever he does "endures forever" (v. 14a). "God has done this, so that all may stand in awe before him" (v. 14c).

Textual Theme and Goal

Whybray writes, "The theme of the whole section is unmistakably and emphatically proclaimed by the occurrence of the key word *'ēt* [time] no less than twenty-nine times in the first eight verses and also by its recurrence in v. 11a."[27] The frequent repetition of this keyword certainly gives us a clue to the theme of this passage. The question is, however, What does the author intend to say about time? Is it about humans discerning the right time to act or about God setting the times, or a combination of the two? Although the passage speaks about "workers" (v. 9), it nowhere makes explicit the point that people should act at the right time. On the contrary, it clearly makes the point that God set the times; in fact, "he has made everything suitable for its time" (v. 11). The key verse is found in the conclusion, "I know that whatever God does endures forever . . . ; God has done this, so that all should stand in awe before him" (v. 14). These considerations lead to the following thematic statement: *The sovereign God set the times forever so that people will stand in awe before him.*

The author's goal in presenting this message to Israel is implied in God's goal stated in verse 14, "so that all should stand in awe before him." But the author's goal is more than simply to encourage Israel to stand in awe before God.

---

26. Brown, *Ecclesiastes*, 42.
27. Whybray, *Ecclesiastes*, 65-66.

With his lengthy poem on the times and the following arguments he seeks to *convince* Israel to stand in awe before God. We can therefore formulate the author's goal as follows: *to convince the Israelites to stand in awe before their sovereign God.*

Ways to Preach Christ

How can we move from the stated theme to Jesus Christ in the New Testament? This passage contains neither a promise of the coming Messiah nor a type of Christ. That leaves five ways to explore. Since redemptive-historical progression and longitudinal themes are again intertwined, we shall combine them under one head.

Redemptive-Historical Progression/Longitudinal Themes

This combination probably offers the best way to Christ in the New Testament. Iain Provan observes, "That God, not mortal beings, controls the 'times' is a fundamental biblical conviction. Thus the biblical account of Israel's past does not focus primarily on the social and political forces that drive history or on the great heroes who are said to shape its direction. It portrays the past, rather, as an entity shaped by God, who acts in grace and judgment, in the midst of all the actions of its human and other participants."[28] One can trace this theme of God controlling the times in the Old Testament from Genesis to Malachi[29] and on into the New Testament.

At the appointed time, also called "the fullness of time," God sent his Son Jesus to this world. Paul writes, "But when *the fullness of time* had come, God sent his Son, born of a woman, born under the law, in order to redeem those who were under the law, so that we might receive adoption as children" (Gal 4:4-5). Jesus began his ministry by preaching, "*The time is fulfilled,* and the kingdom of God has come near; repent, and believe in the good news" (Mark 1:15). When the authorities tried to arrest Jesus, John reports that "no one laid hands on him, because *his hour* had not yet come" (John 7:30). But Jesus' time soon came: "Now before the festival of the Passover, Jesus knew that *his hour* had come to depart from this world and go to the Father" (John 13:1). Jesus told his disciples to "go into the city to a certain man, and say to him, 'The Teacher says, *My time* is near; I will keep the Passover at your house with my disciples'"

---

28. Provan, *Ecclesiastes*, 94-95.
29. See ibid.

(Matt 26:18). Later Paul writes, "For while we were still weak, at *the right time* Christ died for the ungodly" (Rom 5:6).

Jesus rose from the dead, promised to come again, and ascended into heaven. He had predicted that before his Second Coming there would be a time of great tribulation: "at *that time* there will be great suffering, such as has not been from the beginning of the world until now, no, and never will be." But "*immediately after* the suffering of those days. . . . the sign of the Son of Man will appear in heaven, and . . . [people] will see the Son of Man coming on the clouds of heaven with power and great glory. And he will send out his angels with a loud trumpet call, and they will gather his elect from the four winds, from one end of heaven to the other" (Matt 24:21, 29-31).

While we live in these in-between times, Paul urges us, "In the presence of God, who gives life to all things, and of Christ Jesus, who in his testimony before Pontius Pilate made the good confession, I charge you to keep the commandment without spot or blame until the manifestation of our Lord Jesus Christ, which he will bring about at *the right time* — he who is the blessed and only Sovereign, the King of kings and Lord of lords" (1 Tim 6:13-15).

Analogy

As the Teacher made the point that God set the times, so Jesus teaches that God set the time for "the coming of the Son of Man": "About that day and hour no one knows. . . , but only the Father" (Matt 24:36). But whereas the Teacher drew the conclusion that therefore we should stand in awe of God, Jesus draws the conclusion that therefore we must "keep awake" and "be ready" (Matt 24:42, 44).

New Testament References

In addition to the references mentioned above, one might also consider Matthew 16:1-4. Just after Jesus had cured many people and fed the four thousand (Matt 15:29-39), "the Pharisees and Sadducees came, and to test Jesus they asked him to show them a sign from heaven. He answered them, 'When it is evening, you say, "It will be fair weather, for the sky is red." And in the morning, "It will be stormy today, for the sky is red and threatening." You know how to interpret the appearance of the sky, but you cannot interpret the *signs of the times*. An evil and adulterous generation asks for a sign, but no sign will be given to it except the sign of Jonah.'" "The signs of the times" Jesus has in mind are his arrival, his preaching, and his miracles; these signs show that the long-awaited kingdom of God has come near. Even as Jesus began his ministry, he proclaimed, "*The time is fulfilled,* and the kingdom of God has come near; repent, and believe in the good news" (Mark 1:15).

Contrast

There is no contrast between the message of the Teacher and that of the New Testament.

Sermon Theme and Goal

Since the New Testament does not change the author's theme, the sermon theme can be identical: *The sovereign God set the times forever so that people will stand in awe before him.*

The author's goal in presenting this message to Israel is equally valid today: *to convince the hearers to stand in awe before the sovereign God.* This goal points to the need addressed in this sermon: people do not stand in awe before God.

Sermon Exposition

One can begin the sermon with a contemporary illustration of people not standing in awe before God. An atheist denies the very existence of God; insults God; uses God's name in vain. A modern scientist claims that true science must explain the origin of the cosmos without reference to God. A televangelist seeks to manipulate God, frequently using God's name and Jesus' name in healing services, ultimately to enrich himself. A Christian speaks to God in prayer as if God were a mere pal. A theologian dissects the nature of God as if God were a creature. In our busyness all of us have times when we think we alone are in charge and forget God.

When the Teacher wrote this message to Israel, they, too, were busy buying and selling, making fortunes and losing them, thinking they alone were in charge. They did not stand in awe before God. The Teacher begins to counter this problem innocently enough by reminding Israel and us today that there is a time for everything.

Chapter 3:1, "For everything there is a season, and a time for every matter under heaven." For everything there is an appropriate time. Human life is not haphazard. There is a proper "time for every matter under heaven."

He illustrates his point with a poem about the times. This poem mentions the word "time" twenty-eight times. There's a time for this and a time for that

— twenty-eight times. "It sounds like a clock that, inexorably and independent of the wishes of people, keeps ticking and striking. Whatever happens happens, and there is nothing you can do about it."[30]

The poem starts with the times that begin and end every human life. Verse 2, "a time to be born, and a time to die." We did not decide to be born, let alone the *time* to be born. And we don't decide the time to die. The time to be born and the time to die are beyond our control.

The poem matches this first pair with a second pair:

(a time to be born, and a time to die;)
    a time to plant, and a time to pluck up what is planted.

Again, we don't control the time to plant nor the time to pluck up what is planted. We plant our fruit trees at the appropriate time, and when the trees get old and no longer bear fruit, we pluck them up. We plant our annual flowers in the spring and in the fall we pluck them up again. We are free, of course, to plant our flowers at a time other than the appropriate time. We can decide to plant our flowers in the middle of the winter. We are free to ignore the appropriate times, but that would be foolish. We are free to plant whenever we wish, but we cannot control the appropriate time.

Verse 3, "a time to kill, and a time to heal." Again, we don't control this appropriate time. We cannot kill any time. But there are appropriate times to kill; for example, for self-defense in a time of war. But there are also appropriate times to heal, that is, to preserve life when the war is over and a peace treaty has been signed.

Paired up with "a time to kill, and a time to heal" is "a time to break down, and a time to build up." We can think again of a time of war. "An attacking army tears down buildings, but after hostilities cease, they are built once again."[31] But we can also think more broadly: "In ancient Palestine construction often required dismantling of existing stone structures."[32] The same is true today in our inner cities. Buildings are broken down, imploded, in order to make way for more modern buildings. "A time to break down, and a time to build up."

Verse 4,

a time to weep, and a time to laugh;
    a time to mourn, and a time to dance

30. Loader, *Ecclesiastes*, 35.
31. Longman, *Book of Ecclesiastes*, 115. Longman cautions, "This case cannot be pressed too strongly since the words are widely used outside battle contexts."
32. Crenshaw, *Ecclesiastes*, 94.

There are appropriate times to weep and appropriate times to laugh. The second line intensifies the time to weep: this is a time to mourn. At a funeral of a loved one we not only weep but mourn deeply. But then, again, there is a time when it is not just appropriate to laugh but to be so exuberant that it is appropriate to dance for joy.[33]

Verse 5,

> a time to throw away stones,
> and a time to gather stones together.

Again we can think of a time of war. "During war rocks were thrown on cultivable fields to render the fields useless."[34] Those who have been to Israel will recall that even today one of the striking features of Palestine is the multitude of rocks. We read in 2 Kings that Israel in its war with Moab was instructed, "Every good piece of land you shall ruin with stones"; and Israel complied: "On every good piece of land everyone threw a stone, until it was covered" (3:19, 25). As a result the Moabites could neither sow their fields nor reap a harvest. "In peacetime rocks had to be cleared from a field before cultivation; on the hillsides these stones were usually arranged in terraces to prevent erosion, catch the rain, and allow it to penetrate the dry soil."[35]

The line paired with "a time to throw away stones, and a time to gather stones together" is "a time to embrace, and a time to refrain from embracing." One can also relate this line to times of war and peace. In a time of war one refrains from embracing the enemy, while in a time of peace one can embrace the enemy.[36] But one can also think of this more broadly: there are appropriate times to embrace, as when one gets married, and appropriate times to refrain from embracing, as when one has leprosy or another disease thought to be contagious.

Verse 6, "a time to seek, and a time to lose." There is an appropriate time to seek, that is, to acquire possessions,[37] and an appropriate time to lose possessions. "The reference may belong to the household, where women searched for something (like the lost coin in Jesus' parable) that had been misplaced. One can easily think of several circumstances where searching was timely and where

---

33. See Loader, *Ecclesiastes*, 36, with references to Psalm 114:4, 6, where the same verb is used.

34. Crenshaw, *Ecclesiastes*, 94. Cf. Fox, *A Time to Tear Down*, 208.

35. Ibid. See Isaiah 5:2.

36. This interpretation is justified because the inverted parallelism (A B, B′A′) is in line with the inverted parallelism of verse 8, and also links the parallelism between the seventh and fourteenth lines of the poem: in a time of war "to throw away stones"; in a time of peace "to gather stones together" (v. 5a) and "a time for war, and a time for peace" (v. 8b).

37. See Murphy, *Ecclesiastes*, 34.

an unsuccessful search finally justified a decision to consider the object permanently lost."[38]

This line is paired with "a time to keep, and a time to throw away." There is an appropriate time to keep possessions, but there is also an appropriate time "to throw away," to discard possessions. An ancient source "mentions jettisoning merchandise from a ship in a storm."[39] Think of the sailors on Jonah's ship throwing the cargo into the sea to lighten the ship in the storm. Even today, with a downturn in the market, people may think this is the appropriate time to jettison certain stocks. Certainly for most older couples there comes a time for "downsizing."

Verse 7, "a time to tear, and a time to sew." This line clearly refers to ancient practices of expressing sorrow. When people mourned the death of a loved one, they would express their sorrow by tearing their clothes. For example, when Reuben thought that his younger brother Joseph had been killed, "he tore his clothes." When Jacob later thought that his favored son Joseph was dead, he "tore his garments" (Gen 37:29, 34).[40] But when the time of mourning was over, they would mend their clothes again.

This line is paired with the line, "a time to keep silence, and a time to speak." People expressed their sorrow for losing a loved one by keeping silence. The friends of Job "sat with him on the ground seven days and seven nights, and no one spoke a word to him, for they saw that his suffering was very great" (Job 2:13). When the time of mourning was completed, it was again "a time to speak." But "a time to keep silence" need not be restricted to a time of sorrow. "The focus . . . may be connected with the very important wisdom theme of knowing the proper time to speak and to refrain from speaking."[41]

The final lines of the poem are in verse 8,

a time to love, and a time to hate;[42]
a time for war, and a time for peace.

"A time to hate" links up with "a time for war," while "a time to love" links up with "a time for peace." The poem ends with these major contrasts: "a time for

---

38. Crenshaw, *Ecclesiastes*, 95. Seow, *Ecclesiastes*, 162, points out that "the verb [for losing] is used in Jer 23:1 of shepherds who give up on their sheep — let them perish."

39. The Targum; Fox, *Ecclesiastes*, 22.

40. See also 2 Samuel 1:11; 3:31; and 13:31.

41. Longman, *Book of Ecclesiastes*, 117, with references to Proverbs 10:19; 13:3; 16:24; 17:27; 21:23; 25:11, and especially 15:23.

42. "Even hatred has its time, as demonstrated in the psalms that imprecate unnamed enemies (e.g., Pss 58:6-11; 137:7-9; 139:19-22; cf. Eccl 2:18). Each activity has its relative worth and suitability, its 'place' in the grand providential scheme." Brown, *Ecclesiastes*, 41. Of course, Jesus said, "You have heard that it was said, 'You shall love your neighbor and hate your enemy.' But I say to you, Love your enemies . . ." (Matt 5:43-44).

war, and a time for peace." "According to the Midrash [a Jewish exposition], this pair sums up several of the others, namely uprooting/planting, seeking/losing, tearing down/building up, slaying/healing, ripping/sewing, and hating/loving."[43]

The poem sounds very much like the poem about the cycles of nature in chapter 1,

A generation goes, and a generation comes. . . .
The sun rises and the sun goes down. . . .
The wind blows to the south, and goes around to the north. . . . (1:4-6)

As we see these repeated cycles in nature, so we can observe set times for life on earth:

A time to be born, and a time to die;
a time to plant, and a time to pluck up what is planted — and so on.

And as the Teacher raised the question in chapter 1, "What do people gain from all the toil at which they toil under the sun?" (1:3), so here he raises the question in 3:9, "What gain have the workers from their toil?" The expected answer is the same. Workers gain nothing from their toil. Did you notice how one time cancels out another? "A time to be born, and a time to die." Nothing left. A time to plant our flowers in the spring and a time to pluck them up in the fall. Nothing gained. "A time to break down and a time to build up." Nothing changed. "What gain have the workers from their toil?" Absolutely nothing.[44]

So far the Teacher has not said anything about the how and why of the times. He has merely illustrated that there is a time for everything and that these times cancel out each other. But who set these times? And why?

In the next section the Teacher will answer these important questions. He writes in verses 10 and 11, "I have seen the business[45] that God has given to everyone to be busy with. He has made everything suitable for its time." The sovereign God has set the times. He is the one who "has made *everything* suit-

---

43. Fox, *Ecclesiastes*, 22.

44. "As the streams flow continually into the sea without effect (1:7), so unremitting toil continues without even the *prospect* of securing tangible gain. Within a state of existence fraught with the endless recycling of human activity (3:2-8), the matter of gain remains forever a *non sequitur.*" Brown, "'Whatever Your Hand Finds to Do,'" *Int* 55/3 (2001) 277.

45. "The 'business' in question is described in the following verse: trying to understand what God brings to pass, which is undoubtedly a hopeless task." Fox, *Ecclesiastes*, 22. Cf. Ecclesiastes 8:17, "Then I saw all the work of God, that no one can find out what is happening under the sun. However much they may toil in seeking, they will not find it out; even though those who are wise claim to know, they cannot find it out."

able for its time." The "everything" refers back to verse 1, "For everything there is a season, and a time. . . ." That includes the times of birth and death, of planting and plucking up, of war and peace. God sovereignly set all these times.

God also set the time when Jesus would be born. The New Testament calls this "the fullness of time." Paul writes, "But when *the fullness of time* had come, God sent his Son, born of a woman, born under the law, in order to redeem those who were under the law, so that we might receive adoption as children" (Gal 4:4-5). Jesus was very much aware of the times set by God. He began his ministry by preaching, "*The time is fulfilled,* and the kingdom of God has come near; repent, and believe in the good news" (Mark 1:15). Jesus also knew that God had set a time for his death. Shortly before his crucifixion, Jesus told his disciples to "go into the city to a certain man, and say to him, 'The Teacher says, My *time* is near; I will keep the Passover at your house with my disciples'" (Matt 26:18). That night Jesus changed the Old Testament Passover into the Lord's Supper. He "took a cup, and after giving thanks he gave it to them, saying, 'Drink from it, all of you; for this is my blood of the (new) covenant, which is poured out for many for the forgiveness of sins. I tell you, I will never again drink of this fruit of the vine until *that day* when I drink it new with you in my Father's kingdom'" (Matt 26:27-29).

Jesus died and, at the appointed time (Mark 8:31), rose from the dead. Before Jesus ascended into heaven, he met with his disciples. They asked him, "Lord, is this *the time* when you will restore the kingdom to Israel?" Jesus replied, "It is not for you to know *the times* or periods that the Father has set by his own authority." God has sovereignly set the times. And it is not for mere creatures to know these times. But the angels assured the disciples, "This Jesus, who has been taken up from you into heaven, will come in the same way as you saw him go into heaven" (Acts 1:6-7, 11). In God's time, Jesus will come again to establish God's kingdom on earth in perfection. God "has made everything suitable for its time."

The Teacher continues in verse 11, "moreover, he has put a sense of past and future into their minds, yet they cannot find out what God has done from the beginning to the end." Just as Jesus said to his disciples, "It is not for you to know the times," so the Old Testament Teacher declares that human beings "cannot find out what God has done from the beginning to the end." We do not know what God has done in the distant past nor what he will do in the far-off future.

True, the Teacher also says here that "God has put a sense of past and future [literally, 'eternity'] into . . . [our] minds." Unlike animals who live only for the present, we can study the past and contemplate the future. God has given us the kind of self-consciousness that enables us to transcend the present and reflect on the past and the future.[46] Yet we cannot comprehend the whole picture. "We are like the desperately nearsighted, inching their way along some great tapestry or fresco in the attempt to take it in. We see enough to recognize something of its quality, but the grand design escapes us, for we can never stand back far enough to view it as its Creator does, whole and entire, *from the beginning to the end*."[47]

Since we are unable fully to understand the meaning of God's times, the Teacher concludes in verses 12 to 13, "I know that there is nothing better for them than to be happy and enjoy themselves as long as they live; moreover, it is God's gift that all should eat and drink and take pleasure in all their toil." This advice is an echo of his earlier conclusion: since all human endeavors are vanity, "there is nothing better for mortals than to eat and drink, and find enjoyment in their toil. This also is from the hand of God" (2:24). In this case, since human beings cannot understand the times God set, let alone control them, it is best to concentrate on the present: enjoy God's gifts of food, drink, and toil![48]

But there is more. Verse 14 is the key verse in this passage: "I know that whatever God does[49] endures forever;[50] nothing can be added to it, nor anything taken from it; God has done this, so that all should stand in awe before him." Here finally we get an answer to the question *why* God set the times. The Teacher says, "Whatever God does endures forever." The times God set are permanent and unchangeable.[51] "Nothing can be added to it, nor anything taken from it." We cannot add anything to the past, nor can we take anything away from it. By the same token, we cannot add anything to the future, nor can we take anything away from it. The point is "that what God wants to do will invariably be done, and no human being can hope to alter the course of things by sheer effort."[52]

"God has done this," the Teacher concludes in verse 14, "so that all should

---

46. "Human beings are endowed with the facility to step back from immediate situations and particular events that vie for their attention to catch a glimpse of the totality of existence, including their own. Such is the mark of self-consciousness. Yet they remain ignorant of any purposeful providence that underlies the totality. . . . The capacity to transcend oneself, in fact, points to the conundrum of human existence for Qohelet. Human beings are endowed with the capacity to look beyond the immediacy of life, to suspend oneself, however delicately, above the fray to sense the eternal but are never quite able to grasp the meaning of it all." Brown, *Ecclesiastes*, 43, 44.

47. Kidner, *A Time to Mourn*, 39.

48. "Once the search for ultimate meaning in life is thwarted, the best course is to seek the little, sensual pleasures of life." Longman, *Book of Ecclesiastes*, 121.

49. "By this expression he [the Teacher] certainly refers to 'making' (. . . v. 11) everything appropriate for its time, and thus he refers back to vv. 1-8." Longman, ibid., 123.

50. "Eternal. That is, not bound by time and invariably coming to pass (cf. *lĕʿôlām* in 1:4). The meaning of *ʿôlām* is clarified by the next line: one can neither add nor take away from all that God will do." Seow, *Ecclesiastes*, 164.

51. See Murphy, *Ecclesiastes* 35.

52. Seow, *Ecclesiastes*, 174,

stand in awe before him." This is why God has set the times: "so that all should stand in awe before him." This was God's purpose[53] in setting the times. God's times make us aware of our helplessness: we cannot control the times. God's times make us aware of our total dependence on God: we do not even *know* the times. Awareness of our helplessness and dependence makes us stand in awe before God. He is the sovereign God who controls all things. Jesus says, "Are not two sparrows sold for a penny? Yet not one of them will fall to the ground apart from your Father. And even the hairs of your head are all counted" (Matt 10:29-30). God set the times; he controls all things.

In verse 15 the Teacher reiterates one more time his point that God controls the times: "That which is, already has been; that which is to be, already is"; that is, the present was already in the past and the future is already in the present. In other words, "past, present, and future are bound together."[54] The end of verse 15 repeats this notion, "God seeks out what has gone by,"[55] that is, God seeks out the events of the past and brings them back into existence.[56] The thought is similar to that of the opening poem: "What has been is what will be, and what has been done is what will be done; there is nothing new under the sun" (1:9). Not only do God's times "endure forever" (v. 14a), but they form a coherent whole (v. 15).

The point is that God is in control of the times. God is in control! And, as verse 14 states, "he has done this [i.e., set the times forever], so that all should stand in awe before him." The sovereign God set the times forever, it says literally, "so that all should fear him" — so that all should revere God; so that all should honor God as the sovereign God.[57]

---

53. Fox translates, "God *intends* for people to fear him (thus *še* introduces a purpose clause)." *A Time to Tear Down*, 212-13.

54. Ogden, *Qoheleth*, 57.

55. I am following the interpretation given in the translation of the NRSV. One can also move to a different interpretation by way of the footnote, "Heb. *what is pursued*." The question is, What is it precisely that God seeks out? Seow, *Ecclesiastes*, 174, writes: "The final phrase . . . seems to suggest that it is God who will take care of what is pursued, namely, all those matters that are beyond human grasp." Cf. ibid., 166. Cf. Brown, *Ecclesiastes*, 46, "Only God successfully seeks out and apprehends whatever is sought (by God or human being). Only God determines the result, such as who will win the battle, who will receive another's gain, and who will succeed (cf. Prov 16:1, 9; 21:31)."

56. Cf. Murphy, *Ecclesiastes*, 30, "The reference then is to the past or the events of the past, which God will call back into existence, in line with the thought of v. 15a." See ibid., n. 15, for various options for interpreting this difficult sentence. Crenshaw, *Ecclesiastes*, 100, suggests that "God ensures that events which have just transpired do not vanish into thin air. God brings them back once more, so that the past circles into the present." Cf. Blenkinsopp, "Ecclesiastes 3:1-15," *JSOT* 66 (1995) 62-63, "God seeks out what has been driven away, that is to say that God recalls occurrences which have moved from the future into the present and thence into the past so that they may be recycled eventually in a new present."

57. "Reverence of God is founded upon an acute awareness of one's finitude vis-a-vis God,

Why is it that we often do not stand in awe of God? Why is it that we often think that we alone are in charge and forget God? Why is it that even when we remember God and approach him in prayer, we do so with a lack of awe and reverence? Sometimes we talk to God as if he were a mere pal; at other times we may seek to manipulate God. Why is it that we often fail to revere God?

Could it be that we do not stand in awe of God because we cannot see him? When we see lightning strike close by, we stand in awe. When we see a tornado approaching, we hunker down in fear. When Israel saw the lightning on Mount Sinai and heard the thunder, "all the people who were in the camp trembled" (Exod 19:16). But when the signs of God's awesome presence were gone, they soon rebelled against God.

Given our failure to stand in awe before God, the Teacher urges us to consider the hand of God we see in creation around us. God set the times to which we are subject. God set the time for our birth and the time for our death and every appropriate time in between. In other words, God is in control and we are completely dependent on him. When we reflect deeply on God's greatness and our own dependence on God, we are bound to "stand in awe before him."

Jesus also taught us to stand in awe before God. Jesus said, "Do not fear those who kill the body but cannot kill the soul; rather fear him who can destroy both soul and body in hell" (Matt 10:28). Jesus also instructed us to address God as "our Father *in heaven*" (Matt 6:9). God is *in heaven*.[58] This means that God is wholly other from us his creatures. He is infinite while we are finite. He has all authority while we are his subjects. He controls the times while we are subject to the times.

There is only one way to approach this God, and that is with awe. Whether we seek God in personal prayer or worship him with his people, whether we study his word or study his creation, there is only one way to approach God — and that is with reverence and awe. As the author of Hebrews puts it, "Therefore, since we are receiving a kingdom that cannot be shaken, let us give thanks, by which we offer to God an acceptable worship with *reverence and awe*; for indeed our God is a consuming fire" (Heb 12:28-29). We should always approach God with reverence and awe.[59]

---

wholly Other and wholly sovereign. . . . Awe is the appropriate response to the *mysterium tremendum*." Brown, *Ecclesiastes*, 45. Cf. Murphy, *Ecclesiastes*, lxiv, "The fundamental meaning is reverence before the numinous, the *tremendum* (Exod 20:18-21)."

58. Cf. Ecclesiastes 5:2, "God is in heaven, and you upon the earth."

59. A meditation based on this research is found in Appendix 3, pp. 315-16 below.

CHAPTER 5

Working in a Wicked World

Ecclesiastes 3:16–4:6

Better is a handful with quiet
than two handfuls with toil,
and a chasing after wind.

(Eccl 4:6)

This passage deals with working in a world filled with cutthroat competition, wickedness, oppression, and envy. Since we all need to work, this is a good preaching text anytime, but especially for the Sunday before Labor Day. A major challenge will be to discover some logical progression of thought in a passage that, at first reading, seems disjointed. Also, the meaning of some words and sentences is not clear. For example, How is God "testing" human beings? (3:18); what is the meaning of "Who can bring them to see what will be after them?" (3:22); and what precisely is "a handful with *quiet*"? (4:6). And finally, how does one handle concepts which are contrary to the teachings of the New Testament — concepts such as humans having "no advantage over the animals" (3:19); humans and animals all going "to one place" (3:20); and the dead being "more fortunate than the living" (4:2)?

Text and Context

Ecclesiastes 3:16 begins a new literary unit with its "Moreover I saw" and the topic changing from the times God set to the wickedness on earth. The question is, Where does this unit end? Most commentators treat 3:16-22 as one unit and 4:1-16 as another. Verse 22 indeed forms a natural conclusion to this section: "So I saw that there is nothing better than that all should enjoy their

88

work, for that is their lot." One could, therefore, select as a preaching text Ecclesiastes 3:16-22. The problem with this selection in a series of sermons on Ecclesiastes is that the Teacher's repetition of the theme of enjoying one's work leads to virtually the same sermon theme as that of Ecclesiastes 1:12–2:26 (see above). Moreover, chapter 4:1 continues with the topic of wickedness, this time in the form of oppression. Crenshaw, therefore, discusses the unit of 3:16–4:3 under the heading, "The Tears of the Oppressed."[1] Again, it would be possible to preach a sermon on this unit, but it leaves 4:4-6 as an orphan. Based on the refrain, "This also is vanity and a chasing after wind" (4:4) and "a chasing after wind" (4:6), 4:4-6 forms the conclusion of a larger unit that runs from 3:1 to 4:6[2] and therefore should be included in this preaching text. Although these verses dealing with toil seem to move on to a different topic than oppression, toil coming from "one person's envy of another" (4:4) is a form of oppression.[3] Moreover, the conclusion, "Better is a handful with quiet" (4:6), nuances the earlier conclusion, "there is nothing better than that all should enjoy their work" (3:22). We shall, therefore, select Ecclesiastes 3:16–4:6 as our preaching text.

This passage is linked to the foregoing as well as to the following. Syntactically, the Teacher establishes the link to the foregoing with his observation, "I saw something *else*."[4] In terms of contents, his statement that God "has appointed a time for every matter" (3:17) picks up on his earlier theme of God setting the times (3:1-15). He raises here for the first time the thought of wickedness in the world (3:16) — a view he will raise again in the sequel (5:8; 8:10-15; 9:13-16; 10:5-7). He also mentions here for the first time that "God will judge the righteous and the wicked" (3:17) — a belief he will revisit later (11:9) and which will also be reiterated in the last verse of the book: "God will bring every deed into judgment, including every secret thing, whether good or evil" (12:14). He also states here for the first time that at death "all go to the same place" (3:20) — a conviction he will mention again later (6:6; 9:10). The Teacher repeats in 3:22 his earlier advice "to eat and drink, and find enjoyment in their toil" (2:24; cf. 3:12-13) — advice he will reiterate in the sequel (5:18-20; 8:15; 9:7-9; 11:8-9).

1. Crenshaw, *Ecclesiastes*, 101-6.
2. See the analysis of Wright on p. 21 above. So also Murphy, *Wisdom Literature*, 136.
3. See Brown, *Ecclesiastes*, 49.
4. Heb. *'ôd*. Provan, *Ecclesiastes*, 92. Cf. Longman, *Book of Ecclesiastes*, 126.

Literary Features

This passage is made up of several wisdom forms. The Teacher begins with an observation about wickedness in this world ("I saw under the sun," 3:16), which he follows with a reflection about God's judgment ("I said in my heart," 3:17). He follows this reflection with another reflection on God showing us that we are but animals ("I said in my heart," 3:18) and a conclusion to enjoy our work (3:22).

In 4:1 the Teacher adds another observation ("Again I saw . . . under the sun"), this one about oppressions in the world. This observation leads to a reflection ("I thought," 4:2) which includes a "better than" proverb (4:3).

Finally, in 4:4 the Teacher adds another observation/reflection[5] ("Then I saw"), this one about toil motivated by envy. This reflection includes a proverb about fools (4:5) and another "better than" proverb (4:6).[6]

In addition to the literary forms, repetition provides clues for arriving at the author's message. In 3:16 the Teacher uses synonymous parallelism to highlight the wickedness he observed "under the sun":

> Moreover I saw under the sun that in the place of justice,
> *wickedness was there,*
> and in the place of righteousness,
> *wickedness was there* as well.

In similar fashion, the Teacher highlights in 4:1 the oppressions he also observed "under the sun." This time he repeats three times a form of the word "oppression" and twice that there was no one to comfort them:

> Again I saw all the *oppressions* that are practiced under the sun.
> Look, the tears of the *oppressed* —
> *with no one to comfort them!*
> On the side of their *oppressors* there was power —
> *with no one to comfort them.*

Textual Structure

The literary forms discovered above enable us the trace the structure of the text, which will help us see the flow of the Teacher's argument.

---

5. As can be seen in this passage, observation sometimes precedes a reflection proper, at other times it is part of the reflection.

6. See Longman, *Book of Ecclesiastes*, 126-38.

I. Observation: I saw under the sun in the place of justice, wickedness (3:16)
  A. Reflection: God will judge the righteous and the wicked (3:17a)
    1. Reason: for God has appointed a time for judgment (3:17b)
  B. Further reflection: God is showing people that they are but animals (3:18)
    1. Reason: for the fate of humans and that of animals is the same (3:19a)
      a. As one dies, so dies the other (3:19b)
        i. they all have the same breath (3:19c)
        ii. humans have no advantage over the animals (3:19d)
        iii. for all is vanity (3:19e)
      b. All go to one place (3:20a; cf. 6:6)
        i. All are from the dust, and all turn to dust again (3:20b; cf. 12:7)
        ii. No one knows whether the human spirit goes upward (3:21)
  C. Conclusion: there is nothing better than that all should enjoy their work (3:22a)
    1. for work is our lot (3:22b)
    2. We don't know what will be after us (3:22c)
II. Observation: Again I saw all the oppressions that are practiced under the sun (4:1a)
  A. Reflection: I saw the tears of the oppressed (4:1b)
    1. with no one to comfort them (4:1c)
  B. On the side of their oppressors there was power (4:1d)
    1. with no one to comfort them (4:1e)
  C. Conclusion: the dead are more fortunate than the living (4:2)
    1. but better than both are the unborn (4:3a)
      a. for they have not seen the evil deeds that are done under the sun (4:3b)
III. Observation/Reflection: I saw that all toil comes from a person's envy (4:4a)
  A. This also is vanity and a chasing after wind (4:4b)
  B. Fools fold their hands (do not work) (4:5a)
    1. and consume their own flesh (4:5b)
  C. Better is a handful with quiet (4:6a)
    1. than two handfuls with toil (4:6b)
      a. and a chasing after wind (4:6c)

Theocentric Interpretation

This passage has only two references to God. Observing the all-pervasive wickedness in his society, the Teacher responds in a proverb with the Bible's standard answer to wickedness:[7]

> God will judge the righteous and the wicked,
>   for he has appointed a time for every matter,
>   and for every work. (3:17)

But further reflection leads the Teacher beyond this standard answer: "God is testing them to show that they are but animals" (3:18).

Textual Theme and Goal

The Teacher begins by highlighting the wickedness he observes under the sun. In the very place where one would expect to find justice, in the courts of justice, there was wickedness:

> In the place of justice, wickedness was there;
>   and in the place of righteousness, wickedness was there as well. (3:16)

After he gives the standard response to wickedness — "God will judge the righteous and the wicked" — the Teacher further reflects that by not uprooting wickedness God is testing humans to show them that they are but animals. Since humans die just like the animals, and since we don't know whether at death the human spirit goes upward or downward, he concludes that "there is nothing better than that all should enjoy their work" (3:22).

Next the Teacher observes wickedness in the form of oppressions. Graphically he paints "the tears of the oppressed — with no one to comfort them!" (4:1). He concludes that the dead, who no longer see this wickedness, are better off than the living who observe it every day. "But better than both is the one who has not yet been and has not seen the evil deeds that are done under the sun" (4:3).

Finally, the Teacher observes yet another form of wickedness: "All toil and all skill in work come from one person's envy of another" (4:4). Envy is the engine that drives our work ethic. How does one react properly to this reality? Fools give one answer by giving up on work — with the tragic result that they eat their own flesh (4:5). Others are consumed by their envy and become slaves

---

7. See pp. 98-99, n. 12 below.

to their toil in order to gather as much as possible. Unfortunately, this attitude results in "toil and a chasing after wind" (4:6). The Teacher's answer to this problem of work being motivated by envy falls between the responses of lazy fools giving up on work and of workaholics toiling for *two* handfuls: "Better is a handful with quiet" (4:6), or "tranquility" (TNIV), or "peace of mind" (NEB).

We can summarize the Teacher's message in one sentence: *In view of the wickedness, oppressions, and envy in this world, enjoy your work with quietness.*

This passage reveals quite clearly the question behind the text. The Teacher is sending this message primarily to young, male readers who live in a volatile world and are enamored by the possibilities of making a fortune.[8] Because the Teacher repeatedly and vividly paints the wickedness in this world, his goal is more than simply to encourage his readers to do this or that. His goal is *to urge his readers, in view of the wickedness, oppressions, and envy in this world, not to slave away in ruthless competition with their neighbors*[9] *but to enjoy their work and its fruit with quietness.*

Ways to Preach Christ

How can we move in the sermon from the Teacher's theme "to enjoy our work with quietness" to Jesus Christ in the New Testament? There is no promise of Christ in this passage, nor is there a type of Christ. This leaves five possible options to explore. Since redemptive-historical progression and longitudinal themes are again intertwined, we shall combine them in this investigation.

Redemptive-Historical Progression/Longitudinal Themes

Although one can trace through the Old Testament to Jesus Christ in the New Testament the theme of finding enjoyment in our work (see pp. 54-56 above), it would be better here to trace the more specific theme of enjoying one's work with *quietness*. We can begin with the Garden of Eden, where meaningful work was rewarded with the pleasure of eating "freely of every tree in the garden" (Gen 2:16). Although Adam and Eve's desire to be "like God" (Gen 3:5) robbed them of this tranquil setting, God promised to bring his people into another "garden of the LORD" (Gen 13:10): "I have come down to deliver them from the

---

8. "Here it is useful to remember that Qohelet's original audience was probably composed of young men anxious to 'make it' in an urban society that was very far from the biblical ideal for community, namely, the kinship-based villages of their ancestors." Davis, *Proverbs, Ecclesiastes, Song of Songs,* 190.

9. "One person's envy of another" (4:4) is literally of "one's neighbor."

Egyptians, and to bring them up out of that land to a good and broad land, a land flowing with milk and honey" (Exod 3:8). In this land, in contrast to Egypt, Israel can enjoy the fruit of its work in quietness and trust. Here they can confidently confess:

The LORD is my shepherd,
   I shall not want.
He makes me lie down in green pastures;
   he leads me beside still waters;
he restores my soul. (Ps 23:1-3)

The ideal in Israel was a return to the tranquil setting of Paradise: everyone living in safety, "all of them under their vines and fig trees" (1 Kings 4:25; cf. Isa 36:16; 65:21-25).

In the New Testament, John the Baptist warned the soldiers who came to him for advice: "Do not extort money from anyone by threats or false accusation, and be satisfied with your wages" (Luke 3:14). Jesus warned similarly, "Take care! Be on your guard against all kinds of greed; for one's life does not consist in the abundance of possessions" (Luke 12:15). Jesus urged his followers to switch their focus in life from possessions to the kingdom of God. He said, "Strive first for the kingdom of God and his righteousness, and all these things [food, drink, and clothing] will be given to you as well" (Matt 6:33).

Paul later writes, "I have learned to be content with whatever I have. I know what it is to have little, and I know what it is to have plenty. In any and all circumstances I have learned the secret of being well-fed and of going hungry, of having plenty and of being in need. I can do all things through him who strengthens me" (Phil 4:11-13). He also exclaims, "There is great gain in godliness combined with contentment; for we brought nothing into the world, so that we can take nothing out of it; but if we have food and clothing, we will be content with these" (1 Tim 6:6-8). But like the Teacher in Ecclesiastes, Paul also warns against dropping out of the workforce: "We hear that some of you are living in idleness, mere busybodies, not doing any work. Now such persons we command and exhort in the Lord Jesus Christ to do their work quietly and to earn their own living. Brothers and sisters, do not be weary in doing what is right" (2 Thess 3:11-13).

Analogy

The Teacher's message of enjoying your work with quietness is echoed in the New Testament. Paul writes the Thessalonians, "We urge you, beloved, . . . to aspire to live quietly, to mind your own affairs, and to work with your hands, as we directed you, so that you may behave properly toward outsiders and be dependent on no one" (1 Thess 4:10-12). Paul urges this instruction "through the Lord Jesus" (1 Thess 4:2).

In his first letter to Timothy, Paul stresses the importance of contentment. He writes, "Of course, there is great gain in godliness combined with contentment; . . . if we have food and clothing, we will be content with these. But those who want to be rich fall into temptation and are trapped by many senseless and harmful desires that plunge people into ruin and destruction. For the love of money is a root of all kinds of evil, and in their eagerness to be rich some have wandered away from the faith and pierced themselves with many pains" (1 Tim 6:6-10). The author of Hebrews echoes this sentiment: "Keep your lives free from the love of money; and be content with what you have" (Heb 13:5). In order to establish the connection with Jesus directly, one would have to link the last two passages to Jesus' teachings on the danger of the love of money and the value of contentment (e.g., Matt 6:19-33).

New Testament References

The New Testament does not quote or allude to this passage from Ecclesiastes.

Contrast

Some of the Teacher's ideas in this passage show a startling discontinuity with the teachings of the New Testament. The Teacher does not see any evidence that the death of humans is different from that of animals. He writes, "For the fate of humans and the fate of animals is the same; as one dies, so dies the other. They all have the same breath, and humans have no advantage over the animals; for all is vanity. All go to one place; all are from the dust, and all turn to dust again. Who knows whether the human spirit goes upward and the spirit of animals goes downward to the earth?" (3:19-21). In contrast, the New Testament teaches that the human spirit survives death. Paul writes: "For we know that if the earthly tent we live in is destroyed, we have a building from God, a house not made with hands, eternal in the heavens. . . . So we are always confident; even though we know that while we are at home in the body we are away from the Lord — for we walk by faith, not by sight. Yes, we do have confidence, and we would rather be away from the body and at home with the Lord" (2 Cor 5:1, 6-8).[10]

The Teacher seems to have an idea that God has set an appropriate time for

---

10. Cf. Philippians 1:21-23, "For to me, living is Christ and dying is gain. If I am to live in the flesh, that means fruitful labor for me; and I do not know which I prefer. I am hard pressed between the two: my desire is to depart and be with Christ, for that is far better."

judgment, but his view of the finality of death leaves no room for a judgment after death. By contrast, the New Testament teaches that the final judgment will take place after our death and resurrection. Jesus declares, "The hour is coming when all who are in their graves will hear his [Jesus'] voice and will come out — those who have done good, to the resurrection of life, and those who have done evil, to the resurrection of condemnation" (John 5:28-29).

In addition to these contrasts, we should also mention the contrast between the Teacher's message to enjoy our work with quietness in a wicked world and the New Testament message to oppose wickedness. The Old Testament law already urged Israel to oppose injustice. For example, "You shall not render an unjust judgment; you shall not be partial to the poor or defer to the great: with justice you shall judge your neighbor" (Lev 19:15-16; cf. Deut 16:20). The prophets especially called for justice. Micah preached,

> "He has told you, O mortal, what is good;
>   and what does the LORD require of you
> but to do justice, and to love kindness,
>   and to walk humbly with your God?" (Mic 6:8-9)

And Amos cried out,

> Let justice roll down like waters,
>   and righteousness like an ever-flowing stream. (Amos 5:24)

In his Sermon on the Mount, Jesus proclaimed,

> "Blessed are those who hunger and thirst for *righteousness,*
>   for they will be filled. . . .
> Blessed are those who are persecuted for *righteousness' sake,*
>   for theirs is the kingdom of heaven." (Matt 5:6, 10)

Jesus scolded the religious leaders who perverted justice: "Woe to you Pharisees! For you tithe mint and rue and herbs of all kinds, and neglect *justice* and the love of God; it is these you ought to have practiced, without neglecting the others" (Luke 11:42-43).

Sermon Theme and Goal

We formulated the textual theme as, "In view of wickedness, oppressions, and envy in this world, enjoy your work with quietness." But "contrast" above shows that in an unjust world, Jesus, as well as the Old Testament, demands much more of us than simply to enjoy our work with quietness. Jesus clearly requires our engagement in this world to fight wickedness in all its forms and to promote justice. The question is, Should we change the sermon theme in this direction of promoting justice? In other words, should we emphasize the *discon*tinuity between the Teacher's message and that of Jesus (contrast), or should we opt for the continuity (analogy)?

Although we may be tempted to shift the theme to the promotion of justice because it seems much more relevant and demanding, this procedure is problematic because the preaching text from Ecclesiastes would not support this new theme. Moreover, if one wishes to preach on the theme of promoting justice in this wicked world, one can find many preaching texts in the Old as well as the New Testament that address this issue directly and forcefully.

In preaching on this passage from Ecclesiastes, however, we should highlight the continuity between the Teacher's message and that of Jesus. The main advantage is that the chosen preaching text will support the sermon theme. Moreover, the Teacher's message of enjoying our work with quietness is no less relevant than switching to the theme of promoting justice. In a wicked world where many people hate their work, call it a rat race, and seek to opt out (retire) as soon as possible or become enslaved by their work, this message is extremely relevant. So we shall keep the textual theme as our sermon theme: *In view of the wickedness, oppressions, and envy in this world, enjoy your work with quietness.*

We formulated the Teacher's goal as, "to urge his readers, in view of the wickedness, oppressions, and envy in this world, not to slave away in ruthless competition with their neighbors but to enjoy their work and its fruit with quietness." Our goal in preaching the sermon should be in line with the author's goal and match the sermon theme. Since we were able to adopt the author's theme for the sermon theme, we can also make his goal our sermon goal: *to urge our hearers, in view of the wickedness, oppressions, and envy in this world, not to slave away in ruthless competition with their neighbors but to enjoy their work and its fruit with quietness.*

This goal discloses the need that should be addressed in this sermon. The need is that many people today do not enjoy their work but slave away in ruthless competition with their neighbors. The sermon should answer the question, How should God's people work in a society filled with wickedness, oppressions, and envy?

Sermon Exposition

How should Christians work in a dog-eat-dog world? The competition is fierce out there. Companies compete with companies as they seek to control the market. They are out to destroy each other. Within companies, workers compete with each other as they seek to climb the corporate ladder. They, too, are often out to destroy each other. No holds barred!

How should Christians work in a dog-eat-dog world? Some seek to escape "the rat race" by retiring as soon as possible to a gated community. Others join the rat race and give all their time and energy to the company. They sell their soul to the company. The competition is fierce out there: no holds barred!

Things were not much different when the Teacher wrote Ecclesiastes. Because of expanding international trade the economy was booming. Fortunes could be made overnight and lost even faster. The competition was fierce and ruthless. How should God's people work in a world filled with wickedness, oppressions, and envy?

The wise Teacher who wrote Ecclesiastes reflects on this dilemma. He is well aware of the wickedness in this fallen world. He begins in chapter 3:16, "Moreover I saw under the sun that in the place of justice, *wickedness was there,* and in the place of righteousness, *wickedness was there* as well." "In the place of justice," that is, in the court of justice. If anywhere in the world one would expect justice, it would be in the court of justice. In the Western world a court of law can often be identified by a sculpture of a woman holding a set of scales. The woman is Lady Justitia. She weighs carefully what is just and what is unjust, what is right and what is wrong. If anywhere in this world one would expect justice, it would be in a court of law. But the Teacher observes just the opposite: "in the place of justice, wickedness was there." To emphasize the point he repeats: "and in the place of righteousness, wickedness was there as well." Wickedness was all-pervasive in that society.

It was a terrible situation. Wickedness. Wickedness! Isaiah describes this wickedness in the place of justice: they "acquit the guilty for a bribe, and deprive the innocent of their rights!"[11] The Teacher himself writes in Ecclesiastes 5:8, "If you see in a province the oppression of the poor and the violation of justice and right, do not be amazed at the matter." Wickedness is so pervasive in society, he says, that we should not be amazed at the matter.

Yet it is not right. Something is terribly wrong when wickedness is found even in the court of justice. Something is terribly wrong when judges "acquit the guilty for a bribe and deprive the innocent of their rights." Something is terribly wrong when the wicked prosper and the poor are oppressed. Does it pay to be wicked?

The Teacher reflects on this question and first answers the way the Bible often answers this question.[12] Verse 17, "I said in my heart, God will judge the

---

11. Isaiah 5:23; cf. 1:21.
12. See, e.g., Genesis 18:25, "Shall not the Judge of all the earth do what is just?";

righteous and the wicked, for he has appointed a time for every matter, and for every work." That's a good answer. The wicked will not get away with their evil deeds. There is still a God out there, and God sees their evil deeds. "God will judge the righteous and the wicked," that is to say, God will determine who is righteous and who is wicked. The Teacher is not talking about God's final judgment at the end of time. He has no clear idea of a final judgment after death. He is simply saying that "God will judge in God's own time."[13] In his own time, God will set things straight. "God will intervene on behalf of the victims of injustice."[14] For, as he has elaborated in the first half of chapter 3, God is in charge of the times; he has set the times, "a time to be born, and a time to die" (3:2). Moreover, God "has made everything suitable for its time" (3:11). So there must also be a time when "God will judge the righteous and the wicked, for he has appointed a time for every matter" (3:17). But we don't know when that time is. From what we can observe in life, that time is not now. The wicked continue to prosper and the poor continue to be oppressed.

This thought leads the Teacher to a further reflection. Verse 18, "I said in my heart with regard to human beings that God is testing them to show that they are but animals." God's postponement of judgment on wickedness allows God to test[15] humans to see whether they are indeed inclined to all evil. As the Teacher will say in Ecclesiastes 8:11, "Because sentence against an evil deed is not executed speedily, the human heart is fully set to do evil."[16] The increasing wickedness in human society shows people "that they are but animals." Animals have no concept of right or wrong, of justice or injustice. By allowing wickedness to fester in human society God is testing people so that it will be evident "that they are but animals."

Many ancient examples of barbarian, animal behavior can be given. Modern examples of animal behavior include Hitler's holocaust in Europe, Saddam

---

Deuteronomy 1:17, "the judgment is God's"; Job 19:29, "Wrath brings the punishment of the sword, so that you may know there is a judgment"; Psalm 9:8, the Lord "judges the world with righteousness; he judges the people with equity"; Psalm 94:2, "Rise up, O judge of the earth; give to the proud what they deserve!"

13. Seow, *Ecclesiastes*, 166. So also Murphy, *Ecclesiastes*, 36.

14. Ogden, *Qoheleth*, 60. Other commentators, such as Loader, *Ecclesiastes*, 43, think that "the judgment of God over the two parties at law can refer only to death, which comes over both without discrimination." This interpretation raises more questions than it answers.

15. "The precise nuance of the divine purpose remains ambiguous. . . . If it is taken to mean testing, this could consist in the manifest injustice in human affairs (v. 16), which shows whether human beings will throw off moral restraint since there is no principle of justice at work in their experience (cf. 8:11)." Murphy, *Ecclesiastes* 36.

16. Cf. Revelation 22:10-11, "And he said to me, 'Do not seal up the words of the prophecy of this book, for the time is near. Let the evildoer still do evil, and the filthy still be filthy, and the righteous still do right, and the holy still be holy.'"

Hussein's gassing of his own people in Asia, and current rebellions promoting raping and killing in Africa and South America.

The Teacher supports the idea that humans "are but animals" with two arguments. The first is that the "fate,"[17] the destiny, of humans and animals is the same. Verse 19, "For the fate of humans and the fate of animals is the same; as one dies, so dies the other. They all have the same breath, and humans have no advantage over the animals; for all is vanity." The destiny of humans and animals is the same. They both die. This is because they all have the same breath, the same life breath. When God takes away this life breath, they die.[18] The Teacher concludes that therefore "humans have no advantage over animals; for all is vanity." Human life as well as animal life is "vanity." It is fleeting, transitory.[19] Humans are like animals in that they have no advantage over animals with respect to death.

His second argument to support his statement that humans "are but animals" is that at death humans as well as animals go to the same place. Verse 20, "All go to one place; all are from the dust, and all turn to dust again." "All are from the dust, and all turn to dust again" is a reference to Genesis 3, where God punished with death the human attempt to be like God: "You are dust, and to dust you shall return" (Gen 3:19). The one place to which humans as well as animals go is the dust.[20]

But is there not something special about humans? In verse 21 the Teacher raises the question, "Who knows whether the human spirit goes upward and the spirit of animals goes downward to the earth?" The expected answer to this question is, No one knows. When we observe the death of a human being and the death of an animal, we cannot tell whether the spirit of the one goes upward and that of the other downward.

The New Testament, of course, moves beyond the Old Testament and clearly teaches that the human spirit survives death. At the death of his friend

---

17. "The key word of this verse . . . is fate *(miqreh)*. But, as in 2:14, this is not some malignant and impersonal force. 'Fate' is simply what happens to a person or to any living creature; and the final 'happening,' both for men and animals, is death." Whybray, *Ecclesiastes*, 79.

18. "Humans and animals share the same *rûaḥ*, 'spirit' or 'lifebreath.' All living beings have a body (commonly called 'flesh') and a *rûaḥ*. This is not an immortal 'soul,' but the lifebreath . . . , an animating force that gives and preserves life. When God takes this away, the creature dies (Ps 104:29; Job 34:14-15)." Fox, *Ecclesiastes*, 26.

19. "The meaning of *hābel* would probably be 'fleeting,' 'ephemeral,' or 'transient.'" Crenshaw, *Ecclesiastes*, 104. So also Murphy, *Ecclesiastes*, 79.

20. Some commentators, e.g., Whybray, *Ecclesiastes*, 80, state that "the reference [of 'to one place'] is to Sheol: cf. 9:10." Although this interpretation is possible, the context here refers to returning to the dust. Cf. Murphy, *Ecclesiastes*, 37, "The 'one place' to which all go is specified by the 'dust' (cf. 6:6), although Qohelet readily acknowledges the existence of Sheol (9:10). The theme of return to the dust is frequent (Job 10:9; 34:15; Pss 104:29; 146:4; Sir 40:11)."

Lazarus, Jesus comforted Martha: "I am the resurrection and the life. Those who believe in me, even though they die, will live" (John 11:25). Later Jesus said to his disciples, "If I go and prepare a place for you, I will come again and will take you to myself, so that where I am, there you may be also" (John 14:3). Jesus and the New Testament teach that the human spirit or soul survives death.

But the Teacher's point is this: when we observe the world from a secular perspective ("under the sun," 3:16), we cannot tell at the death of human beings that their spirit, in distinction from that of the animals, goes upward. So through the festering wickedness in this world God shows human beings that "they are but animals." They are not at all like God. They have the same fate as animals: they die. And they go to the same place as the animals do: they return to the dust.

How then should God's people work during their short lives on this wicked earth? The Teacher offers this advice in verse 22: "So I saw that there is nothing better than that all should enjoy their work, for that is their lot; who can bring them to see what will be after them?" "There is nothing better than that all should *enjoy their work*." The Teacher has given this advice before. In chapter 2:24 he wrote, "There is nothing better for mortals than to eat and drink, and find enjoyment in their toil." In chapter 3:12 he advocated, "I know that there is nothing better for them than to be happy and enjoy themselves as long as they live."

In this passage he focuses specifically on our work and the possessions gained by that work.[21] He says in verse 22, "I saw that there is nothing better than that all should enjoy their work, for that is their lot." All of us have to work to make a living. So we may as well enjoy our work and its fruits. For, he asks, "Who can bring them to see what will be after them?" Again the expected answer is, No one. No one can bring us to see what will be after us, that is, after our death.[22] From our observations of life on earth, no one knows whether at death the human spirit goes upward, and no one knows what will be after our death. So we may as well make the best of our short life on this earth and enjoy our work and its fruits.

---

21. "Hebrew *ma'ăśāv* (lit. 'his works'), what one has earned and now owns." Fox, *Ecclesiastes*, 26.

22. "'*aḥărāyw* has been understood in three ways: (1) 'After him,' with reference to what happens to an individual after his death (Delitzsch, Crenshaw). (2) 'After him,' with reference to what will happen on earth after one's death (Rashbaum, Murphy). . . . (3) 'Afterwards,' with reference to what will happen on earth within the individual's lifetime (Podechard, Gordis, Fox 1987). . . . In the present context, following upon a verse that declares human ignorance of what follows death, the first alternative is probably in view." Fox, *A Time to Tear Down*, 217. Cf. Longman, *Book of Ecclesiastes*, 131, "The phrase *after them* is a circuitous manner of saying 'after their death.' As above [v. 21], Qohelet here is uncertain whether (and probably doubts that) life continues after death. No one knows for certain."

But that is not the end of his advice. The Teacher cannot let go of the wickedness in this world. He comes back to it again with his graphic description of oppressions in human society. Three times he refers to oppression: "oppressions," "oppressed," and "oppressors." "In the Bible, oppression involves cheating one's neighbor of something (Lev 6:2-5 . . .), defrauding him, and robbing him. . . . Oppression is accumulation — the seeking after profit — without regard to the nature, needs, and rights of other people."[23]

The Teacher writes in chapter 4:1, "Again I saw all the *oppressions* that are practiced under the sun. Look, the tears of the *oppressed* — with no one to comfort them! On the side of their *oppressors* there was power — with no one to comfort them." "Look, the tears of the oppressed." People are suffering terribly. They cry themselves to sleep each night. And there is "no one to comfort them!" The Teacher adds, "On the side of their oppressors there was power," and then he repeats for emphasis, "with no one to comfort them," that is, the oppressed. There is no one to comfort the oppressed by protecting them from the abuse of their oppressors.[24]

This wickedness of no one coming forward to help oppressed people crying for help is so disgusting that the Teacher concludes in verse 2, "I thought the dead, who have already died, more fortunate than the living, who are still alive." The dead, at least, no longer have to witness this awful display of wickedness in human society. But, he adds in verse 3, "better than both is the one who has not yet been, and has not seen the evil deeds that are done under the sun." The unborn are better off than either the living or the dead because they have "not seen the evil deeds that are done under the sun": the unborn have not seen that human beings for the sake of their own profit will ignore the tears of the oppressed.[25]

The Teacher so far has mentioned two forms of wickedness: wickedness even in the courts of justice and people being oppressed and no one stepping

23. Provan, *Ecclesiastes*, 103.

24. Davis, *Proverbs, Ecclesiastes, Song of Songs*, 189, is wrong when she understands the repetition of "with no one to comfort them" as no one to comfort the oppressed and no one to comfort the oppressor: "Slave and slave owner, prisoner and prison guard, battered woman and abusive man — both are to be pitied, for they are in the same system, 'with no one to comfort them.'" On the contrary, the repetition highlights the plight of the oppressed. Cf. Brown, *Ecclesiastes*, 48, "By itself, the first mention of 'comfort' in verse 1 might convey merely the sense of consolation. Its second occurrence, however, suggests more than simply providing the proverbial tissue to dry the victim's tears. Here, the comforter takes on an active role aimed at protecting the powerless from further abuse by the powerful. The consoler, in short, is an advocate. . . . Such advocacy entails an investment of power in behalf of the powerless."

25. "If Qohelet's gloom strikes us as excessive at this point, we may need to ask whether our more cheerful outlook springs from hope and not complacency. While we, as Christians, see further ahead than he allowed himself to look, it is no reason to spare ourselves the realities of the present." Kidner, *Time to Mourn*, 44.

forward to help them. Finally he mentions another form of wickedness that pervades society. It is envy. In chapter 4:4 he writes, "Then I saw that all toil and all skill in work come from one person's *envy* of another." The TNIV translates, "I saw that all toil and *all achievement* spring from one person's envy of another." The focus is on our toil and its achievement. What drives our toil and our achievement? Here for the first time the Teacher exposes what lies behind our toil. It is envy. "Envy inspires competition and thus twists the noble sense of vocation into an exercise in rivalry, into an upward and onward quest in the pursuit of dominance, leading even to violence. The envy of another (literally 'one's neighbor') flies in the face of the great command found in Leviticus and on the lips of Jesus to 'love your neighbor as yourself' (Lev 19:18b; Matt 22:39)."[26]

Yet envy drives our business world. We try to outdo each other, often to the detriment of the other. In the corporate world, people will climb over corpses to reach the top. Proverbs 27:4 says, "Wrath is cruel, anger is overwhelming, but who is able to stand before jealousy?" "This also," the Teacher concludes, "is vanity and a chasing after wind." Our ruthless competition with each other to gain ever more stuff is vanity, he says. It is futile! It's "a chasing after wind" — that is to say, it leaves us empty-handed.

How can God's people work in such a wicked, competitive world? The Teacher graphically sketches the three options we have. Since we usually work with our hands, he sketches the three options with three positions of our hands. The first option is that of folded hands. Verse 5,

Fools *fold their hands*
    and consume their own flesh.

People who fold their hands cannot use their hands for work. Folded hands show that people do not want to work. These people want to opt out of the workforce. This is not a good option. The Teacher calls these people "fools." The book of Proverbs warns these people: "A little sleep, a little slumber, a little folding of the hands to rest, and poverty will come upon you like a robber, and want, like an armed warrior" (Prov 6:10-11; 24:33-34). The Teacher puts the resulting poverty in even more graphic form: "Fools fold their hands and *consume their own flesh.*"[27] They end up eating themselves. Since there is nothing else to eat, they will eat up their savings and then they will die. They are "fools." Dropping out of the workforce is not a wise option.

The second option is that of hands cupped open to acquire as much as pos-

---

26. Brown, *Ecclesiastes*, 49.

27. "Qohelet is using the grotesque imagery of self-cannibalism to speak of self-destruction. Fools who are so lazy will end up devouring themselves." Seow, *Ecclesiastes*, 179.

sible. When children come for Halloween treats they often cup their hands to-gether. Two cupped hands can hold much more than one open hand.[28] Verse 6:

> Better is a handful with quiet
>> than *two handfuls* with toil,
>> and a chasing after wind.

At first sight, the "two handfuls" looks very desirable. Who would not rather have two handfuls instead of one? In our society we soon learn that bigger is better: More money is better than less; a Cadillac Escalado is better than a Ford Escort; a mansion is better than a shack; a bigger business is better than a small one. Bigger is better. Two handfuls are better than one.

But there is a downside to selecting the two handfuls. It comes, the Teacher says, "with toil and a chasing after wind." In order to gain the two handfuls, people have to resort to toil without rest: work, work, work.[29] And in the end it turns out to be "a chasing after wind." People end up with two handfuls of wind, that is, two handfuls of nothing.

The third option is one handful. Verse 6, "Better is *a handful* with quiet." A handful is a very small amount.[30] But if it comes with "quiet," with "tranquil-ity" (TNIV), with "peace of mind" (NEB), this is the way the Teacher recom-mends for God's people to work in a wicked world. "Better is a handful with quiet than two handfuls with toil, and a chasing after wind."

The Teacher's counsel here follows that of other Old Testament wisdom sayings:

> Better is a little with the fear of the LORD
>> than great treasure and trouble with it. (Prov 15:16)

> Better is a little with righteousness
>> than large income with injustice. (Prov 16:8)

> Better is a dry morsel with quiet
>> than a house full of feasting with strife. (Prov 17:1)[31]

28. "Qohelet imagines a single open palm versus two hands cupped to hold the maximum amount." Crenshaw, *Ecclesiastes,* 109.

29. "For Qohelet, an individual's incessant drive to work, even for his or her self-enrichment, is no different from the oppression wielded by a ruthless taskmaster. . . . Without the benefit of rest, even self-employment is self-enslavement." Brown, *Ecclesiastes,* 50.

30. "Hebrew *mĕlō'-kap* refers to a very small amount (cf. 1 Kgs 17:12). The emphasis is on the limited nature of a handful, not on the fullness." Seow, *Ecclesiastes,* 180.

31. Cf. Psalm 37:16, "Better is a little that the righteous person has than the abundance of many wicked."

The Teacher's advice, then, is not only the conclusion given in chapter 3:22 that "there is nothing better than that all should enjoy their work." Because work in our society is driven by envy, we still have to make choices as to what we will work for. Will we fold our hands and opt out of the workforce? Or will we cup both hands and become "workaholics"? Or will we be content with one handful?

The Teacher counsels,

> Better is a handful with quiet
>> than two handfuls with toil,
>> and a chasing after wind.

His point, then, is that in view of the many forms of wickedness in this world we should be satisfied with one handful and enjoy our work with quietness.

In our world today we can observe the same forms of wickedness the Teacher saw. In law courts around the world we see wickedness. In countless countries, we see "the tears of the oppressed — with no one to comfort them!" In the business world, we see that work is driven by envy — envy which results in cutthroat competition. The Teacher enjoins us: In view of the wickedness, oppressions, and envy in this world, enjoy your work with quietness.

But is this enough? Is it enough in a wicked world simply to enjoy our work with quietness? No, it is not enough. Many Old Testament prophets as well as Jesus (e.g., Matt 25:31-46) urge us to fight for justice, to comfort and help the oppressed.[32] But that is another sermon.

The point of *this* passage is that we ought to be content with one handful and enjoy our work with quietness. Jesus also warns against the desire to acquire *two* handfuls. He says, "Take care! Be on your guard against all kinds of greed; for one's life does not consist in the abundance of possessions" (Luke 12:15). Jesus tells the parable of the rich fool who thought he could lay up "ample goods" for many years. The man was rich, but God called him a fool. "So it is," says Jesus, "with those who store up treasures for themselves but are not rich toward God" (Luke 12:21).

Jesus wants us to focus our lives not on gathering possessions but on *God,* on promoting the kingdom of God and his righteousness. What then about food and drink and clothing? "Do not worry" about these, Jesus says, "for it is the Gentiles who strive for all these things; and indeed your heavenly Father knows that you need all these things. But strive *first* for the kingdom of God and his righteousness, and all these things will be given to you as well" (Matt 6:31-33).

---

32. As does the Teacher, Jesus also assumes that "you always have the poor with you" (Mark 14:7).

In agreement with Jesus' teaching, the apostle Paul also urges Christians to be content with what they have. He writes, "Of course, there is great gain in godliness combined with contentment; . . . If we have food and clothing, we will be content with these. But those who want to be rich fall into temptation and are trapped by many senseless and harmful desires that plunge people into ruin and destruction. For the love of money is a root of all kinds of evil, and in their eagerness to be rich some have wandered away from the faith and pierced themselves with many pains" (1 Tim 6:6, 8-10). The author of Hebrews echoes this sentiment: "Keep your lives free from the love of money; and be content with what you have" (Heb 13:5).

Even today, with all the wickedness we observe in this world, the advice of the Old Testament Teacher should be heeded:

> Better is a handful *with quiet*
>   than two handfuls with toil,
>   and a chasing after wind.

Enjoying our work with quietness will enable us to experience again a little bit of the tranquility of Paradise. We can work with quietness, with peace of mind, trusting that our heavenly Father will provide us our food, drink, clothing, and housing. In a desert of wickedness — ruthless competition, a rat race, a dog-eat-dog world — we can experience an oasis of joy and tranquility when we don't follow the crowd in working to pile up possessions. Enjoy your work with quietness, and your heavenly Father will provide your every need.

CHAPTER 6

Working Together

Ecclesiastes 4:7-16

Two are better than one,
because they have a good reward for their toil.

(Eccl 4:9)

Ecclesiastes 4:7-16 is a good antidote to the individualism that infects our society and which also contaminates the Christian community. One of the challenges again is to select a proper textual unit. Although it is clear that this passage contains three subunits (vv. 7-8, 9-12, and 13-16), the question is how many of these constitute the preaching text. If we choose all three subunits, the question is, What theme ties them together? Whybray, for example, does not acknowledge "thematic continuity" between the first two units[1] — let alone all three — and deals with each section separately. A further challenge is interpreting the third unit, about the wise youth and the foolish king (vv. 13-16). Scholars are pessimistic about solving this riddle. Murphy writes, "Any translation, and hence interpretation, of verses 13-16 is uncertain, because of the vagueness of the text."[2] And a final challenge is to preach Christ from a text that does not even mention God.

---

1. "There is no *thematic* continuity here." Whybray, *Ecclesiastes*, 86.
2. Murphy, *Ecclesiastes*, 42. Cf. Fox, *Ecclesiastes*, 30: "The Hebrew text of this passage is very difficult. . . . In the Hebrew, it is often unclear what the pronouns and verbs refer to, and it is not even certain how many 'youths' appear in the story, whether two or three." Cf. Delitzsch, *Ecclesiastes*, 280, "Gratz thinks vv. 13-16 ought to drive expositors to despair." For a clear overview of the different opinions among commentators, see A. D. Wright, "The Poor but Wise Youth and the Old but Foolish King," 142-48.

Text and Context

Ecclesiastes 4:7 begins a new unit with its "Again, I saw vanity under the sun. . . ." This unit about the toil of a solitary individual concludes at verse 8 with the inclusio, "This also is vanity and an unhappy business." One could select this subunit as a preaching text, but the next unit about the value of having a companion (vv. 9-12) complements the first about the solitary individual. It is tempting, therefore, to select as a preaching text just the verses 7 to 12. This would simplify the formulation of the theme and avoid the many difficulties of correctly interpreting the following unit about the wise youth and the foolish king. The problem with this option is that the Teacher has clearly sought to link this third unit to the foregoing units. Provan observes, "The closing verses of chapter 4 (vv. 13-16), although their precise relationship with what precedes them has puzzled many commentators, seem clearly connected with what precedes by theme and by language (notice the common reference to what is 'better' in vv. 6, 9, 13; the reference to the 'second person' [*šēnî*] in vv. 8 and 15, . . . and the occurrence of 'there was no end to all' [*'ên qēṣ lěkol*] in vv. 8 and 16)."[3] Moreover, cutting the preaching text off at verse 12 leaves verses 13-16 as an orphan, for 4:16 ends the larger unit with "this also is vanity and a chasing after wind," while 5:1 begins a new unit with a different topic. We therefore select as our preaching text Ecclesiastes 4:7-16.

As to its context, the topic of toil of verses 4-6 is continued in this passage in verses 7-9. The "better than" of verse 6 is repeated in verses 9 and 13. His "eyes are never satisfied" (v. 8) harks back to 1:8, "the eye is not satisfied," and will be raised again in 5:10, "The lover of money will not be satisfied with money." The anecdote about the poor but wise youth seems similar to the anecdote of 9:15-16, "Now there was found in it a poor wise man, and he by his wisdom delivered the city. Yet no one remembered that poor man." The "yet those who come later will not rejoice in him" (v. 16) seems to echo 1:11, "The people of long ago are not remembered" (cf. 2:16).

Literary Features

Noting the forms of wisdom literature in this text will help us sketch the "Textual Structure" below. "Again, I saw" (v. 7) indicates that this is an observation beginning a reflection. The reflection consists of an anecdote about a solitary

---

3. Provan, *Ecclesiastes*, 106-7. Cf. Murphy, *Wisdom Literature*, 137, "This unit [4:7-16] is held together by the repetition of the key word, 'two' (*šēnî*, vv. 8, 10, 15; *šěnayim*, vv. 9, 11, 12), and the characteristic phrase, 'vanity and striving after wind,' terminates the unit."

miser and includes his rhetorical question, "For whom am I toiling and depriving myself of pleasure?" This unit ends with the exclamation, "This also is vanity" (v. 8), which forms an inclusio with the "vanity" of verse 7.

The next unit begins with a "better than" proverb ("Two are better than one"; v. 9), which is supported with three illustrations (vv. 10-12a). The Teacher clinches the point of each illustration respectively with a woe oracle (v. 10b), a rhetorical question (v. 11b), and a concluding proverb ("A threefold cord is not quickly broken"; v. 12b).

The final unit again begins with a "better than" proverb ("Better is a poor but wise youth than an old but foolish king"; v. 13). This is followed by an anecdote (vv. 14-16b) and concluded with the refrain, "Surely this also is vanity and a chasing after wind" (v. 16c).

It is again important to take note of repetitions since these will help us discern the Teacher's theme. The word "vanity" is repeated three times (vv. 7, 8, and 16), as is the word "toil" (vv. 8 [twice] and 9). But the primary keywords in this passage are the numbers one and two (second). The Teacher uses "one" *(eḥād)* five times (vv. 8, 9, 10, 11, and 12), and "two," "second" *(šēnî, šĕnayim)* six times (vv. 8 ["solitary" is literally "and not a second"], 9, 10, 11, 12, and 15).

Textual Structure

The forms discovered in our literary analysis enable us to sketch the textual structure:

I. Observation/Reflection: Again, I saw vanity under the sun (4:7)
  A. Anecdote of one without a second, without sons or brothers (4:8a)
      1. yet there is no end to all his toil (4:8b)
      2. his eyes are never satisfied with riches (4:8c)
  B. Question: For whom am I toiling, depriving myself of pleasure? (4:8d)
  C. Conclusion: This also is vanity and an unhappy business (4:8e)
II. Proverb: Two are better than one (4:9a)
  A. because they have a good reward for their toil (4:9b)
      1. For if they fall, one will lift up the other (4:10a)
          a. but woe to one who is alone and falls and does not have another to help (4:10b)
      2. Again, if two lie together, they keep warm (4:11a)
          a. but how can one keep warm alone? (4:11b)
      3. Two will withstand one (note reversal, 4:12b)
          a. though one might prevail against another (4:12a)
  B. Concluding proverb: A threefold cord is not quickly broken (4:12c)

III. Proverb: Better is a poor but wise youth than an old but foolish king who will no longer take advice (4:13)
    A. Anecdote supporting the proverb
        1. For one can come out of prison to reign (4:14a)
           a. even though born poor in the kingdom (4:14b)
        2. All the living follow that youth who replaced the king (4:15)[4]
        3. There was no end to all those people whom he led (4:16a)
    B. The brevity of political fame: Those who come later will not rejoice in him (4:16b)
    C. Conclusion: Surely this also is vanity and a chasing after wind (4:16c)

Theocentric Interpretation

This section can be very brief because there is no reference to God in this passage. Since wisdom literature reflects the "customary orders" in God's creation, however, the advice given by the inspired Teacher can be understood as God's advice on how people should live in order to be in tune with his created order.[5]

Textual Theme and Goal

The selected preaching text contains three subunits. One way to discover the textual theme is to observe the structure of the text. As we can see above, the overall structure of the text is a simple chiasm, A B A, with the focal point on B.

    A. Anecdote of a solitary rich person whose life is vanity
        B. Proverb: Two are better than one
    A′. Anecdote of a popular king whose life is vanity

The Teacher also shows that he intends to emphasize B by supporting the proverb "Two are better than one" with no fewer than three illustrations. So we could formulate the theme of this passage simply as, "Two are better than one."

In order to confirm our initial attempt at a theme, we should check if this theme is indeed the thread that holds the three units together. The anecdote of the rich person without a companion, ringed by "vanity," confirms that "two

---

4. In view of the uncertainty of translating the Hebrew (see p. 107, n. 2 above), I am for now following the translation (and interpretation) of the NRSV.
5. See von Rad, *Wisdom in Israel*, 92-95.

are better than one." Although the anecdote of the king who is forgotten is more difficult to fit in, it ends with an even larger sense of isolation than that of the rich person: from "no end to all those people whom he led," to "those who come later will not rejoice in him" (4:16b). And here, too, the verdict is, "Surely, this also is vanity and a chasing after wind" (4:16c). This verdict of vanity confirms the textual focus on "Two are better than one."

This theme, however, does not do full justice to the whole text. Although it would be a good theme for verses 9-12, it fails to give sufficient emphasis to the isolation experienced by the rich man and the king (the bookends). To cover this emphasis fully, we can formulate the textual theme as follows, *Since working alone is futile, we ought to cooperate with others.*

The Teacher's goal can be derived from the theme as well as the historical circumstances behind the text. These circumstances, we have seen, were an economy that was driven by selfish individualism. Fortunes could be quickly made and lost. People competed with each other out of "envy of another" (4:4). It was a dog-eat-dog world. In that setting, the Teacher seeks to encourage his readers to cooperate with others. More than this, since he uses three telling illustrations to support his point, he seeks not only to encourage his readers but to *persuade* them. So we can formulate the Teacher's goal as, *to persuade his readers not to go it alone but to cooperate with others.*

Ways to Preach Christ

In order to preach a Christocentric sermon, preachers have frequently subjected this passage to allegorical interpretation. "Ambrose saw Christ as the one who lifts up his companion (v. 10) and warms him (v. 11), and the one who went from the house of bondsman to be king (v. 13). Jerome has also seen the Trinity in Qohelet's saying concerning the threefold cord."[6] More recently, Matthew Henry's commentary made this point: "Two together are a threefold cord; where two are closely joined in holy love and fellowship, Christ will by his Spirit come to them, and make the third, as he joined himself to the two disciples going to Emmaus; then there is a threefold cord that can never be broken."[7]

We can avoid allegorical interpretation and still preach a Christocentric sermon by investigating the seven Christocentric ways. This passage contains

---

6. Jarick, *Gregory Thaumaturgos' Paraphrase,* 359-60, n. 49, quoted by Longman, *Book of Ecclesiastes,* 143.

7. Matthew Henry and Thomas Scott, *Commentary on the Holy Bible,* Vol. 3 (Grand Rapids: Baker, 1960 rpt.), 413.

neither a promise of Christ nor a type of Christ. Redemptive-historical progression and contrast also fail to provide a solid bridge to Christ in the New Testament. This leaves us with three options to explore: analogy, longitudinal themes, and New Testament references.

Analogy

The question is, Did Jesus, like the Old Testament Teacher, also teach that working alone is vanity and that we should cooperate with others? Jesus certainly opposed greed — an extreme form of selfishness that isolates us from one another. Jesus' parable of the rich fool reminds us of the anecdote about the rich man in our passage. The rich fool also had "ample goods laid up for many years." For all we know he had no companion ("second one") with whom to share his wealth, for God said to him, "This very night your life is being demanded of you. And the things you have prepared, whose will they be?" (Luke 12:19-20). God's question in Jesus' parable sounds very much like the rich man's question in our text, "For whom am I toiling?" (4:8). In any event, Jesus warned, "Do not store up for yourselves treasures on earth, where moth and rust consume and where thieves break in and steal" (Matt 6:19). Instead he commanded us, "You shall love your neighbor as yourself" (Matt 22:39). When Jesus was subsequently asked, "Who is my neighbor?" he told the parable of the good Samaritan. The neighbor was "the one who showed him mercy." Jesus clinches his point: "Go and do likewise" (Luke 10:29, 37).

Jesus himself sent out his disciples not as individuals but "two by two" (Mark 6:7). He also instructed his followers, "If you are not listened to, take one or two others along with you, so that every word may be confirmed by the evidence of two or three witnesses. . . . Truly I tell you, if two of you agree on earth about anything you ask, it will be done for you by my Father in heaven. For where two or three are gathered in my name, I am there among them" (Matt 18:16, 19-20).

Longitudinal Themes

One can also move to Christ by tracing the theme of companionship from the Old Testament to Jesus in the New Testament. God created human beings for companionship. In Paradise God declared, "It is not good that the man should be alone; I will make him a helper as his partner" (Gen 2:18). God created humans as social beings. They are made to work together and help each other. "Israel is called out of Egypt to model for the world the way in which a righteous community should function."[8] God gave Israel many laws requiring care for one's neighbor, the climax being, "You shall love your neighbor as yourself" (Lev 19:18). The Teacher echoes this law in Ecclesiastes 4 by calling solitary living "vanity," futile, and useless and by illustrating that "two are better than one."

Jesus acknowledged this wisdom by gathering disciples around him and sending them out "two by two" (Mark 6:7). Jesus also reiterated the love commandment, "You shall love your neighbor as yourself" (Matt 22:39). The early Christians gave expression to this love commandment by being together and having "all things in common; they would sell their possessions and goods and distribute the proceeds to all, as any had need" (Acts 2:44-45). Paul instructs the church, "If then there is any encouragement in Christ, any consolation from love, any sharing in the Spirit, any compassion and sympathy, make my joy complete: be of the same mind, having the same love, being in full accord and of one mind. Do nothing from selfish ambition or conceit, but in humility regard others as better than yourselves. Let each of you look not to your own interests, but to the interests of others" (Phil 2:1-4; see also 1 Cor 12–13 concerning the church as the one body of Christ with many members).

New Testament References

The New Testament does not quote or allude to this passage. But one can also look for passages in the New Testament that make a point similar to that of the Teacher (see the New Testament passages supporting the two ways above). Accordingly, one can also consider using as a bridge to Christ the story of Jesus and Zacchaeus. Zacchaeus is described as "a chief tax collector" and being "rich." He reminds us of the rich man in Ecclesiastes 4. When Jesus invites himself to Zacchaeus's house for dinner, Zacchaeus welcomes him and says, "Look, half of my possessions, Lord, I will give to the poor; and if I have defrauded anyone of anything, I will pay back four times as much." Zacchaeus declares that he will give up his solitary hunt for riches at the expense of his neighbors and return to following God's law, which required that a thief make restitution, "four sheep for a sheep" (Exod 22:1). Little wonder Jesus says to him, "Today salvation has come to this house, because he too is a son of Abraham" (Luke 19:1-9). Through Jesus, Zacchaeus discovered that God created us not as solitary gold diggers but as social creatures who are obliged to help each other.

---

8. Provan, *Ecclesiastes*, 110. See there also for various laws requiring care for the neighbor.

Sermon Theme and Goal

We formulated the textual theme as, "Since working alone is futile, we ought to cooperate with others." Because the New Testament, as we have seen, supports this theme, the textual theme can function as the sermon theme: *Since working alone is futile, we ought to cooperate with others.*

We formulated the Teacher's goal as, "to persuade his readers not to go it alone but to cooperate with others." We can keep the same goal for the sermon: *to persuade our hearers not to go it alone but to cooperate with others.* This goal reveals the target for this particular sermon: the need addressed is the rugged, selfish individualism in our culture and its effects on Christians.

Sermon Exposition

The sermon introduction can tell the story of a contemporary person who walked over corpses to become rich. Then raise the question, Could it be that this selfish individualism is also rubbing off on the church and its members?

Israel often exhibited selfish individualism. When God brought Israel out of Egypt to form God's covenant people, he commanded them over and over not to exploit their neighbors: "You shall not steal. You shall not bear false witness against your neighbor. You shall not covet your neighbor's house . . . or anything that belongs to your neighbor" (Exod 20:15, 17). "You shall love your neighbor as yourself" (Lev 19:18). Centuries later, the prophets had to warn Israel time and again not to exploit their neighbors but to care for them: "What does the LORD require of you but to do justice, and to love kindness, and to walk humbly with your God?" (Mic 6:8).

The Teacher in Ecclesiastes also addresses this issue of selfish individualism. As we read in chapter 4:4, just before our text, "I saw that all toil and all skill in work [all achievements] come from one's person's *envy* of another." People worked not just to keep up with the Joneses but in order to get ahead of the Joneses. People were interested only in enriching themselves. They had no concern for their needy neighbor. It was a world of cutthroat competition.

The Teacher begins in chapter 4:7-8, "Again, I saw vanity under the sun: the case of solitary individuals, without sons or brothers; yet there is no end to all their toil, and their eyes are never satisfied with riches." The Teacher calls attention to a case that he calls "vanity," that is, futility, uselessness. This is the case of a solitary individual. The original reads, "There is a person and he has no second."[9]

---

9. "The Hebrew phrase, *who was all alone* (*'eḥād wě'ên šēnî*), is a general one indicating that the man had no friend, no business partner, no wife (contra all those commentators who have

He is all alone in his pursuits; "he has no second," no companion. The text says that he is even "without sons or brothers," that is, "the two closest male relations across two generations and also the two relatives who might benefit from his toil through inheritance."[10] This person has cut off all relationships in order to concentrate on the single goal of his life: to gain riches for himself. "Afflicted with an insatiable appetite for wealth, the loner is consumed by work."[11]

This thirst for wealth refers back to verse 6 just before our text. "Better is a handful with quiet than two handfuls with toil and a chasing after wind." Many people today are dissatisfied with one handful. They want more and more: two handfuls at least. But, we are warned, two handfuls come "with toil."

The Teacher writes in verse 8 that for this greedy person, "there is *no end* to all his toil." Why is there "no end to all his toil"? Because, the Teacher continues, "his eyes are never satisfied with riches" (v. 8; cf. 1:8).[12] "The eye, the organ of desire, cannot be satisfied."[13] This leads to ever more toil to satisfy his eyes. This person is caught in a vicious cycle; "there is no end to all his toil."

Finally the rich man wakes up to his predicament. He asks himself the crucial question, "For whom am I toiling and depriving myself of pleasure?" The expected answer is, No one. He has "no second," no companion, who can benefit from all his riches. He does not even have sons or brothers who would benefit from inheriting his estate. He is all alone. And he does not even benefit himself, for, as he says, he is depriving himself "of pleasure." He finds no pleasure in life. Work offers no pleasure for him because he has become a slave to toil. Eating and drinking offer no pleasure for him because he hardly takes time to eat and drink. Rest offers no pleasure for him because he is driven by toil and has little time for rest. "There is no end to all his toil."[14]

The Teacher sums up at the end of verse 8, "This also is vanity and an unhappy business." This person's life is "vanity," literally "vapor." His life is futile, useless. It is insubstantial[15] because he is all alone: "he has 'no second' — no

---

tried to specify one of these relationships)." Longman, *Book of Ecclesiastes*, 140. Seow, *Ecclesiastes*, 188, points out that "the medieval commentator, Rashbam, speculates that this verse refers to misers who refuse to accept anyone as a partner because they do not want to share their wealth."

10. Longman, ibid.

11. Brown, *Ecclesiastes*, 51. Cf. Proverbs 18:1.

12. "In v. 8ab *gam* is a coordinating conjunction. . . . In other words, there are two factors in this man's behavior: external — he never ceases working — and internal — he is never satisfied with what he has." Fox, *Qohelet*, 204.

13. Crenshaw, *Ecclesiastes*, 110.

14. "The competitive spirit which drives one to greater performance needs to be balanced against the danger of compulsive action. When work becomes an unreflective drive for riches, it ceases to have meaning." Ogden, *Qoheleth*, 69.

15. "Both occurrences of *hebel* in 4:7-8 refer to the insubstantiality of vapor to describe work that is futile." Miller, "Power in Wisdom," 157, n. 35.

one with whom to share the fruits of his labor in any manner; his toil benefits no one else."[16] The Teacher concludes that this solitary rich man's life is "an unhappy business."

Contrast this solitary person's life with that of a person who *has* "a second," a companion. Verse 9 *"Two* are better than one, because they have a good reward for their toil." "Two are better than one." When it comes to riches, the Teacher has said in 4:6, more is *not* better: "Better is a handful [one] with quiet than two handfuls with toil." But when it comes to human relationships, more is better: "Two are better than one." "The 'one' to which he refers is undoubtedly the solitary worker whose goal is the accumulation of material gain, which cannot ultimately provide satisfaction. Of more value . . . are the 'two' who at least can share the fruits of their work."[17]

In fact, two can do much more than share the fruits of their work. The Teacher gives three illustrations of how two people as partners can help each other. First, verse 10, "For if they fall, one will lift up the other; but woe to one who is alone and falls and does not have another to help." The Teacher is thinking here of people traveling in the Middle East. This can be dangerous, especially on dark nights. No streets or streetlights. Not even flashlights. Walking on trails that frequently follow the edge of ravines, people can easily stumble and plunge down the embankment. The landscape is also dotted with pits — bitumen pits (cf. Gen 14:10) or concealed pits to trap animals.[18] In one of his parables, Jesus referred to the danger of falling into these pits. He asked, "Can a blind person guide a blind person? Will not both fall into a pit?" (Luke 6:39). So it was dangerous to travel alone in the Middle East. But "two are better than one. . . . For if they fall [i.e., if one or the other falls[19]], one will lift up the other." Because they are together, they can help each other and survive. "But woe to one who is alone and falls and does not have another to help." That solitary person will perish. Today we still apply this wisdom of two being better than one. When children go off to camp, they are taught the "buddy system": each child is paired up with another so that they can help each other. "Two are better than one."

The Teacher's second illustration follows in verse 11, "Again, if two lie together, they keep warm; but how can one keep warm alone?" This illustration is also taken from the dangers of traveling in the Middle East. Travelers often

16. Wright, "The Poor but Wise Youth," 148-49. Cf. Brown, *Ecclesiastes*, 51, "The vanity of it all is that unremitting determination and single-minded diligence reap not self-fulfillment but self-deprivation."

17. Ogden, "The Mathematics of Wisdom," *VT* 34/4 (1984) 450.

18. See Ecclesiastes 10:8; Proverbs 26:27; 28:10.

19. "The Hebrew is strictly plural ('If they fall . . .'), but occasionally the plural may 'denote an indefinite singular' and thus mean 'If either of them should fall. . . .'" Eaton, *Ecclesiastes*, 94.

spent the night outdoors. When Jacob fled from Esau's fury he traveled north until the sun had set. Then he slept outdoors with a stone for a pillow (Gen 28:11). But how does one keep warm on frigid nights? People did not carry sleeping bags or blankets. All they had for a covering was their cloak (see Exod 22:26-27). On cold nights that was not enough. So people would lie together, sharing their cloaks and their body heat. "Two are better than one," for they can lie together and "keep warm; but how can one keep warm alone?"

The Teacher adds a third illustration in verse 12, "And though one might prevail against another, two will withstand one." Again, this illustration is taken from the dangers of traveling in the Middle East. Away from the safety of towns and cities, there was the danger of robbers who roamed the countryside. Think of Jesus' parable about a man who went from Jerusalem to Jericho. "He fell into the hands of robbers, who stripped him, beat him, and went away, leaving him half dead" (Luke 10:30). By himself the man did not have a chance. "Though one [robber] might prevail against another [person], two [partners] will withstand one [robber]." Even today, we act on this wisdom by advising people never to jog or walk alone.

These three illustrations give three instances of the advantages of being together with "a second one." But they apply in a much broader area than that of traveling. Already in Paradise God said, "It is not good that the man should be alone. I will make a helper as his partner" (Gen 2:18). God created us not as loners but as social beings. There are many advantages for a husband and wife to work together, to complement each other in running the household, in raising a family, and finally in retiring together. Research today shows that in contrast to singles, "married people live longer and are healthier throughout those extra years."[20] There are also many advantages for business partners to work together and to complement each other in running their business. There are many advantages to having a pilot *and* copilot at the controls of an airplane rather than a solitary pilot.

The Teacher sums up his message at the end of verse 12 with a proverb, "A threefold cord is not quickly broken." The Teacher "is likely alluding to a well-known ancient Near Eastern proverb concerning the benefits of friendship."[21] A threefold cord is a rope with three strands twisted together. A single cord can easily be broken. As we have seen in the illustrations, one alone cannot survive a fall, cannot keep warm on a cold night, and cannot withstand a robber. A single cord can easily be broken. Two cords combined are much stronger. As we have

20. As reported in *Time*, January 28, 2008, 75. The article explains that "studies have linked marriage to lower rates of cardiovascular disease, cancer, respiratory disease and mental illness. Marriage helps both spouses cope better with stress."

21. Longman, *Book of Ecclesiastes*, 143. See also Fox, *A Time to Tear Down*, 223.

seen in the illustrations: two can survive a fall, can keep warm, and can overcome a robber. But three cords woven together would be even stronger. "A threefold cord is not quickly broken."

From the repetition of two, two, two, the Teacher moves to the climax of three.[22] The move from two to three may be "a hint that there is nothing sacrosanct about the pair and that companionship may operate within larger numbers."[23] There are many advantages for a basketball team when its players work together instead of performing as individual stars. There are many advantages for the church when its members work together, complementing each other by using their individual gifts to benefit the church. Since working alone is futile, the Teacher's message is that we ought to cooperate with others.

God created human beings for companionship — as social beings. God gave Israel many laws which required that they care for their neighbor. These laws reached a climax in Leviticus 19, "You shall love your neighbor as yourself" (Lev 19:18). In the New Testament, Jesus reiterated that we should not be selfish loners but care for our neighbors. Jesus also commanded us, "You shall love your neighbor as yourself" (Matt 22:39). Jesus himself acted on the wisdom that "two are better than one." Rather than remaining a solitary figure, he gathered disciples around him. Moreover, he sent them out "two by two" (Mark 6:7). Jesus also instructed his followers, "If you are not listened to, take one or two others along with you, so that every word may be confirmed by the evidence of two or three witnesses. . . . Truly I tell you, if two of you agree on earth about anything you ask, it will be done for you by my Father in heaven. For where two or three are gathered in my name, I am among them" (Matt 18:16, 19-20).

The early Christians were not loners. Luke reports that "all who believed were together and had all things in common; they would sell their possessions and goods and distribute the proceeds to all, as any had need" (Acts 2:44-45). Paul pleaded with the church, "If then there is any encouragement in Christ, any consolation from love, any sharing in the Spirit, any compassion and sympathy, make my joy complete: be of the same mind, having the same love, being in full accord and of one mind. Do nothing from *selfish* ambition or conceit, but in humility regard *others* as better than yourselves. Let each of you look *not to your own* interests, but to the interests of *others*" (Phil 2:1-4). The church is a community. Even though the church has many members, the many members form one body — the body of Christ. As members we have to work together for the common good (1 Cor 12–13).

---

22. "The numerical sequence x, x + 1, is fairly common in the Old Testament (cf. Eccl 11:2; Amos 1:3, etc.) and generally indicates a full measure of what is being referred to." Eaton, *Ecclesiastes*, 95.

23. Ibid.

The Old Testament Teacher follows up his message with a final story. Verse 13, "Better is a poor but wise youth than an old but foolish king, who will no longer take advice." The old but foolish king is a tragic figure. Proverbs 12:15 says, "Fools think their own way is right, but the wise listen to advice." In Israel the elderly were considered wise. Certainly the king should be wise. But here is "an old but foolish king, who will no longer take advice." This foolish king is as isolated as the rich man in the first story. The rich man devoted his whole life to gathering riches and cast off his companions, even his sons and brothers. He was a solitary figure, without "a second one." The "old but foolish king . . . will no longer take advice." He has fired his advisers.[24] He will go it alone. He, too, is a solitary figure; he has no "second one." Or is there "a second one"? Yes there is. He is the successor to the old king.[25] He is waiting in the wings, that is, in prison.

Verse 14 reads, "One[26] can indeed come out of prison to reign, even though born poor in the kingdom." The poor but wise youth can come out of prison to reign as king. One example of such a wise youth coming "out of prison to reign" was the "youth" (Gen 37:30) Joseph coming out of prison in Egypt and rising to rule the nation. Pharaoh said to him, "See, I have set you over all the land of Egypt" (Gen 41:41).[27]

Verse 15 continues, "I saw all the living who, moving about under the sun, follow that youth who replaced the king." "All the living" followed "that youth [the second][28] who replaced the king." He was not solitary like the old but fool-

---

24. The old but foolish king "makes himself vulnerable to being replaced by one who is receptive to wise counsel." Brown, *Ecclesiastes*, 53. See Proverbs 15:22, "Without counsel, plans go wrong, but with many advisers they succeed." Cf. Proverbs 11:14, "Where there is no guidance, a nation falls, but in the abundance of counselors there is safety."

25. "The primary point of the narrative in its present context is that a 'second' is not always an advantage." Wright, "The Poor but Wise Youth," 154.

26. The question is, Who is the "one," the "he"? Is it the foolish king or the wise youth? Wright, "The Poor but Wise Youth," 152, argues that the old king remains the subject of the story: "He (the king) came forth from prison and poverty; the youth would stand in his (the king's) place; he (the king) was over all of them; those later will not rejoice in him (the king)." Other commentators argue that it is the wise youth who becomes king (see Eaton, *Ecclesiastes*, 96, with references to Gordis and Aalders; and Longman, *Book of Ecclesiastes*, 146). Since the ambiguity does not change the point of the story, I will follow the interpretation of the NRSV, which happens to be the interpretation of the majority of commentators.

27. Most commentators argue that the Teacher does not have a specific historical figure in mind. Ogden is one of the exceptions. "One further piece of evidence that Qohelet has the Joseph story in mind is his use on several occasions (7:9; 8:8; 10:5) of a term *šallîṭ*, used on only one other occasion, in Gen 42:6, as a term descriptive of Joseph's office as counselor." *Qoheleth*, 72.

28. Because of the word "the second," many commentators argue that there are two youths (some even three youths) in the anecdote, youth A (v. 13) and youth B (v. 15). See, e.g., Murphy, *Ecclesiastes*, 42-43; Whybray, *Ecclesiastes*, 89-90; Longman, *Book of Ecclesiastes*, 146-47; Fox, *Ec-*

ish king. He was one with all the people he led. This wise youth made a wise king. Verse 16 says, "there was no end to all those people whom he led." Commentators have wondered about phrases like "all the living" following that youth, and "no end to all those people whom he led." Is it hyperbole? Is it exaggeration? Probably. But it makes us think again of Joseph, of whom we read in Genesis 41:57, "All the *world* came to Joseph in Egypt to buy grain, because the famine became severe throughout the world."

The Teacher has in mind a great, wise king such as Joseph. But he continues in verse 16, "Yet those who come later will not rejoice in him." People will become critical and no longer follow the king.[29] They will reject him. Political fame is short-lived. "People are fickle and may cast their palms before a new arrival, only to cry 'Crucify him!' a few days later."[30]

With his statement that "those who come later will not rejoice in him," the Teacher may suggest that the wise king is soon forgotten. In chapter 9:15 the Teacher tells a similar story about a poor but wise man: "Now there was found in it [the city] a poor wise man, and he by his wisdom delivered the city. Yet *no one* remembered that poor man." As the Teacher said in chapter 2:16, "There is no enduring remembrance of the wise or of the fools, seeing that in the days to come all will have been long forgotten" (cf. 1:11). Again we can think of Joseph. Such great wisdom; such a great king. But we read in Exodus 1:8, "Now a new king arose over Egypt, who did not know Joseph." Those who came after Joseph had forgotten him. Such a great king — yet forgotten.

The Teacher concludes, "Surely this also is vanity and a chasing after wind." Even a life guided by wisdom, even a life that reaches the pinnacle of human achievement, even a life that is exalted by the adoration of millions, is futile, useless in the end. The Teacher also calls it "a chasing after wind." It is empty, insubstantial. The great king and his wonderful deeds are forgotten.

With this story, the Teacher is warning us that there is a limit to where wisdom will get us in this life. Certainly, he warns against going it alone. That surely is futile! Two are better than one in many ways. A threefold cord is even better: it "is not quickly broken." We ought to cooperate with others in this life.

---

clesiastes, 31; and Seow, *Ecclesiastes,* 191. Wright, "The Poor but Wise Youth," 149-50, offers a compelling argument for a single youth. "The meaning of the word 'the second' in v. 15 is determined by its use in vv. 8 and 10 where it was last employed. . . . It means 'companion' or 'associate' as all translators recognize. There is no youth B in the story, because the word 'second' is not used in an enumerative sense (i.e., second, third, fourth) but in the sense of 'companion/associate.' The youth described as 'the second' is not a second to the youth mentioned in v. 13. . . . He is second to the king, i.e., an associate or in this case a future successor."

29. "The idiom ['rejoice in him'] . . . may indicate acceptance of the king's rule." Seow, *Ecclesiastes,* 192. Cf. Judges 9:19.

30. Eaton, *Ecclesiastes,* 96.

But we ought to realize also that this earthly life will come to an end, and then our greatest accomplishments will soon be forgotten. The realization of the brevity of our legacy on this earth should keep us humble even as we work together with others.

Thus the Teacher challenges us not to work just by and for ourselves but to work humbly with and for others. To go it alone is futile. To work together offers many advantages. Jesus also urges us not to live for ourselves but to "love our neighbor as ourselves" (Matt 22:39). Paul says that we are all members of one body — the body of Christ. As members of one body, we cannot go it alone but must work together. "The eye cannot say to the hand, 'I have no need of you,' nor again the head to the feet, 'I have no need of you'" (1 Cor 12:21).

Our culture is marked by rugged individualism. This selfish trait also tends to seep into the church. But Christians cannot be individualists because we are members of a community. We are all members of the body of Christ. As members of the body of Christ we ought to work together for the coming kingdom of God on earth. All our individual accomplishments will be forgotten in the future, but what we do together for God's kingdom will last. Paul encourages us, "Therefore, my beloved, be steadfast, immovable, always excelling in the work of the Lord, because you know that in the Lord your labor is *not in vain*" (1 Cor 15:58).

CHAPTER 7

Worshiping in God's House

Ecclesiastes 5:1-7[1]

Guard your steps
when you go to the house of God.

(Eccl 5:1)

Ecclesiastes 5:1-7 is unique in Ecclesiastes because it focuses on worship in God's temple. It is an ideal preaching text for countering the contemporary trend of turning the worship of God into folksy entertainment or a gaudy spectacle. The major challenge in preaching this passage is to gain a proper understanding of some obscure phrases. Take, for example, the sentence, "To draw near to listen is better than the sacrifice offered by fools" (5:1). What is this "sacrifice offered by fools"? Longman asks, "Since he is encouraging listening and not an alternative to sacrifice, does this mean that all sacrifices are those of fools? Or is there a certain type of sacrifice that is foolish?"[2] Even more difficult to interpret is the next line, which reads literally, "for they do not know how to do evil." Is the Teacher saying that fools "do not know how to do evil"?[3] And how does one handle in the sermon 5:7a, "With many dreams come vanities and a multitude of words"? The NRSV notes, "Meaning of Heb uncertain." The "NAB and NEB omit it altogether."[4]

---

1. In the Hebrew Bible this is chapter 4:17–5:6.

2. Longman, *Book of Ecclesiastes*, 150.

3. Fox, *Qohelet*, 210-11, acknowledges frankly, "The end of 4:17 [Heb.] is a crux. . . . Since MT is clear and grammatically feasible, I translate the sentence without understanding the point of its context."

4. Eaton, *Ecclesiastes*, 100. Crenshaw, *Ecclesiastes*, 118, observes, "No solution seems entirely satisfactory."

Text and Context

The boundaries of this textual unit are quite easily identified. Ecclesiastes 5:1 begins a new literary unit with, "Guard your steps when you go to the house of God." Going "to the house of God" indicates a new topic. Moreover, the "guard your steps" signals "a new literary unit by the change in tone. The language of reflection in 4:1-16 gives way to the language of instruction in 5:1-7."[5] The only question is where this unit ends. A few commentators extend the text to verse 9 because verses 8 to 9 continue "the address style of the second person — exactly like the rest of the poem that precedes them."[6] But the Teacher elsewhere employs a bridge from one unit to the next — necessitating a decision whether the bridge should be included with the first preaching text or the second (see, e.g., 3:16-17; 8:16-17; 9:11-12; and 11:7-8). In this case, he indicates that verses 1 and 7 are a unit by forming an inclusio with the imperatives, "Guard your steps when you go to the house of God" (v. 1) and "Fear God" (v. 7). The concise imperative, "Fear God!" forms a powerful conclusion to the literary unit. In addition, in verse 8 he switches from the topic of temple worship to "the oppression of the poor." Therefore we can select Ecclesiastes 5:1-7 as our preaching text.

Since this passage gives advice on a completely new topic, there are only a few connections with its context. In this passage the Teacher uses the word "fool" three times. He has written about fools before (2:14, 15, 16, 19; 4:5, 13), and will do so again later (6:8; 7:6, 17, 25; 10:2, 3, 12, 14, 15). More importantly, the concluding admonition, "Fear God," echoes an earlier conclusion that God set the times "so that all should stand in awe before him" (literally, "should fear him"; 3:14). The same theme of fearing God will be mentioned again in the sequel (7:18; 8:12-13), and finally in the conclusion of the book (12:13).

Literary Features

This passage contains several wisdom forms. The imperatives indicate that the overall form is that of instruction.[7] The Teacher "uses four admonitions or imperatives relating to cultic activity. Each is supported by a motive clause, and in addition there are quotations or comments which add force to the appeal."[8] We can picture the basic structure as follows:

---

5. Seow, *Ecclesiastes*, 197.
6. Loader, *Ecclesiastes*, 57. So also Crenshaw, *Ecclesiastes*, 115.
7. Murphy, *Wisdom Literature*, 138-39.
8. Ogden, *Qoheleth*, 75. The four admonitions are found in 5:1; 5:2; 5:4; and 5:6.

I. Admonition
   A. Motive clause (reason for obeying the admonition)
      1. Additional supporting proverb(s)

The first admonition, "Guard your steps when you go to the house of God," is supported by a motive clause consisting of a "better than" proverb: "to draw near to listen is better than the sacrifice offered by fools" (v. 1). The second admonition consisting of synonymous parallelism, "Never be rash with your mouth, nor let your heart be quick to utter a word before God,'" is supported by a motive clause consisting of a proverb with antithetic parallelism, "for God is in heaven and you upon earth" (v. 2), as well as a proverb with synonymous parallelism, "For dreams come with many cares, and a fool's voice with many words" (v. 3). The third admonition, "Do not delay fulfilling . . . [your vow to God]," is supported by the motive clause, "for he has no pleasure in fools," and concluded with a "better than" proverb: "It is better that you should not vow than that you should vow and not fulfill it" (v. 5). The final admonition consisting of synthetic parallelism, "Do not let your mouth lead you into sin, and do not say before the messenger that it was a mistake," is supported by a motive clause in the form of a rhetorical question, "Why should God be angry at your words . . . ?" (v. 6), as well as a proverb with synonymous parallelism, "With many dreams come vanities and a multitude of words" (v. 7), and is concluded with the imperative, "Fear God."[9] These wisdom forms will help us in sketching the structure of the text.

Repetition may again provide clues to the author's theme. It is worth noting that in this short passage the Teacher mentions "God" six times while he refers to the "fool" three times. Graham Ogden states, "The tenor of the admonitions and the mention of the fool on three occasions would suggest that Qohelet is concerned that people avoid the kinds of mistakes the fool might make in this cultic area. Frequent use of vocabulary relating to verbal communication (*'āmar, dābār, peh, qôl, nēder)* [to utter, word, mouth, voice, vow] focuses the issue about the dangers of incautious speech to which the fool is especially prone."[10]

Textual Structure

The best expository preaching has been described with the vivid image of the preacher touching the text "with a silver hammer, and it immediately broke up

---

9. For some of these forms, see Longman, *Book of Ecclesiastes*, 151-56.
10. Ogden, *Qoheleth*, 75-76.

into natural and memorable divisions."[11] At this stage in our study we look for the "natural divisions" and subdivisions in the preaching text. In this passage the four admonitions provide the main points of the textual structure:

I. Guard your steps when you go to the house of God (v. 1a)
    A. Reason: To draw near to listen is better than the sacrifice offered by fools (v. 1b)
        1. for they do not know how to keep from doing evil (v. 1c)
II. Do not be rash with your mouth (v. 2a)
    nor let your heart be quick to utter a word before God
    A. Reason: for God is in heaven, and you upon earth (v. 2b)
    B. Conclusion: therefore let your words be few (v. 2c)
    C. Proverb supporting the command:
    For dreams come with many cares (v. 3)
      and a fool's voice with many words
III. Do not delay fulfilling a vow you make to God (v. 4a)
    A. Reason: for God has no pleasure in fools (v. 4b)
    B. Conclusion: Fulfill what you vow (v. 4c)
    C. Proverb supporting command:
    It is better that you should not vow (v. 5)
      than that you should vow and not fulfill it
IV. Do not let your mouth lead you into sin (v. 6a)
    and do not say before the messenger that it was a mistake
    A. Reason: why should God be angry at your words (v. 6b)
      and destroy the work of your hands?
    B. Proverb supporting the command:
    With many dreams come vanities (v. 7a)
      and a multitude of words (cf. v. 3)
    C. Conclusion: but fear God (v. 7b)[12]

Theocentric Interpretation

As mentioned, this passage refers to God no fewer than six times — a remarkable concentration for the book of Ecclesiastes. This concentration is due to the fact that this passage deals with behavior in God's temple. Most important is the

11. W. R. Nicoll, describing the sermons of Alexander McLaren; quoted by John Stott, *Between Two Worlds: The Art of Preaching in the Twentieth Century* (Grand Rapids: Eerdmans, 1982), 230.

12. Cf. Murphy, *Wisdom Literature*, 138, who outlines this passage A through J, and Fletcher, "Ecclesiastes 5:1-7," *Int* 55/3 (2001) 296.

Teacher's theological statement, "for God is in heaven, and you upon earth" (v. 2). This conviction of God's transcendence is the foundation for all four admonitions. "An awareness of divine transcendence sustains an economy of human discourse, Qohelet claims. If God were utterly immanent, residing wholly within one's heart, as some today might claim, then free license would be given for human discourse and imagination to run rampant, so Qohelet's logic would suggest. . . . 'God is in heaven,' and the gulf that separates the creature from the Creator mandates spareness of speech that reflects integrity and proper reverence. As wholly Other, God holds people accountable for what they say and do."[13]

Textual Theme and Goal

Michael Fox claims that "the main theme of the present unit is caution in making vows. The remarks about going to the Temple, offering sacrifices, avoiding rash speech, and fearing God are all organized around this theme and should be interpreted in this context."[14] But his proposal is much too restricted, for we see in the textual structure above that vows are not mentioned until the third main point.

We must formulate a theme that covers all the points made in this passage: guarding your steps, listening, praying, fulfilling your vow, not calling your vow a mistake, and fearing God. All these components are held together by the theme of worshiping God in his temple. As Seow puts it, "The common issue in these verses is one's attitude before God, with Qohelet counseling caution, reverence, restraint, moderation, and sincerity. The emphasis throughout the passage is on the necessity of respecting the distance between humanity and God, an emphasis that is encapsulated by the admonitions 'watch your steps' (5:1 . . .) and 'fear God' (5:7 . . .)."[15] These two imperatives, we have seen, form an inclusio for our text. Therefore we can capture the various elements in this text with the overarching theme: "Worship God in his house with fear."

Since themes ought to be as clear as crystal, however, we have to clarify the word "fear," which is open to misunderstanding. Perdue speaks for those who understand "fear" as "dread," "terror," "being afraid of God." He writes, "Unlike the meaning of the phrase in Proverbs, Qohelet understands that 'fear of God' is dread, even terror, evoked by the unfathomable sovereign of human history."[16] But, given the four admonitions, it makes little sense to say, "Worship

---

13. Brown, *Ecclesiastes*, 56.

14. Fox, *Ecclesiastes*, 32. Cf. his *Qohelet*, 209.

15. Seow, *Ecclesiastes*, 197.

16. Perdue, *Wisdom Literature*, 201. Cf. Shepherd, "Ecclesiastes," 304, who says that Qohelet does not mean "what the frame-narrator means in 12:13 when he says 'fear God,' though he uses identical words. . . . Qohelet's admonition here is not that one should have a 'reverential' fear of God but that one should be truly afraid of God." Cf. Longman, *Book of Ecclesiastes*, 124.

God in his house with terror or dread." Moreover, there is no valid reason for understanding the Teacher's use of the phrase "fear God" differently from the way it is understood in the Epilogue (12:13) and elsewhere in the Old Testament.[17] To fear God is to revere God, to stand in awe of God, to approach God with reverence.[18] We can therefore formulate the textual theme as follows, *Worship God in his house with reverence!*

The Teacher's goal in sending this message is more pressing than simply to encourage the Israelites to do something. The imperatives indicate that he is commanding them, urging them. So we can formulate the textual goal as follows, *to urge Israel to worship God in his house with reverence.*

Ways to Preach Christ

Since this passage contains neither a promise nor a type of Christ, we shall explore the five other ways to Jesus Christ in the New Testament.

Redemptive-Historical Progression

The Teacher urges Israel to worship God in his house with reverence. God's house in those days was the second temple. In Old Testament times people were required to bring their sacrifices (5:1) to the temple in Jerusalem. But Jesus' coming brought about a major change with respect to the animal sacrifices and the place of worship. When the Samaritan woman said to Jesus, "Our ancestors worshiped on this mountain, but you say that the place where peo-

---

17. The different interpretations are due to different presuppositions. See above, pp. 8-9. Cf. Whybray, *Ecclesiastes*, 75, "The idea that Qohelet's concept of the 'fear of God' is essentially different from its usual meaning in the Old Testament (devotion to God, worship of God, or willing obedience to his commandments) is an idea derived from a particular interpretation of Qohelet's thought in general rather than from his actual use of the phrase. His meaning is that God rightly demands 'fear' from men in the sense of recognition of his essential difference from his creatures (cf. 5:2)."

18. "The notion of the 'fear of God' . . . does not connote absolute terror. Rather, the concept of the fear of God here, as elsewhere in Israelite wisdom literature, stresses the distance between divinity and humanity." Seow, *Ecclesiastes*, 174. Cf. Whybray, "Qoheleth as a Theologian," 264, "The commonly held view that the 'fear of God' that Qohelet commended to his readers was fear — that is, terror — in the most literal sense cannot be sustained: it has no basis in the text." Cf. Provan, *Ecclesiastes*, 118, "The reader is exhorted to hold on to reality: 'Stand in awe of God.'" Cf. Von Rad, *Wisdom in Israel*, 66, "The modern reader must . . . eliminate, in the case of the word 'fear,' the idea of something emotional, of a specific, psychical form of the experience of God."

ple must worship is in Jerusalem," he responded, "Woman, believe me, the hour is coming when you will worship the Father neither on this mountain nor in Jerusalem. . . . The hour is coming, and is now here, when the true worshipers will worship the Father in spirit and truth" (John 4:20-23). People can now worship the Father wherever two or three are gathered in Jesus' name (Matt 18:20).

The Teacher also exhorts us, "let your words be few," because of the distance between God and us: "God is in heaven, and you upon earth." But with the coming of Jesus, the Mediator, the distance between God and us has been bridged. Jesus instructed his followers concerning prayer, "I will do whatever you ask in my name, so that the Father may be glorified in the Son. If in my name you ask me for anything, I will do it" (John 14:13-14). Paul, too, writes that through Christ Jesus we "have access in one Spirit to the Father" (Eph 2:18). The author of Hebrews encourages us likewise, "Therefore, my friends, since we have confidence to enter the sanctuary by the blood of Jesus, by the new and living way that he opened for us through the curtain (that is, through his flesh), and since we have a great priest over the house of God, let us approach with a true heart in full assurance of faith, with our hearts sprinkled clean from an evil conscience and our bodies washed with pure water" (Heb 10:19-22).

Analogy

The Teacher urges us to worship God in his house with reverence because "God is in heaven, and you on earth." Jesus also teaches us to remember that God is in heaven; in fact, he teaches us to address God as, "Our Father in heaven" (Matt 6:9). During his ministry on earth, Jesus also urged reverent worship in the temple. When Jesus found that the temple courts had been turned into a marketplace, he "drove out all who were selling and buying in the temple, and he overturned the tables of the money changers and the seats of those who sold doves. He said to them, 'It is written, "My house shall be called a house of prayer"; but you are making it a den of robbers'" (Matt 21:12-13).

We should also note analogies in the details of the Teacher's instructions and those of Jesus. Like the Old Testament Teacher, Jesus urges us to let our words be few: "When you are praying, do not heap up empty phrases as the Gentiles do; for they think that they will be heard because of their many words. Do not be like them, for your Father knows what you need before you ask him" (Matt 6:7-8).

Concerning vows, Jesus calls the scribes and Pharisees "hypocrites" and "blind guides" for teaching that one need not fulfill all vows. They taught,

"Whoever swears by the sanctuary is bound by *nothing*, but whoever swears by the gold of the sanctuary is bound by the oath" (Matt 23:16; cf. v. 18). In fact, concerning "the vows you have made to the Lord," Jesus said, "Do not swear at all, either by heaven, for it is the throne of God, or by the earth, for it is his footstool. . . . Let your word be 'Yes, Yes' or 'No, No'" (Matt 5:33-37).

Like the Old Testament Teacher, Jesus also instructs us to "fear God." He said, "Do not fear those who kill the body but cannot kill the soul; rather fear him who can destroy both soul and body in hell" (Matt 10:28).

Longitudinal Themes

The Teacher insists that we worship God with reverence by listening rather than speaking. The great commandment for God's old covenant people was, "*Hear*, O Israel: The LORD is our God, the LORD alone. You shall love the LORD your God with all your heart, and with all your soul, and with all your might" (Deut 6:4-5). God's command to hear is repeated many times in the Old Testament (e.g., Deut 4:10; 5:1; 6:3, 4; 9:1; 12:28; 20:3; 31:12, 13; Isa 1:10; 7:13; 28:14). Provan observes, "Without hearing there can be no understanding of the kingdom of God; thus Jesus repeats, 'He who has ears, let him hear' (e.g., Matt 11:15; 13:9, 43; John 8:47)."[19]

New Testament References

In addition to the New Testament references supporting the above ways to Christ, one may also be able to use Hebrews 12:28-29, "Therefore, since we are receiving a kingdom that cannot be shaken, let us give thanks, by which we offer to God *an acceptable worship with reverence and awe; for indeed our God is a consuming fire.*"

Contrast

Except for the contrasts noted under redemptive-historical progression above, there is no contrast between the message of the Teacher and that of the New Testament.

---

19. Provan, *Ecclesiastes*, 119. See also Revelation 2:7, 11, 17, 29; 3:6, 13, 22.

Sermon Theme and Goal

We formulated the textual theme as, "Worship God in his house with reverence!" In our text God's "house" is understood as God's temple. As noted above, Jesus' coming changes the place of worship from the temple in Jerusalem to wherever two or three are gathered in his name (Matt 18:20; John 4:20-23). But since we still speak of each of these gathering places as "a house of worship," we can keep the textual theme for the sermon theme: *Worship God in his house with reverence!*

The Teacher's goal was, "to urge Israel to worship God in his house with reverence." Our goal in preaching this sermon can be practically the same: *to urge the hearers to worship God in his house with reverence.*

The sermon goal reveals the need addressed in this sermon: people are not worshiping God with reverence. Provan observes that "'worship services' provide little opportunity for silent awe in the presence of God but plenty of opportunity for performance on the part of a select few professional speakers and musicians, who fill all the space with their words and sounds." He also notes the inroads our narcissistic culture is making into the church. "A survey of sermons by evangelical ministers between 1985 and 1990 suggests, in fact, that over 80 percent of these made God and his world spin around the surrogate center of the self. This is related to the professionalization of the ministry, in which the fulcrum around which ministry turns is no longer God but the church, which itself thus turns out to be a kind of idol."[20]

Sermon Exposition

One can begin the sermon with a contemporary illustration of the need addressed. Many come to church without the proper reverence. Some come out of custom or superstition; others come to be entertained; still others come to be seen and heard.

Such was the case also in Israel. People still came to the temple, but they failed to approach God with reverence. Worshiping God had become a mere formality. In fact, we know from Malachi[21] that Israel dishonored God in his temple. Whereas God required his people to bring their best animals to be sacrificed, they brought as offerings what they could not use themselves: blind, lame, and sick animals. Instead of blessing his worshipers, God said, "*Cursed* be

---

20. Ibid., 121 and 122.

21. Malachi wrote his book around 430 B.C. — a date a century or two before that of Ecclesiastes.

the cheat who has a male in the flock and vows to give it, and yet sacrifices to the Lord what is blemished" (Mal 1:14). In addition, people were quick to make vows to God; they were quick to make promises to God but also quick "to retract them later when they realized the implication of their words (see Prov 20:25)."[22]

Against this background of God cursing his worshipers, we hear the urgency of the Teacher's message in Ecclesiastes. He gives Israel a series of commands about their conduct in worshiping God in his temple. He begins in chapter 5:1, "Guard your steps when you go to the house of God." Be careful when you go to the temple. Think of what you are about to do. You are not just dropping in on a neighbor for a friendly chat. You are not just passing time with a friend. You are going to "the house of *God*." You are going to the place where the almighty Creator stoops down to meet with you. "Guard your steps!" Think of Moses meeting God at the burning bush. God said to him, "Remove the sandals from your feet, for the place on which you are standing is holy ground" (Exod 3:5). "Guard your steps!"

How should we guard our steps? The Teacher explains in the next line, "to draw near to listen is better than the sacrifice offered by fools." In the temple, while sacrifices were offered to God, "silence reigned, fostering a sense of divine presence and human receptivity."[23] Then the priest would read from God's law and explain what was read. He would offer prayers, and the people would respond with songs. And finally the priest would place God's blessing on his people. "To draw near to *listen* is better than the sacrifice offered by fools."

Fools refers to those who bring unacceptable sacrifices to God. People are fools when they bring to God what they cannot use themselves: blind, lame, and sick animals. Fools also "believe that their sacrifices will automatically cancel out their sins without the need for repentance."[24] Fools, the Teacher says at the end of verse 1, "do not know how to keep from doing evil." They do evil even when they go to the house of God.[25]

---

22. Seow, *Ecclesiastes,* 200. Seow, ibid., 200-201, continues, "The Mishnah in fact tells of a series of excuses that people gave when they failed to fulfil their vows (*Ned.* 9)."

23. Brown, *Ecclesiastes,* 55.

24. Whybray, *Ecclesiastes,* 93, "The 'fools' whom Qohelet has in mind are presumably those who believe that their sacrifices will automatically cancel out their sins without the need for repentance, and so are offering sacrifice which is itself essentially wicked and deserving God's anger." Provan, *Ecclesiastes,* 116-17, suggests, "The 'sacrifice of fools' is . . . careless observance of religion, unattached to any genuinely Godward movement of the soul and enacted out of custom, peer pressure, or habit." Shepherd, "Ecclesiastes," 302, argues, "By designating listening as the more appropriate thing to do in God's presence, the implication is that the 'sacrifice of fools' is excessive talk; this implication becomes explicit in v. 2." The latter two interpretations do not take "sacrifice" literally but understand the word as a metaphor.

25. The Hebrew reads literally, "for they do not know of doing evil." The NRSV interprets

The point is this: we should come to God's house first of all to *listen* to what God has to say to us.[26] Many times, God said to Israel: "*Hear*, O Israel."[27] Israel was to listen first of all to God's instruction. Jesus also tells his church repeatedly, "He who has ears, let him hear."[28] Paul writes that "faith comes from what is *heard*, and what is heard comes through the word of Christ" (Rom 10:17). And James admonishes, "Let everyone be quick to *listen*, slow to speak" (1:19). We should come to God's house first of all to listen.

The second point the Teacher makes about worshiping God with reverence deals with prayer. He writes in verse 2, "Never be rash with your mouth, nor let your heart be quick to utter a word before God." The phrase "before God" "usually means in the Temple, in God's presence."[29] So we should not be rash with our mouth, we should not be quick to speak when we pray in God's house.

Why does the Teacher caution us to be restrained in our speaking before God? He answers, "For God is in heaven, and you upon earth." The Teacher wants us to remember the tremendous distance between God and us. God is in heaven, we on earth. God is far above us, far superior to us. God is the almighty Creator King. Even when we meet human kings or queens we are not supposed to be quick to speak. So we should certainly control our tongue when we meet with almighty God in his house. We are mere earthlings. We show our reverence for God when we are not quick to speak.[30]

The Teacher repeats his command at the end of verse 2: "therefore let your words be few." His first point for reverent worship was, "Draw near to *listen*." His second point, "Let your words be *few*" because God is in heaven. Jesus also teaches us to let our words be few. He instructs, "When you are praying, do not heap up empty phrases as the Gentiles do; for they think that they will be heard because of their *many* words. Do not be like them, for your Father knows what you need before you ask him." And then, interestingly, Jesus says, "Pray then in this way: Our Father in *heaven*" (Matt 6:7-9). Like the Old Testament Teacher, Jesus reminds us that God is in heaven and we are on earth. So out of reverence

---

this as, "for they do not know how to keep from doing evil"; the NASB has, "for they do not know they are doing evil"; and the TNIV has, "who do not know that they do wrong." Since this phrase is not a major point and so as not to confuse your hearers, I think it best to follow the translation of the pew Bible.

26. Many commentators link this verse with 1 Samuel 15:22, "to obey is better than sacrifice," and equate listening with obedience. But the contrast in this context is between listening and being "rash with your mouth." "In contrast to the approach of noisy fools, it is better that one should listen, rather than speak." Seow, *Ecclesiastes*, 194.

27. E.g., Deuteronomy 4:10; 5:1; 6:3, 4; 9:1; 12:28; 20:3; 31:12, 13; Isaiah 1:10; 7:13; 28:14.

28. E.g., Matthew 11:15; 13:9, 43; John 8:47; Revelation 2:7, 11, 17, 29; 3:6, 13, 22.

29. Fox, *Ecclesiastes*, 33.

30. "For the Teacher the supreme act of impiety is the presumption that one can be in a position of control when dealing with God." Garrett, *Proverbs, Ecclesiastes*, 311.

for almighty God, our words should be few. But Jesus adds that our words *can* be few because we are praying to "our *Father* in heaven," and "your Father knows what you need before you ask him."

The Teacher supports his second point, "Let your words be few," with a proverb in verse 3, "For dreams come with many cares, and a fool's voice with many words." The proverb assumes that many concerns will lead to dreams. The one follows from the other. So a fool's voice leads to "many words."[31] As in his first point where he contrasted the drawing near to listen with "the sacrifice offered by *fools*," so here he contrasts his advice, "Let your words be few," with that of a *fool's* voice which speaks "with many words." Later in his book the Teacher will say that "fools talk on and on" (10:14). We should not be fools in our worship of almighty God.

Having made the points that we worship God with reverence when we come to his house, first, to listen, and second, to use few words in prayer, the Teacher moves on to his third point. This point has to do with vows. Verse 4, "When you make a vow to God, do not delay fulfilling it; for he has no pleasure in fools." Again the Teacher refers to fools. God has no pleasure in fools, so we should be wise when we worship almighty God. And we are wise when we do not delay fulfilling a vow made to God. The Teacher alludes here to the law of God in Deuteronomy 23:21-22 which reads, "If you make a vow to the LORD your God, do not postpone fulfilling it; for the LORD your God will surely require it of you, and you would incur guilt. But if you refrain from vowing, you will not incur guilt" (cf. Num 30:2). A vow is usually a conditional promise made to God. If God will do something for the worshiper, then the worshiper will do such and such for God.[32] For example, the barren Hannah vowed: "O LORD of hosts, if only you will look on the misery of your servant, and remember me, and not forget your servant, but will give to your servant a male child, then I will set him before you as a nazirite until the day of his death" (1 Sam 1:11). When God answered her prayer with the conception and birth of Samuel, she kept her vow by bringing him "to the house of the LORD at Shiloh" and "lending" him "to the LORD; as long as he lives, he is given to the LORD" (1 Sam. 1:24, 28). Hannah fulfilled her vow as soon as she could — after she had weaned little Samuel.

Unfortunately, worshipers were tempted *not* to fulfill their vow after God had granted their request. So the Teacher continues in verse 5, "It is better that you should not vow than that you should vow and not fulfill it." The New Testa-

---

31. See Whybray, *Ecclesiastes*, 94.

32. "Temple vows were a common feature of Old Testament worship and involved promises to consecrate such things as sacrifices or money to God in return for granting a request in prayer (Lev 7:16-17; 22:18-23; 27:1-25; Num 6). The temptation presented to the worshiper was to avoid fulfilling the vow once the prayer had been answered." Provan, *Ecclesiastes*, 117.

ment offers a striking example of God's anger when people do not fulfill their vows. Ananias and Sapphira apparently vowed that they would give the proceeds from the sale of some property to the church for distribution to the needy. But secretly they kept part of the proceeds for themselves. Peter said to Ananias, "While it remained unsold, did it not remain your own? And after it was sold, were not the proceeds at your disposal?" For lying to God both were punished with death, "and great fear seized the whole church and all who heard of these things" (Acts 5:4, 11).

The Jewish tradition underscored the seriousness of making vows to God by swearing by some object. As we today may swear an oath with a hand on the Bible, they would swear by heaven, or earth, or by the sanctuary, or the gold of the sanctuary, or by the altar, or the gift on the altar. Jesus faulted the scribes and Pharisees for making clever distinctions between such vows, for some vows had to be fulfilled while others could be disregarded. For example, they taught, "Whoever swears by the sanctuary is bound by *nothing*, but whoever swears by the *gold* of the sanctuary is bound by the oath" (see Matt 23:16-22). Jesus, in contrast, taught that all vows to God must be fulfilled. But Jesus simplified matters. Concerning "the vows you have made to the Lord," he said, "Do not swear at all, either by heaven, for it is the throne of God, or by the earth, for it is his footstool, or by Jerusalem, for it is the city of the great King. . . . Let your word be 'Yes, Yes' or 'No, No'; anything more than this comes from the evil one" (Matt 5:33-37).

Today in church we still make vows to God. When we marry in church, we promise before God to live together as husband and wife "till death do us part." When we present our children for baptism, we promise to instruct them in the Christian faith and lead them into Christian discipleship. When we are ordained as officers in the church, we promise to fulfill this calling faithfully. We may also make private promises to God in church: "If God will heal me, I will. . . ." And in a surprising number of hymns we make promises to God. For example, "O Jesus, I have promised to serve thee to the end";[33] "Take my silver and my gold; not a mite would I withhold";[34] "Teach me, O Lord, your way of truth, and from it I will not depart";[35] "We come with offerings to his house, and here we pay the solemn vows we uttered in distress";[36] "Forth in your name, O Lord, I go my daily labor to pursue — you only, Lord, resolved to know in all I think or speak or do";[37] "I will follow you all of my days."[38] The

33. John E. Bode, 1869.
34. Frances R. Havergal, 1874.
35. Psalm 119:33.
36. Psalm 66:13-14.
37. Charles Wesley, 1749.
38. Rich Mullins, 2005.

point is, we must keep these promises if we are indeed to worship God with reverence.

This admonition is so serious that the Teacher reinforces it in his final point. Verse 6, "Do not let your mouth lead you into sin, and do not say before the messenger that it was a mistake." The Teacher here seems to be referring to people making vows to pay a certain sum to the temple treasury. When they failed to pay what they had promised, a priest or some other messenger from the temple would visit them to remind them of their vow.[39] Then people might respond that their vow was "a mistake." They claimed that their vow was unintentional.[40] This conduct was foolish. Did they really think that God would not see through this ruse? The Teacher asks, "Why should God be angry at your words, and destroy the work of your hands?" God will punish people for not fulfilling their vows, and he will punish them for coming up with lame excuses.

The Teacher concludes with verse 7, "With many dreams come vanities and a multitude of words;[41] but fear God." The first part of this verse seems to be another proverb that supports the point that we should not let our mouth lead us into sin.[42] As many dreams are vanities, that is, empty and futile, so a multitude of words in worship is empty and futile. Even our worship of God can be without substance, futile, because of "a multitude of words."

Consequently the Teacher concludes with a final command: "But fear God!" Instead[43] of empty words, "fear God." The book of Proverbs highlights that "the fear of the Lord is the beginning of wisdom" (1:7; cf. 9:10; 31:30). The Teacher says, the fear of God is the beginning of reverent *worship*. Fear of God does not mean that we should be afraid of God or terrified at coming into his

---

39. For this interpretation, see Longman, *Ecclesiastes*, 154, and Crenshaw, *Ecclesiastes*, 117. Leupold, *Exposition of Ecclesiastes*, 121-22, understands the "messenger" to be the priest who is being asked to make an "error offering" to dispose of the sin. Whybray, *Ecclesiastes*, 96, concurs that the "messenger" "refers to the priest to whom the (in this case false) confession is made."

40. For the distinction between intentional and unintentional sins, see Leviticus 4:2-35 and Numbers 15:22-31.

41. "There is no verb in the Hebrew text, and three nouns — dreams, 'futilities' (*hebel* in the plural) and words — stand together simply linked by *we* (usually 'and'), suggesting that they constitute a list." Whybray, *Ecclesiastes*, 96. The lack of a verb leads to many different translations and interpretations (see Seow, *Ecclesiastes*, 197). For example, the TNIV translates, "Much dreaming and many words are meaningless." As before with verse 3, I think it best in the sermon to follow the translation/interpretation of the pew Bible.

42. "The verse opens with *kî* ['for,' omitted in most translations], which I here take in a causal sense, identifying the first part of the verse as a motive clause. It gives a final reason for caution in cultic observance." Longman, *Book of Ecclesiastes*, 156.

43. "Qohelet insists that *instead* (the *kî* is adversative) his hearer/reader should *fear God*." Ibid.

presence. Fear of God means that we revere God, that we stand in awe of him, that we come into his presence with reverence.

Jesus agrees with the Old Testament Teacher that we should worship God in his house with reverence. Jesus became very angry when he found that the temple courts had been turned into a marketplace. We read in Matthew 21 that he "drove out all who were selling and buying in the temple, and he overturned the tables of the money changers and the seats of those who sold doves. He said to them, 'It is written, "My house shall be called a house of prayer"; but you are making it a den of robbers'" (Matt 21:12-13). "My house shall be called a house of prayer."

We should worship God in his house with reverence. Reverence for God will cause us to guard our steps when we go to the house of God. Reverence for God will cause us to draw near to *listen* rather than to blabber like fools. Reverence for God will cause us not to be rash with our mouth. Reverence for God will cause us not to delay fulfilling any promises we have made to God. Reverence for God will cause us not to come up with lame excuses for not fulfilling our promises. In short, reverence for God will make our worship truly awesome.

CHAPTER 8

The Love of Money

Ecclesiastes 5:8–6:9[1]

The lover of money will not be satisfied with money;
nor the lover of wealth, with gain.

(Eccl 5:10)

Ecclesiastes 5:8–6:9 concludes the first half of the book of Ecclesiastes.[2] It is an ideal preaching text for countering the materialism of our society and its impact on the church and its members. As with the other preaching texts, it confronts preachers with several challenges. Since "there is no agreement among scholars on the boundaries of the passage,"[3] the first issue to resolve is the selection of a proper textual unit. If 5:8-9 is indeed part of the textual unit, the next question is how "the oppression of the poor" (v. 8) is related to "the lover of money" (v. 10). We also run into the problem of interpreting some obscure Hebrew words and phrases. For example, what is the meaning of 5:9, "a king for a plowed field"?[4] Moreover, should one understand phrases like "all their days they eat in darkness" (5:17) literally or figuratively? And finally, as we shall see, the structure of this passage raises an important question for the form of the sermon.

---

1. In the Hebrew Bible this is 5:7–6:9.

2. See Wright's analysis on p. 21 above.

3. Seow, *Ecclesiastes*, 215.

4. "The meaning of this verse is totally obscure." Crenshaw, *Ecclesiastes*, 119. The NRSV notes, "Meaning of Heb uncertain."

Text and Context

We begin by looking for the boundaries of the preaching text. Where does the literary unit begin? Some commentators judge that 5:8-9 belong to the preceding unit (5:1-7),[5] while others argue that they are an independent unit.[6] These commentators, then, would start the larger unit at 5:10. But other commentators begin the unit at 5:8.[7] There is similar disagreement about the end of the unit — some ending it at 5:20, others at 6:9, and still others at 6:12.

Whatever unit we select, it is clear from the contents that the Teacher's exclamation, "This is what I have seen to be good . . ." (5:18-20), is the climax of the preaching text. A good preaching text, therefore, would be 5:10-20. However, according to Wright's analysis of the structure of Ecclesiastes (see p. 21 above), 6:9, with a final repetition of the double "this also is vanity and a chasing after wind," marks the end of the first half of the book. We are left, therefore, with two questions: Should we include 6:1-9 in our preaching text and add 5:8-9 to its beginning?

The answer to these questions was elusive until 1989, when Daniel Fredericks published an article entitled, "Chiasm and Parallel Structure in Qoheleth 5:9 [Eng. 5:10]–6:9."[8] Highlighting parallel Hebrew words, Fredericks argued for the following chiastic structure: A (5:10-12); B (5:13-17); C (5:18-20); C' (6:1-2); B' (6:3-6); and A' (6:7-9).[9]

In 1997 Seow refined Fredericks' proposal by including 5:8-9 in the chiasm and centering it on 5:20. He noted the following parallels:[10]

A 5:8-12	A' 6:7-9
the poor (v. 8)	the afflicted (v. 8)
not satisfied (v. 10)	not satisfied (v. 7)
what accomplishment (v. 11)	what advantage (v. 9)
seeing of their eyes (v. 11)	seeing of eyes (v. 9)

B 5:13-17	B' 6:3-6
he sired a son (v. 14)	he sires a hundred (v. 3)
going as he came (v. 15)	he came . . . he went (v. 4)
he eats in darkness (v. 17)	he goes in darkness (v. 4)

---

5. E.g., Crenshaw, *Ecclesiastes*, 115, and Loader, *Ecclesiastes*, 57.

6. E.g., Whybray, *Ecclesiastes*, 97, and Longman, *Book of Ecclesiastes*, 156-59.

7. Seow, *Ecclesiastes*, 215, who mentions Beek and Ravasi. Shepherd, "Ecclesiastes," 305, acknowledges the chiastic structure (see below) but still divides 5:8-20 and 6:1-9.

8. Fredericks, "Chiasm and Parallel Structure in Qoheleth 5:9–6:9," *JBL* 108/1 (1989) 17-35.

9. Ibid., 18. Murphy, *Ecclesiastes*, 49-50, for the most part agrees with Fredericks's analysis. For a similar division from 5:10 to 6:12, see Fox, *Qohelet and His Contradictions*, 213.

10. Seow, *Ecclesiastes*, 217.

C 5:18-19   C′ 6:1-2
good (v. 18)   evil (v. 1)
God has given (v. 19)   God gives (v. 2)
this is a gift (v. 19)   this is a sickness (v. 2)

D 5:20
must not remember much
God preoccupies/responds with joy in their heart

Consequently, Seow proposed the following chiastic structure:[11]

A   People Who Cannot Be Satisfied (5:8-12)
    B   People Who Cannot Enjoy (5:13-17)
       C   What Is Good (5:18-19)
          D   Enjoy the Moment (5:20)[12]
       C′   What Is Bad (6:1-2)
    B′   People Who Cannot Enjoy (6:3-6)
A′ People Who Cannot Be Satisfied (6:7-9)

All these parallels cannot be a coincidence. The Teacher must have deliberately structured Ecclesiastes 5:8–6:9 as a chiasm. Since the author intended to present these verses as a unit, we should use the whole unit as our preaching text.

As to the context, the Teacher begins this text with the oppression of the poor and injustice in the land (5:8) — a topic first raised in 4:1-3. He stresses that "the lover of money will not be satisfied with money," nor will the human appetite be "satisfied" (5:10; 6:7). He made a similar point earlier: "the eye is not satisfied with seeing" (1:8); and specifically about solitary individuals toiling hard: "their eyes are never satisfied with riches" (4:8). The Teacher concludes that we should enjoy our food, drink, and toil (5:18-20), as he had done earlier (2:24-26; 3:12-13, 22) and will do again in the sequel (8:15 and 9:7-10).

11. Ibid. See also Stephen Brown, "The Structure of Ecclesiastes," *EvRT* 14/3 (1990) 201-2.
12. Seow's summary of verse 20, "Enjoy the Moment," really summarizes the whole subunit of verses 18-20.

Literary Features

In addition to the repetitions, parallels, and chiastic structure listed above, we should also take note of other literary forms in this passage. The Teacher begins with an instruction about oppression of the poor and injustice, including the prohibition, "do not be amazed at the matter" (5:8), and a proverb about the king (5:9). He follows this with a proverb about the lover of money not being satisfied (synonymous parallelism) and his confirmation, "This also is vanity" (5:10). The Teacher continues with a proverb about the increase of goods and the increase of those who eat them (synonymous parallelism) and his confirmation with the rhetorical question, "What gain has their owner but to see them with his eyes?" (5:11). He closes this section with a fourth proverb comparing the sweet sleep of laborers with the lack of sleep of the rich (antithetic parallelism; 5:12).

The Teacher continues with a reflection on "a grievous ill that I have seen under the sun" (5:13a). He relates an anecdote about a rich person who lost his riches in a bad venture and has nothing to pass on to his offspring (5:13-17). He includes in the anecdote a popular saying (5:15) similar to Job 1:21, "Naked I came from my mother's womb, and naked I shall return there," as well as another rhetorical question, "What gain does he have for toiling for the wind?" (5:16).

Next the Teacher offers a reflection on what he has "seen to be good: it is fitting to eat and drink and find enjoyment in all the toil with which one toils . . ." (5:18-19). He concludes this reflection with the assurance that "God keeps them occupied with the joy of their hearts" (5:20).

The Teacher next offers another reflection on what he has seen to be evil "under the sun" (6:1). Here he relates an anecdote about a person who has everything one's heart could desire, "yet God does not enable him to enjoy these things" (6:2). He also calls this "a grievous ill" (6:3; cf. 5:13). In this anecdote he uses hyperbole: "a hundred children" and living "a thousand years twice over" (6:3, 6).

The Teacher concludes this passage with a proverb about the appetite not being satisfied (synthetic parallelism; 6:7), two rhetorical questions (6:8), a "better than" proverb (6:9a), and his final assessment, "this also is vanity and a chasing after wind" (6:9b).[13]

If we superimpose our findings on the chiastic structure, we find that even the wisdom forms roughly confirm the chiasm:

---

13. For some of these identifications I am indebted to Murphy, *Wisdom Literature*, 138; and Longman, *Book of Ecclesiastes*, 156-75.

A   People Who Cannot Be Satisfied (5:8-12)   *instruction/four proverbs*
   B   People Who Cannot Enjoy (5:13-17)   *reflection/anecdote*
      C   What Is Seen to Be Good (5:18-19)   *reflection*
         D   Enjoy the Moment (5:20)   *conclusion*
      C′   What Is Seen to Be Evil (6:1-2)   *reflection*
   B′   People Who Cannot Enjoy (6:3-6)   *anecdote*
A′   People Who Cannot Be Satisfied (6:7-9)   *two proverbs*

Textual Structure

With the chiastic structure and literary forms in mind, we are ready to expose the logical outline of the text.

I. Instruction: Do not be amazed at the oppression of the poor (5:8a) and the violation of justice and right
  A. Reason: For the high official is watched by a higher (5:8b)
    1. Still, a king may be an advantage for a land (5:9)
  B. Proverb: The lover of money will not be satisfied with money (5:10) nor the lover of wealth, with gain
    1. This also is vanity
    2. When goods increase, so do its consumers (5:11)
    3. The poor sleep well, while the rich cannot sleep (5:12)

II. Reflection on "a grievous ill" (5:13-17)
  A. Anecdote about an owner losing his riches in a bad venture (5:13b-14a)
    1. He has nothing to support his son (5:14b)
    2. He has no gain from all his toil (5:15-16)
    3. He ends up eating in darkness and resentment (5:17)

III. Reflection on what is seen to be good (5:18-20)
  A. It is fitting to eat and drink and find enjoyment in toil (5:18a)
    1. This is our lot (5:18b)
    2. God gives wealth and possessions as well as the ability to enjoy them (5:19)
  B. Reason: For they will not brood over the days because God gives them joy (5:20)

IV. Reflection on what is seen to be evil: "a grievous ill" (6:1-6)
  A. Anecdote about a rich person who lacks nothing (6:2a)
    1. But God does not enable him to enjoy his wealth (6:2b)

B. A person may have a hundred children and live long, and yet have no joy (6:3a)
   1. A stillborn child is better off than he (6:3b-6)
      a. For it has not known anything (6:4-5a)
      b. It finds rest rather than the rich person (6:5b)
V. Proverb: All human toil is for the mouth (6:7),
                yet the appetite is not satisfied
  A. Reason: For the wise have no advantage over fools (6:8a)
   1. Yet the poor may have an advantage over the rich (6:8b)
  B. Proverb: Better is the sight of the eyes than the wandering of desire (6:9a)
   1. The wandering of desire (the human appetite) is vanity (6:9b) and a chasing after wind

Theocentric Interpretation

Derek Kidner writes, "At first sight this [passage] may look like the mere praise of simplicity and moderation; but in fact the key word is God, and the secret of life held out to us is openness to him: a readiness to take what comes to us as heaven-sent, whether it is toil or wealth or both."[14] It is indeed remarkable that in this relatively brief passage the Teacher mentions God no fewer than six times and that he places these at the heart of the passage: "the few days of the life God gives us" (5:18); "God gives wealth and possessions and . . . enables [us] to enjoy them . . . — this is the gift of God" (5:19); "God keeps them occupied with the joy of their hearts" (5:20); "those to whom God gives wealth, possessions, and honor . . . , yet God does not enable them to enjoy these things" (6:2).

It is clear that this passage centers on God: the sovereign God gives us our life, our wealth and possessions, and the ability to enjoy them. The Teacher emphasizes that God is the great Giver by repeating in 5:19, "this is the gift of God." God is good: he keeps people "occupied with the joy of their hearts" (5:20). But God can also withhold these gifts: the poor are oppressed (5:8); the "few days" of our life will come to an end (5:18); God can also withhold the joy (6:2). God can do all this because he is sovereign.

Textual Theme and Goal

The center of a chiastic structure frequently focuses on the theme. In this passage the center is the conclusion in 5:20, God keeps people occupied with joy.

14. Kidner, *Time to Mourn*, 58.

But this conclusion is reached via warnings about pursuing wealth and encouragement to enjoy God's daily gifts of food, drink, and toil. Therefore the question is: Is the focus of this passage on *God* giving joy or on the encouragement that *we* enjoy God's daily gifts, or both? I think we can keep the dual focus in the sermon: the Teacher's message is, Enjoy God's daily gifts, and after we have followed his advice we will acknowledge that it was God who gave us this joy. But for the sake of a unified sermon we should formulate a single theme. Taking into account the Teacher's warnings about wealth, we can make the textual theme, *Instead of pursuing wealth, enjoy God's daily gifts.*

As to the goal in sending this message, Ellen Davis states that the Teacher "shows more awareness of the dangers of amassing wealth than any other Old Testament writer. This reflects the fact that in the third century B.C.E., many Jews were eager to participate in the highly aggressive mercantile economy developed by the Ptolemaic rulers in Egypt, whose power extended over Palestine."[15] Against this historical background, the Teacher's dual[16] goal was *to warn Israel against pursuing wealth and to encourage them instead to enjoy God's daily gifts.*

Ways to Preach Christ

With the theme in mind, we must now ask how we can carry it forward to Jesus Christ in the New Testament. Redemptive-historical progression does not offer a strong bridge; neither does promise-fulfillment, typology, or contrast. This leaves three possible ways to explore: analogy, longitudinal themes, and New Testament references.

Analogy

Analogy supported by New Testament references offers the most obvious bridge from the Old Testament Teacher's message to the New Testament Teacher Jesus, for on many occasions Jesus warned against pursuing wealth. He said, "No one can serve two masters; for a slave will either hate the one and love the other, or be devoted to the one and despise the other. You cannot serve God and wealth" (Matt 6:24).

Jesus warned his disciples, "Take care! Be on your guard against all kinds of

---

15. Davis, *Proverbs, Ecclesiastes,* 196. See also pp. 9-11 above.
16. Although a sermon, for the sake of its unity and movement, should have a single theme, that single message can have a dual goal or application.

greed; for one's life does not consist in the abundance of possessions." To underscore his point, Jesus told them the parable of the rich fool who built bigger barns to store all his grain and his goods. The rich fool said, "Soul, you have ample goods laid up for many years; relax, eat, drink, be merry." But God said to him, "You fool! This very night your life is being demanded of you. And the things you have prepared, whose will they be?" Jesus concluded, "So it is with those who store up treasures for themselves but are not rich toward God" (Luke 12:15-21).

Jesus also told the parable of the sower whose seed fell into different kinds of soil: on the path, in rocky ground, among the thorns, and in good soil. For our purposes, the relevant point is the seed that fell among the thorns, for Jesus later explained, "As for what was sown among thorns, this is the one who hears the word, but the cares of the world and *the lure of wealth choke the word*, and it yields nothing" (Matt 13:22).

Moreover, Jesus told his disciples, "How hard it will be for those who have wealth to enter the kingdom of God! . . . It is easier for a camel to go through the eye of a needle than for someone who is rich to enter the kingdom of God." When the disciples wondered, "Then who can be saved?" Jesus responded, "For mortals it is impossible, but not for God; for God all things are possible" (Mark 10:23, 25-27). It takes no one less than almighty God to save the rich.

Jesus also warned his followers, "Do not work for the food that perishes, but for the food that endures for eternal life, which the Son of Man will give you" (John 6:27).[17] Therefore Jesus urged the crowd, "If any want to become my followers, let them deny themselves and take up their cross and follow me. For those who want to save their life will lose it, and those who lose their life for my sake, and for the sake of the gospel, will save it. For what will it profit them to gain the whole world and forfeit their life? Indeed, what can they give in return for their life?" (Mark 8:34-38).

In addition, Jesus taught his followers that they need not worry about food and drink. He pointed out that "it is the *Gentiles* who strive for all these things." Instead of striving for food and drink, Jesus assured his followers: "Indeed your heavenly Father knows that you need all these things. But strive first for the kingdom of God and his righteousness, and all these things will be given to you as well" (Matt 6:32-33). The implication is that instead of worrying about food and drink, we should rely on God and enjoy his good gifts every day. In fact, Jesus taught that even when we suffer persecution we can "rejoice and be glad"

---

17. In his first letter, John writes similarly, "Do not love the world or the things in the world. The love of the Father is not in those who love the world; for all that is in the world — the desire of the flesh, the desire of the eyes, the pride in riches — comes not from the Father but from the world. And the world and its desire are passing away, but those who do the will of God live forever" (1 John 2:15-17).

(Matt 5:12). Paul similarly instructed the church, "Rejoice in the Lord always; again I will say, Rejoice" (Phil 4:4).

Longitudinal Themes

One can trace from the Old Testament to the New the longitudinal theme of finding enjoyment in God's daily gifts of food, drink, and work — as we did in Chapter 3 above, pp. 54-55. Since this passage, in addition, warns against pursuing wealth, we can also trace the theme of the danger of pursuing wealth. In his law God warned, "You shall not covet your neighbor's house; you shall not covet your neighbor's wife, or male or female slave, or ox, or donkey, or anything that belongs to your neighbor" (Exod 20:17). The prophets also warned against the pursuit of wealth. For example, Isaiah proclaimed,

> Woe to you who add house to house
> > and join field to field
> till no space is left
> > and you live alone in the land.
> The LORD Almighty has declared in my hearing:
> "Surely the great houses will become desolate,
> > the fine mansions left without occupants" (Isa 5:8-9, TNIV).[18]

Wisdom literature contains similar warnings against pursuing wealth, not only in Ecclesiastes but also in Proverbs. For example, Proverbs 23:4-5 warns,

> Do not wear yourself out to get rich;
> > be wise enough to desist.
> When your eyes light upon it, it is gone;
> > for suddenly it takes wings to itself,
> > flying like an eagle toward heaven.

And Proverbs 28:22 states,

> The miser is in a hurry to get rich
> > and does not know that loss is sure to come.

The New Testament continues this theme. Many times Jesus warned against the pursuit of wealth (see "Analogy" above). Paul prescribed that "a bishop must be above reproach, . . . and not a lover of money" (1 Tim 3:3). In 1 Timothy 6 Paul echoes many of the Teacher's thoughts in our text. Paul calls his own words, "the

---

18. The NRSV has changed the sharp warning, "Woe to you," into the sterile, "Ah, you."

sound words of our Lord Jesus Christ" (1 Tim 6:3): "Of course, there is great gain in godliness combined with contentment; for *we brought nothing into the world, so that we can take nothing out of it;* but if we have *food* and clothing, we will be content with these. But *those who want to be rich fall into temptation and are trapped by many senseless and harmful desires that plunge people into ruin and destruction.* For *the love of money is a root of all kinds of evil,* and in their eagerness to be rich some have wandered away from the faith and *pierced themselves with many pains. . . .* As for those who in the present age are rich, command them not to be *haughty,* or to set their hopes on *the uncertainty of riches,* but rather on *God who richly provides us with everything for our enjoyment*" (1 Tim 6:6-10, 17).

New Testament References

In addition to the New Testament references above, one can also consider using some other words of Paul. Concerning joy, Philippians 4:4, 7: "Rejoice in the Lord always; again I will say, Rejoice. . . . And the peace of God, which surpasses all understanding, will guard your hearts and your minds in Christ Jesus" (Phil 4:4, 7). And concerning contentment, Philippians 4:12-13: "I have learned to be content with whatever I have. . . . In any and all circumstances I have learned the secret of being well-fed and of going hungry, of having plenty and of being in need. I can do all things through him who strengthens me."[19]

Sermon Theme and Goal

We formulated the textual theme as, "Instead of pursuing wealth, enjoy God's daily gifts." Since the New Testament does not change this message, we can use the textual theme as the sermon theme: *Instead of pursuing wealth, enjoy God's daily gifts.*

We formulated the Teacher's goal as, "to warn Israel against pursuing wealth and to encourage them instead to enjoy God's daily gifts." The sermon goal can be similar: *to warn the hearers against pursuing wealth and to encourage them instead to enjoy God's daily gifts.* This goal discloses the need addressed: people are tempted to pursue wealth and thus fail to enjoy God's daily gifts.

Sermon Form

The form of the text, as we have seen, is a chiasm. This raises the question whether an expository sermon should follow the chiastic form or change it to a

---

19. We should not use all of these New Testament passages in the sermon, of course. We may be able to use some of them in the liturgy to resonate with the preaching text and sermon.

more conventional form for Western hearers — that is, rearrange the parts so that the climax of 5:18-20 comes at the end instead of in the middle. We can accomplish this change by combining each of the parallel pairs (such as A and A') as points in the sermon. This rearrangement can be pictured as follows:

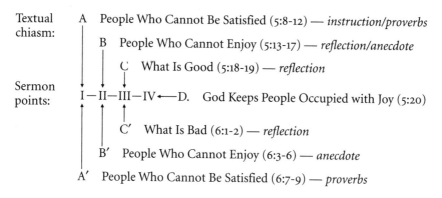

Textual chiasm:

A People Who Cannot Be Satisfied (5:8-12) — *instruction/proverbs*

    B People Who Cannot Enjoy (5:13-17) — *reflection/anecdote*

      C What Is Good (5:18-19) — *reflection*

Sermon points:

I — II — III — IV ← D. God Keeps People Occupied with Joy (5:20)

      C' What Is Bad (6:1-2) — *reflection*

    B' People Who Cannot Enjoy (6:3-6) — *anecdote*

A' People Who Cannot Be Satisfied (6:7-9) — *proverbs*

This rearrangement of the text has several advantages: we can combine the seven textual points into four sermon points; we can highlight the similarities and differences between the parallel parts; and we can end the sermon with the climax of the passage. A disadvantage, of course, is that we need to switch back and forth in the sermon from one part of the text to the other. We can reduce this switching, however, by combining C' and B' (6:1-2 and 3-6), so that it parallels the reflection and anecdote of B (5:13-17). We can also combine C and D as the final point (5:18-20).

The resultant sermon outline is a clear three-point sermon:

I. People who pursue wealth will not be satisfied (5:8-12; 6:7-9) — *instruction/proverbs*
II. The evil of people not enjoying life (5:13-17; 6:1-6) — *two reflections/two anecdotes*
III. Enjoy God's daily gifts (5:18-20) — *reflection*

Sermon Exposition

In all times and places people seem to be interested in accumulating wealth. People want to get rich. In the past, thousands joined the gold rush. Today people search for high paying jobs. Some strive to be CEO of a corporation so they will receive rich bonuses and stock options. Others go to casinos to hit the jackpot. When the lottery goes over a hundred million dollars, people flock to the stores to buy more tickets. They are always searching for more. Some preachers even tap into this human craving for wealth. They promise that God will bless their hearers with health and wealth if only they will step out in faith and send in some "seed money."

There was also a hunger for riches when the Teacher wrote Ecclesiastes. The land of Israel had become a province in the huge empire ruled by the Ptolemies from Alexandria, Egypt. International trade was booming. Some people struck it rich; others would do anything to become rich. The Teacher wants to warn God's people against pursuing riches and to encourage them to enjoy God's daily gifts.

He presents his message in a form favored in the ancient Near East. It is called a chiasm. We can picture a chiasm as a step pyramid:

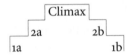

The Teacher ascends the pyramid by making points 1a and 2a until he reaches the climax at point 3. Then he descends on the other side of the pyramid by making parallel points: 2b and 1b. In the West we prefer a more linear structure, making various points and ending with the climax. In this sermon, therefore, we shall combine the parallel steps, such as 1a and 1b and end with the climax.

The first point the Teacher makes is that people who pursue wealth will not be satisfied. But he begins this point in a strange way. He writes in chapter 5:8, "If you see in a province[20] the oppression of the poor and the violation of justice and right, do not be amazed at the matter." The Teacher wants to warn against the pursuit of wealth, but he begins with the poor. Why does he begin with the poor? And why does he write about them the way he does? We might have expected to read, "If you see in a province the oppression of the poor and the violation of justice and right, *do something about it!*" But the Teacher advises, "Do not be amazed at the matter." Why should we not be amazed?

Because, he explains, "the high official is watched by a higher, and there are yet higher ones over them." "'Watched by' means that the high and mighty 'look out for' one another, so the poor have no chance for justice."[21] The high officials are concerned only with lining their own pockets. They have no con-

20. "Kohelet speaks as a resident of a *medinah,* a province in an empire. This is probably the Hellenistic Ptolemaic empire, ruled from Alexandria." Fox, *Ecclesiastes*, 35. See also p. 143 above.

21. Van Leeuwen, Note on Ecclesiastes 5:8 in *The Harper Collins Study Bible.* Seow, *Ecclesiastes*, 203, translates this line literally as "an arrogant one is above an arrogant one, (and) arrogant ones have watched over them all."

cern at all for the poor. In fact, they fleece the poor for whatever they can get their hands on, even if that action violates justice.[22] With so much corruption in government, the Teacher says, *"Do not be amazed"* that you see "the oppression of the poor and the violation of justice and right." It is all the result of greed — the greed and graft of arrogant higher officials.

"But all things considered," he continues, "this is an advantage for a land: a king for a plowed field." It may be that these rich people bought up land as an investment[23] and let it lie fallow. Thus the poor would be deprived even of their right to glean the fields for food. So it would be an advantage for a land if the king restored the land to its proper use, namely, to produce food. This would provide food not only for the owner but also for the poor. Unfortunately, human greed for riches prevents justice for the poor. So "do not be amazed" when you see "the oppression of the poor and the violation of justice."

Next the Teacher warns those who seek to be rich. Verse 10, "The lover of money will not be satisfied with money; nor the lover of wealth, with gain." This verse, with its repetition of "the lover of money" and "the lover of wealth," focuses on those who place money and wealth before anything else in their lives. They live for the money — never mind if it violates justice. They pursue money as their goal in life.

But it is an unattainable goal. The Teacher warns that they "will not be satisfied."[24] "Wealth itself is not the problem here, but the insatiability of those who love money. There is always more that they want, always something else."[25] The Teacher sums up his point on the pursuit of money: "This also is vanity," that is to say, it is like pursuing a vapor; it is empty; it is futile; it does not satisfy.

Like the Teacher, the apostle Paul warns, "The *love* of money is a root of all kinds of evil, and in their eagerness to be rich some have wandered away from the faith and pierced themselves with many pains" (1 Tim 6:10). Paul calls this teaching "the sound words of our Lord Jesus Christ" (1 Tim 6:3). Jesus himself warned his disciples, "Take care! Be on your guard against all kinds of greed; for

22. "In the provincial government the officers extract as much revenue as possible from lesser officers, who turn to the peasantry for their annual dues." Crenshaw, *Ecclesiastes*, 118.

23. This is suggested by Seow, *Ecclesiastes*, 219. See Isaiah 5:8 for the evil of joining "house to house" and adding "field to field, until there is room for no one but you." Cf. Brown, *Ecclesiastes*, 58-59. Garrett, *Proverbs, Ecclesiastes*, translates, "But in all, an advantage for a land is this: a king, for the sake of agriculture." So as not to confuse the hearers on a relatively minor point, I am following the translation and interpretation of the NRSV. If the pew Bible is the TNIV, one may have to include the king with the arrogant, greedy officials, for it translates, "The king himself profits from the fields." In the sermon, of course, one does not have to comment on *every* verse as I do in this commentary.

24. "The saying does not deny that the acquisitive person obtains money, but that he or she will find satisfaction." Crenshaw, *Ecclesiastes*, 121.

25. Seow, *Ecclesiastes*, 219.

one's life does *not* consist in the abundance of possessions." To underscore his point, Jesus told the parable of the rich fool who built bigger barns to store all his grain and his goods. The rich fool said, "Soul, you have ample goods laid up for many years; relax, eat, drink, be merry." But God said to him, "You fool! This very night your life is being demanded of you. And the things you have prepared, whose will they be?" Jesus concluded, "So it is with those who store up treasures for themselves but are not rich toward God" (Luke 12:15-21).

In verse 11 the Teacher writes, "When goods increase, those who eat them increase; and what gain has their owner but to see them with his eyes?" When goods increase, so do its consumers. When people become rich, they will need a maid to clean their house, a gardener to trim their lawn, a nanny to watch their kids, a chauffeur to drive their car, an accountant to keep their books, a broker to invest their money, a body guard to protect themselves and their family. All these people and more have to be paid. In addition, the tax man will require a good cut, and charities will fill their mailboxes with requests for donations. They will also discover that they have many so-called friends who would like to relieve them of their money. "When goods increase, those who eat them increase; and what gain has their owner?" Nothing! There is no gain. All the owner can do is "to see them with his eyes." The owner merely gets to watch as others consume his goods. There is no gain for the owner.

Not only is there no gain for the owner of wealth, but riches are also a liability. Verse 12, "Sweet is the sleep of laborers, whether they eat little or much; but the surfeit [the abundance] of the rich will not let them sleep." The "laborers" may well refer to the oppressed poor mentioned in verse 8.[26] Sometimes they have only very little food to eat. But whether they eat little or much, they sleep well. In contrast, "the surfeit of the rich will not let them sleep." The rich worry about their riches. They see it slipping away as more and more people want a piece of the pie. They fret whether their investments are safe. They are anxious about a recession. Will they lose everything for which they have worked so hard? Such thoughts are enough to keep them awake at night.[27]

In this first point, the Teacher has given three reasons why people who pursue wealth will not be satisfied: "the lover of money will *not be satisfied* with money"; "when goods increase *those who eat them increase*"; and "the surfeit of the rich *will not let them sleep.*"

In his final point, the last step down the pyramid, the Teacher adds more people who will not be satisfied pursuing wealth. He writes in chapter 6:7, "All human toil is for the mouth, yet *the appetite is not satisfied.*"[20] "All human toil is

---

26. See Seow, *Ecclesiastes,* 220.

27. Cf. Ecclesiastes 4:6, "Better is a handful with quiet than two handfuls with toil."

28. Cf. Proverbs 16:26, "The appetite of workers works for them; their hunger urges them on."

for the mouth." We work in order to eat. "Yet the appetite is not satisfied." Come morning, we feel hungry again. The appetite here refers not only to our appetite for food but also our appetite for wealth. Our appetite for wealth and possessions will never be satisfied.[29]

He asks in 6:8, "For what advantage have the wise over fools?" The expected answer to this rhetorical question is, None. With respect to their appetite for food and riches, neither the wise nor fools will ever be satisfied.[30]

But the poor, amazingly, have an advantage. Verse 8, "And what do the poor have who know how to conduct themselves before the living?" Somehow the poor know how to conduct themselves properly. What do the poor have that guides them to proper behavior? The answer is given in 6:9, "Better is the sight of the eyes than the wandering of desire [or appetite]."[31] The poor live by the sight of their eyes; they are content with what they *have;* the poor enjoy their daily bread.

The lovers of money, in contrast, are not content with God's daily gifts of food, drink, and work. Their wandering desire always wants more and more. Their appetite will never be satisfied. The Teacher judges, "this also is vanity and a chasing after wind."[32] The wandering desire is futile; it comes up empty as if one had been "chasing after wind."

Having made his point that people who pursue wealth will not be satisfied, the Teacher moves to a second point: it is evil when people do not enjoy their life. For this point we'll have to turn back to chapter 5:13: "There is a grievous ill that I have seen under the sun: riches were kept by their owners to their hurt, and those riches were lost in a bad venture; though they are parents of children, they have nothing in their hands." The Teacher calls this "a grievous ill," literally "a sickening evil." These people *kept* their riches. They did not enjoy them; they hoarded them. They remind us of the rich fool in Jesus' parable (Luke 12:15-21). He built bigger barns to store all his grain and his goods, thinking that he had it made for many years to come. These people, too, kept their riches but then lost them in a bad venture. It could have been a bank failure, or an investment that

---

29. "'Mouth' and 'appetite' . . . do not, of course, refer to the hunger for food alone (5:11), but rather to a diffuse yet painful yearning for possessions of all sorts." Fox, *Qohelet and His Contradictions,* 221. Seow, *Ecclesiastes,* 227, argues that "the implication of what Qohelet is saying is that the insatiability of the rich is not only self-destructive, it poses dangers to others who fall prey to their greed. Here, as in the mirror section (5:8-12) . . . , personal greed has social consequences. The author is thinking of the oppressive rich, who will gobble up anything and anyone. . . . Greed endangers the world."

30. Seow, *Ecclesiastes,* 227, understands this verse differently: "The wise are no less vulnerable than the fool before the gaping gullet of the insatiable oppressors. Everyone is endangered by the greedy!"

31. The Hebrew word *nephesh* is translated in 6:7 as "appetite" and in 6:9 as "desire."

32. This is the last time the double vanity formula is used in Ecclesiastes.

soured, or a war, or a recession — there are many ways to lose one's wealth. The point is that overnight these rich people became poor. Verse 14 emphasizes, "They have nothing in their hands." A lifetime of toil, a lifetime of hoarding — and it's all gone — down the drain. "They have nothing in their hands." What makes it even worse is that "they are parents of children."[33] And now they have nothing to pass on to their children.

Verse 15 graphically describes their failure: "As they came from their mother's womb, so they shall go again, naked as they came; they shall take nothing for their toil, which they may carry away with their hands." This statement makes us think of Job. Job was extremely wealthy, but he lost it all in one day. An enemy army killed his servants plowing the fields and carried away his oxen and donkeys. Lightning burned up his shepherds and his sheep. Another enemy killed his last servants and carried off his camels. And finally a great wind destroyed the house occupied by his children and killed them all. Having lost all his possessions as well as his children, Job lamented, "Naked I came from my mother's womb, and naked shall I return there." But Job was a pious man. He still worshiped God and said, "The LORD gave, and the LORD has taken away; blessed be the name of the LORD" (Job 1:21).

Not so the rich man in Ecclesiastes. The Teacher repeats in verse 16, "This also is a grievous ill [literally, "a sickening evil"]: just as they came, so shall they go; and what gain do they have from toiling for the wind?" The answer is, Nothing! They have no gain. "They shall take nothing for their toil." The Teacher likens their toiling for riches to "toiling for the wind." You can grab for the wind, try to catch it in your hands, but it slips right through your fingers. So it is with pursuing wealth: it slips right through your fingers. Just one bad venture and it is all gone. A lifetime wasted.

And what is the end result? The Teacher observes in verse 17, "Besides, all their days they eat in darkness, in much vexation and sickness and resentment." The rich who have lost their riches eat in darkness.[34] In biblical times, eating was a social event. When Abraham was approached by three strangers, he rushed out to meet them and invited them to a sumptuous dinner (Gen 18:6-8). When the prodigal son returned home, the father rushed out to meet him and welcomed him with a lavish banquet (Luke 15:23). Eating together was a cele-

---

33. In order to be gender inclusive, the NRSV and TNIV translate the Hebrew singulars as plurals. Unfortunately, in doing so they lose the contrast between 5:14 and 6:3. The NASB retains the contrast by translating respectively: "he had fathered a son," and "If a man fathers a hundred *children.*"

34. I take verse 17 to be the conclusion of the anecdote of the rich person who lost his riches in a bad venture. Other commentators, e.g., Seow, *Ecclesiastes*, 222, understand the verse to speak of rich people who still possess their riches — an interpretation that I find unconvincing.

bration, a social event. But the rich who have lost their riches eat all alone in darkness. Their so-called friends have left them; the house has been foreclosed; gas and electricity have been cut off.

"They eat in darkness." They can no longer afford to light their lamps at night. But the term "darkness" connotes more than the lack of light. Ultimately, "darkness" stands for death.[35] The rich who have lost their riches eat in darkness. Their life is over. There is no joy in their life. They may as well be dead.[36]

Reflecting on their wasted life, thinking of what might have been, "they eat in darkness, in much vexation and sickness and resentment." The Teacher piles up the painful consequences of such a wasted life: vexation, sickness, resentment. . . .[37] Who would want to end up like that?

In chapter 6 the Teacher adds another story of a rich person who does not enjoy life. Chapter 6:1, "There is an *evil* that I have seen under the sun, and it lies heavy upon humankind: those to whom God gives wealth, possessions, and honor, so that they lack nothing of all that they desire, yet God does not enable them to enjoy these things, but a stranger enjoys them. This is vanity; it is a grievous ill [literally again, "a sickening evil"]. A man may beget a hundred children, and live many years; but however many are the days of his years, if he does not *enjoy* life's good things, or has no burial, I say that a stillborn child[38] is better off than he."

This story is even more tragic than the one about the rich man who lost his riches in a bad venture. Here is a person to whom God has given wealth, possessions, and even honor.[39] He has everything his heart desires. The other rich person had only one son;[40] this one has a hundred children. The other rich person lived relatively few years; this one lives many years. God has richly blessed this man. Many children and a long life are what every Israelite desired.[41]

But there is a problem: God does not enable this person to enjoy God's daily gifts. In contrast to chapter 5:19 where God was said to enable rich people to enjoy God's gifts, in 6:2 we read that "God does *not enable*" this rich person to enjoy

35. See n. 43 below.
36. "The gist of the idea is that these people, though they are alive, go through life as if they were already dead." Seow, *Ecclesiastes*, 222.
37. "The cascade of emotion in this verse draws the reader into this poor soul's torment, recreating in the reader a sense of terror at the prospect of such a condition." Salyer, *Vain Rhetoric*, 319. Cf. Provan, *Ecclesiastes*, 128, "For those who pursue gain, then, and who oppress the poor in doing so . . . there is no contented consumption, but only dissatisfaction, restlessness, frustration, affliction, and anger."
38. Cf. Job 3:16.
39. God promised Solomon "riches, possessions, and honor" (2 Chron 1:12).
40. See n. 33 above.
41. "Long life and abundance of offspring are characteristic indicators of God's blessing in the Bible (e.g., Job 42:12-17; Ps 127:3-5; Prov 28:16)." Provan, *Ecclesiastes*, 129.

his wealth and possessions. The Teacher does not explain how God withholds joy — perhaps through the rich person's constant worrying (see 5:12).

In any event, the Teacher writes in verse 3, "but however many are the days of his years, if he does *not* enjoy life's good things, or has no burial, I say that a stillborn child is better off than he." This person has a miserable life because "he does not enjoy life's good things." In addition, he has a miserable death because he "has no burial."[42] "A stillborn child is better off than he," the Teacher claims.

A stillborn child better off than that rich person? This is a shocking comparison. In verses 4 and 5 the Teacher explains why the stillborn child is better off than the rich man who "does not enjoy life's good things." "For it [the stillborn child] comes into vanity and goes into darkness, and in darkness its name is covered;[43] moreover it has not seen the sun or known anything; yet it finds rest rather than he." A stillborn child comes and goes before it experiences the harsh realities of life. It does not see the light of day or know anything about the pain of life in this world. "A long life without enjoyment . . . is far worse than no life at all."[44] Moreover, the rich man has no proper burial and therefore cannot find rest.[45] But the stillborn child "finds rest."

The Teacher continues in verse 6, "Even though he [the rich man] should live a thousand years twice over, yet enjoy no good — do not all go to one place?" Imagine that the rich man would live an unheard-of 2,000 years. What a tremendous blessing from God. But if he would not *enjoy* any of God's good gifts in all these years, his life would still be futile and empty. For even that long life would come to an end. "All go to one place." "Dust to dust." All die and return to the earth. To have lived so long and yet not to have enjoyed God's good gifts — what a waste!

The Teacher has powerfully made two points. First, people who pursue wealth will not be satisfied. And second, it is evil when people do not enjoy their life. Now he is ready to make his major point: we are to enjoy God's daily gifts.

In contrast to this "vanity and grievous ill," the Teacher exclaims in chapter 5:18, "This is what I have seen to be *good*." Life does not have to end in such tragedies. "This is what I have seen to be good: it is fitting to eat and drink and find

---

42. "To die unburied was the mark of a despised and unmourned end (cf. Jer 22:18-19)." Eaton, *Ecclesiastes*, 106.

43. "Covering the name with darkness (v. 4) is idiomatic for non-existence or death; the name is the person. In 6:10 giving the name means to call into existence, to create." Murphy, *Ecclesiastes*, 54. Cf. Loader, *Ecclesiastes*, 68, "Stillborn children come and go in darkness, total nonparticipants in the drama of life."

44. Brown, *Ecclesiastes*, 65.

45. In the Old Testament God required prompt burial (Deut 21:22-23). God's punishment sometimes consisted of no burial (see 1 Kings 13:22; Jer 16:6).

enjoyment in all the toil with which one toils under the sun the few days of the life God gives us; for this is our lot."[46] The emphasis here falls on "enjoyment." Find enjoyment in the common things of life. It is true that God has given us but few days on this earth. There is nothing we can do about this. But there is something we can do about *how* we live those few days on earth. We can use them to pursue money and end up with vexation, sickness, and resentment. Or we can begin every morning with the goal of enjoying the day God is giving us. We can start with the common, everyday things, the Teacher suggests: find enjoyment in our food, our drink, and our toil. We don't have to be rich to find something to enjoy each day.

But what about people who are rich? The Teacher has similar advice for them in verse 19, "Likewise all to whom God gives wealth and possessions and whom he enables to enjoy them, and to accept their lot and find *enjoyment* in their toil — this is the gift of God." Notice how the Teacher stresses that it is "the gift of God": "God *gives* wealth and possessions" followed by, literally, "God *gives* the ability to eat[47] from them," and he sums up with, "this is the gift of God." The point is this: wealth in itself is not evil; it is a gift of God. But wealth as *an end* in itself is a "sickening evil." Pursuing wealth as an end in itself will lead people to ruin. But one can accept wealth as a gift from God[48] and "eat from it," that is, enjoy it and use it to help others.[49]

The Teacher, then, encourages all of us to enjoy God's daily gifts such as food and drink and work. Instead of pursuing riches, we should pursue daily enjoyment. When we do this, we will discover that even our joy is a gift from God. It's similar to the thought in the hymn, "I sought the Lord, and afterward I knew he moved my soul to seek him, seeking me."[50] I sought enjoyment and afterward I knew that God gave that enjoyment.

In verse 20 the Teacher states the benefit of this godly way of living: "For they will scarcely brood over the days of their lives, because God keeps them occupied with the joy of their hearts." If God keeps us occupied, every day of our

---

46. "It is good for a person to eat and drink and to 'see the good' . . . in all toil. These things are, in themselves, our *helĕq*, our 'share' in or 'reward' from life (NIV 'lot,' 5:18)." Provan, *Ecclesiastes*, 128.

47. Cf. 5:11, 12, 17, 18, (19 here), and 6:2.

48. "The person who recognizes God as the center of life is free to enjoy life as a gift precisely because he has not given his heart to something less than God. The capacity to enjoy is here declared to come from putting first things first and to be God-given." Ryken, *The Literature of the Bible* (Grand Rapids: Zondervan, 1974), 256.

49. "Those who spend money on other people or charities are the happiest, says a University of British Columbia psychology department study. . . . Regardless of how much income a person earned, those who spent money on others reported greater happiness." *The Grand Rapids Press*, April 8, 2008, E3.

50. Anonymous, 1878.

lives, with the joy of our hearts, then we will seldom reflect on the few days God has given us. Even when we encounter difficulties, as we undoubtedly will, joy will dominate our lives.[51]

The Teacher's message is clear: we have a choice between two ways of life. We can spend our life pursuing wealth, but this never satisfies and in the end leads to disaster. Or we can focus on enjoying God's gifts every day. Instead of pursuing wealth, the Teacher encourages us to enjoy God's daily gifts.

In the New Testament Jesus also gives us the choice between these two ways of life. He teaches us, "No one can serve two masters; for a slave will either hate the one and love the other, or be devoted to the one and despise the other. You cannot serve God and wealth" (Matt 6:24). Jesus also warns us against spending our lives in the pursuit of wealth. He cautions us, "Take care! Be on your guard against all kinds of greed; for one's life does not consist in the abundance of possessions" (Luke 12:15). Jesus offers the alternative to greed: "Do not work for the food that perishes," he says, "but for the food that endures for eternal life, which the Son of Man will *give* you" (John 6:27).

But should we not work hard to earn our daily food and drink? Jesus does not think so. He says that "it is the *Gentiles* who strive for all these things." Instead, Jesus urges us, "Strive first for the kingdom of God and his righteousness, and all these things [such as food and drink] will be *given* to you as well" (Matt 6:32-33). Just like the Old Testament Teacher, Jesus sees food and drink as gifts from God. If we strive for the kingdom of God, God will *give* us food and drink and whatever we need to live on this earth.

Spending our life pursuing wealth is not only a waste of our brief time on earth but will lead to certain disaster. Instead we ought to focus our lives on the kingdom of God and his righteousness. Then we can enjoy God's gifts to us every day: food and drink, work and health, family and friends, forgiveness and salvation. The apostle Paul urges us, "Rejoice in the Lord *always;* again I will say, *Rejoice*" (Phil 4:4).

---

51. "Regardless of the type of problem encountered in life in this enigmatic and painful world, we have only one wise response: to grasp life as divine gift, and to seek within it the divine portion which is available." Ogden, *Ecclesiastes*, 87-88.

CHAPTER 9

How to Handle Adversity

Ecclesiastes 6:10–7:14

In the day of prosperity be joyful,
  and in the day of adversity consider;
God has made the one as well as the other.

(Eccl 7:14)

This passage begins the second half of the book of Ecclesiastes.[1] The first
half ended with the seventh and final refrain, "This also is vanity and a chasing after wind" (6:9).[2] The second half begins with two questions: "Who
knows what is good for mortals?" and "Who can tell them what will be after
them under the sun?" (6:12). The first question the Teacher will explore in
chapters 7:1 to 8:17 in four sections that each conclude with the phrase, "not
find out" (7:14, 24, 29; 8:17). The second question is the focus of four sections
in chapters 9:1 to 11:6 that each contain the refrain, "do not know" (9:12;
10:15; 11:2, 6).[3]

Ecclesiastes 6:10–7:14 is an extremely relevant preaching text for times of
adversity. In preparing to preach this text, however, it may be difficult to
come up with a brief, single theme that encompasses the many ideas expressed in this passage. But an even greater challenge will be to understand
the meaning intended by the Teacher. Because of the many proverbs in this
passage, some commentators assume that the Teacher, in Murphy's words, is
"dialoguing with traditional wisdom, and modifying it."[4] They think that the

1. This center was noticed already by the Masoretes, who made a note of it in the margin of
the Hebrew Bible.
2. See 1:14; 2:11, 17, 25; 4:4, 16; 6:9. "Seven" is the Hebrew number of completeness.
3. See the analysis of Addison Wright cited on p. 19 above.
4. Murphy, *Ecclesiastes*, 62. Murphy adopts the dialogue approach of N. Lohfink but ac-

157

Teacher preaches "against the text" of traditional wisdom. Their assumption is that he opposes and seeks to undercut traditional wisdom. For example, Seow claims that the Teacher "quickly challenges the seriousness of the proverb [7:1]. He does so by carrying the assumption of the saying to its absurd conclusion. . . . The author employs the rhetoric of subversion. . . . The sayings are perhaps deliberately ludicrous. By their sheer absurdity, Qohelet challenges the audacity of anyone to tell others what is good and how to have an advantage in life."[5]

But the assumption that the Teacher uses a "rhetoric of subversion" is just that — an assumption.[6] The problem is that this presupposition can make the Teacher say the opposite of what he wrote; in other words, it could subvert the intention of the Teacher. Moreover, this approach assumes that we can know for certain which proverbs are traditional wisdom and which are the Teacher's own compositions. As Fox explains, "The weakness of this approach is its arbitrariness in separating out traditional wisdom from Qohelet's. And it sometimes involves projecting a notion of traditional wisdom from Qohelet's words which is not actually found in 'traditional wisdom.'"[7]

Text and Context

It is not difficult to establish the parameters of the textual unit. After the final, "This also is vanity and a chasing after wind" (6:9), 6:10 begins a new section. However, according to Murphy, "most commentaries recognize 7:1-14 as a unit."[8] The question is, therefore, what to do with 6:10-12. Do these verses belong to the literary unit of 7:1-14? Seow calls attention to the repetition of key expressions at the beginning and end of the larger unit:[9]

---

knowledges that "Chapter 7 is perhaps the most difficult chapter in a difficult book. Among other reasons, it is difficult because the words and sayings seem to be clear — but the way Qohelet is using them is another matter." Ibid., 66.

5. Seow, *Ecclesiastes*, 244, 246. Cf. Perdue, *Wisdom Literature*, 204, "These sayings [7:1-4] appear to be subversive aphorisms, sayings that seek to overturn the conventional worldview and its undergirding by the social knowledge of the wisdom tradition." Cf. Shepherd, "Ecclesiastes," 317, "In these verses [7:5-7] some traditional wisdom is dispensed and then subverted." Cf. Loader, *Ecclesiastes*, 82, "We have to conclude, therefore, that the Preacher's opposition to the generally optimistic teachers of wisdom never relaxes."

6. See Chapter 1, p. 9 above.

7. Fox, *A Time to Tear Down*, 250. See also his argument on p. 255, that "Murphy, along with many other commentators, misinterprets these verses [7:8-10]."

8. Murphy, *Ecclesiastes*, 66.

9. Seow, *Ecclesiastes*, 241.

6:10-12	7:10-14
whatever happens (*mah-ššehāyâ*, v. 10)	how is it? *meh hāyâ*, v. 10
they cannot (*lō'-yûkal*, v. 10)	who can? (*mî yûkal*, v. 13)
advantage (*yōtēr*, v. 11)	advantage (*yōtēr*, v. 11)
like a shadow (*kassēl*, v. 12)	as a shadow (*běṣēl*, v. 12)
afterwards (*'aḥărāyw*, v. 12)	after them (*'aḥărāyw*, v. 14)

It appears that 6:10–7:14 is the literary unit. We can, therefore, begin the preaching text with 6:10 and end it with 7:14, which has the key concluding refrain, "not find out."

In this passage the Teacher picks up several ideas he raised earlier. The idea, "Whatever has come to be has already been named" (6:10), is a more profound form of the Teacher's earlier expressions, "There is nothing new under the sun" (1:9) and "That which is already has been" (3:15). The Teacher previously explored the question, "Who knows what is good for mortals? (6:12a) in 2:3-26. Earlier he also raised the question, "Who can tell them what will be after them?" (6:12b; cf. 7:14) in 3:22, and he will raise it again in 8:7 and 10:14. The Teacher also alluded to his view that the day of death is better than the day of birth (7:1b) in 4:2 and 6:3. Moreover, he expressed earlier his conviction that no one "can make straight what he [God] has made crooked" (7:13) in 1:15.

Perhaps the most helpful comment about the context of this passage is that it "appears to intentionally echo the poem about time in 3:1-15. Specific echoes and allusions include references to 'death,' 'birth,' 'mourning,' 'laughter,' 'destroying' (*'ibbēd*), 'good times,' 'bad times,' 'what God has done' (*ma'aśēh 'ĕlōhîm*), etc. It seems that in 7:1-14 the author is offering practical advice in response to the poem about time. Yes, there is 'a time to be born and a time to die' (3:2); but 'the day of death is better than the day of birth' (7:1). . . . Yes, there is 'a time to weep and a time to 'laugh' (*śḥq*) . . . (3:4); but 'sorrow is better than laughter (*śḥq*)' (7:3). . . ."[10]

Literary Features

Although this passage begins and ends with prose (6:10-12; 7:13-14), it centers on proverbs (7:1-12).[11] The subunit of 6:10-12 is presented in the form of a reflection, while verses 7:1-14 most likely are in the form of instruction.[12]

10. Dorsey, *Literary Structure*, 195. Dorsey also observes on p. 196, "As with the earlier poem about time, this unit comprises fourteen poetic verses that appear to form seven smaller units of two verses apiece."

11. This is the first of three major lists of proverbs in Ecclesiastes. The other two are found in 9:17–10:4 and in 10:8–11:4.

12. Murphy, *Wisdom Literature*, 139-40. Because of the verb *rā'â* (see, consider) in 7:13 (cf.

In 6:12 the Teacher raises the rhetorical questions, "Who knows what is good for mortals?" and "Who can tell them what will be after them?"[13] With the proverbs he seeks to answer the first question by repeating the word "good" *(ṭôb)* many times. But the answer is by no means simple. In this section we find a high concentration[14] of "better than" (in Hebrew, "more good than") proverbs, which introduce a degree of relativism. Frequently "one must choose the lesser of two evils, or at least settle for a situation that falls far short of ideal."[15]

Most of the proverbs are composed with synonymous parallelism (7:1, 6, 7, 8, 11), but three use antithetic parallelism (7:2, 4, 5) and one employs synthetic parallelism (7:12).[16] Many lines of these proverbs also contain an artful internal structure. For example, 7:1a reveals both inverted parallelism (A B B′ A′) and assonance:[17]

ṭôb	šēm	mi-šemen	ṭôb
good	a name	from oil	good

Assonance is also found in "verse 5 *(šîr, šēmaʿ, ʾîš)* and verse 6 *(šîr, kĕsîl, sîrîm)*, and the *rûaḥ, nûaḥ* terms in verses 8-9."[18]

Repetition of keywords is often a clue to the theme of a passage. In 7:1-14 the words are "good/better" *(ṭôb),* repeated a total of eleven times; "wise/wisdom," six times; "heart," five times; "fool," four times; "sorrow/anger," three times; and "laughter" and "house of mourning," twice each.[19]

Textual Structure

In this section we seek to determine the logical flow of the passage; in other words, we seek to detect the main points and the supporting sub-points. Whybray warns, "Attempts to see a logical progression of thought throughout the section are probably wasted."[20] But one cannot formulate the theme of a

---

1:14, 17; 3:10, 8:17) Ogden, *Qoheleth,* 110, calls 7:13-14 a reflection. But the fact that *rāʾâ* is in the imperative mood argues for classifying it as an instruction rather than the Teacher's reflection.

13. The Teacher raises another rhetorical question in 7:13.

14. "Five of the sixteen occurrences of the 'better than' proverb occur here." Salyer, *Vain Rhetoric,* 335.

15. Davis, *Proverbs, Ecclesiastes, Song of Songs,* 199.

16. For these distinctions, see p. 33 above. Eaton, *Ecclesiastes,* 111, argues for synthetic parallelism also in verse 7. See n. 53 on p. 173 below.

17. Assonance is resemblance of sound in words or syllables.

18. Ogden, *Qoheleth,* 99.

19. See Whybray, *Ecclesiastes,* 112, and Murphy, *Wisdom Literature,* 140.

20. Whybray, ibid.

passage nor prepare an *expository* sermon without detecting some form of logical coherence. Even though it may be difficult, therefore, we cannot avoid this step of outlining the textual structure. Following the text as closely as possible, I suggest the following outline:

I. The human predicament: no one knows what is good for mortals (6:10-12)
  A. Whatever has come to be has already been predetermined by God (6:10a)
  B. We are not able to dispute with a stronger one, that is, God (6:10b)
   1. Reason: For *(kî)* the more words, the more vanity (6:11a)
   2. Conclusion: So disputing with God is not good (6:11b)
  C. No one knows what is good for mortals (6:12a)
   1. Reason: For no one can tell them what will be after them (6:12b)
II. Still, there are some things that are better ("more good") than others (7:1-12)
  A. Thinking about our death is better than living in denial (7:1-2)
   1. The day of death is better than the day of birth (7:1)
   2. It is better to go to the *house of mourning* than to the house of feasting (7:2a)
    a. Reasons:
     i. For death is the end of everyone (7:2b, c)
     ii. and the living will lay it to heart
   3. Sorrow is better than laughter (7:3a)
    a. Reason: For by sadness of countenance the heart is made glad (7:3b)
   4. The heart of the wise is in the *house of mourning* (7:4) but the heart of fools is in the house of mirth
  B. It is better to hear the rebuke of the wise than the song of fools (7:5)
   1. Reason: For the laughter of fools (7:6b)
    a. is like the crackling of thorns under a pot (7:6a)
    b. This also is vanity (7:6c)
  C. The end of a matter is better than its beginning (7:7-10)
   1. Oppression makes the wise foolish (7:7) and a bribe corrupts the heart
   2. Better is the end of a thing than its beginning (7:8a)
   3. The patient in spirit are better than the proud in spirit (7:8b)
    a. Do not be quick to anger (7:9a)
     i. Reason: For anger lodges in the bosom of fools (7:9b)
    b. Do not say, "Why were the former days better?" (7:10a)
     i. Reason: For it is not from wisdom that you ask this (7:10b)

D. Wisdom is an advantage (7:11-12)
   1. Wisdom is as good as an inheritance (7:11),
      an advantage to those who see the sun
      a. Reason: For the protection of wisdom is like that of money
         (7:12a)
   2. The advantage of knowledge is that wisdom gives life (7:12b)
III. Conclusion: Consider the work of God in times of adversity (7:13-14)
   A. Consider the work of God (7:13a)
      1. No one can make straight what he has made crooked (7:13b)
   B. In the day of prosperity be joyful (7:14a)
   C. In the day of adversity consider that God has made this time too
      (7:14b)
      1. so that mortals may not find out anything that will come after them
         (7:14c)

Theocentric Interpretation

It may appear that the Teacher refers to God only in the conclusion, but, be it
obliquely, he refers to God in the introduction as well. The Teacher begins this
passage with the words, "Whatever has come to be has already been named"
(6:10). Who "named" what has come to be? God did. Seow points out that
"here, as so often in Ecclesiastes, passive verbs are used to refer obliquely to
what the deity does."[21] In New Testament studies this is called the "divine passive."[22] So the Teacher begins by claiming that God in the past already determined the present and that God knows what human beings are.

Next the Teacher states that these human beings "are not able to dispute
with those who are stronger." Unfortunately, the NRSV's custom of turning Hebrew singulars into plurals disguises the real meaning. The Hebrew reads literally that these human beings "are not able to dispute with one who is stronger"[23] — which must be God.[24] The Teacher may well have been thinking of

21. Seow, *Ecclesiastes*, 232. Cf. p. 241, "What is meant is that God has designated and God
has known, although the deity is not explicitly mentioned."

22. See my *Modern Preacher*, 295, for references and examples.

23. "The NRSV translation of v. 10 is misleading; the word is a grammatical singular and
clearly refers to God (compare the argument in Job 9)." Davis, *Proverbs, Ecclesiastes, Song of
Songs*, 197. Huwiler, "Ecclesiastes," 197, adds, "The lack of explicit mention of God may be an
expression of human (even Qohelet's) inability to contend with this stronger one, or it may be
a rhetorical ploy by which the readers are pushed to take responsibility for their own infer-
ences."

24. See Seow, *Ecclesiastes*, 250, and Loader, *Ecclesiastes*, 72.

Job, who disputed with God. God has set out our course; we cannot dispute with God; and no one but God "knows what is good for mortals while they live the few days of their vain life" (6:12).

After a series of proverbs about what is better, the Teacher concludes with two admonitions: First, "Consider the work of God": we cannot make straight what he has made crooked (7:13). Second, "In the day of prosperity be joyful, and in the day of adversity consider; God has made the one as well as the other" (7:14). God has made both good and bad times.

Textual Theme and Goal

The wide array of ideas in this passage makes it difficult to discern a single focus. Do we concentrate on the opening that God has predetermined whatever comes to be (6:10) — an idea that is reiterated in the conclusion that God has made good as well as bad times (7:14)? Or do we highlight the idea that we cannot tell "what will be after us under the sun" — an idea set forth at the end of the introduction (6:12) and at the end of the passage (7:14)? Or, turning to the proverbs, do we highlight death (7:1-4) or wisdom and folly (7:4-12)?[25] Or can we combine these two topics under one theme such as, "We should be wise in times of suffering"?[26] Or do we select as our theme the important conclusion, "In the day of prosperity be joyful, and in the day of adversity consider that God has made the one as well as the other" (7:14)?

In trying to discover the theme of a preaching text, we have to look for the golden thread that runs through the entire passage. The Teacher frequently signals this thread by repeating a keyword. In our passage, we have seen, the keyword used most often is *ṭôb* (good/better). The introduction raises a key question: "Who knows what is *good* for mortals?" The expected answer is: No one, because humans do not know "what will be after them under the sun" (6:12). Still, some things in life are "more good" than others — an idea the Teacher demonstrates with his "better than" proverbs. And he concludes with the advice to be joyful in times of prosperity and to consider in times of adversity that

---

25. Longman, *Book of Ecclesiastes*, 179, states, "Two themes dominate vv 1-12 and unify the section: death (vv 1b, 2, 4, and perhaps 8) and wisdom and folly (vv 4, 5, 6, 7, 9, 10, 11, 12)."

26. Leupold, *Exposition of Ecclesiastes*, 145 and 156, follows this direction with his headings, "Counsel for Days of Suffering" and "Wisdom, a Fine Regulative in Days of Suffering." On p. 157 he mentions especially "mourning" (7:2), "a situation that causes men to grow angry" (7:9), deeming the past better (7:10), God making things "crooked" (7:13) and advice for "the day of adversity" (7:14). He could have added "death" (7:1), "sorrow" (7:3), "sadness" (7:4), "house of mourning" (7:2, 4), "rebuke" (7:5), "oppression" (7:7), "bribe" (7:7), and we don't know what the future holds (6:12; 7:14).

God has also made these times, "so that mortals may not find out anything that will come after them" (7:14). We can capture this line of thought in the following theme: "Since God has sovereignly set the times of prosperity and the times of adversity, and since humans do not know what the future holds, people should not only be joyful in times of prosperity but also look for the good in times of adversity." But this is a dual theme, reflecting as it does the dual conclusion, "In the day of prosperity be joyful, and in the day of adversity consider that God has made the one as well as the other" (7:14). The Teacher earlier focused on being joyful and will do so again, but in this passage he concentrates on the time of adversity and suffering: humans live but a few days, their days are like "a passing shadow," "vain [brief] life," "death," "house of mourning," "sorrow," "rebuke," "oppression," "bribe," impatience, "anger," "former days better," no one "can make straight what God has made crooked," and "the day of adversity." Therefore we can formulate the theme as follows: "Since God has sovereignly set the times of prosperity and the times of adversity, and since humans do not know what the future holds, in the day of adversity people should look for what is relatively good." But this theme formulation is still too complex to provide good focus for the sermon. We can arrive at a better focus by simplifying the theme as follows: *Since God has sovereignly set the times, in times of adversity people should look for what is relatively good.*

Since the Teacher's literary forms are mainly instruction and proverbs, his goal is to *teach* something; more specifically, *to encourage suffering people to show their trust in the sovereign God by looking for what is relatively good in times of adversity.*

Ways to Preach Christ

Usually the strongest bridge to Jesus Christ in the New Testament is to carry forward the author's theme. So the main question is, Did Jesus also teach people to look for some good in times of adversity? Or did Jesus demonstrate this attitude in his life on earth? Since the passage has neither a promise of Christ nor a type of Christ, we shall investigate the ways of redemptive-historical progression, analogy, longitudinal themes, New Testament references, and contrast.

Redemptive-Historical Progression

In this passage the Teacher frequently mentions death. He did not know, as we do after Jesus' resurrection and the teachings of the New Testament, that people live on beyond death. William Brown writes, "Qohelet reminds the church that faith in Christ entails facing the fulness of death. . . . The hope of the resurrection does not rest on the denial of death, but on the full acceptance of death's all-encompassing scope. As death marks the beginning of wisdom's journey for Qohelet, so death in baptism marks the beginning of the journey of faith."[27]

Loader uses redemptive-historical progression by ascribing to the Teacher the concept of a capricious God. He writes, "The Preacher holds his reader captive in the tense domain of futility: man is simply prey to the arbitrariness of God. The solution . . . lies in Christ. By his coming he has demonstrated that there is more to be known of God than there was in the time of the Preacher; that God is not just a capricious apportioner of human fortune; that everything that happens, though subject to his rule, is by no means always his will. . . . We can now still be happy in days of prosperity, but in times of adversity we need no longer, in resignation, lie down before the superior Power. Although he is in heaven and we are on earth (5:2), there is now a way open to him (John 14:6). Therefore there is now a wisdom and there are now riches whose value is absolute and not relative (see 1 Cor 1:30; Eph 1:17-18)."[28]

Analogy

The Old Testament Teacher discerns some relative good in events we usually think of as bad: death, sorrow, the house of mourning, rebuke, the day of adversity. Remarkably, in Jesus' teachings we find a similar emphasis on good aspects of suffering on this earth. In the Beatitudes Jesus called those who suffer "blessed":

> Blessed are those who *mourn,* for they will be comforted.
> Blessed are those who are *persecuted* for righteousness' sake,
>   for theirs is the kingdom of heaven (Matt 5:4, 10).

> Blessed are you who are *poor,*
>   for yours is the kingdom of God.
> Blessed are you who are *hungry* now,
>   for you will be filled.
> Blessed are you who *weep* now,
>   for you will laugh.

27. Brown, *Ecclesiastes,* 75.

28. Loader, *Ecclesiastes,* 86. Because of the continuity between the Old and the New Testaments of seeing a relative good in suffering (see "Longitudinal Themes" below) and because I disagree with Loader's premise that makes him preach against the Teacher's text, in the "Sermon Exposition" we shall not use his moves to Christ.

Blessed are you when people *hate* you, and when they exclude you, revile you, and defame you on account of the Son of Man. Rejoice in that day and leap for joy, for surely your reward is great in heaven (Luke 6:20-23).

Longitudinal Themes

We can trace from the Old Testament to the New Testament the teaching that there is some good in suffering. The Old Testament sees suffering mostly as God's punishment. Human disobedience resulted in Adam and Eve being driven out of Paradise, pain in childbearing, toil to eke out a living, and death (Gen 3:16-19, 23). When Israel sinned against God, God punished them with suffering: the sword and a plague (Exod 32:28, 35). If Israel continued to disobey, God warned, he would punish them with terror, consumption and fever, famine, defeat by enemies, wild animals, and pestilence, and by making the land desolate and the cities waste (Lev 26:14-33). Suffering was by and large a negative experience for Israel. Yet there was also good in their suffering. God used it to bring Israel back into God's fold (see, e.g., Judg 3:7-30 and Isa 40:1-2). The Teacher also argues that there is a positive aspect to human suffering: people can look for what is relatively good in times of adversity.

The New Testament continues this theme. Jesus calls those who suffer "blessed," but he provides a different reason from that of the Old Testament Teacher. Jesus tends to point to the future that awaits, "Blessed are those who mourn, for they *will be* comforted" (see the list above). Paul echoes this thought, "I consider that the sufferings of this present time are not worth comparing with the glory about to be revealed to us" (Rom 8:18-19). Elsewhere Paul writes, "We do not lose heart. Even though our outer nature is wasting away, our inner nature is being renewed day by day. For this slight momentary affliction is preparing us for an eternal weight of glory beyond all measure, because we look not at what can be seen but at what cannot be seen; for what can be seen is temporary, but what cannot be seen is eternal" (2 Cor 4:16-18).

Peter similarly encourages suffering Christians, "But rejoice insofar as you are sharing Christ's sufferings, so that you may also be glad and shout for joy when his glory is revealed" (1 Pet 4:13). And John passes on the good news, "'Blessed are the dead who from now on die in the Lord.' 'Yes,' says the Spirit, 'they will rest from their labors, for their deeds follow them'" (Rev 14:13-14).

New Testament References

The appendix of the Greek New Testament lists Ecclesiastes 7:9 with a reference to James 1:19, "You must understand this, my beloved: let everyone be quick to listen, slow to speak, slow to anger." This reference, of course, refers to a single verse rather than the theme of the passage. On the theme of finding good in suffering, we can consider James 1:2-5, "My brothers and sisters, whenever you face trials of any kind, consider it nothing but joy, because you know that the testing of your faith produces endurance; and let endurance have its full effect, so that you may be mature and complete, lacking in nothing. If any of you is lacking in wisdom, ask God, who gives to all generously and ungrudgingly, and it will be given you."

Contrast

Under redemptive-historical progression and longitudinal themes above we noted several contrasts in details. Another contrast is that the Teacher instructs his readers to look for some good in times of adversity in part because they do not know what the future holds. By contrast, Jesus and the New Testament teaches us to look for the good in adversity because of what our future holds: the perfect kingdom of God.

Sermon Theme and Goal

We formulated the Teacher's theme as follows, "Since God has sovereignly set the times, in times of adversity people should look for what is relatively good." Although Jesus and the New Testament changes the reason for looking for what is good in suffering (see "Contrast" above), they do not contradict the Teacher's theme. We can, therefore, adopt the Teacher's theme as the sermon theme: *Since God has sovereignly set the times, in times of adversity people should look for what is relatively good.*[29]

We formulated the Teacher's goal as, "to encourage suffering people to show their trust in the sovereign God by looking for what is relatively good in times of adversity." The sermon goal can be identical: *to encourage suffering people to show their trust in the sovereign God by looking for what is relatively good in times of adversity.* This goal points to the need addressed: people fail to trust God sufficiently to see any good in adversity.

29. We should avoid the temptation of toning down the point of the Teacher by bringing in other considerations such as: it is Satan who brings about suffering; lamenting to God is proper (see the many Psalms of lament); in answer to prayer, God can change his mind (e.g., Hezekiah's receiving another fifteen years [2 Kings 20:1-6]). These are all worthy themes for other sermons. But in *this* sermon we should maintain the Teacher's sharp point, which is a legitimate strand of thought in the Old as well as the New Testament.

Sermon Exposition

The introduction of the sermon can illustrate the need addressed. One can briefly tell the story of a person who suffered much and thought of it as a totally negative experience. For example, one can retell the story of Job losing all his possessions and all his children in one day and cursing the day of his birth (Job 3:1-10). But this story deals with such extreme suffering that people may not be able to relate. So it may be better to tell a story about contemporary suffering — as long as the introduction sets the tension between the negative way in which we tend to experience suffering and the surprising message of the Teacher and of Jesus.

The Teacher begins his message in chapter 6:10, "Whatever has come to be has already been named,[30] and it is known what human beings are." What does he mean by, "Whatever has come to be has already been *named*"? He is thinking of God naming things at the creation: Day, Night, Sky, Earth, Seas, and so on. "To 'give the name' to a thing is to make it exist, and hence dependent."[31] "Whatever has come to be has already been named." In other words, whatever happens in the present was already predetermined by God in the past.

The Teacher continues, "and it is known what human beings are." God knows what human beings are: he created them, he named them "Adam," that is, from *'adāmāh,* from the ground (Gen 2:7). As the Psalmist writes, "He knows how we were made; he remembers that we are dust" (Ps 103:14). God knows that humans are weak and finite. God himself declared, "You are dust, and to dust you shall return" (Gen 3:19).

Humans are so weak, the Teacher continues, "that they are not able to dispute with those who are stronger." The Hebrew here is literally, "*one* who is stronger." So the TNIV translates, "No one can contend with some*one* who is stronger." The stronger one is God. God is the powerful Creator of the universe; he called all things into being; he named them; he called humans into being; he named them "earthlings," made from earth. Mere earthlings cannot dispute with the Creator of the universe.

Job found that out. After he lost all his possessions and all his children, he tried to dispute with God.[32] But in the end, Job had to "repent in dust and ashes" (Job 42:6). Even when they suffer greatly, mere creatures cannot dispute with God. Isaiah records the words of the LORD, "Woe to you who strive with your Maker, earthen vessels with the potter! Does the clay say to the one who fashions it, 'What are you making'? or 'Your work has no handles'?" (Isa 45:9).

30. Cf. 3:15, "That which is, already has been."
31. Murphy, *Ecclesiastes,* 58. Cf. Longman, *Book of Ecclesiastes,* 177, "In the OT, naming captures the essential nature of a person or thing. Thus, to name is to have knowledge and control of something or someone."
32. See Job 9:32-35; 13:20-28; 16:18-22; 23; 31:35-37.

Paul echoes this sentiment in Romans 9:20, "But who indeed are you, a human being, to argue with God? Will what is molded say to the one who molds it, 'Why have you made me like this?'" Mere creatures are not able to dispute with their Creator.

The Teacher shows the futility of disputing with God in verse 11, "The more words, the more vanity, so how is one the better?" Arguing with God does not help, for God has sovereignly set the times: "a time to be born, and a time to die; . . . a time to weep, and a time to laugh; a time to mourn, and a time to dance" (Eccl 3:2, 4). The more words one uses in arguing with God, the more vanity, that is, the more futility. It is wasted breath. "So how is one better?" One is not better off at all. There is no profit or gain[33] in disputing with God.[34]

"For," the Teacher continues in verse 12, "For who knows what is good for mortals while they live the few days of their vain life, which they pass like a shadow?" Human beings live but a few days on this earth. Their life is "vain," literally "breath": it is short-lived like the breath you see on a winter day. Now you see it, now you don't. That's how quickly our life speeds by. We are also said to "pass like a shadow." Psalm 144:4 uses the same image: human beings "are like a breath; their days are like a passing shadow." A shadow can move very quickly, "like a shadow of a bird in flight."[35] It's here one minute and gone the next. A shadow also lacks substance. That's our life on earth: it passes like a shadow: swiftly, leaving no evidence of ever having impacted the earth.

The key question the Teacher raises is this: "Who knows what is good for mortals?" The expected answer is, No one but God. No human being knows what is good for people. Since they do not know what is good for them, it is implied, they must accept submissively what God sends them.[36]

"For who can tell them what will be after them under the sun?" This is the second rhetorical question. The expected answer again is, No one can tell human beings what will be after them. The Teacher means to say that no one can tell us what tomorrow will bring.[37] Will it be a day of prosperity? Or a day of adversity? Will we be happy? Or will we be mourning? We just don't know. The future is

---

33. *Yitrôn,* as in 1:3 and 3:9, "what gain."

34. "The quest for eloquence fails for two reasons: first, echoing a theme he has already emphasized more than once, the predetermination and recurrence of all events, and second, the fact that in the last resort power rests in God, not in the human tongue." Crenshaw, *Ecclesiastes,* 131.

35. Fox, *Ecclesiastes,* 43, with a reference to Rashi.

36. Whybray, *Ecclesiastes,* 111.

37. "'*aḥărāyw* means 'afterwards,' 'in the future,' here with reference to future events in one's lifetime. . . . Moreover, in 7:14b, which reiterates 6:12b, the future in question is clearly within this life." Fox, *Qohelet,* 225. Cf. Murphy, *Ecclesiastes,* 59, "Qohelet does not have in mind the mystery of 'life after death,' but rather how things will turn out while one still lives on earth. He is speaking of what will come 'under the sun.'"

hidden. We don't know what is good for us, and we don't know what the future holds. If the Teacher were a pessimist, he would now give up in despair.

But the Teacher is not a pessimist. He has graphically sketched our predicament in order to show us that *wisdom* can detect some good even in times of adversity. He gives us a series of proverbs that repeat nine times the word "good" or "more good," that is, "better." He begins in chapter 7:1, "A good name is better than precious ointment, and the day of death, than the day of birth." That's a startling statement! We can understand that "a good name is better than precious ointment."[38] You can buy precious ointment while you cannot buy a good name. But we don't immediately understand that the day of death is better than the day of birth. To us it seems that the day of death is filled with sadness while the day of birth is filled with joy. Most of us would say that the day of birth is better than the day of death. But the Teacher flips this around: the day of death is better than the day of birth. Why?

The Teacher said something like this also in chapter 4. There he reflected on all the oppressions practiced on this earth and looked at "the tears of the oppressed — with no one to comfort them!" He concluded, "I thought the dead who have already died, more fortunate than the living, who are still alive" (4:1-2). The dead are better off than the living because they no longer have to witness the injustice, pain, and tears we see on this earth. In a similar fashion he says in this passage that the day of death is better than the day of birth. The day of birth is the beginning of a lifetime of witnessing the tears of the oppressed and of being oppressed oneself. But the day of death marks the end of witnessing the suffering of others and of one's own suffering.[39]

In verse 2 the Teacher continues this theme of death: "It is better to go to the house of mourning than to go to the house of feasting." Is it really better to go to a funeral home than to a wedding reception? Few of us would say so. Why does the Teacher again reverse our likes and dislikes? This time he gives the reason why he thinks "it is better to go to the house of mourning." "For," he writes, "this [i.e., death] is the end of everyone, and the living will lay it to heart."

We all know that, unless the Lord returns first, we will die some day. But we don't like to think about it. We try to avoid this morbid topic. We would rather live in denial. But when we go to a funeral home, we can no longer deny the reality of death. We are reminded: Yes, I, too, will die one day. "And the living will lay it to heart," that is to say, they will keep it in mind and live their days accordingly.[40]

38. Cf. Proverbs 22:1, "A good name is to be chosen rather than great riches."

39. Another explanation is "that our reputation [name] is not secure until we die and can no longer blemish it (Rashbam)." Fox, *Ecclesiastes*, 43.

40. "Death as human destiny should be deeply rooted in the inner person and be grasped by mind, emotions, and will. . . . Recognizing the brevity and preciousness of life, we should live life *seriously*." Provan, *Ecclesiastes*, 139.

William Brown writes, "The inescapable reality of death is for . . . [the Teacher] the point of departure for life (v. 2b). Death orients the self toward authentic, rather than false, living. The end of life is, as it were, the ground of being in . . . [his] ethic of finitude. Death must be accepted fully, the sage contends, in order to live the good life, however minimal it may seem."[41]

Some Eastern monasteries not only bury their deceased monks but retrieve their bones later and display them in a prominent place inside the monastery. In fact, some skulls are arranged so that living monks and visitors can touch them. The experience of touching these skulls is not at all morbid but a sober reminder that *our* earthly lives will also end one day. The Psalmist taught Israel to pray, "So teach us to count our days that we may gain a heart of wisdom" (Ps 90:12). It makes sense, therefore, to say that it is better to go to a funeral home than to a wedding reception. In the funeral home we will be confronted with the reality of death, which can lead to the wisdom of counting each day and not wasting it. In times of adversity, the Teacher points out, there is still some good. We can learn to treasure each day.

In verse 3 he adds, "Sorrow is better than laughter." Again he reverses our likes and dislikes, for we would prefer laughter to sorrow. But by "laughter" he does not mean here the enjoyment he recommends throughout his book. By "laughter" he means "to behave in a frivolous manner."[42] Earlier he exclaimed, "I said of laughter, 'It is mad,' and of pleasure, 'What use is it?'" (2:2). So here he argues that "sorrow is better than laughter, for," and this is his reason, "by sadness of countenance the heart is made glad."

We probably wonder, How in the world does sadness of countenance make the heart glad? "Sadness of countenance" is found in funeral homes because people are confronted with the reality of death. But "it is better to go to the house of mourning" (7:2) because the reality of death will teach people to treasure their days. So sadness of countenance makes the heart glad because it enables us to seize each day and live it to the full.

The New Testament, similarly, sees no contradiction between sadness of countenance and a glad heart. Paul writes that he is "sorrowful, yet always rejoicing" (2 Cor 6:10). Jesus calls those who mourn and those who weep, "blessed." He proclaims, "Blessed are those who mourn, for they will be comforted" (Matt 5:4), and "Blessed are you who weep now, for you will laugh" (Luke 6:21). And James writes, "My brothers and sisters, whenever you face *trials* of any kind, consider it nothing but *joy,* because you know that the testing of your faith produces endur-

41. Brown, *Ecclesiastes,* 73,

42. Fox, *Ecclesiastes,* 44. Cf. Ogden, *Qoheleth,* 103, "The laughter envisioned is presumably a general term for empty hilarity (cf. Prov 14:13), as distinct from the profound enjoyment *(śmḥ)* which Qohelet advocates throughout."

ance; and let endurance have its full effect, so that you may be mature and complete, lacking in nothing. If any of you is lacking in wisdom, ask God, who gives to all generously and ungrudgingly, and it will be given you" (Jas 1:2-5; cf. Rom 5:3-4).

In verse 2 the Teacher said, "It is better to go to the house of mourning than to go to the house of feasting." In verse 4 he comes back to these two houses: "The heart of the wise is in the house of mourning; but the heart of fools is in the house of mirth." The "heart" refers to the center of a human being. Proverbs says, From the heart "flow the springs of life" (Prov 4:23). "The 'heart' represents the seat of intelligence and volition (cf. 1:13, 17; 2:3; 8:9, 16)."[43] Now the Teacher claims that "the heart of the wise is in the house of mourning." The house of mourning has become a schoolhouse for learning about the essence of life. The wise live their lives with the reality of their death in mind. Fools, by contrast, seek to avoid thinking about their death. Therefore "the heart of fools is in the house of mirth." Perhaps the wild parties in the house of mirth will drown out thoughts of death.

In these first four verses of chapter 7, the Teacher has focused on the very topic most people seek to avoid: death! According to Genesis 3, death is God's punishment for human disobedience: "You are dust, and to dust you shall return" (Gen 3:19). Death is tragic. Death is the climax of human suffering. But the Teacher shows that the wise can detect some good even in death: "the day of death" is better than "the day of birth"; "it is better to go to the house of mourning than to go to the house of feasting"; "sorrow is better than laughter"; and "the heart of the wise is in the house of mourning."

In verse 5 the Teacher continues to contrast the wise and fools. "It is better to hear the rebuke of the wise than to hear the song of fools." "The rebuke of the wise" is "'constructive criticism,' whose purpose is to correct a behaviour pattern that is morally questionable, or detrimental."[44] As Proverbs 12:1 states, "Whoever loves discipline loves knowledge, but those who hate to be rebuked are stupid."[45] So one can learn from "the rebuke of the wise." But what does one learn from "the song of fools"? These are the songs that are sung in the house of mirth.[46] Think back to the songs we have heard at parties. It is not likely that we learned anything important.[47]

---

43. Brown, *Ecclesiastes*, 74. Cf. Raymond C. Van Leeuwen's "Excursus: The 'Heart' in the Old Testament," in *The New Interpreter's Bible Old Testament Survey* (Nashville: Abingdon, 2005), 244-45.

44. Ogden, *Qoheleth*, 104.

45. Cf. Proverbs 13:1, 18; 17:10.

46. "It has been maintained that *the song of fools* means 'the song of praise and flattery,' 'the compliments showed by fools' (cf. GNB, NEB). But since the word *song (šîr)* is always used for quite literal songs (more than seventy times in the Old Testament), it is more likely that the reference is to the songs of jubilation in the house of festivity." Eaton, *Ecclesiastes*, 110.

47. "In the ancient world, as in the modern world, people sang songs to escape the prob-

The Teacher is not impressed by the songs of fools, nor by their laughter. In verse 6 he paints a scathing picture of the laughter of fools. "For like the crackling of thorns under a pot, so is the laughter of fools." "Thorns were rapidly burning, easily extinguishable fuel in the ancient world (Ps 58:9). Thus fools' laughter is a sudden flame, a fine display of sparks, accompanied by plenty of noise, but soon spent and easily put out."[48] The Teacher judges that this laughter[49] "also is vanity." It is short-lived, like the flame of thorns, and useless.[50]

But the wise are not safe either. Verse 7, "Surely oppression makes the *wise* foolish, and a bribe corrupts the heart." The Teacher mentions specifically oppression — or "extortion" (TNIV) — and bribery. In Chapter 4 he raised the issue of oppression in the context of people toiling out of "envy of one another." He came to the conclusion that it was "vanity and a chasing after wind" (4:4). Here he sees oppression or extortion as such a great temptation for humans that even the wise might engage in this evil pursuit and become fools.[51] For even wise people are tempted by riches. They also long for more possessions. To increase their wealth they might even stoop to extortion and bribery.[52] But the Teacher rebukes those who fall for this temptation, "Surely oppression [extortion] makes the wise foolish, and a bribe corrupts the heart."[53]

---

lems of life. But most of the time these popular songs do not help a person to face reality; they are hollow, both spiritually and morally, and have nothing to offer except a bit of momentary entertainment." Goldberg, *Ecclesiastes*, 90.

48. Eaton, *Ecclesiastes*, 110. "The pun 'Like the sound of *sîrîm* (thorns) under the *sîr* (pot, cauldron)' is caught by Moffatt's 'Like nettles crackling under kettles.'" Ibid.

49. Because the antecedent of "this" is not clear, some commentators extend the judgment of "vanity" back to the whole argument and even forward to what follows. See Fox, *A Time to Tear Down*, 253, for the various possibilities.

50. "Song and laughter can be enjoyable and beneficial. It is the fact that it stems from the lips of a fool that denies it value." Ogden, *Qoheleth*, 104.

51. The question here is whether the wise are *causing* oppression or *suffering from* oppression. Commentators are divided on this issue (see the two positions in n. 53 below). I choose for the former since suffering from oppression does not necessarily make the wise foolish but causing oppression certainly makes them foolish.

52. "The wise person who joins the insane race after possessions, compromising integrity in the process, becomes just as much a fool as the wise person who joins with fools in empty laughter." Provan, *Ecclesiastes*, 141.

53. "Extortion requires payment from someone in return for silence, and bribery is the receipt of money from someone in return for some desired action. The former makes the wise person a fool by surrendering control of life to another; the latter clouds one's judgment by introducing bias." Longman, *Book of Ecclesiastes*, 187. Taking a different tack, Eaton, *Ecclesiastes*, 111, notes: "Verses 1-14 . . . deal with the suffering of oppression, not its exercise. It is better, therefore, to see here not synonymous parallelism (expressing the same thought) but synthetic parallelism (taking the thought further). The first line, then, speaks of a pressure which oppression may exert on the faithful; the second goes further and provides an example of how a wise man may be 'made mad' by another kind of folly."

Because of the danger that even the wise can be sidetracked in life, the Teacher continues in verse 8, "Better is the end of a thing than its beginning" (cf. 7:1). "The end of a thing" here should be understood as the "outcome," the "end product."[54] In English we have a similar saying: "All's well that ends well."[55]

The Teacher adds in verse 8, "The patient in spirit are better than the proud[56] in spirit." The patient in spirit are in it for the long haul. They will avoid knee-jerk reactions. They are willing to withhold judgment until they see "the end of a thing."[57] When adversity strikes, they will bear it patiently and wait for the outcome.

The Teacher, therefore, advises in verse 9, "Do not be quick to anger, for anger lodges in the bosom of fools." Fools are not patient. They quickly fly off the handle. When things do not go their way, they explode with anger. Proverbs 12:16 says, "Fools show their anger at once, but the prudent ignore an insult."[58] In the New Testament, James alludes to this warning from the Teacher. James writes, "You must understand this, my beloved: let everyone be quick to listen, slow to speak, *slow to anger*" (1:19). Jesus also warns against angry outbursts: "I say to you that if you are angry with a brother or sister, you will be liable to judgment . . . ; and if you say, 'You fool,' you will be liable to the hell of fire" (Matt 5:22). "Anger," says the Teacher, "lodges in the bosom of fools." "The fool coddles his vexation [in his bosom], nurtures it, lets it grow, while all along, of course, it is gnawing at him."[59] Fools nourish their anger until it explodes.

The Teacher refers to another instance of impatience in verse 10: "Do not say, 'Why were the former days better than these?' For it is not from wisdom that you ask this." When we experience "the day of adversity" (v. 14), when we fall upon hard times, it is so easy for us to complain, "Why were the former days better than these?" But in doing so we express our dissatisfaction with the present. We are impatient, not willing to wait to see how things turn out in the end. The Teacher instructs us that we should not ask this question, "for," he says, "it

---

54. Eaton, *Ecclesiastes*, 111.

55. "One cannot know whether a matter will be successful until it has run a full course, for obstacles tend to retard, if not frustrate, informed efforts." Crenshaw, *Ecclesiastes*, 136.

56. The Hebrew reads literally, "Better a long spirit than a tall spirit." Fox, *Ecclesiastes*, 46. Longman, *Book of Ecclesiastes*, 187, speaks of "length of spirit" and "height of spirit." To bring this to expression, he suggests the translation, "Better long patience than soaring pride."

57. "A wise person will not react immediately to circumstances but will take a longer term view, waiting to see the full measure of a matter before deciding how to respond." Provan, *Ecclesiastes*, 141. Cf. Eaton, *Ecclesiastes*, 111, "The proverb implies that times of trial may be purposeful, that they are confined to limited seasons, that the end-product makes them worth while."

58. Cf. Proverbs 14:29, "Whoever is slow to anger has great understanding, but one who has a hasty temper exalts folly."

59. Fox, *Qohelet*, 230.

is not from wisdom that you ask this." "To complain . . . about the degeneracy of the times is to show a lack of patience and self-control which is the mark of a fool rather than of a wise man."[60]

In verses 11 and 12 the Teacher sings the praises of wisdom: "Wisdom is as good as an inheritance, an advantage to those who see the sun." When we hear the word "inheritance," we should think of land. When God gave Israel the promised land, the land was "apportioned for inheritance" (Num 26:53). Each family (except the Levites) received an inheritance of land. This portion of land was to pass on from father to son or daughter and to remain in the family. Even if a family fell upon hard times and was forced to sell their land, they could only sell the crop years remaining till the year of jubilee. For in the "year of jubilee you shall return, every one of you, to your property" (Lev 25:13). The land was a permanent possession.[61] In an agricultural society, land meant food; land meant security; land meant stability. The inheritance of land meant that one could survive times of adversity. So "wisdom is as good as an inheritance, an advantage to those who *see the sun*," that is, an advantage to those who are living. Through wisdom one can survive times of adversity.

The Teacher explains further in verse 12, "For the protection of wisdom is like the protection of money." He compares the protection of wisdom to the protection of money. Money can, to some extent, protect people from hardship. In a time of famine, money can safeguard people from hunger. In a time of unemployment, money can shelter people from losing their homes to foreclosure. So money can protect people to some extent from adversity. Similarly, wisdom can protect people "from the hard realities of life."[62]

But wisdom has an advantage over money. The Teacher adds in verse 12, "and the advantage of knowledge is that wisdom gives life to the one who possesses it." "Wisdom gives *life* to the one who possesses it." Money by itself does not give life. In fact, in chapter 5:17 the Teacher has shown that money by itself leads to eating "in darkness, in much vexation and sickness and resentment." But wisdom gives life. How? "It gives a higher life which cannot be smothered or submerged by the floods of suffering that may surge over" a person.[63]

The Teacher is not talking about eternal life but about life on this earth. For him even this "higher life" will end in death. It will be centuries later when another wise Teacher will teach us about eternal life. Jesus said, "And this is eternal life, that they may know you, the only true God, and Jesus Christ whom you

---

60. Whybray, *Ecclesiastes*, 117.

61. "The permanence of such a possession is emphasized. This treasure abides with a man through all manner of vicissitudes." Leupold, *Exposition of Ecclesiastes*, 158.

62. Longman, *Book of Ecclesiastes*, 190. In n. 65, Longman adds, "This is also supported by the parallel in the following sentence, which states that wisdom *preserves the life of its possessor.*"

63. Leupold, *Exposition of Ecclesiastes*, 159.

have sent" (John 17:3). The life Jesus gives finally overcomes death. Jesus said, "I am the resurrection and the life. Those who believe in me, even though they die, will live, and everyone who lives and believes in me will never die" (John 11:25-26).

But the Old Testament Teacher did not yet have this insight. He struggled with the issue of how we can live a good life on this earth knowing that there is so much suffering and certain death. He has shown that there is still a relative good, even in suffering: "the day of death" is better than "the day of birth"; "it is better to go to the house of mourning than to go to the house of feasting"; "sorrow is better than laughter"; and "the heart of the wise is in the house of mourning." He has stated that "it is better to hear the rebuke of the wise than . . . the song of fools." But he also warned that "oppression makes the wise foolish." He reiterated, "better is the end of a thing than its beginning." This led him to recommend patience, to "not be quick to anger," and not to complain, "Why were the former days better than these?" Finally he has shown the advantage of wisdom: it protects us from the harshness of life; in fact, having gone through the crucible of suffering, wisdom gives a more vigorous form of life.

Now the Teacher is ready to conclude his message. He exhorts us in verse 13, "Consider the work of God; who can make straight what he has made crooked?" "Consider the work of God!" God is the sovereign God who has made all things. Some of these things appear "crooked" to us. In this passage the Teacher has referred to death, mourning, and sorrow. We experience these things as "crooked."[64] But these "crooked things," too, are "the work of God."[65] And no one can make straight what God "has made crooked." It would be the height of arrogance and foolishness for us to try to change the work of God. We have no choice but to take the long view and accept also suffering from the hand of God.

This consideration leads the Teacher to his final advice. Verse 14, "In the day of prosperity be joyful, and in the day of adversity consider; God has made the one as well as the other, so that mortals may not find out anything that will come after them." "In the day of prosperity be joyful!" The Teacher has given this advice before and will do so again. But in this passage he has concentrated on human suffering. What do we do "In the day of adversity"?

---

64. "Verse 13 is speaking not of moral crookedness but of the shapes of things and events which we find awkward but should accept from God. It includes his judgments . . . but also presumably many of life's trials, as the next verse (14) suggests." Kidner, *Time to Mourn*, 68.

65. Cf. Isa 45:7, I form light and create darkness,
        I make weal and create woe;
        I the Lord do all these things.
In writing about "the sufferings of this present time," Paul also acknowledges that it was God who subjected the creation to "futility" (Rom 8:18-20).

His advice is, "Consider: God has made the one as well as the other, so that mortals may not find out anything that will come after them." God has made both the day of prosperity and the day of adversity, but in such a way that we cannot find out what will come after us. We do not know what the future holds, so we certainly cannot control the future. All we can do is to accept prosperity as well as adversity as it comes from the hand of God.[66] We don't know what the future holds. We simply have to trust our God who holds the future.[67]

Paul writes to the Romans, "If God is for us, who is against us? He who did not withhold his own Son, but gave him up for all of us, will he not with him also give us everything else? . . . Who will separate us from the love of Christ? Will hardship, or distress, or persecution, or famine, or nakedness, or peril, or sword? . . . No, *in* all these things we are more than conquerors through him who loved us. For I am convinced that neither death, nor life, . . . nor anything else in all creation, will be able to separate us from the love of God in Christ Jesus our Lord" (Rom 8:31-39).[68] Paul claims that we are more than conquerors not *in spite of* our suffering but *in* our suffering. He explains that this is so because neither death, no matter how tragic, nor life, no matter how difficult, can separate us from the love of God in Christ Jesus our Lord. Since the love of God in Christ is always with us, we can search and find some good even in the day of adversity.

66. "The day of misfortune provokes an awareness that mortals are profoundly limited, irredeemably finite in both knowledge and power. They cannot dispute with the one who is stronger (6:11). . . . Their place is to welcome the good with joy and accept adversity when it comes, both wrought by God. . . . The human subject can only take what comes and no more. To defy the bad in bitter protest, as Job does, only tears the self in anger, Bildad observes (Job 18:4)." Brown, *Ecclesiastes*, 80.

67. "This effect on man is designed by God for the very purpose that man may recognize how little he can do, and how cheerfully he ought to trust God. Such an attitude is the attitude of true wisdom." Leupold, *Exposition of Ecclesiastes*, 162.

68. Written at a time of great suffering, the Heidelberg Catechism of 1563 asks, "How does the knowledge of God's creation and providence help us?" It answers, "We can be *patient* when things go against us, *thankful* when things go well, and for the future we can have good *confidence* in our faithful God and Father that nothing will separate us from his love" (Q. & A. 28).

CHAPTER 10

How to Act in a Paradoxical World

Ecclesiastes 7:15-29

Do not be too righteous. . . .
Do not be too wicked.

(Eccl 7:16-17)

This is one of those passages that sets preachers to pacing in their studies, wringing their hands: What does it mean? How do we preach it? The temptation will be great to either skip over it or to preach on just a few verses. Roland Murphy states, "It is hard to be satisfied with any commentary on this section [7:15-24]; it is very difficult to understand." And regarding 7:25-29 he adds, "This is one of the more difficult and perhaps one of the more notorious passages in Ecclesiastes."[1] Yet it is an extremely relevant passage that deals with some of the most perplexing questions we have: Why do some good people die young while some criminals live to a ripe old age? Therefore it will be worth our while, and that of the church, to put some hard work into understanding and proclaiming the message God sends us in this word.

The challenges for preaching this passage begin with the translation of some Hebrew words. Take, for example, 7:18, which the NRSV translates as, "It is good that you should take hold of the one, without letting go of the other; for the one who fears God *shall succeed with both.*" The TNIV translates the last part, "Whoever fears God *will avoid all extremes,*" with a footnote, "Or *will follow them both.*" The NASB is different again: "For the one who fears God *comes forth with both of them.*" What's a preacher to do when committees of expert translators disagree substantially? Moreover, it is not at all clear to what "the one" and "the other" ("both") refer. Is it the "righteous" of verse 16 and the

---

1. Murphy, *Ecclesiastes,* 72 and 77.

"wicked" of verse 17? Does the Teacher mean to say that we should follow both righteousness and wickedness? And this is only one of several ambiguities. What does the Teacher mean with his first recommendation, "Do not be too righteous" (v. 16)? And how are we to understand verse 28, "One man among a thousand I found, but a woman among all these I have not found."[2]

Aside from difficulties in translation and interpretation, it will be a challenge to detect the coherence of this passage[3] and to formulate a single theme that encompasses the various ideas. Also, in preaching this passage, preachers may be tempted to drift away from the theme when they try to apply it to the present situation, either charging the Teacher with male chauvinism or seeking to defend him from this charge.

Text and Context

Commentators are not agreed on the boundaries of this unit. Although most of them agree that a new unit starts at 7:15,[4] they disagree on where it ends. Fox writes, "Most commentators (including Delitzsch, Barton, Podechard, Gordis, and Zimmerli) close this unit at v. 29, others at 8:1 (Hertzberg, Galling, Lauha, Ellermeier, et al.)."[5] After recounting various possibilities, Murphy concludes, "There is simply no certain solution. . . . Our translation ends with 7:29 because of the occurrence of the telling phrase 'find out.'"[6] We shall select as our preaching text 7:15-29 not only because "find out" are the usual concluding words in this section of Ecclesiastes but also because verse 29 has a similar reference to what "God made," as did the conclusion of the prior unit (v. 14).[7]

As to the context, the prior unit ended with, "consider; God has made the one [the day of prosperity] as well as the other [the day of adversity]" (7:14). The present unit begins in 7:15 with the statement that the Teacher has seen both adversity (early death) and prosperity (long life). The Teacher struggles

2. "The statement is a notorious crux for the interpreter. It is difficult to explain it as anything other than a misogynistic remark, although some scholars have proffered nonderogatory interpretations or insisted that Qohelet is quoting a well-known attitude only to reject it." Seow, *Ecclesiastes*, 273.

3. Fox, *Ecclesiastes*, 49, writes concerning 7:19, "This verse disrupts the connection between verse 18 and 20. It makes better sense after verse 12. It perhaps belonged there originally and should be read in that context (Ginsberg)."

4. "This verse is taken by almost all the commentators to be the beginning of a new section: 7:15-22." Whybray, *Ecclesiastes*, 119.

5. Fox, *Qohelet*, 237.

6. Murphy, *Ecclesiastes*, 75.

7. Moreover, to finish the unit with the question of 8:1a makes for a weak ending. For reasons for including 8:1 with the following literary unit, see pp. 201-2 below.

with this paradox: while God promised that those who keep his law will prolong their life (e.g., Exod 20:12), some righteous people die young and some wicked people "prolong their life."[8] He will return to this enigma in chapter 8:12-14. He assures his readers in 7:18 that "one who fears God shall succeed with both." Earlier he mentioned the fear of God in 3:14 and 5:7, and he will do so again in 8:12-13, while an editor will highlight it in 12:13. His praise of the strength of wisdom (7:19) anticipates the anecdote about the poor wise man (9:13-18). He also states that he has "tested by wisdom" (7:23) — a point he made earlier in 1:13 and 2:3 and will make again in 8:16. But his testing by wisdom results in failure because "what is, is far off, and deep, very deep" (7:24) — a point similar to that made in 7:14c.

Literary Features

Although some of the literary forms are hard to classify, the Teacher uses a rich variety of forms in this passage. The "I have seen" in 7:15 indicates that the passage begins with a reflection. The reflection contains an observation that some righteous people perish while some wicked people prolong their life (v. 15b). This observation, which is a paradox,[9] is followed by admonitions not to be too righteous and not to be too wicked, each concluded with a rhetorical question (vv. 16 and 17). Verse 18 is an instruction to take hold of both. Verse 19 is probably a proverb about wisdom, and verse 20 another about sinning. Verse 21 is an instruction not to give heed to everything people say, followed by "the motive" (vv. 21b-22).[10] Verses 23 to 24 probably form another reflection, this one about the failure of wisdom to understand reality. Verse 25 follows up with another reflection ("I turned my mind") about searching out "the sum of things, and to know that wickedness is folly." He found several things: he "found more bitter than death the woman who is a trap" (v. 26), but he could not find "the sum" (vv. 27-28). He also found (proverb) "one man among a thousand" but "a woman among all these I have not found" (v. 28). His conclusion is that God made human beings upright but that they strayed (v. 29).

The Teacher uses A-B-C A′ B′ C′ parallelism in verses 16 and 17:

v. 16	v. 17
Do not be too righteous,	Do not be too wicked,
and do not act too wise;	and do not be a fool;
why should you destroy yourself?	why should you die before your time?

8. For other biblical authors struggling with this paradox, see Psalm 73 and Job 21.

9. Murphy, *Wisdom Literature*, 141.

10. See Murphy, *Ecclesiastes*, 69.

At the same time he uses synonymous parallelism in verse 16a, b, which equates "righteous" and "wise," and in verse 17a, b, which equates "wicked" and "fool." The Teacher probably uses hyperbole in verse 19, "Wisdom gives strength to the wise more than ten rulers that are in a city";[11] and again in verse 28, "One man among a thousand I found, but a woman among all these I have not found." Hyperbole means, of course, that these statements should not be understood literally but as purposeful exaggeration.

Repetition of keywords may be important for detecting the theme of this passage. The noun *ḥokmâ*, is found three times as "wisdom" (vv. 19, 23, and 25), and the same root twice as "wise" (vv. 19, 23). The verb *(lō) māṣā*, "(not) find out," is repeated eight times in the second half of this passage (vv. 24, 26, 27 [2x], 28 [3x], 29). The word *ḥešbôn*, is found twice as "sum of things" (vv. 25, 27) and once *(ḥiššĕbōnôt)* as "schemes" (v. 29).

Textual Structure

Although it is difficult to detect logical coherence, the literary features will help us outline the structure of this passage.

I. Reflection on a paradox concluded with an instruction (vv. 15-18)
   A. Observation:
      there are righteous people who perish
         and there are wicked people who prolong their life (v. 15)
   B. Parallel admonitions (vv. 16, 17):
      1. Do not be too righteous (v. 16a, b)
         and do not act too wise;
        a. Reason: why should you destroy yourself? (v. 16c)
      2. Do not be too wicked (v. 17a, b)
         and do not be a fool;
        a. Reason: why should you die before your time? (v. 17c)
   C. Instruction: It is good that you should take hold of both (v. 18a)
      1. Reason: for the one who fears God shall succeed with both (v. 18b)
II. Proverbs about wisdom and sinning concluded with an instruction (vv. 19-22)
   A. Proverb: Wisdom gives strength to the wise (v. 19)
         more than ten rulers in a city
   B. Proverb: There is no one on earth so righteous as to do good (v. 20)
         without ever sinning

11. Whybray, *Ecclesiastes*, 122, compares it with 1 Samuel 1:8, "Am I not more to you than ten sons?"

   C. Instruction: Do not give heed to everything that people say (v. 21a)
     1. Reason: or you may hear your servant cursing you (v. 21b)
     2. Reason: for *(kî)* you know that many times you have cursed others (v. 22)
III. Reflection on using wisdom to understand reality (vv. 23-24)
   A. He said, "I will be wise" (v. 23a)
   B. Conclusion: wisdom was far from him (v. 23b)
   C. The reasons for his failure:
     1. That which is (paradoxical reality), is far off (v. 24a)
     2. It is deep, very deep (v. 24b)
     3. No one can find it out (v. 24c)
IV. Reflection on seeking to understand wisdom, the sum of things, and folly (vv. 25-29)
   A. He turned his mind to search out wisdom and the sum of things (v. 25)
       and to know that wickedness is folly and that foolishness is madness
   B. What he found and did not find:
     1. He found more bitter than death the woman who is a trap (v. 26a)
       a. whose heart is snares and nets (v. 26b)
       b. whose hands are fetters (v. 26c)
       c. one who pleases God escapes her (v. 26d)
         but the sinner is taken by her (v. 26e)
     2. He did not find the sum of things (vv. 27-28a)
     3. He found one man among a thousand (v. 28b)
       but a woman among all these he did not find (v. 28c)
     4. This alone is what he found (v. 29a):
       a. God made human beings straightforward (v. 29b)
         but they have devised many schemes (v. 29c)

Theocentric Interpretation

In this passage, the Teacher mentions God several times. Following his instruction to "take hold of the one, without letting go of the other," he adds the motive clause, "for one who fears God shall succeed with both" (v. 18). He also assures his readers that the "one who pleases God escapes" the stalking woman (v. 26). And in his conclusion he rejects the notion that God is responsible for the evil in this world: "See, this alone I found, that God made human beings straightforward, but they have devised many schemes" (v. 29).

Textual Theme and Goal

There is no easy way to uncover the main theme of this passage. We have to examine the meaning of its individual parts, consider the flow from one to the other, and test what idea holds these parts together. The Teacher opens this passage with a significant reflection on a major paradox for Israel: while God promised a long life to the righteous,[12] "there are righteous people who perish in their righteousness," and the reverse, while God threatened to cut off evildoers,[13] "there are wicked people who prolong their life in their evil-doing" (v. 15). How can one explain this reversal of retribution? And is there then any point to being righteous? The Teacher's advice is: "Do not be too righteous/too wise and do not be too wicked/a fool" (vv. 16, 17), but "take hold of the one, without letting go of the other; for the one who fears God shall succeed with both" (v. 18).

A key issue for discerning the correct theme is to identify the antecedents of "the one," and "the other" in verse 18. The easy answer is to relate them back to verse 16, "Do not be too righteous, and do not act too wise." Then the Teacher might be interpreted to say, "It is good to hold on to righteousness, and not to let go of wisdom. . . . Both righteousness and wisdom are achieved through the fear of God."[14] The problem with this interpretation is that the Teacher does not say in verse 16, "Be righteous and be wise," but "Do *not* be too righteous, and do *not* act too wise." Moreover, the synonymous parallelism of "righteous" and "wise" practically equates the two and thus diminishes the duality that is required for taking "hold of the one, without letting go of the other."

"The one" and "the other" can only relate to the two pieces of advice given in verses 16 and 17: "Do not be too righteous/too wise" and "Do not be too wicked/a fool."[15] In order to avoid misunderstanding, the Teacher next affirms that though "wisdom gives strength to the wise" (v. 19), even the righteous cannot "do good without ever sinning" (v. 20). One example of this is that we ourselves have "cursed others" (v. 22).

That still leaves the question how to explain this reversal of retribution. Why do some righteous people die young while some wicked people prolong their life? "All this," says the Teacher, "I have tested by wisdom" (v. 23). "That

12. E.g., Exodus 20:12; Deuteronomy 4:40; 5:33; 6:2; 11:9; 25:15; 32:47; Proverbs 3:1-2.
13. E.g., Genesis 6:5-7; 19:24-26; Exodus 12:29; 14:26-31; Psalms 55:23; 73:18.
14. E. Carson Brindle, "Righteousness and Wickedness in Ecclesiastes 7:15-18," *AUSS* 23/3 (1985) 256-57.
15. "The verse is difficult because the pronouns are indefinite. It is most likely, however, that *this* and *that (zeh . . . zeh)* refer to the two lines of advice given in vv. 16 and 17." Longman, *Book of Ecclesiastes,* 197.

which is," that is, the paradoxical reality we experience, "is far off, and deep, very deep. Who can find it out?" (v. 24). This is where we pick up the trail of the Teacher's eightfold repetition of "finding out" and "not finding out" (vv. 24, 26, 27 [2x], 28 [3x], 29), and the threefold repetition of "sum of things"/"schemes" (vv. 25, 27, 29). He turns his mind "*to know* and *to search out* and *to seek* wisdom and the sum of things, and to know that wickedness is folly" (v. 25).

The first thing he finds is a wicked woman (the Temptress of Proverbs) who traps people. "One who pleases God escapes her, but the sinner is taken by her" (v. 26). It does not pay to be wicked after all! The Teacher continues trying to find "the sum of things," but he cannot find it (vv. 27-28). He did find "one [righteous] man among a thousand, but a woman among all these" he did not find (v. 28). He concludes, "See, this alone I found, that God made human beings straightforward [upright], but they have devised many schemes" (v. 29).

It is apparent that the formulation of the textual theme has to cover the Teacher's advice on how to live in this paradoxical world and the results of his search to find an explanation. We might formulate the theme as follows, "The Teacher reflects on the anomalies of life." But this is merely a statement of what he is doing. The homiletical theme should state in a single sentence what is his message for his readers. Basically he seems to make two points: (1) seeing that bad things happen to some good people and good things to some bad people, do not be too righteous nor too wicked (vv. 15-22); and (2) by wisdom one cannot understand "the sum" of this paradoxical reality (vv. 23-29). For a single theme, we have to subordinate one of these points under the other. I take the first point to be the most important and relevant. Therefore the theme becomes: "Since we cannot make sense of this paradoxical world, those who fear God should not be too righteous/too wise nor too wicked/fools." The Teacher's use of synonymous parallelism between "too righteous" and "too wise" and between "too wicked" and "a fool" allows us to simplify the theme by selecting only the first entry of each pair. The theme then becomes, "Since we cannot make sense of this paradoxical world, those who fear God should not be too righteous nor too wicked." But the meaning of "too righteous" and "too wicked" is not entirely clear. For "too righteous" we have to choose between "self-righteous" and "superrighteous." As we shall see, in this context "superrighteous" is the better term. The phrase "too wicked" is easier because it is literally "very wicked." Therefore we can clarify the theme as follows: *Since we cannot make sense of this paradoxical world, those who fear God should not be superrighteous nor very wicked.*

The Teacher's goal in sending this message is *to warn his readers not to be superrighteous nor very wicked.*

Ways to Preach Christ

How can we link the stated theme to Jesus Christ in the New Testament? Since this passage contains neither a promise nor a type of Christ, we shall investigate the remaining five ways.

Redemptive-Historical Progression

"The fear of the LORD is the beginning of wisdom," the Old Testament proclaims (e.g., Prov 1:7; 9:10; 31:30). When God gave Israel his law, he made his presence known by thunder and lightning, a thick cloud, fire and smoke, so that the people "trembled" and "feared" God (Exod 19:16-18; 20:20). God required his people to obey his law, to be righteous, promising them a long life (e.g., Exod 20:12). If they really feared God, they would not seek to prolong their lives for themselves by trying to be superrighteous (think of the Pharisees), and, obviously, they would not seek to be very wicked. In this passage, the Teacher concludes that "the one who fears God shall succeed with both" (Eccl 7:18) — with both not being superrighteous nor very wicked. The history of Israel shows, however, that they frequently did not fear God and chose often to be very wicked. True righteousness is out of reach for sinful creatures (Eccl 7:20, 22; Job 28, 38–42).

Jesus' coming to this world enables his followers to be truly righteous and wise because they can be clothed with the righteousness and wisdom of Christ. Paul writes, "We proclaim Christ crucified, a stumbling block to Jews and foolishness to Gentiles, but to those who are the called, both Jews and Greeks, Christ the power of God and the wisdom of God. . . . He is the source of your life in Christ Jesus, who became for us *wisdom* from God, and *righteousness* and sanctification and redemption" (1 Cor 1:23-24, 30; cf. Rom 3:21-22; Eph 4:22-24).

Analogy

The Teacher warned his readers against being superrighteous. In Jesus' days the Pharisees tried to be superrighteous by splitting up God's law into numerous rules and regulations. Like the Old Testament Teacher, Jesus warned them, "Why do you break the commandments of God for the sake of your tradition? . . . You hypocrites! Isaiah prophesied rightly about you when he said: 'This people honors me with their lips, but their hearts are far from me; in vain do they worship me, teaching human precepts as doctrines'" (Matt 15:3-8). "Woe to you, scribes and Pharisees, hypocrites! For you tithe mint, dill, and cummin, and have neglected the weightier matters of the law: justice and mercy and faith" (Matt 23:23). Trying to be superrighteous does not guarantee entrance into the kingdom of God. Jesus said to his followers, "For I tell you, unless your righteousness exceeds that of the scribes and Pharisees, you will never enter the kingdom of heaven" (Matt 5:20).

Jesus also warned those who chose to be very wicked. For example, he warned the cities that failed to repent: "Woe to you, Chorazin! Woe to you, Bethsaida!" (Matt 11:21; cf. 23:13-33). He declared to those who failed to feed the hungry, "Depart from me into the eternal fire prepared for the devil and his angels" (Matt 25:41). He told the parable of the wicked slave whose master "will cut him in pieces and put him with the hypocrites, where there will be weeping and gnashing of teeth" (Matt 24:51).

Longitudinal Themes

We can trace through the Old Testament to Christ in the New Testament the obligation that God-fearers should not seek to prolong their lives themselves by being superrighteous; instead they should trust God to fulfill his promises. Nor should they be very wicked, of course. Paul connects God's demands in the Old Testament with those in the new age inaugurated by Christ: "'Come out from them, says the Lord, and touch nothing unclean; then I will welcome you, and I will be your father, and you shall be my sons and daughters, says the Lord Almighty.' Since we have these promises, beloved, let us cleanse ourselves from every defilement of body and of spirit, making holiness perfect in *the fear of God*" (2 Cor 6:17–7:1; cf. Rom 12:1-2).

New Testament References

The appendix of the Greek New Testament identifies Romans 3:10 as a New Testament reference to Ecclesiastes 7:20. Paul writes in Romans 3:10, "As it is written, 'There is no one who is righteous, not even one.'" This appears to be a direct quote from Ecclesiastes 7:20,[16] which Paul connects with Christ by way of redemptive-historical progression: "But now, apart from law, the righteousness of God has been disclosed, and is attested by the law and the prophets, the righteousness of God through faith in Jesus Christ for all who believe" (Rom 3:21-22).

---

16. Paul's words, "there is no one righteous," *ouk estin dikaios,* are identical to the Septuagint translation of Ecclesiastes 7:20.

Contrast

There may be a few contrasts between details in the Teacher's teaching and that of Jesus. Depending on one's interpretation there may be a contrast between the Teacher's advice, "Do not be too righteous" (7:16), and Jesus' upholding the ideal: "Be perfect, therefore, as your heavenly Father is perfect" (Matt 5:48; cf. Matt 5:20). Also, whereas the Teacher could not find one upright woman among a thousand (7:28), Jesus found several women who could tell the apostles the good news of his resurrection (Luke 24:10).

Sermon Theme and Goal

We formulated the textual theme as, "Since we cannot make sense of this paradoxical world, those who fear God should not be superrighteous nor very wicked." The New Testament does not contradict this message. Therefore we can keep the textual theme as the sermon theme: *Since we cannot make sense of this paradoxical world, those who fear God should not be superrighteous nor very wicked.*[17]

The Teacher's goal in sending this message was "to warn his readers not to be superrighteous nor very wicked." With a slight change we can make the Teacher's goal the sermon goal: *to warn our hearers not to be superrighteous nor very wicked.*

This goal discloses the need addressed: since people don't understand why bad things happen to some good people while some wicked people seem to prosper, they are tempted either to try even harder to be righteous or to give up on Christian faith and living. The sermon introduction can begin directly with verse 15 since this verse, together with contemporary examples, sets the tension for hearing the entire passage.

Sermon Exposition

In chapter 7:15 the Teacher begins this passage by focusing on a major puzzle that confronts us all. He writes, "In my vain life I have seen everything; there are righteous people who perish in their righteousness, and there are wicked people who prolong their life in their evildoing." Even though his life has been vain,

---

17. Technically, this is a dual theme: "Not . . . nor. . . ." We can turn this into a single theme: "Avoid the extremes of being too righteous and too wicked," but we can justify bending the rules a little for the sake of gaining greater clarity for the theme and being more direct.

that is, brief, he has been around long enough to observe this paradox: some righteous[18] people die young while some wicked people become old.

This does not seem right, does it? God had promised that those who kept his law would prolong their life. Even in the Ten Commandments, God promised, "Honor your father and your mother, so that your days *may be long* in the land that the LORD your God is giving you" (Exod 20:12). Elsewhere God promised, "You must follow exactly the path that the LORD your God has commanded you, so that you may live, and that it may go well with you, and that you may live *long* in the land that you are going to possess" (Deut 5:33).[19]

Although this promise was frequently fulfilled, there are also cases where we don't see that fulfilment. Sometimes God's people died young. Think of Abel being killed by Cain. The righteous Abel died young while the murderer Cain married, had children, and, as far as we know, lived to a ripe old age. Or think of the righteous Naboth, who refused to sell his "ancestral inheritance" to King Ahab. For doing the right thing, he was stoned to death (1 Kings 21:1-14). In the early church, the young deacon Stephen witnessed bravely for Christ. As a result he also was stoned to death (Acts 7:59).

We all know of examples in our own day. A young seminary student has dedicated his life to God's service. After years of preparation, he is ready to become a preacher when he is killed in a head-on collision. A young, Christian mother is stricken by cancer and dies. Children die in tornadoes, cyclones, and earthquakes. Meanwhile hardened criminals live to a ripe old age. It does not seem right, does it? How can God allow this travesty of justice?

The Psalmist despairs,

> Such are the wicked;
>> always at ease, they increase in riches.
> All in vain I have kept my heart clean
>> and washed my hands in innocence.
> For all day long I have been plagued,
>> and am punished every morning. (Ps 73:12-14)

"All in vain I have kept my heart clean." All in vain have I tried to obey God's law. All in vain have I tried to do the right thing. The Israelites were acutely aware of this paradox of the righteous suffering and dying young while the wicked prospered. If obedience to God's law was all in vain, why bother? Why not give it up?

18. "In the vocabulary of the wisdom tradition, 'the righteous' is one who simply does the right things (Prov 10:1-4; 12:10; 28:1; 29:7), says the right things (Prov 10:11-21, 30-31), and has the right thoughts and attitudes (Prov 12:5; 13:5; 15:28)." Seow, *Ecclesiastes*, 267.

19. Cf. Deuteronomy 4:40; 6:2; 11:9; 25:15; 32:47; Proverbs 3:1-2.

Christians today face the same temptation. Followers of Christ do not always live to a ripe old age. Sincere Christians are not immune to cancer. They are not immune to injuries. They are not immune to being hurt by disasters. When people observe this anomaly, they may think that God is punishing them. And so they try hard to be *more* righteous. Or, conversely, they are tempted to give up the Christian faith and life. What's the use anyway?

That's the issue the Teacher is dealing with in this passage. When we see bad things happening to good people, should we try harder to please God? Or should we give up on Christian living? The Teacher's advice may surprise us. He writes in verses 16 and 17, "Do not be too righteous, and do not act too wise; why should you destroy yourself? Do not be too wicked, and do not be a fool; why should you die before your time?"

What does he mean by "Do not be too righteous"? At first hearing, this advice seems to run counter to Jesus' teachings, "Blessed are those who hunger and thirst for righteousness" (Matt 5:6); "Be perfect, therefore, as your heavenly Father is perfect" (Matt 5:48). Surely the Teacher is not opposed to being righteous!? Some commentators have tried to solve this problem by understanding him to say, "Do not be *self*-righteous."[20] But neither the Hebrew nor the context allows for this interpretation.[21] We can detect what the Teacher means by going back to verse 15, where he observed that "there are righteous people who perish *in their righteousness.*" Since God had promised a long life to the righteous, some Israelites may have thought that these people who died young were not righteous enough. Therefore they may have drawn the conclusion that they themselves should be *more* righteous: that they should pursue righteousness with greater vigor in order to prolong their life.

It is to this temptation that the Teacher responds, "Do not be too righteous," that is, Do not try to be superrighteous. For no matter how righteous we become, we can never force God to prolong our life because of our righteousness.[22] The goal of perfect righteousness is beyond us. We cannot prolong our lives by working harder at right living. The Teacher reminds us in verse 20, "Surely there is no one on earth so righteous as to do good without ever sin-

---

20. Especially Whybray, *Ecclesiastes*, 120: "His warning is not against righteousness and wisdom, but against *self*-righteousness and *pretensions* to wisdom."

21. See E. Carson Brindle, "Righteousness and Wickedness in Ecclesiastes 7:15-18," *AUSS* 23/3 (1985) 254-56; Fox, *Qohelet*, 233; Longman, *Book of Ecclesiastes*, 195-96; Seow, *Ecclesiastes*, 267; and John H. Choi, "Doctrine of the Golden Mean in Qoh 7:15-18," *Bib* 83/3 (2002) 360-61.

22. The Teacher rejects "overconfidence in righteousness and wisdom. He has in mind specifically the notion that it is possible for one to be so righteous that one could always avert destruction and extend life (v. 15b)." Seow, *Ecclesiastes*, 267. Cf. ibid., 269. The Teacher is addressing "the impossibility of super-righteousness among mortals. . . . That is the hubris that one must avoid. . . . That attitude is the very opposite of the fear of God."

ning." In verse 22 he adds, "Your heart knows that many times you have yourself cursed others." "Straining for perfection is presumptuous, a refusal to accept human limitations."[23] The Teacher "exposes all efforts to fulfill the absolute ideals of righteousness as self-serving attempts to reap glory. A life obsessed with righteousness, in fact, blinds a person to his or her own sinfulness."[24]

From "Do not be too righteous," the Teacher moves on to a similar thought:[25] "and do not act too wise," or, "Do not act superwise." The pursuit of wisdom in excess can be as disastrous as the pursuit of righteousness in excess. People should not pursue wisdom "hoping to gain an edge over God and force his hand."[26] Moreover, there is a negative side to wisdom. As the Teacher concluded in chapter 1:18,

> For in much wisdom is much vexation,
>   and those who increase knowledge increase sorrow.

The Teacher warns against this fanatic pursuit of being righteous and wise by raising the question, "Why should you destroy yourself?" Those who think that they can prolong their life by being superrighteous and superwise are headed for destruction. Proverbs 16:18 states, "Pride goes before destruction, and a haughty spirit before a fall."

In verse 17 the Teacher sketches the other side of the coin: "Do not be too wicked [literally, Do not be very wicked], and do not be a fool; why should you die before your time?" People might think, if righteousness cannot guarantee a long life, why not throw caution to the wind and become very wicked? But the Teacher warns, "Do not be too wicked, and do not be a fool, why should you die before your time?" To aim to be very wicked is to be a fool.[27] Then you will likely die before your time.

Since the Teacher warns against being "too wicked," does he imply that we should aim to be a little bit wicked? The answer is, No. The Teacher knows that after the Fall into sin we are flawed creatures. As we noted earlier, he observes in verse 20, "Surely there is no one on earth so righteous as to do good without ever sinning." We are all sinners. Perfect goodness is beyond us. Even the best of our works are tainted by sin. Against this background of our inherent sinfulness, the Teacher advises us not to be "very wicked." In other words, he warns us

---

23. Fox, *Ecclesiastes*, 48-49.

24. Brown, *Ecclesiastes*, 81.

25. Synonymous parallelism between "righteous" and "wise." Seow, *Ecclesiastes*, 267, notes that in the wisdom tradition "the one who is righteous is wise and the one who is wise is righteous. The terms are virtually synonymous (see Prov 10:31-32)."

26. Provan, *Ecclesiastes*, 152.

27. Note the synonymous parallelism between being "very wicked" and "a fool."

not to *choose* to be wicked, not to choose to sin *deliberately*.[28] For that will more than likely lead to an early death. Think of the many criminals who die young; the gang members who are shot on the street; the drug dealers who are killed in their homes. "While some sin in everyone's life is inevitable, those who embrace evil as a way of life are destroyed by it."[29]

In verse 18 the Teacher recommends, "It is good that you should take hold of the one, without letting go of the other; for the one who fears God shall succeed with both." What does he mean by taking "hold of the one, without letting go of the other"? What is "the one" and what is "the other"? "The one" and "the other" must relate to the two pieces of advice given in verses 16 and 17: "Do not be too righteous/too wise" and "Do not be too wicked/a fool."[30] The Teacher, therefore, recommends two things in verse 18, "Take hold of the one," that is, Do not try to be superrighteous and superwise," for that is impossible for sinners. But, at the same time, "Do not let go of the other," that is, Do not choose to be very wicked, for that is to be a fool.

The key to living in a world where some godly people die young and some wicked become old — the key to living in such a paradoxical world is to fear God. "For," the Teacher says at the end of verse 18, "the one who fears God shall succeed with both." First, people who fear God will not try to prolong their life by trying to be superrighteous. Since even the most righteous people are sinners, that would be impossible. Moreover, since God has set the time to be born and the time to die, trying to prolong our life by being superrighteous would be arrogant.[31] And second, people who fear God will not try to be very wicked. Instead, those who fear God will naturally seek to live in obedience to God.

In verse 16 the Teacher warned, among other things, against trying to be "too wise." As if to make sure that we do not misunderstand this verse, he begins the next section by highlighting the value of wisdom. Verse 19, "Wisdom gives strength to the wise more than ten rulers that are in a city." The rulers of cities were powerful figures. Today we might think of rulers of nations. They have the power to make decisions that affect the lives of millions. Their decisions can mean wealth or poverty, health or illness, life or death for many. Now the Teacher says that "wisdom gives strength to the wise more than *ten* rulers

---

28. Goldberg, *Ecclesiastes*, 97.

29. Garrett, *Proverbs, Ecclesiastes, Song of Songs*, 323.

30. See p. 183, n. 15 above.

31. "Godly fear . . . is neither a matter of fanatical fear that raises the bar of moral conduct to unattainable or obsessive levels, nor a matter of indifference or moral complacency. Rather, the fear of God is based on an acute awareness of human finitude and a realistic assessment of life's vicissitudes." Brown, *Ecclesiastes*, 82.

that are in a city." Ten rulers is a full number of rulers.[32] They are superstrong. But wisdom gives even more strength to the wise.

In chapter 9:14-18 the Teacher will tell a short story about the strength of wisdom: "There was a little city with few people in it. A *great* king came against it and besieged it, building *great* siegeworks against it. Now there was found in it a poor wise man, and he *by his wisdom* delivered the city." The Teacher concludes, "So I said, 'Wisdom is better than might. . . .' The quiet words of the wise are more to be heeded than the shouting of a ruler among fools. Wisdom is better than weapons of war. . . ." The wisdom of the poor wise man was stronger than the strength of the great king who built great siegeworks. "Wisdom gives strength to the wise more than ten rulers that are in a city."

But there is another side to the coin, and that is that even the wise are imperfect. Verse 20, "Surely there is no one on earth so righteous as to do good without ever sinning." Paul may be referring to this passage when he writes "that all, both Jews and Greeks, are under the power of sin, as it is written, 'There is no one who is righteous, not even one'" (Rom 3:9-10). Even the most righteous people sin.

The Teacher continues by giving an example of the universality of sin. He begins with the advice in verse 21, "Do not give heed to everything that people say." Do not pay attention to everything people say. The reason for this advice is, "or you may hear your servant cursing you." And you know that he may curse you because[33] (v. 22) "your heart knows that many times you have yourself cursed others." Remember the time someone criticized you unfairly. Remember the time someone on the highway cut you off, almost causing an accident. Remember the time you lost your temper and called your brother or sister stupid or something worse. Sin is universal. Even the most righteous sin by falling short of the mark.

In verse 23 the Teacher returns to the subject of wisdom. Even though "wisdom gives strength to the wise more than ten rulers that are in a city" (v. 19), human wisdom has its limits. He writes in verse 23, "*All this* I have tested by wisdom; I said, 'I will be wise,' but it was far from me." The "all this" refers to the foregoing discussion, especially trying to understand the paradox of verse 15 that "there are righteous people who perish in their righteousness, and there are wicked people who prolong their life in their evildoing." He tested this ob-

---

32. "Many commentators understand this [ten officials] as a reference to the *deka protoi* who, according to Josephus (*Ant.* 20.8, 11), were even in Jerusalem as well as in Hellenistic cities." Murphy, *Ecclesiastes*, 71. Longman, *Book of Ecclesiastes*, 198, thinks that it is "extremely unlikely that Qohelet has in mind a specific historical situation in 7:19; it is more likely that the ten-to-one ratio is hyperbole."

33. "Verse 22 provides the motive clause (note *For* [*kî*]) for v 21. . . . 'Your heart knows' . . . is an idiom for what later would be called the 'conscience.'" Longman, *Book of Ecclesiastes*, 199.

servation by wisdom. He said, "I will be wise." This was no flippant remark; he was determined to acquire true wisdom.[34] And indeed, he accomplished something. He was able to give advice on how to live with the paradox that bad things happen to some good people and good things happen to some bad people. He warned us not to let this paradox lead us to choose a wrong way of living: "Do not be too righteous," that is, do not try to prolong your life by being superrighteous, and "do not too be too wicked," that is, do not sin deliberately. Fearing God will enable us to avoid both of these extremes. In this puzzling world we should simply seek to live in obedience to God, realizing all along that we cannot be perfect.

Thus the Teacher was able to arrive at some good advice. But he wanted to dig deeper. He wanted to understand why it is that some good people die young while some bad people live to a ripe old age. "I said, 'I will be wise,' but it was far from me." It was "beyond my grasp" (NEB). This all-encompassing wisdom was far from him. Why was it beyond his grasp?

In verse 24, he gives the reasons, "That which is, is far off, and deep, very deep; who can find it out?" "That which is," that is, the puzzling, paradoxical reality[35] we experience when we see a Christian mother die young while a hardened criminal lives to a ripe old age. "That which is, is far off, and deep, very deep." The Teacher portrays the mysteries of reality both horizontally and vertically: horizontally it is far off — as when one looks over the ocean and there is no end in sight. Vertically, reality is also "deep, very deep" — again like the ocean, we cannot fathom it. It is beyond our understanding why God directs or allows things to happen the way they do.[36] As the LORD said in Isaiah,

> For as the heavens are higher than the earth,
> so are my ways higher than your ways
> and my thoughts than your thoughts.[37]

---

34. Crenshaw, *Ecclesiastes*, 145. Whybray, *Ecclesiastes*, 123, notes. "Qohelet is here using the concept of wisdom or 'being wise' in two different senses: in a superficial sense he is wise, while in a deeper sense he is not." Cf. Ogden, *Qoheleth*, 118, The Teacher "asserts not that wisdom of any kind is utterly beyond human reach, but that a wisdom which transcends all limits, which can lift the sage above the boundaries of human thought and experience, is unattainable."

35. Some commentators identify "that which is" with absolute wisdom. In the context of verse 15, however, it seems to refer to reality as we experience it, the riddle of life. "That which is — that is, life's bewildering reality — is far off and extremely deep." Loader, *Ecclesiastes*, 91.

36. "The argument of Ecclesiastes demands that we refer 'That which is' not only to all that exists . . . , but also to the very way in which it is constituted by God. It is all that exists as God controls and decrees it that is beyond the Preacher's comprehension." Eaton, *Ecclesiastes*, 115.

37. Isaiah 55:9. Cf. Romans 11:33.

The Teacher says, "That which is, is far off, and deep, very deep; who can find it out?" "Who can find it out?" No one!

Yet the Teacher is not ready to give up his search. He will be very deliberate about it. Verse 25, "I turned my mind *to know* and *to search out* and *to seek* wisdom and the sum of things, and to know that wickedness is folly and that foolishness is madness." What he seeks to know is, first, "wisdom and the sum of things," that is, the kind of wisdom that makes sense of the whole of reality. And, secondly, he seeks to know the opposite of wisdom, namely the foolishness of wickedness. If God made "everything suitable for its time" (3:11), why does wickedness even exist and how does it fit in with the sum of things? Did God create wickedness? The Teacher has set himself a gigantic task.

As he goes about his search he "finds" four things. The first thing he finds is the great temptation of wickedness. Remember, he warned us against being very wicked. In verse 26 he pictures this wickedness as "the woman who is a trap," that is, "the foolish woman" sketched in the book of Proverbs, the seductive adulteress, the personification of Folly.[38] He writes, "I found more bitter than death the woman who is a trap, whose heart is snares and nets, whose hands are fetters." This woman is a hunter. She herself is "a trap." Her heart, the center of her being, is guided by the instincts of a hunter, setting snares and nets to catch the unwary. Her hands are fetters, binding victims so no escape is possible. This woman is "a composite image of Folly herself."[39] Proverbs 7 sketches "a young man without sense" being trapped:

> Right away he follows her,
>> goes like an ox to the slaughter,
>> or bounds like a stag toward the trap. . . .
> He is like a bird rushing into a snare,
>> not knowing that it will cost him his life.

The temptation of wickedness! Proverbs warns earnestly,

> Do not let your hearts turn aside to her ways;
>> do not stray into her paths.

---

38. Proverbs 9:13-18,
> The foolish woman is loud;
>> she is ignorant and knows nothing. . . .
> But they do not know that the dead are there,
>> that her guests are in the depths of Sheol.

Cf. Proverbs 2:16-19; 5:20; 6:24-35; 7:5-27; 23:27-28.

39. "The *femme fatale* is not . . . an individual woman. She is not necessarily a specific type of woman or women in general. Rather, she is a composite image of Folly herself." Seow, *Ecclesiastes*, 272.

For many are those she has laid low,
>   and numerous are her victims.
Her house is the way to Sheol,
>   going down to the chambers of death.[40]

In our world there is a great danger of falling into the hands of wickedness. In today's context we can liken wickedness to a black hole in space. A black hole gradually sucks in and destroys everything that comes within range. Once something is caught, there is no escape possible. Wickedness in this world has the same fatal attraction. Sniffing some drugs to feel good may not seem so bad at first, but before long one is a drug addict. Watching pornography may seem rather innocent at first, but soon it will become an addiction. Visiting a casino for a bit of gambling may seem like fun, but this too can lead to a destructive addiction. Even something perfectly acceptable in our society, the pursuit of wealth, can lead to an addiction. Earlier the Teacher warned against the pursuit of wealth: "The lover of money will not be satisfied with money, nor the lover of wealth, with gain" (5:10; cf. 2:22-23). Being addicted to something means that one is no longer in control. Wickedness is in control, and it is practically impossible to escape.

Yet the Teacher is not pessimistic about the outcome. He writes at the end of verse 26, "One who pleases God escapes her, but the sinner is taken by her." The good news is that "one who pleases God escapes" the lure of wickedness. We are not space rocks inescapably drawn into a black hole. We can escape the powerful suction of evil. Those who *please* God escape wickedness. The Teacher mentioned God's being pleased also in chapter 2: "To the one who *pleases* him God gives wisdom and knowledge and joy" (2:26). Now he adds another item to the list of God's gifts: those who please God escape the pull of evil and its disastrous consequences. As Jesus said, "My sheep hear my voice. I know them, and they follow me. I give them eternal life, and they will *never* perish. *No one* will snatch them out of my hand" (John 10:27-28).

So the first thing the Teacher found in his search was this tempting, destructive form of wickedness from which only those who please God escape. The second thing he found, ironically, was something he did not find. Verse 27, "See, this is what I found, says the Teacher, adding one thing to another to find the *sum*, which my mind has sought repeatedly, but I have *not* found." He added one thing

---

40. Proverbs 7:22-27. "The sages exploited, one-sidedly, the dangers that women posed to men (without exploring the need to investigate the blame that attached to the males)." Murphy, *Ecclesiastes*, 76. Without making a major issue of this in the sermon, one can, after explaining the text, provide more balance by adding illustrations of wickedness in our society perpetrated by men: pimps, Johns, and men involved in sex trafficking children. Note that the Teacher shows great appreciation for women in 9:9.

to another like an accountant to find the sum of things, that is, the principles that govern the universe. He was not content to simply repeat what others had found, but tried "to form his own conclusions on the basis of phenomena which he . . . himself observed."[41] And his major observation was that "there are righteous people who perish in their righteousness, and there are wicked people who *prolong* their life in their evil-doing" (7:15). In his investigation he also found a form of wickedness that *destroys* all but those who please God (7:26). How do these phenomena fit into the sum of things? He says that his mind sought it repeatedly, "but I have not found." Not even the wise Teacher can find the sum of things. He cannot make sense of this paradoxical world. Why do bad things happen to good people? He does not know.

But he does find a third thing. He writes in the second half of verse 28, "One man among a thousand I found, but a woman among all these I have not found." The Hebrew (and NRSV translation) is not clear on what he was looking for. But the context of wickedness (v. 26) and God's having made human beings upright (v. 29) makes clear that he was searching for upright people.[42] Therefore the TNIV translates,

> I found one upright man among a thousand,
> but not one upright woman among them all.[43]

Printing this sentence as poetry is illuminating. Could the Teacher be quoting an existing proverb? Whybray thinks that probably "this is a conventional saying quoted by . . . [the Teacher] himself . . . , possibly to emphasize the seriousness of the problem which he is discussing, and which he has sought repeatedly to solve: the apparent universality of human depravity and folly."[44] Are there some upright people to be found in this wicked world? Using hyperbole, he reports that he found only "one upright man among a thousand but not one upright woman[45] among them." Whether the Teacher quotes an existing proverb or composes one himself, his point is that he has found virtually no upright persons.

41. Whybray, *Ecclesiastes,* 126.
42. Murphy, *Ecclesiastes,* 77.
43. "While perhaps undermining Qohelet's subtlety, the NIV correctly makes explicit Qohelet's meaning, as is clear by looking at the use of 'upright' *(yāšār)* in the next verse." Longman, *Book of Ecclesiastes,* 206.
44. Whybray, *Ecclesiastes,* 126-27.
45. Fox, *Ecclesiastes,* 51, suggests that the Teacher may have intended his remark "as a wisecrack rather than a solemn statement." I think it is better to acknowledge the male chauvinism of that culture which, for the Teacher, would be lessened somewhat if he were quoting an existing proverb. In any event, I would not give much space in the sermon to this issue since it is not the point of this passage.

So the Teacher found first an alluring wickedness in this world; second he found that he could not find the sum of things; and third he found virtually no upright persons. In verse 29 he reports his final finding: "See, this alone I found, that God made human beings straightforward, but they have devised many schemes." "See, this *alone* I found." This is the single point in all his searching that is of prime importance. "God made human beings straightforward," or, as the TNIV translates, "God created humankind upright." God is not to blame for the wickedness we find in this world. And God is not to blame for the lack of upright persons on this earth. He made human beings upright.

The Teacher here clearly refers to the creation story of Genesis: "Then God said, 'Let us make humankind in our image, according to our likeness.' . . . God saw everything that he had made, and indeed, it was very good" (Gen 1:26, 31). Human beings were made upright. How is it then that we see so much wickedness in this world and so few upright people? Well, the Teacher says, "they [human beings] have devised many schemes." Here he is using a play on the words "sum of things." He writes that "he has tried to use wisdom to find 'the scheme [sum] of things,' but all he could discover was that human beings are all 'schemers.'"[46]

He is thinking of the Genesis stories about the Fall into sin. Adam and Eve fell for the first scheme to be "like God" and "wise" (Gen 3:5, 6). That scheme failed miserably. Instead of becoming wise, they acquired the knowledge of "good and evil" and experienced the evil of pain, suffering, and death (Gen 3:16-22). Next people schemed to control their destiny by building a city and developing agriculture, art, and technologies (Gen 4:17-22). That scheme also failed. "The LORD saw that the wickedness of humankind was great in the earth, and that every inclination of the thoughts[47] of their hearts was only evil continually" (Gen 6:5), and the LORD sent a great flood. After the flood they schemed to build "a city, and a tower with its top in the heavens . . . ; otherwise we shall be scattered abroad upon the face of the whole earth." That scheme also failed when the LORD confused their language and "scattered them abroad over the face of all the earth" (Gen 11:4, 9). One scheme after another. Even in the time of Israel's prophets, Isaiah had to admit, "All we like sheep have gone astray; we have all turned to our own way" (Isa 53:6).

Thus the most important finding of the Teacher in searching for "the sum of things" is that God is not to blame for the wickedness we see in this world. He made human beings upright, but they deliberately devised many schemes

---

46. Farmer, *Who Knows What Is Good?* 179. After twice using the word ḥešbôn (the sum of things), in 7:29 the Teacher uses ḥiššĕbōnôt (schemes).

47. Longman, *Book of Ecclesiastes,* 207, points out that the word "thoughts" "is related to the word translated 'devices' ['schemes'] here in Ecclesiastes in that both are words formed from the verbal root ḥšb ('to think, to calculate')."

that led to pain, suffering, and death. This is an answer, but it does not solve the problem "that there are righteous people who perish in their righteousness" (7:15). It is true that the punishment for the original sin was death (Gen 2:17; 3:19). But when righteous people die young, it is not because they are worse sinners than others. The Teacher says in verse 15 "that there are righteous people who perish *in their righteousness.*" Why "righteous people perish in their righteousness" the Teacher cannot figure out. Jesus also died at a young age, in his early thirties. We read that Jesus, before his excruciating suffering and death, "began to be grieved and agitated." Was his early death really necessary? But in the end, Jesus entrusted his life, and death, to his Father's will: "My Father, if this cannot pass unless I drink it, your will be done" (Matt 26:37, 42).

The Teacher's message is this: Since we cannot make sense of this paradoxical world, we should entrust ourselves to God. We should not try to prolong our life by trying to be superrighteous. Nor should we give up on the Christian life by becoming very wicked. We should not be superrighteous nor sin deliberately.

When Jesus was on earth, he proclaimed the same message. Jesus warned that those who sinned deliberately and those who did not repent would be cast into hell: "Woe to you, Chorazin! Woe to you, Bethsaida!" (Matt 11:21; cf. 24:48-51; 25:41). At the same time Jesus warned the Pharisees who aimed to be superrighteous: "Woe to you, scribes and Pharisees, hypocrites! For you tithe mint, dill, and cummin, and have neglected the weightier matters of the law: justice and mercy and faith. It is these you ought to have practiced without neglecting the others. You blind guides! You strain out a gnat but swallow a camel" (Matt 23:23-24).[48] Paul also writes about the attempts of these religious leaders to be superrighteous: "I can testify that they have a zeal for God, but it is not enlightened. For, being ignorant of the righteousness that comes from God, and *seeking to establish their own,* they have not submitted to God's righteousness. For Christ is the end of the law so that there may be righteousness for everyone who believes" (Rom 10:2-4). The obsession to establish their own righteousness is later found among ascetics who separated themselves from the world in order to obtain righteousness through isolation, flagellation, and dedication to prayer.

---

48. In Philippians 3:6-9 Paul describes himself: ". . . as to righteousness under the law, blameless. Yet whatever gains I had, these I have come to regard as loss because of Christ. More than that, I regard everything as loss because of the surpassing value of knowing Christ Jesus my Lord. For his sake I have suffered the loss of all things, and I regard them as rubbish, in order that I may gain Christ and be found in him, not having a righteousness of my own that comes from the law, but one that comes through faith in Christ, the righteousness from God based on faith."

Even today, the warning is to the point: "Do not be too righteous." Jesus said, "I have come to call not the righteous but sinners" (Matt 9:13). It is impossible for us to be so righteous that God simply must give us a long life, let alone eternal life. But by believing in Jesus, we can be clothed with *his* righteousness. Paul writes that God "is the source of your life in Christ Jesus, who became for us *wisdom* from God, and *righteousness* and sanctification and redemption" (1 Cor 1:30). And Christ promised to give us not a long life on earth but *eternal* life. He said, "My sheep hear my voice. I know them, and they follow me. I give them *eternal* life, and they will *never* perish" (John 10:27-28). "Do not be too righteous" and "Do not be too wicked." Rather, hear Jesus' voice, follow him, and you will receive eternal life.

CHAPTER 11

Use Wisdom but Know Its Limitations

Ecclesiastes 8:1-17

The wise mind will know the time and way. . . .
Then I saw all the work of God,
that no one can find out what is happening under the sun.
However much they may toil in seeking, they will not find it out;
even though those who are wise claim to know,
they cannot find it out.

(Eccl 8:5, 17)

Ecclesiastes 8 is a passage particularly relevant for people who act unwisely and for those who think that wisdom should answer all the questions we have. But in preaching this passage one faces difficulties similar to those in the last chapter. Here, too, the problems begin with the translation of Hebrew words and phrases. Verse 3, for example, can be translated in two different ways: the NRSV translates it as, "Do not be terrified; go from his [the king's] presence, do not delay when the matter is unpleasant, for he does whatever he pleases," while the TNIV translates, "Do not be in a hurry to leave the king's presence. Do not stand up for a bad cause, for he will do whatever he pleases."[1] In addition to these ambiguities, most translators consider verse 10 one of "the most difficult in the book."[2]

1. Another example is verse 9b, which the NRSV translates, "one person exercises authority over another to the other's hurt," while the TNIV translates, "There is a time when a man lords it over others to his own hurt" (with a note, "Or to their"). When the Hebrew allows for either translation and the issue is not a major point for the sermon, I suggest that preachers simply follow the translation of the pew Bibles. If it is a major point, it would be well not to give one's own translation but to quote another respectable Bible version.

2. Longman, *Book of Ecclesiastes,* 218, writes, "This verse vies for the most difficult in the

Another challenge in interpreting this passage is to discern the intention of the Teacher. Some commentators consider verses 2-5 quotations from traditional wisdom which the Teacher critiques with verses 6-9.[3] Others, such as Roland Murphy, assume a dialectical pattern in which "verses 2-4 modify verse 1; 6-12a modify verse 5; [and] 14-15 are in opposition to 12b-13."[4] By contrast, Michael Fox states that the Teacher "does not oppose or present antitheses to the doctrines of traditional wisdom. It is not even clear that he recognizes a difference. He is not 'using traditional wisdom against itself.' He is just using it."[5] The different presuppositions of interpreters regarding the Teacher's use of traditional wisdom will lead to different understandings of his intended meaning.[6]

An additional challenge for preachers is to detect coherence between the parts in this passage and to formulate a single theme that encompasses the various ideas.

Text and Context

As indicated in the last chapter, commentators are not agreed on the placement of 8:1. Does it (or part of it) belong to the former literary unit (7:15-29) or to the present one (8:1-17)? There are good reasons for including 8:1 with the present literary unit. First, the catchword *dābār* of verse 1, "a thing," is repeated in verse 3, "matter," verse 4, "word," and verse 5, "harm," "(evil) thing." Second, the word *pēsher*, "interpretation," in verse 1a, "is used elsewhere in the Hebrew Bible only with reference to the interpretation of dreams or signs by courtiers in the service of foreign rulers," especially Joseph and Daniel. This indicates "the importance of verse 1a for the argument of 8:1b-9 — a text dealing specifically with wisdom, royal authority, and knowledge of the future."[7] Third, "the rhetorical question 'who knows' anticipates the assertion that 'no one knows' (v. 7) and, eventually, also the admission at the end of the passage that the wise who think they know are not able to discover anything (v. 17)."[8] And finally, the question

---

book and thus I begin its exposition by admitting that certainty eludes every honest interpreter, even though the problems are often hidden behind smooth English translations." Cf. Eaton, *Ecclesiastes*, 121.

3. For detailed references, see Scott C. Jones, "Qohelet's Courtly Wisdom: Ecclesiastes 8:1-9," *CBQ* 68 (2006) 211-12, n. 2.

4. Murphy, *Ecclesiastes*, 82.

5. Fox, *A Time to Tear Down*, 275. See also his comments on p. 280 against Crenshaw's position.

6. See pp. 8-9 above.

7. Jones, "Qohelet's Courtly Wisdom: Ecclesiastes 8:1-9," *CBQ* 68 (2006) 213.

8. Seow, *Ecclesiastes*, 290.

of verse 1a, "Who is like the wise man?" forms an inclusio with verse 17b, "even though those who are wise claim to know, they cannot find it out." The "cannot find it out," three times in verse 17, is the key phrase that also concluded the last section (7:29). We can, therefore, select as our preaching text Ecclesiastes 8:1-17.

Several ideas in this text recall similar sentiments earlier in the book. The notion that "every matter has its time" (v. 6) picks up the thought of 3:1, 17, "there is a time for every matter under heaven." The question, "who can tell them how it will be?" (v. 7) repeats the questions of 3:22 and 6:12, "who can tell them what will be after them?" The claim that "no one has power over the wind" (v. 8) reminds us of the Teacher's description of our lack of power with the repeated phrase, "a chasing after wind" (1:14, 17; 2:11, 17, 26; 4:4, 16; 6:9). The enigma that the wicked are not punished but prolong their life (vv. 10-12a) was raised earlier in 3:16; 4:1; and 7:15. The Teacher's conviction that God will reward those who fear him but will punish the wicked (vv. 12b-13) is similar to the sentiments raised in 7:17-18. His commendation of enjoyment (v. 15) he made earlier in 2:24-26; 3:12-13, 22; 5:18-20, and will make again in 9:7-9 and 11:7-9. The Teacher's statement, "I applied my mind to know wisdom, and to see the business that is done on earth" (v. 16), is found in similar words in 1:13. And finally, his repeated claim in verse 17 about human inability to find out "all the work of God" ("no one can find out what is happening") harks back to 1:14-18; 3:11; 7:14, 24, 27-28; and will come up again in 11:5.

Literary Features

The passage begins with two rhetorical questions and a proverb,[9] all cast in synonymous parallelism:

> Who is like the wise man?
>   And who knows the interpretation of a thing?
> Wisdom makes one's face shine,
>   and the hardness of one's countenance is changed.

This is followed by an "instruction concerning conduct before the king."[10] The instruction begins with an imperative, "Keep the king's command!" (v. 2) and gives the reason for doing so. It includes another rhetorical question, "Who can say to him, 'What are you doing?'" (v. 4). Verse 5 completes the instruction with what appears to be another proverb,[11] this one with synthetic parallelism:

9. See Jones, "Qohelet's Courtly Wisdom: Ecclesiastes 8:1-9," *CBQ* 68 (2006) 217, n. 25.
10. Murphy, *Wisdom Literature*, 142.
11. See Fox, *Qohelet*, 245.

Whoever obeys a command will meet no harm,
    and the wise mind will know the time and way.

Verses 6 to 9 are a reflection (see v. 9, "All this I observed") on human inability to know the future. It includes another rhetorical question in verse 7, "Who can tell them how it will be?" Verse 8 is a "numerical saying"[12] giving four examples of human powerlessness (inability).

Verses 10 to 15 are another reflection (v. 10, "Then I saw"), this one on injustice: the wicked are praised (v. 10), "prolong their lives" (v. 12), and "are treated according to the conduct of the righteous" (v. 14). In the middle of this reflection on injustice, the Teacher inserts the traditional assurance, "yet I know that it will be well with those who fear God . . . , but it will not be well with the wicked" (vv. 12-13). Verse 14, especially, is artfully constructed with inverted parallelism within an inclusio of vanity:

There is a vanity that takes place on earth,
that there are *righteous* people who are treated according to the conduct of
the *wicked,*
    and there are *wicked* people who are treated according to the conduct
    of the *righteous.*
I said that this also is vanity.

The Teacher concludes this reflection by commending "enjoyment, for there is nothing better for people under the sun than to eat, and drink, and enjoy themselves."[13]

The unit ends with a final reflection (v. 16, "When I applied my mind . . . to see the business that is done on earth") on human inability to know all the work of God. It concludes emphatically with a threefold repetition of, "they cannot find it out" (v. 17). The statement that even "those who are wise . . . cannot find it out" (v. 17) forms an inclusio with 8:1, "Who is like the wise man?"

As to repetition of keywords, we have already noted that the Teacher concludes this text with a threefold "they cannot find it out." He also uses the words "wise"/"wisdom" five times (vv. 1 [2x], 5, 16, and 17). In addition, he uses a form of *šlṭ,* "power," four times: "The word of the king is powerful" (v. 4); "No one has power over the wind . . . , or power over the day of death" (v. 8); and, "one person exercises authority [power] over another to the other's hurt" (v. 9). Further, in this passage he uses the word "vanity" three times (vv. 10 and 14 [2x]).

12. Cf. Proverbs 30:4, 11-14, 18-19, 21-31. Whybray, *Ecclesiastes,* 133.
13. "The last time that the *'ên ṭôb* or, 'There is nothing better,' saying is used." Ogden, *Qoheleth,* 139.

Textual Structure

The analysis of the literary forms will help us in sketching the structure of the text.

I. Instruction about using wisdom before the king (vv. 1-5)
   A. The value of wisdom (v. 1)
      1. The wise know the interpretation of a thing (v. 1a, b)
      2. Proverb: Wisdom makes one's face shine (v. 1c, d)
   B. Keep the king's command! (v. 2a)
      1. Reason: because of your sacred oath (v. 2b)
   C. Do not be terrified! (v. 3a)
      1. Go from his presence when the matter is unpleasant (v. 3b)
         a. Reason: for he does whatever he pleases (v. 3c)
         b. Reason: for the word of the king is powerful (v. 4a)
            i. no one can say to him, "What are you doing?" (v. 4b)
   D. Proverb: Whoever obeys a command will meet no harm (v. 5)
                and the wise mind will know the time and way
II. Reflection on human inability to know the future and to control the present (vv. 6-9)
   A. Every matter has its time and way (v. 6a)
      1. although the troubles of mortals lie heavy upon them (v. 6b)
   B. People do not know what is to be (v. 7a)
      1. Reason: for no one can tell them how it will be (v. 7b)
   C. People do not even have power over the present (v. 8)
      1. No one has power over the wind to restrain the wind (v. 8a)
      2. No one has power over the day of death (v. 8b)
      3. There is no discharge from the battle (v. 8c)
      4. Wickedness does not deliver those who practice it (v. 8d)
   D. The Teacher observed all of the above (v. 9a)
      1. while one person exercises power over another to the other's hurt (v. 9b)
III. Reflection on injustice on earth (vv. 10-15)
   A. Example of injustice: The wicked receive a proper burial and are praised (v. 10)
      1. This also is vanity
   B. The human heart is fully set to do evil (v. 11b)
      1. because sentence against an evil deed is not executed speedily (v. 11a)
   C. Sinners do evil a hundred times and prolong their lives (v. 12a)

    D. Yet the Teacher knows:
        1. that it will be well with those who fear God (v. 12b)
            a. because they stand in fear before him (v. 12c)
        2. but it will not be well with the wicked (v. 13a)
              neither will they prolong their days like a shadow (v. 13b)
            a. because they do not stand in fear before God (v. 13c)
    E. Another injustice (vanity):
        Some righteous people are treated like the wicked (v. 14a)
            while some wicked are treated like the righteous (v. 14b)
        1. This also is vanity (v. 14c)
    F. Conclusion: So I commend enjoyment (v. 15a)
        1. Reason: for there is nothing better than to eat, drink, and enjoy (v. 15b)
            a. for this will go with them through the days God gives them (v. 15c)
IV. Reflection on human inability to know all the work of God (vv. 16-17)
    A. The Teacher applied his mind to know wisdom (v. 16a)
        1. His eyes did not see sleep, neither day nor night (v. 16b)
    B. Contemplating all the work of God, he saw (v. 17a)
        1. that no one can find out what is happening under the sun (v. 17b)
        2. they will not find it out (v. 17d)
            a. however much they may toil in seeking (v. 17c)
        3. they cannot find it out (v. 17f)
            a. even though those who are wise claim to know it (v. 17e)

Theocentric Interpretation

The first five verses of this passage deal with how to survive in the employ of a powerful, unpredictable king. The Teacher concludes his advice with the assurance: "the wise mind will know the time and way" (v. 5b). He supports this assurance with the repetition in verse 6, "For every matter has its time and way." Although God is not mentioned at this point,[14] we recall that God is the one who has set the times (3:1-15). Human beings "do not know what is to be" (v. 7). They don't even have power over the wind or the day of death. But God, we recall, is all powerful and controls the wind as well as the day of death (3:2). He is sovereign.

    But how, then, can we account for the injustice we see in this world? The wicked are buried honorably and receive praise (v. 10). The wicked "prolong their lives" (v. 12a). Why does the divine King allow such injustice? At this point the Teacher begins to mention God explicitly. "Yet I know that it will be well

---

14. In verse 2 "your sacred oath" is literally "your oath to (or before) God."

with those who fear God, because they stand in fear before him, but it will not be well with the wicked . . . , because they do not stand in fear before God" (vv. 12-13). The Teacher concludes by again commending enjoyment, "for this will go with them in their toil through the days of life that God gives them under the sun" (v. 15). This does not answer the question of how to square the sovereign rule of the divine King with the injustice we observe on earth. The Teacher has no good answer. In fact, he writes, "I saw all the work of God, that no one can find out what is happening under the sun. However much they may toil in seeking, they will not find it out; even though those who are wise claim to know, they cannot find it out." We know that the sovereign God controls all that happens on earth, but we cannot find out all the work of God.

Textual Theme and Goal

The repetition of certain keywords and the structure of the text will help us discern the overarching theme of this passage. In analyzing the structure of the text, we noticed four divisions:

I. Use wisdom in dealing with a powerful, presumably fickle, king (vv. 1-5)
II. We don't know the future and are powerless in controlling the present (vv. 6-9)
III. We see grave injustice in this world, yet can still enjoy the life God gives (vv. 10-15)
IV. Even the wisest people cannot find out all the work of God (vv. 16-17)

Especially important for discerning the overall theme of this passage is the inclusio of verses 1 and 17 that bracket this passage: the opening of the value of wisdom and the threefold repetition in the conclusion that wisdom cannot find out all the work ("doings") of God. The Teacher makes two main points concerning wisdom: First, use wisdom in dealing with a powerful, fickle king, and second, in view of our inability to know the future or control the present as well as our inability to make sense of the injustice in this world, human wisdom cannot find out all the work of God.

For a single focus, we have to formulate an overarching theme covering the two points or subsume one point under the other. Both the extent of the second point (vv. 6-17) and the threefold repetition "cannot find out" in verse 17 argue for subsuming the first point under the second. We can therefore formulate the theme of this passage as follows, *Although we should use wisdom to survive in a dangerous, unjust world, wisdom does not enable us to find out all the work of God.*

The goal of this message must be discerned against the backdrop of the historical circumstances. The passage itself hints that the hearers of this message suffer under unpredictable, powerful rulers (v. 3; cf. 10:6) and witness the prosperity and praise of the wicked (vv. 10-14; cf. 4:1; 5:8). The goal of the Teacher, then, would be a dual goal:[15] *to encourage his readers to use wisdom in this dangerous, unjust world, while cautioning them concerning the limitations of wisdom.*

Ways to Preach Christ

In this section we brainstorm the legitimate ways we can possibly use to move from this Old Testament message to Jesus Christ in the New Testament. Since the passage contains neither a promise of Christ nor a type of Christ, we shall investigate the remaining five ways: redemptive-historical progression, analogy, longitudinal themes, New Testament references, and contrast.

Redemptive-Historical Progression

In this passage the Teacher deals again (see 7:15) with the enigma of some wicked people being blessed with a long life while some "righteous people . . . are treated according to the conduct of the wicked" (vv. 12a, 14). Although the Teacher confidently confesses, "I know it will be well with those who fear God . . . , but it will not be well with the wicked" (vv. 12b-13), he cannot resolve this problem in his Old Testament setting where he conceives of death as the end for both the righteous and the wicked (see 2:14-16). His conclusion is that not even the wise can find out "all the work of God" (8:17).

But as redemptive history moves forward to the coming of Jesus, his teaching, death, and resurrection, a partial solution comes into view: there is life beyond death. Jesus teaches his disciples about a twofold resurrection: "The hour is coming when all who are in their graves will hear his [the Son of Man's] voice and will come out — those who have done good, to the resurrection of life, and those who have done evil, to the resurrection of condemnation" (John 5:28-29). Jesus also tells the parable of the weeds among the wheat and explains, "The Son of Man will send his angels, and they will collect out of his kingdom all causes of sin and all evildoers, and they will throw them into the furnace of fire, where there will be weeping and gnashing of teeth. Then the righteous will shine like the sun in the kingdom of their Father" (Matt 13:41-43). Jesus reinforces this message by teaching that "the kingdom of heaven is like a net that

---

15. While the theme has to be singular for a unified sermon, the goal can be plural as the single theme is applied in different ways.

was thrown into the sea and caught fish of every kind; when it was full, they drew it ashore, sat down, and put the good into baskets but threw out the bad. So it will be at the end of the age. The angels will come out and separate the evil from the righteous and throw them into the furnace of fire, where there will be weeping and gnashing of teeth" (Matt 13:47-50). In his teaching on the judgment of the nations, Jesus concludes, "And these will go away into eternal punishment, but the righteous into eternal life" (Matt 25:46).

Analogy

As the Old Testament Teacher urged his hearers to be wise in dealing with fickle, powerful rulers, so Jesus said to his disciples, "See, I am sending you out like sheep into the midst of wolves; so *be wise* as serpents and innocent as doves" (Matt 10:16). And just like the Teacher, Jesus also stressed the limitations of human wisdom in trying to find out all the work of God. When Nicodemus wanted a rational answer about the new birth, Jesus said, "Do not be astonished that I said to you, 'You must be born from above.' The wind blows where it chooses, and you hear the sound of it, but you do not know where it comes from or where it goes. So it is with everyone who is born of the Spirit" (John 3:7-8). We do not know; we cannot comprehend all the work of God. Paul echoes this sentiment when he exclaims: "O the depth of the riches and wisdom and knowledge of God! How unsearchable are his judgments and how inscrutable his ways!" (Rom 11:33).

Longitudinal Themes

One can trace from the Old Testament to the New the theme that human wisdom can never fully understand all the work of God. Psalm 145:3 states,

> Great is the LORD, and greatly to be praised;
>   his greatness is unsearchable.

Through Isaiah (55:8-9) the LORD proclaims,

> For my thoughts are not your thoughts,
>   nor are your ways my ways,
>   says the LORD.
> For as the heavens are higher than the earth,
>   so are my ways higher than your ways
>   and my thoughts than your thoughts.

Job 11:7-8 echoes this idea:

> Can you find out the deep things of God?
>> Can you find out the limit of the Almighty?
> It is higher than heaven — what can you do?
>> Deeper than Sheol — what can you know?

In the New Testament, Paul writes, "Since, in the wisdom of God, the world did not know God through wisdom, God decided, through the foolishness of proclamation, to save those who believe" (1 Cor 1:21; cf. 1 Cor 2:6-16; 13:9). Jesus himself thanked his Father, "because you have hidden these things from the wise and the intelligent and have revealed them to infants. . . . No one knows the Father except the Son and anyone to whom the Son chooses to reveal him" (Matt 11:25-27). Nevertheless, "all the work of God," all his doings, remains a mystery for us.

New Testament References

In addition to the New Testament references mentioned above to support the different ways to Christ, the appendix of the Greek New Testament lists as a reference to Ecclesiastes 8:15 ("to eat, and drink, and enjoy themselves") Luke 12:19, where the rich fool says, "relax, eat, drink, be merry." We cannot use this reference, however, because it fails to connect with the theme of this passage. Moreover, it is unlikely that Jesus would place the positive commendation of the Teacher in the mouth of a rich fool.

Contrast

Except for the progression in redemptive history noted above, there is no contrast between the message of this passage and that of the New Testament.

Sermon Theme and Goal

Since the New Testament does not change the textual message, the textual theme can become the sermon theme: *Although we should use wisdom to survive in a dangerous, unjust world, wisdom does not enable us to find out all the work of God.* The goal of the Teacher can also become ours: *to encourage our hearers to use wisdom in this dangerous, unjust world, while cautioning them concerning the limitations of wisdom.*

This goal points to a dual need. On the one hand, there are people who fail to make use of wisdom in getting along in this sinful world. On the other hand, there are people who cannot live with mystery; they think they should be able to find answers to all their questions. We can keep the sermon unified by beginning with our failure to use wisdom and leaving the second need for later in the sermon.

Sermon Exposition

We have all heard of people who lack wisdom, or, at least, who fail to use wisdom. A baseball coach yells in the referee's face until he is thrown out of the game. A lady traveler gives the customs agent at the border a hard time; she is held up for hours while her car and luggage are carefully searched. A driver stopped by a policeman for speeding starts yelling and threatening him; he ends up in a holding cell. An employee loses his cool and swears at his employer; he loses his job.[16] A lack of wisdom! On occasion we ourselves may have acted without using wisdom and paid the consequences.

In Ecclesiastes 8 the Teacher makes two main points about wisdom. His first point is that wisdom helps us survive in a dangerous, unjust world. He begins this chapter by praising wisdom. He asks, "Who is like the wise man?" The expected answer is, No one. No one is as exalted as the wise man. The Teacher follows this up with a second question, "And who knows the interpretation of a thing?" He is thinking of wise men in a royal court interpreting signs or dreams so as to foretell the future for the king.[17] "Who knows the interpretation of a thing?" The expected answer is, No one but a wise person.

Think of Joseph at the court of Pharaoh. Pharaoh had had that strange dream of seven sleek and fat cows coming up out of the Nile river, followed by seven ugly and thin cows. The thin cows ate the fat cows. Then Pharaoh awoke. He fell asleep again and had another dream about seven thin and blighted ears of grain swallowing up seven plump ears of grain. When Pharaoh woke again he was troubled. He called all the wise men of Egypt together to interpret his dreams, but no one could. Then the chief cupbearer remembered that the prisoner Joseph had interpreted *his* dream correctly. He told Pharaoh about Joseph,

16. Instead of a series of examples like this, it is more engaging to tell a single story about the lack of using wisdom — your own story if it happened a long time ago, or a current story that has been broadcast on the news.

17. Jones, "Qohelet's Courtly Wisdom: Ecclesiastes 8:1-9," *CBQ* 68 (2006) 214-15, argues that *pēšer* is not simply "interpretation" but "mantological interpretation," that is, "the future vision disclosed through exegesis." Krüger, *Qoheleth*, 151, n. 7, points out that Genesis 40–41 and Daniel 2, 4, 5, and 7 contain keywords corresponding to *pēšer*.

and Pharaoh summoned Joseph to the palace. Joseph interpreted the dreams for Pharaoh: God would give Egypt seven years of plenty, but would follow these with seven years of famine. Pharaoh said to Joseph, "Since God has shown you all this, there is no one so discerning and *wise* as you" (Gen 41:39). The Teacher asks, "Who knows the interpretation of a thing?" The answer is, Only a wise person like Joseph.[18]

The Teacher continues to praise wisdom in verse 1: "Wisdom makes one's face shine, and the hardness of one's countenance is changed." "The face is an index of the feelings; and a bright face is a sign of happiness or contentment (Prov 15:13)."[19] Wisdom is reflected even in a person's face.

In verses 2 to 5 the Teacher urges his readers to use wisdom in this dangerous world. He zeroes in on those who are in the service of a powerful, unpredictable Eastern king. Verse 2, "Keep the king's command because of your sacred oath." "Your sacred oath" is literally "your oath to (or before) God." With the anointing of a new king, people would swear allegiance to him.[20] So the Teacher instructs people that a wise person will keep the king's command because of the oath of allegiance made before God. He adds in verse 3, "Do not be terrified." "People ought not to be so terrified before the king that they cannot react appropriately."[21] Awkward behavior or speech might provoke the king's anger. People should therefore have a cheerful expression on their face, act pleasantly, and obey the king's command.[22]

The Teacher continues in verse 3, "Go from his presence,[23] do not delay when the matter is unpleasant, for he does whatever he pleases." Rather than argue with the king when he rejects your advice, it is wiser to go quietly from his presence. For the king is sovereign. "He does whatever he pleases." Moreover, as we read in verse 4, "The word of the king is powerful [his word is law], and who can say to him, 'What are you doing?'" No one, of course. The king is not accountable to any other human. So it is wise to "keep the king's command" and to quietly go from his presence when you disagree with him.

In verse 5 the Teacher wraps up his advice with a proverb: "Whoever obeys

18. I have used the Joseph story because it is familiar to people. One can also use the story of Daniel interpreting the dream of King Nebuchadnezzar about the huge statue. See Daniel 2.

19. Whybray, *Ecclesiastes*, 129.

20. See, e.g., 1 Chronicles 29:24.

21. Seow, *Ecclesiastes*, 291.

22. "Before a superior, especially someone whose wrath is swift, it is wise not to display any animosity. Instead, despite one's feelings, it is smart to act pleasantly." Ibid. For a similar interpretation, see Fox, *Qohelet*, 246.

23. The TNIV, by contrast, translates verse 3, "Do not be in a hurry to leave the king's presence. . . ." Since the Hebrew allows for either translation and since this is not a major point, I would simply follow the translation offered in the pew Bibles.

a command will meet no harm, and the wise mind will know the time and way." "Whoever obeys the command" of even a powerful, unpredictable king "will meet no harm." The reason for safety even in such a dangerous situation, says the Teacher, is that "the wise mind will know the time and way." A fool might argue with the king, perhaps even threaten him with the evil consequences that will follow. But "the wise mind will know the time and way." The wise person will know when it is the proper time to speak up and what is the proper procedure[24] (cf. Prov 14:8; 15:23). The Teacher, then, advises us to use wisdom in order to survive in a dangerous, unjust world.

Jesus himself used wisdom for getting out of dangerous spots. One time the Pharisees sought "to entrap" him. They asked him, "Is it lawful to pay taxes to the emperor, or not?" If he said, "Yes, paying taxes to the Romans is lawful," the Jews would be angry with him. If he said, "No," the Romans could charge him with sedition. "Jesus, aware of their malice," called for a coin and asked, "Whose head is this?" They answered, "The emperor's." Then Jesus said, "Give therefore to the emperor the things that are the emperor's, and to God the things that are God's." We read, "When they heard this, they were amazed; and they left him and went away" (Matt 22:15-22).

On another occasion the Pharisees "conspired . . . how to destroy him." Jesus avoided this confrontation by departing "with his disciples to the sea" (Mark 3:6-7). He withdrew because his time had not yet come. Later, when his time had come, he courageously headed for Jerusalem to suffer and die.[25]

Jesus also told his followers that they would face danger and urged them to be wise. He said to his disciples, "See, I am sending you out like sheep into the midst of wolves; so be *wise* as serpents and innocent as doves" (Matt 10:16). Sheep in the midst of wolves are in a precarious situation. The wolves can easily attack and devour defenseless sheep. The sheep have only one line of defense, and that is to be wise.

The disciples soon found out what it meant to be as sheep in the midst of wolves. Shortly after Pentecost Peter and John were arrested, placed in custody, and threatened by the Council (Acts 4). Soon thereafter Peter and the apostles were arrested again, put in prison, and flogged — barely escaping death (Acts 5). Next Stephen was arrested, accused by false witnesses, and stoned to death (Acts 6–7). Sheep in the midst of wolves. "Be wise as serpents and innocent as doves." Whether Christians suffer from open persecution or more subtle opposition, Jesus' command still holds for us today, "Be wise!"

---

24. "The last word of the verse is *mišpāṭ*, a term usually translated 'judgment.' . . . The broader meaning of the Hebrew term is 'standard of behavior.' In our present context it has the sense of 'custom,' 'procedure,' or perhaps even 'assessment.'" Longman, *Book of Ecclesiastes*, 213.

25. Luke 9:51 puts it this way, "When the days drew near for him to be taken up, he set his face to go to Jerusalem."

So the Teacher's first point is that we should use wisdom to survive in a dangerous, unjust world. Some people might take this advice to the extreme and seek to use wisdom to understand all that happens on earth. But this is not possible, the Teacher cautions. While we should use wisdom to survive, his second point is that human wisdom has its limitations: it does not enable us to know all the work, all the doings, of God.

The Teacher concluded verse 5 with the assurance that "the wise mind will know the time and way." In verse 6 he reiterates, "For every matter has its time and way." This reminds us of chapter 3, where we read: "For everything there is a season, and a time for every matter under heaven: a time to be born, and a time to die" (3:1-2). There the Teacher made clear that God sovereignly set the times "so that all should stand in awe before him" (3:14). Here he repeats that "every matter has its time and way," but he adds, "although the troubles of mortals lie heavy upon them." The troubles that lie so heavy upon us are the troubles of not knowing what God has planned for the future. Who knows whether it will be "a time to weep" or "a time to laugh"? Who knows whether it will be "a time for war" or "a time for peace"? (3:4, 8). We cannot control the times that come upon us.[26] Since we don't know what the future holds, we are helpless and troubled.

The Teacher continues in verse 7, "Indeed, they do not know what is to be, for who can tell them how it will be?" Not even wise persons know what the future holds. God's special revelation to Joseph that seven years of plenty would be followed by seven years of famine was an exception to the rule. That exception averted a terrible disaster. But normally we cannot predict when and where famines will strike. Earthquakes, tornadoes, floods, and forest fires also are unpredictable. We don't know when and where they will hit. So we cannot adequately prepare for them. As a result they cause a tremendous amount of damage and pain. "The troubles of mortals" indeed "lie heavy upon them," for "they do not know what is to be."

Our trouble is not only that we do not know the future but that we cannot even control the present. In verse 8 the Teacher enumerates four examples of our powerlessness to control present events. First, "No one has power over the wind to restrain the wind."[27] Those who have suffered through hurricanes or tornadoes will know that feeling of helplessness. We are powerless against a mighty wind.

26. "Everything has an opportune time and a proper way of doing it, yet man cannot know the future, and so can only wait and watch for things to come to pass. Being ignorant, he lacks *siltôn*, control over what befalls him." Fox, *A Time to Tear Down*, 279.

27. *Rûaḥ* can refer to the wind or the life-breath. Crenshaw, *Ecclesiastes*, 152, favors the latter because it is followed by "the day of death." I favor "wind" because in a "numerical saying" one would expect the enumeration of a number of different items (see, e.g., Prov 30:18-19, 21-31).

Second, we do not have "power over the day of death." God has set the time to be born and the time to die (3:2), and there is nothing we can do about it. Doctors may be able to treat our diseases, but in the end the day of death comes for everyone. Again, we are powerless.

Third, "there is no discharge from the battle." Once the battle starts, there is no discharge from the army; we cannot go home and take furlough; we cannot send someone else in our place.[28] Again, we are powerless.

And fourth, "nor does wickedness deliver those who practice it." This is the Teacher's most important observation, for in the context he is puzzled especially about the wicked prospering and prolonging their life (7:15; 8:12). But just as we have no power to restrain the wind, or avoid the day of death, or receive a discharge during the battle, so wickedness will not deliver the wicked. The wicked may seem to flourish; they seem to do whatever they please; no one can stop them. But however powerful, they cannot escape the consequences of their wickedness. Eventually their wickedness will bring them down. There is no escape. All of us are completely powerless.

The Teacher concludes[29] this section in verse 9, where he writes, "All this I observed, applying my mind to all that is done under the sun, while one person exercises authority [power] over another to the other's hurt." The Teacher observed all that is done in the world. He noted that people had better use wisdom to escape the wrath of a fickle king. But he also observed that wisdom has its limitations: people don't know what the future holds; they don't know when disasters will strike. They are powerless to restrain the wind, powerless to change the day of death, powerless to receive a discharge from the battle. Even the wicked, who seem all powerful, cannot be delivered by their wickedness.

But some people, such as the king mentioned earlier, have power over others. How will they use this power? The Teacher observes that "one person exercises authority [power] over another to the other's *hurt*." People with power are bent on pursuing their own interests without regard for the hurt it causes others. Power corrupts, it is said, and absolute power corrupts absolutely. Think of the ruthless killings by tyrants like Adolf Hitler, Saddam Hussein, and Robert Mugabe. Think of the cutthroat competition in the marketplace. What a dangerous, unjust world we live in! People with power over others use it to the others' hurt.

In the next paragraph, the Teacher continues his exploration of injustice in

28. "Here he may be alluding to the common practice among the rich in the Persian period of paying for substitutes to go to war." Seow, *Ecclesiastes*, 293.

29. Although a few commentators (Hengstenberg, Zimmerli, Galling, Murphy) take this verse as the beginning of a new section, most think it concludes the foregoing because "the use of *šālāṭ* [power] links this verse with the preceding ones (8:4, 8)." Crenshaw, *Ecclesiastes*, 153. See also Whybray, *Ecclesiastes*, 134.

this world. Verse 10, "Then I saw the wicked buried; they used to go in and out of the holy place, and were praised in the city where they had done such things. This also is vanity." The Teacher observes the burial of the wicked. Even though they seem to be all powerful, there is also a time for them to die. But even in death, the great equalizer between the wicked and the righteous (2:14-16), the wicked seem to prosper. They are honored with a proper burial (cf. Job 21:32-33).[30] Even though they were wicked, they used to go in and out of the holy place, that is, the synagogue; and now they are honored with a funeral procession that begins at the synagogue.[31] Moreover, they are praised in the city where they did their wicked deeds. "This also is vanity," the Teacher concludes. It doesn't make sense; it is absurd. It almost seems that it pays to be wicked. The wicked can attend the synagogue during their lifetime and at the end of their life be honored with a splendid funeral and the praise of the people.

Moreover, wickedness rarely receives the punishment it deserves. The Teacher says in verse 11: "Because sentence against an evil deed is not executed speedily, the human heart is fully set to do evil." We can relate to this sentiment in North America. Many crimes are never prosecuted. Other crimes are prosecuted but smart lawyers can get their clients off the hook. Other sentences are delayed time after time, often on a technicality. This delay in punishing crime, the Teacher holds, encourages people to do more evil.

In fact, in verse 12 he states that "sinners do evil a *hundred* times and *prolong* their lives." The Teacher here faces the same problem he related in chapter 7:15, "There are righteous people who *perish* in their righteousness, and there are wicked people who *prolong* their life in their evil-doing." How can God allow wicked people to prolong their life in evil-doing? It just doesn't make sense. Human wisdom cannot comprehend this anomaly.

"Yet," the Teacher continues in verse 12, "I know that it will be well with those who fear God, because they stand in fear before him, but it will not be well with the wicked, neither will they prolong their days like a shadow, because they do not stand in fear before God." The Teacher here falls back on the teaching of traditional wisdom. We read in Proverbs 10:27, "The fear of the LORD prolongs life, but the years of the wicked will be short" (cf. Prov 3:2; 9:10-11). Living a life that honors God leads to a long life. In a perfect world, it will be well with the righteous and it will not be well with the wicked. The wicked, says verse 13, will not "prolong their days like a shadow."[32]

---

30. "To die unburied was the mark of a despised and unmourned end (cf. Jer 22:18-19)." Eaton, *Ecclesiastes*, 106.

31. Fox, *A Time to Tear Down*, 284.

32. "The image of the *shadow* is appropriate here because as the day ends the shadows gradually lengthen. Thus, the lives of the wicked will not grow longer as they approach the end of their days." Longman, *Book of Ecclesiastes*, 220.

But we do not live in a perfect world. The Teacher notes in verse 14: "There is a vanity that takes place on earth, that there are righteous people who are treated according to the conduct of the wicked, and there are wicked people who are treated according to the conduct of the righteous. I said that this also is vanity." It just doesn't make sense.[33] Human wisdom cannot comprehend this anomaly.

The Teacher forces us to face the real world. In an ideal world, as verse 13 put it, "It will not be well with the wicked, neither will they prolong their days." In the real world, according to verse 14, "There are righteous people who are treated according to the conduct of the wicked," that is, they will *not* prolong their days, they die young. "And there are wicked people who are treated according to the conduct of the righteous," that is, they live to a ripe, old age.[34]

Faced with this enigma, the Teacher in verse 15 repeats his earlier advice:[35] "So I commend enjoyment, for there is nothing better for people under the sun than to eat, and drink, and enjoy themselves, for this will go with them in their toil through the days of life that God gives them under the sun." In spite of the injustice they see in this world, in spite of the troubling questions they cannot answer, wise people will seek to enjoy themselves in the life God gives them.[36]

Of course, enjoyment in life does not answer all the questions we have. But "the commendation of enjoyment cautions against too much puzzling over the incomprehensible and morally offensive facts of life. In other words, . . . [the Teacher] warns against the attempt to be overwise (7:16). . . . Embracing joy frees him to let God be God, whose trademark is work that exceeds our comprehension."[37]

In the New Testament Jesus offers some answers that were not available to the Teacher in the Old Testament. Jesus teaches us that life does not end with death but that there is life beyond death. At the final judgment both the righteous and the wicked will have to give an account of their deeds. Jesus proclaims, "The hour is coming when all who are in their graves will hear his [Jesus'] voice and will come out — those who have done good, to the resurrection

---

33. The Teacher "'knows' the principle of retribution and nowhere denies it. At the same time, he *also* knows there are cases that violate the rule. It is because . . . [he] holds to the axioms of wisdom and religious tradition that he is shocked by their violation." Fox, *Ecclesiastes*, 59.

34. These glaring exceptions challenge "the theory of reward and retribution, so dear to Deuteronomy. . . . Whoever dispenses reward and punishment has gotten things mixed up." Crenshaw, *Ecclesiastes*, 156.

35. See Ecclesiastes 2:24-26; 3:12-13, 22; and 5:18-20.

36. "Merely to seek pleasure, without due consideration of death or of life as divine gift, is typical of the fool. To enjoy life because it is recognized as God's gift is a sign of wisdom and theological maturity. . . . Both life and its pleasure are God-given." Ogden, *Qoheleth*, 140.

37. Davis, *Proverbs, Ecclesiastes, Song of Songs*, 210.

of life, and those who have done evil, to the resurrection of condemnation" (John 5:28-29). Justice will be served — if not in this life, then in the next.

Jesus teaches this message also in some of his parables. For example, Jesus explains that "the kingdom of heaven is like a net that was thrown into the sea and caught fish of every kind; when it was full, they drew it ashore, sat down, and put the good into baskets but threw out the bad. So it will be at the end of the age. The angels will come out and separate the evil from the righteous and throw them into the furnace of fire, where there will be weeping and gnashing of teeth" (Matt 13:47-50). In the final analysis, it is true that "it will be well with those who fear God [those who revere God] . . . , but it will not be well with the wicked . . . , because they do not stand in fear before God" (8:12-13).

In spite of these answers, we still have our questions. Why do bad things happen in this life to good people? And why do good things happen in this life to bad people? The Teacher tried very hard to find answers to these questions. He writes in verses 16-17, "When I applied my mind to know wisdom, and to see the business that is done on earth, how one's eyes see sleep neither day nor night [that's how hard he tried], then I saw all the work of God, that *no one* can find out what is happening under the sun. However much they may toil in seeking, they will *not* find it out; even though those who are wise claim to know, they *cannot* find it out."

In this final verse he stresses three times: "*no one can find out* what is happening under the sun. However much they may toil in seeking, *they will not find it out*; even though those who are wise claim to know, *they cannot find it out*." Not even the wise, the best-equipped human beings, can find out all the work of God. There are limitations to human wisdom. We cannot find out all of God's doings and why God allows these injustices. As God says in Isaiah (55:8-9):

> For my thoughts are not your thoughts,
>   nor are your ways my ways,
>   says the LORD.
> For as the heavens are higher than the earth,
>   so are my ways higher than your ways
>   and my thoughts than your thoughts.

In the New Testament Paul echoes this sentiment when he exclaims: "O the depth of the riches and wisdom and knowledge of God! How unsearchable are his judgments and how inscrutable his ways!" (Rom 11:33).

The Old Testament Teacher has shown us that although we should use wisdom to survive in a dangerous, unjust world, wisdom does not enable us to know all the work of God. We have to learn to live with our limitations. We simply cannot comprehend "all the work of God." Although we must use our God-given wisdom in life, we must also accept the fact that life on earth presents us with mysteries we cannot fathom.

> God moves in a mysterious way his wonders to perform.
> He plants his footsteps in the sea and rides upon the storm.
>
> Deep in unfathomable mines of never-failing skill,
> he treasures up his bright designs and works his sovereign will. . . .
>
> Blind unbelief is sure to err and scan his work in vain.
> God is his own interpreter, and he will make it plain.[38]

38. William Cowper, 1774.

CHAPTER 12

Enjoy Life!

Ecclesiastes 9:1-12

> *Go, eat your bread with enjoyment,*
> *and drink your wine with a merry heart;*
> *for God has long ago approved what you do.*
> *Let your garments always be white;*
> *do not let oil be lacking on your head.*
> *Enjoy life with the wife whom you love. . . .*
> *Whatever your hand finds to do, do with your might. . . .*
>
> (Eccl 9:7-10)

In this passage the Teacher exhorts his readers for the sixth time to enjoy life. In preaching a series of sermons on Ecclesiastes, a challenge will be to capture in this sermon the unique urgency and scope of this passage so that it does not duplicate other sermons on enjoying life.

Text and Context

There is general agreement that this literary unit begins at 9:1, "All this I laid to heart, examining it all." But where does it end? Some commentators argue that the unit ends at 9:10, "since verse 11 clearly begins a new section . . . [with] 'Again I saw.'"[1] But other commentators include verses 11-12 because they form an inclusio with verses 1-2.[2] Duane Garrett suggests that verses 11-12 are "transi-

---

1. Whybray, *Ecclesiastes*, 139.
2. E.g., Ogden, *Qoheleth*, 155, "Most obvious is the inclusion *'ên/lō yôdēa' hā'ādām* (9:1, 12). A second factor is the use of *ra'a* in 9:3, 12, qualifying human fate."

tional": this text "looks back to previous statements about death when it speaks of the snare that ultimately overtakes us, but it also looks ahead to the following passage, in which wisdom offers no certainty of success in the political realm."[3] Although verses 11-12 constitute a transitional subunit, its content argues for including it with the present unit rather than with the following one. Our preaching text, therefore, is Ecclesiastes 9:1-12.

The Teacher concluded the last unit with his statement, "I saw all the work of God, that no one can find out what is happening under the sun" (8:17). In this unit he continues his reflections on the inscrutability of God's ways. He continues to struggle with his observation that the righteous seem to have no advantage over the wicked, as he did earlier in 8:12a, 14. In the present passage he stresses that "the same fate comes to . . . the righteous and the wicked" (9:2) — a point made earlier in 2:14, "the same fate befalls all of them" (cf. 3:19). Given the inevitability and apparent finality of death, the Teacher commands his readers to enjoy life to the full. He has recommended enjoyment before (2:24-26; 3:12-13, 22; 5:18-20; 8:15, and will do so once more in 11:7-9) but never in such strong terms (imperatives) and so elaborately (bread, wine, wife, and work) as in this passage. The Teacher concludes this section with the reminder that "no one can anticipate the time of disaster" (9:12) — a point made earlier in the passage of the times, especially 3:11, and in 7:14.

Literary Features

This passage contains several literary forms.[4] It begins with a reflection ("examining it all") on how the righteous and their deeds are "in the hand of God" (vv. 1-3). Sadly, the Teacher concludes that "the same fate comes to all, to the righteous and the wicked" (v. 2); "the same fate comes to everyone" (v. 3a): they all "go to the dead" (v. 3b). This reflection is followed by a reflection on the advantages the living have over the dead (vv. 4-6). It contains a proverb,[5] "A living dog is better than a dead lion" (v. 4b). These two reflections, the one flowing from the other, are perhaps linked together with the inclusio "love/hate" (vv. 1 and 6).

The centerpiece of this preaching text is an instruction with commands to enjoy life as much as possible (vv. 7-10).[6] The unit closes with another reflection ("Again I saw"), this one concerning humans being subject to "time and chance" and sudden, unexpected death (vv. 11-12).

3. Garrett, *Proverbs, Ecclesiastes*, 332.
4. See Murphy, *Wisdom Literature*, 144-45.
5. Crenshaw, *Ecclesiastes*, 161.
6. "Verses 7-10 of this chapter offer the longest sequence of imperative verbs, the longest section of *instruction*, in the entire book of Ecclesiastes." Limburg, *Encountering Ecclesiastes*, 107.

We find synonymous parallelism in three of the imperatives:[7]

Eat	your bread	with enjoyment
Drink	your wine	with a merry heart
Enjoy	life	with the wife you love

Metaphors are found in verse 1, "the hand of God" (which is also anthropomorphic), and verse 10, "your hand," as well as in verse 4, the living dog and the dead lion. Similes are found in verse 12, "Like fish . . . , and like birds."

Repetition of keywords may help us discern the thrust of the passage. "Death" is frequently mentioned or alluded to in words like "fate" (vv. 2, 3), "dead" (vv. 3, 4, 5), "die" (v. 5), "Sheol" (v. 10), and "time of calamity" (v. 12). "Under the sun" is mentioned four times (vv. 3, 6, 9, and 11). "Not know," "no knowledge" is repeated four times (vv. 1, 5, 10, and 12). And finally, "enjoyment" is mentioned (v. 7) and alluded to with "merry heart" (v. 7), "white garments" and "oil" (v. 8), and "enjoy" (literally, "see"; v. 9). In addition to these keywords, we should note that the imperative mood is found five times: "Go!" "Eat!" "Drink!" "Enjoy!" and "Do!" (vv. 7, 9, and 10).

Textual Structure

The literary forms again help us discern the textual structure:

I. Reflection on the righteous and the wise being in the hand of God (vv. 1-3)
  A. The righteous and the wise and their deeds are in the hand of God (v. 1a)
    1. Whether it is love or hate one does not know (v. 1b)
  B. Everything that confronts them is vanity (vv. 1c-2a)
    1. since the same fate comes to all (v. 2)
      a. to the righteous and the wicked
      b. to the good [and the evil]
      c. to the clean and the unclean
      d. to those who sacrifice and those who do not sacrifice
      e. as are the good, so are the sinners
      f. those who swear are like those who shun an oath
  C. This is an evil in all that happens under the sun (v. 3)
    1. The same fate comes to everyone (v. 3a)

7. Garcia Bachmann, "A Study of Qoheleth (Ecclesiastes) 9:1-12," *International Review of Mission* 91 (2002) 387.

    2. Moreover, the hearts of all are full of evil (v. 3b)
      a. madness is in their hearts while they live
      b. and after that they go to the dead
  II. Reflection on the advantages the living have over the dead (vv. 4-6)
    A. The living have hope (v. 4)
      1. for a living dog is better than a dead lion
    B. The living know that they will die (v. 5a)
    C. But the dead (vv. 5b-6)
      1. know nothing
      2. have no more reward
      3. even the memory of them is lost
      4. all their passions have already perished
        a. their love
        b. their hate
        c. their envy
      5. never again will they have a share *(portion)* in all that happens
 III. Instruction on how to live in the face of certain death (vv. 7-10)
    A. Go! (v. 7)
      1. Eat your bread with enjoyment!
      2. Drink your wine with a merry heart!
        a. for God has long ago approved what you do.
      3. Let your garments always be white (v. 8)
         do not let oil be lacking on your head
      4. Enjoy life with the wife whom you love! (v. 9)
        a. all the days of the brief life God gives you under the sun
          i. because that is your *portion* in life
            and in your toil at which you toil under the sun
      5. Do with your might! (v. 10)
        a. whatever your hand finds to do
          i. for in Sheol, to which you are going,
            (a) there is no work
            (b) or thought
            (c) or knowledge
            (d) or wisdom
 IV. Reflection on "time and chance" (vv. 11-12)
    A. Observation of unexpected results under the sun (v. 11a)
      1. the race is not to the swift
      2. nor the battle to the strong
      3. nor bread to the wise
      4. nor riches to the intelligent
      5. nor favor to the skillful

B. The reason for these results: time and chance happen to them all
   (v. 11b)
   1. for no one can anticipate the time of disaster (v. 12)
   2. mortals are snared at a time of calamity
      when it suddenly falls upon them
      a. like fish taken in a cruel net
      b. like birds caught in a snare

Theocentric Interpretation

In this preaching text the Teacher mentions the name of God only twice, but
both times it occurs at crucial junctures in his argument. His first reflection is
on the righteous and their deeds being "in the hand of God" (v. 1). At this point,
however, he fails to see much difference between the righteous and the wicked,
for one fate, death, comes to all. Still, there are advantages to being alive: one
can have hope, knowledge, and above all enjoyment. So he commands his readers, "Go, eat your bread with enjoyment and drink your wine with a merry
heart!" He adds the reason why they should enjoy food and drink: "for *God* has
long ago approved what you do" (v. 7).[8] The Teacher adds in verse 9, "Enjoy life
with the wife whom you love, all the days of your vain life that are given you,"
that is, all the days that are given you by God.[9]

Textual Theme and Goal

Verses 2 and 3 repeat that the same fate, namely death, comes to everyone.
Verses 5-6 describe in great detail what the dead do not have any more: "the
dead know nothing; they have no more reward, and even the memory of them
is lost. Their love and their hate and their envy have already perished; never
again will they have any share in all that happens under the sun." With good
reason Crenshaw entitles 9:1-10, "The Shadow of Death."[10] But the Teacher's

8. Many commentators refer to striking similarities between the Teacher's recommendations of enjoyment and the Epic of Gilgamesh as well as ancient Egyptian sources. However, von
Rad, *Old Testament Theology*, Vol. I, p. 457, observes, "In spite of their agreement with similar
utterances from ancient Egypt, these maxims of Ecclesiastes are nevertheless to be distinguished
fairly radically from that often almost cynical hedonism.... For his counsels recommending an
acceptance and enjoyment of the possible in every case contain a pointer to God: they are in fact
the only maxims which bring human action with an almost astonishing directness into connection with a positive will of God — it 'pleases' God (Ecclesiastes 9:7b)."

9. Divine passive, see p. 162 above.

10. Crenshaw, *Ecclesiastes*, 158.

message is not that we live in the shadow of death. The focus of his message comes in verses 7-10, "Enjoy to the fullest the days God gives you!"[11] The imperatives of the text call for an imperative in the main clause of the theme. If we had chosen as our text 9:1-10, the point of the message would come at the climax and we could formulate the theme as follows: "Because we live in the shadow of death, enjoy to the fullest the days God gives you!"

But now that we have chosen as our text 9:1-12, we also have to take into account verses 11-12. These verses speak of the unpredictability of life and the unexpectedness of death: "No one can anticipate the time of disaster. Like fish taken in a cruel net, and like birds caught in a snare, so mortals are snared at a time of calamity, when it suddenly falls upon them" (v. 12). The passage as a whole, then, looks somewhat like a chiastic structure:

A. We all die, and the dead have nothing (vv. 1-6)
   B. Enjoy to the fullest the days God gives you! (vv. 7-10)
A'. Life is unpredictable, and death can strike us unexpectedly (vv. 11-12)

The focus is still on the center, B, but we need to add to the theme the idea of A', that life is unpredictable and that death can strike unexpectedly. These considerations lead to the following theme formulation: *In view of the certainty of death and the unpredictability of life, enjoy to the fullest the days God gives you!*

If possible, the goal of the Teacher should be determined by hearing his message (theme) in its original historical context. If this context was indeed the time of an international economic boom during the rule of the Ptolemies, one can understand that this time, as well as many others, would have been dehumanizing to individuals. Some seek to understand the Teacher's message against this background: "Qohelet's proposal affirms real life in opposition to the dehumanizing rhythm of the Ptolemaic system of elevating the value of production, which cast humans as objects that produced objects, not as complete persons or subjects."[12]

Although this move is possible, it fails to do justice to the specific context offered by the text itself. We will all die and have nothing; moreover, death can capture us suddenly and unexpectedly. Since the main clause in the theme is a command, the appropriate goal is not to teach, or to encourage,

11. See ibid., 162, on verse 7, "Now he switches to imperatives . . . , conveying a greater sense of urgency issuing from Qohelet's reflection on the power of death to extinguish powerful emotions." Seow, *Ecclesiastes*, 302, adds: "The statement that the dead never again will have a portion (v. 6), is answered by the affirmation of enjoyment as the portion of the living (v. 9)."

12. E.g., Elsa Tamez and Gloria Kinsler, "Ecclesiastes: A Reading from the Periphery," *Int* 55/3 (2001) 250-59, specifically 258.

but to *urge*. The goal, then, is, *To urge the readers, in view of the certainty of death and the unpredictability of life, to enjoy to the fullest the days God gives them.*

Ways to Preach Christ

There is no promise of the coming Messiah in this passage, nor is there a type of Christ. Since redemptive-historical progression and longitudinal themes are intertwined, we shall explore them in combination as well as checking analogy, New Testament references, and contrast.

Redemptive-Historical Progression/Longitudinal Themes

The theme that we ought to enjoy to the fullest the life God gives begins in Paradise but is interrupted by the Fall into sin. The joy of eating and drinking, marriage and work (Gen 2:15-25) changed suddenly into eating "by the sweat of your brow," strife for dominance in marriage, "toil" to eke out a living, and certain death (respectively Gen 3:19a, 16b, 17c, and 19b). Yet in his grace the LORD brings his people Israel to a land which was "well watered everywhere like the garden of the LORD" (Gen 13:10) — a land where Israel can experience to some extent the joys of Paradise: fellowship with the LORD, enjoying food and drink, joy in marriage and family, and satisfaction in work (see Chapter 3 above, pp. 54-56).

Because of Israel's sin, God sent them into exile, but in his grace he enabled a remnant to return. God promised them that he would "create new heavens and a new earth": "Be glad and rejoice forever in what I am creating; for I am about to create Jerusalem as a joy, and its people as a delight. . . . They shall plant vineyards and eat their fruit, . . . and my chosen shall long *enjoy* the work of their hands" (Isa 65:17-21). But as yet the certainty of death remained. The Teacher uses this certainty and the seeming finality of death as backdrop to urge his readers to enjoy to the full the life God gives.

Redemptive history jumps forward with Jesus' coming to this world. Jesus teaches that death is not the end but that there is life beyond death (see redemptive-historical progression on pp. 207-8 above). Jesus' own death and resurrection prove the point. But the obligation to enjoy the life God gives still holds. To the extent that it was possible, given his mission, Jesus experienced joy in his life on earth: "the Son of Man came eating and drinking."[13] Jesus pro-

13. Matthew 11:18-19, "For John came neither eating nor drinking, and they say, 'He has a

vided bread for the masses to enjoy (John 6:1-14), and he turned plain water into "good wine" for people to enjoy at a wedding (John 2:9-11).

After his ascension, Jesus made true joy possible by pouring out the Holy Spirit. We read about the church after Pentecost, "Day by day, as they spent much time together in the temple, they broke bread at home and ate their food with *glad and generous hearts*" (Acts 2:46). The "generous hearts" indicates that our joy cannot derive from selfishness. Jesus teaches "the perspective of service. Service to one's fellowmen — with the intent that they too can have joy in life — means faithfulness to him who gives us orders."[14] That joyful service to others leads to our joy being full one day. In Jesus' parable of the talents, the master responds to those who have served faithfully, "Well done, good and trustworthy slave; you have been trustworthy in a few things, I will put you in charge of many things; enter into the *joy* of your master" (Matt 25:21, 23; cf. 25:34-36, "inherit the kingdom prepared for you"). When Jesus comes again, he will usher in "a new heaven and a new earth": "death will be no more; mourning and crying and pain will be no more, for the first things have passed away" (Rev 21:4), and God's people will receive again "permission to eat from the tree of life that is in the paradise of God" (Rev 2:7; cf. 22:1-5, 14).

Analogy

We can also look for analogies between the mandates of the Teacher and the teachings of Jesus. The Teacher taught, "Enjoy life with the wife whom you love" (v. 9a). Although not married himself, Jesus honored marriage with his presence at the wedding in Cana and even turned water into "good wine" (John 2:1-11). The Teacher also taught, "Whatever your hand finds to do, do with your might; for there is no work or thought or knowledge or wisdom in Sheol." Jesus taught similarly, "We must work the works of him who sent me while it is day; night is coming when no one can work" (John 9:4).

New Testament References

For Ecclesiastes 9 the appendix to the Greek New Testament lists two references. For verse 7 it lists Acts 2:46, "Day by day, as they spent much time together in the temple, they broke bread at home and ate their food with glad and generous

---

demon'; the Son of Man came eating and drinking, and they say, 'Look, a glutton and a drunkard, a friend of tax collectors and sinners!' Yet wisdom is vindicated by her deeds."

14. Loader, *Ecclesiastes*, 111.

hearts" — a verse we used in redemptive-historical progression above. For verse 8 it lists Matthew 6:17, where Jesus says, "But when you fast, put oil on your head and wash your face, so that your fasting may be seen not by others but by your Father who is in secret; and your Father who sees in secret will reward you." However, since Jesus' point is not that of enjoyment, this reference is not a good bridge to Christ for our preaching text.

Instead one can think of passages where Jesus speaks of our joy. For example, in John 15:10-11 Jesus says, "If you keep my commandments, you will abide in my love. . . . I have said these things to you so that my joy may be in you, and that your joy may be complete." Or one can think of Paul urging Christians to rejoice: "Rejoice *in the Lord* always; again I will say, Rejoice" (Phil 4:4); "Rejoice always . . . ; for this is the will of God *in Christ Jesus* for you" (1 Thess 5:16).

Contrast

The Teacher's view that we don't know whether our experiences in life are a result of God's love or God's hate (9:1) stands in contrast to the New Testament teachings on God's love. The familiar John 3:16 states that "God so loved the world that he gave his only Son." 1 John affirms that "God's love was revealed among us in this way: God sent his only Son into the world so that we might live through him" (4:9); it further states plainly that "God is love" (4:16). In Romans 8:39 Paul declares that nothing "in all creation will be able to separate us from the love of God in Christ Jesus our Lord." However, in possible continuity with the Teacher's view, the New Testament teaches that "the Lord disciplines those whom he loves" (see 1 Cor 11:32; Heb 12:5-11; Rev 3:19).

The Teacher's totally negative description of death (vv. 5-6) also stands in sharp contrast to the teachings of the New Testament. Jesus says, "I am the resurrection and the life. Those who believe in me, even though they die, will live, and everyone who lives and believes in me will never die" (John 11:25-26). He also teaches his followers, "In my Father's house there are many dwelling places. . . . If I go and prepare a place for you, I will come again and will take you to myself, so that where I am, there you may be also" (John 14:2-3). Because of the death and resurrection of Jesus, Paul struggles with the question which is better for him, life on earth or death. He writes, "I am hard pressed between the two: my desire is to depart and be with Christ, which is far better" (Phil 1:23).

Sermon Theme and Goal

We formulated the textual theme as follows, "In view of the certainty of death and the unpredictability of life, enjoy to the fullest the days God gives you!" Since the New Testament deepens but does not change the specific message of the Teacher, the textual theme can become the sermon theme: *In view of the certainty of death and the unpredictability of life, enjoy to the fullest the days God gives you!*

With a slight change, the Teacher's goal can become our goal: *To urge the hearers, in view of the certainty of death and the unpredictability of life, to enjoy to the fullest the days God gives them.* This goal points to the need addressed in this sermon: people are not enjoying to the fullest the days God gives them.

Sermon Form

The sermon introduction can set the relevance of this sermon by exposing the need addressed. In the sermon body we expose the meaning of the parts and the theme of the preaching text. If our preaching text were 9:1-10, the sermon form could use inductive development by simply following the text from its premises that we all die and the dead have nothing (vv. 1-6) to its conclusion (theme), "Enjoy to the fullest the days God gives you!" (vv. 7-10). But now that we have chosen as our text 9:1-12, we have more options with the sermon form. We can still use inductive development by rearranging the text:

   I. We all die, and the dead have nothing (vv. 1-6)
  II. Life is unpredictable, and death can strike unexpectedly (vv. 11-12)
 III. Enjoy to the fullest the days God gives you! (vv. 7-10)

Or we can follow the textual order so that we use inductive/deductive development:

   I. We all die, and the dead have nothing (vv. 1-6)
  II. Enjoy to the fullest the days God gives you! (vv. 7-10)
 III. Life is unpredictable, and death can strike unexpectedly (vv. 11-12)

In the following presentation, we shall use a third option that consists of inductive/inductive development (inductive vv. 1-6 to the theme in vv. 7-10, then inductive vv. 11-12 to the theme in the New Testament):

   I. We all die, and the dead have nothing (vv. 1-6)
  II. Enjoy to the fullest the days God gives you! (vv. 7-10)

III. Life is unpredictable, and death can strike unexpectedly (vv. 11-12)
IV. Enjoy to the fullest the days God gives you! (New Testament)

The conclusion should clinch the goal of the sermon.

Sermon Exposition

Many people today go through life with little joy. They are anxious about the economy: concerned about being laid off; worried they may lose their home; angry about high gas prices; some wondering where their next meal will come from. Others are anxious about their health: Will the cancer return? Will a stroke leave me paralyzed? Will a matching organ donor be found in time? Still others are anxious about death: Will it involve much suffering? Am I ready to face my Maker? Who will look after the kids?

Anxiety eats away at the joy life can give. Anxiety kills joyful living! That is as true today as it was in the time the Teacher wrote Ecclesiastes. The Teacher has been struggling in chapters 7 and 8 with the question why bad things happen to some good people and good things happen to some bad people. How can a just God allow this to come about? He ended chapter 8 with the conclusion that *no one* can find out all the work of God; "even though those who are wise claim to know, they cannot find it out." Then he begins chapter 9, "All this" — that is, that the righteous sometimes suffer while the wicked prosper, and that we cannot understand God's ways[15] — "All this I laid to heart, examining it all, how the righteous and the wise and their deeds are in the hand of God; whether it is love or hate one does not know."

No matter how much they suffer on earth, "the righteous and the wise and their deeds are in the hand of *God.*" The evil that befalls good people is not outside God's control. God is sovereign. God set the times: "a time to be born and a time to die" (3:2). God is in control. So when good people suffer, it is a perplexing yet consoling thought that "the righteous and the wise and their deeds are in the hand of God." They are in God's care.[16]

The problem is, the Teacher continues, "whether it is love or hate one does not know." That is to say, the righteous and the wise do not know whether what they experience is a result of God's love, God's favor, or of God's hate, God's an-

---

15. Fox, *A Time to Tear Down*, 290: "The opening *kî* is a loose causal particle that explains why the above is said rather than why it is true."

16. "In the hand of God" "is a well-known expression meaning 'at the disposal of' (Gen 14:20; 16:6, etc.), 'under the supervision of' (Gen 9:2, etc.), or 'in the care of' (best here; cf. Est 2:3, 8; Job 12:10; Ps 31:5, etc.)." Eaton, *Ecclesiastes,* 124. Cf. Seow, *Ecclesiastes,* 298, "To be 'in the hand of God' is to be subject to God's power (see Prov 21:1; Deut 33:3; Wis 3:1)."

ger. They do not know because they also experience painful things in life. Sometimes they suffer terribly: as the Teacher put it in chapter 8:14, they are "treated according to the conduct of the wicked." Sometimes they die young: as the Teacher observed in chapter 7:15, "they perish in their righteousness." Looking at what we experience in life, we cannot tell whether God loves us or is angry with us.[17]

The Teacher continues at the end of verse 1, "Everything that confronts them is vanity,"[18] that is, it doesn't make sense. And then he explains with a series of contrasts why our experiences in life don't make sense: "since the same fate [i.e., death][19] comes to all, to the righteous and the wicked, to the good and the evil, to the clean and the unclean, to those who sacrifice and those who do not sacrifice. As are the good, so are the sinners; those who swear are like those who shun an oath."[20]

"The same fate comes to all." That great enemy, death, captures all people: good people as well as bad people.[21] "Moral or immoral, religious or profane, we are all mown down alike."[22]

In verse 3 the Teacher bursts out, "This is an evil in all that happens under the sun, that the *same* fate comes to everyone." It is an evil, isn't it, that good

17. Seow, *Ecclesiastes*, 298, argues that "love or hate" refers to "their works," the deeds of the righteous and wise. But Kidner, *Time to Mourn*, 81, n. 1, argues that "the emphasis on God's inscrutability in 8:17, immediately before this verse, makes it more likely (and more relevant to the argument) that His attitude rather than man's is the issue here." Cf. Murphy, *Ecclesiastes*, 90: "One cannot know from experience, from the way things turn out, whom God truly loves since the same treatment is dealt out to the just and to the wicked alike (vv. 2-3)." Cf. Fox, *Ecclesiastes*, 61, "These are God's emotions, not humans.' Looking at the unjust allocations of fates, we cannot understand God's favor and disfavor. The divine psychology is opaque, as is shown, for example, by the unfair allocation of life spans, described in 8:14."

18. The Hebrew has, "Everything that confronts them is everything" (see NRSV footnote). The Septuagint and other translations have changed the second *hakkōl*, "everything," to *hebel*, "vanity."

19. "Here Qohelet is *not* referring to injustices in this life, but to death as the great leveler." Whybray, *Ecclesiastes*, 141. See Ecclesiastes 2:14-16.

20. Commentators disagree on whether "those who shun an oath" are good or bad. Following the pattern in the series of good followed by bad, some, such as Eaton, *Ecclesiastes*, 125, and Provan, *Ecclesiastes*, 180, argue that shunning an oath must be bad. But Crenshaw, *Ecclesiastes*, 160, argues that the last pair is an exception, "which may have been reversed on the principle of concluding on a favorable note, but more likely is simply a stylistic variation." Thus shunning an oath would be good, and in line with the Teacher's earlier warning against making a vow hastily (5:5). In any event, since this issue is not the Teacher's point but rather that *all*, whether good or bad, die, I would not raise this issue in the sermon.

21. "Just as in 2:13-14 there are contrasting statements to embrace all manner of humanity, in 9:2 the series of contrasts is a literary device emphasizing death's universality." Ogden, *Qoheleth*, 145.

22. Kidner, *Time to Mourn*, 82.

people as well as bad people suffer the tragedy of death? We can sense his outrage.

But the Teacher adds, "Moreover, the hearts of all are full of evil; madness is in their hearts while they live, and after that they go to the dead." When he says, "the hearts of all are full of evil," is he giving a reason why all die?[23] He may have been thinking of God's observation before sending the great flood: "The Lord saw that the wickedness of humankind was great in the earth, and that every inclination of the thoughts of their *hearts was only evil continually*" (Gen 6:5). Because the Lord saw that the human hearts were full of evil, he said, "I will blot out from the earth the human beings I have created" (Gen 6:7).

Perhaps the Teacher is thinking back even further, to Paradise where God gave but one commandment: "Of the tree of the knowledge of good and evil you shall not eat, for in the day that you eat of it you shall die" (Gen 2:17). Adam and Eve disobeyed God's commandment — and death followed: "You are dust, and to dust you shall return" (Gen 3:19). Since we have all inherited this evil disposition of disobeying God, we all deserve to die. The so-called righteous (cf. 7:20) as well as the wicked deserve to die.

The Teacher says, "Madness is in their hearts while they live." It is madness to defy our Creator God. "And after that they go to the dead"; literally, "and afterwards — to the dead!"[24] The life of all persons will suddenly be cut off — and they go to the abode of the dead. It's a somber picture of the destiny of every person.

Still, there are advantages to being alive. The Teacher writes in verse 4, "But whoever is joined with all the living has hope, for a living dog is better than a dead lion." The living have hope[25] that they may still experience some of the joy that the Teacher repeatedly advocates. Today we express this hope in a proverb, "Where there's life, there's hope." The Teacher also uses a proverb to support his point that the living have hope: "For a living dog is better than a dead lion." In

---

23. Many commentators, e.g., Loader, *Ecclesiastes*, 108, and Seow, *Ecclesiastes*, 304, argue that the fact that both good and evil people die leads to the hearts of all being full of evil. In other words, Why be righteous when we all die anyway? They point to the supposed parallel in 8:11, where the delay of judgment leads to more evil. But the argument that the delay of judgment leads to more evil is quite different from an argument that the *same* judgment leads to all being evil. The latter, as we can see from history, is simply not true. The Teacher never gives up on the distinction in life between the righteous and the wicked.

24. Whybray, *Ecclesiastes*, 141. Cf. Longman, *Book of Ecclesiastes*, 227, "The abrupt syntax at the end of the verse is intentional and reflects the suddenness of death in the midst of life."

25. This same word, *biṭṭāḥôn*, is translated as "confidence" in 2 Kings 18:19 (par. Isa 36:4). Many commentators, e.g, Fox, *Qohelet*, 258, deny that the word implies hope, as expressed in the NRSV and TNIV. Garrett, *Proverbs, Ecclesiastes, Song of Songs*, 331, n. 207, by contrast, holds that "*biṭṭāḥôn* and its cognates always have the positive sense of hope, security, or confidence about the future. See A. Jepsen, *bāṭach, TDOT* 2:88-94."

the ancient Near East a dog was not a pet but a despised, unclean scavenger.[26] Today we might think of a rat — a loathsome creature. By contrast, the lion, like today, was admired as king of the animal world. Now the Teacher says that the living have hope, for a living scavenger dog is better than a dead lion. In other words, even a dog's life is better than death; even a miserable life is better than death, for the living have hope.

Moreover, the Teacher says in verse 5, "The living know that they will die,[27] but the dead know nothing." The living have "consciousness"; "the living are self-aware";[28] they "*know* that they will die, but the dead know *nothing*." In addition, the dead "have no more reward": they have nothing to look forward to; they have no future. "And even the memory of them is lost": their past accomplishments are forgotten by those who live later. They have no past and no future. It's as if they had never lived.

Verse 6, "Their love and their hate and their envy have already perished"; that is, their passions[29] — their love, hate, and envy — have been extinguished. "Never again will they have any share [portion] in all that happens under the sun." This is probably the starkest biblical description of the dead: they are gone; no more rewards; soon forgotten; their passions perished; no more portion in life.

Against this dark background of death, the Teacher has some important advice for the living. Verse 7, "Go, eat your bread with enjoyment, and drink your wine with a merry heart; for God has long ago approved what you do." The Teacher has encouraged us before to enjoy the life God gives us, but here he is most urgent. We cannot waste a day. He brings to expression the urgency by casting his advice in the form of commands: Go! Eat! Drink! Enjoy! Do!

The first command is, "Go!" It's a wakeup call. There's no time to waste. Stop your complaining! Stop nursing your anger! Stop brooding about your problems! Get over your anxiety! "Go!"[30]

---

26. "The dog . . . was a despised scavenger (Exod 22:31; 1 Kings 14:11), notorious for its uncleanness (Prov 26:11); a Sumerian proverb states: 'He who esteems highly dogs which are clever is a man who has no shame." Eaton, *Ecclesiastes*, 126.

27. Since this statement follows upon the one that says that the living having "confidence," some commentators, e.g., Crenshaw, *Ecclesiastes*, 161, view it as "irony": "Although many commentators view this theoretical knowledge as positive, Qohelet's words appear ironic." Cf. Loader, *Ecclesiastes*, 109.

28. Longman, *Book of Ecclesiastes*, 228.

29. The Teacher sees "love, hate, and envy (or, more probably, rivalry or striving for success in life — cf. 4:4). . . . as the strong passions which, admirable or not, form the mainspring of human activities. Better to participate in the stimulating ferment of life than to be dead, with no passions and no activities at all!" Whybray, *Ecclesiastes*, 143.

30. The Teacher "urges his readers to embrace the good in life before it is too late, to seize the day before death seizes the self." Brown, *Ecclesiastes*, 93.

The Teacher's second command is, "Eat your bread with *enjoyment!*" Don't rush through your meals. Don't gulp down your food like a pig. God made us so that we not only need food in order to live but so that we can enjoy it. He has provided us with a rich variety of delicious fruit, vegetables, and grain. "Eat your bread with enjoyment!"

"And drink your wine with a merry heart." God has also provided a rich variety of drinks for us to enjoy. In Israel wine was a favorite. In other countries it may be coffee or tea. The point is not that we should necessarily drink wine, but that we should enjoy whatever we drink. "Drink your wine with a merry heart!"

Some people think that this advice is the same as the pagan slogan, "Let us eat and drink, for tomorrow we die" (Isa 22:13; 1 Cor 15:32). But this slogan is shallow and selfish. The Teacher's advice is much more profound. He writes in verse 7, "Go, eat your bread with enjoyment, and drink your wine with a merry heart; *for* [because] God has *long ago* approved what you do." Long ago God approved our enjoyment of food and drink. The Teacher is probably thinking of the creation story.[31] God placed the first human creatures in a beautiful garden and gave them many plants and fruit for food (Gen 1:29; 2:16). In other words, God not only created human beings with the need for food but he provided food with great variety for their enjoyment. Psalm 104:15 states, "The LORD gives wine to gladden the human heart, oil to make the face shine, and bread to strengthen the human heart." So if we enjoy our meals, God approves. Long ago God approved because he created us to enjoy our food and drink. God is pleased when we enjoy his provisions.[32]

The Teacher continues in verse 8, "Let your garments always be white; do not let oil be lacking on your head." In a hot climate, white garments would reflect the heat of the sun, and oil would keep the skin from drying out. Here the white garments and oil are symbols of joy.[33] When people were distraught they showed it by wearing sackcloth and putting ashes on their head (see 2 Sam 13:19). When people were joyful they showed it by wearing *white* clothes and putting *oil* on their head.[34] In our culture we might show

---

31. "Long ago" or "already": "This may mean that the enjoyment of God's gifts is something which God has decreed from the beginning (cf. 5:18 [MT 17], 'for this is his lot')." Whybray, *Ecclesiastes*, 144.

32. "Everything created by God is good, and nothing is to be rejected, provided it is received with thanksgiving" (1 Tim 4:4). Cf. Ogden, *Qoheleth*, 152, "God wills that we enjoy his basic provisions, for he is the one who provides them (cf. 2:24 etc.)."

33. White garments are worn by the church triumphant as a symbol of joy (Rev 3:4, 5; 7:9). For oil as a symbol of joy, Psalm 45:7 speaks of God anointing the king with "the oil of gladness." Cf. Isaiah 61:3, "the oil of gladness instead of mourning," and Psalm 23:5, "You anoint my head with oil; my cup overflows."

34. Jesus taught his followers to use oil on their heads even when fasting so that fasting

our joy by wearing colorful clothes and having a neat hairdo and a smile on our face.

In verse 9 the Teacher becomes more specific: "Enjoy[35] life with the wife whom you love, all the days of your vain [brief] life that are given you under the sun, because that is your portion[36] in life and in your toil at which you toil under the sun." "Enjoy life with the wife whom you love!" Again, the Teacher may well be thinking of the first garden where God made the woman as a partner for the man for mutual, "one flesh" intimacy (Gen 2:18-25).[37]

Iain Provan reminds us that "there has always been within the Christian tradition an ascetic tendency that understands true spirituality as involving the shunning of created things (e.g., food, wine, sex) rather than the enjoyment of these things in thankfulness to God who has blessed us with them. . . . [The Teacher] helps us see that the latter is the true spirituality."[38] Enjoying God's good gifts is true spirituality.

The Teacher adds one more command, verse 10, "Whatever your hand finds to do, do with your might; for there is no work or thought or knowledge or wisdom in Sheol, to which you are going." Sheol is the abode of the dead. So the Teacher reminds his readers again that death awaits. "There is no work or thought or knowledge or wisdom in Sheol." All the more reason to "do with your might" "whatever your hand finds[39] to do" (cf. Pss 6:5; 30:9). "Whatever your hand finds to do" refers to opportunity. "If you have a chance to do something, do it now, because who knows what the future will bring."[40] For the

---

would not become a public display. "Whenever you fast, do not look dismal, like the hypocrites. . . . When you fast, put oil on your head and wash you face . . ." (Matt 6:16-18). See also Luke 7:46, "You did not anoint my head with oil, but she has anointed my feet with ointment."

35. Hebrew *rĕ'ēh*, "see." "In 2:1 and 3:13 where its meaning is of the same order as here, the notion of seeking or looking for pleasure in what one does is marked by the addition of the adjective *ṭôb*, 'good.' Although in this present case the *ṭôb* is omitted, yet the sense of seeking pleasure can be detected." Ogden, *Qoheleth*, 153. The immediate context certainly calls for the translation, "Enjoy!"

36. "People ought to enjoy life precisely because life is ephemeral. This, he [the Teacher] says, is the *portion* of humanity in life (v. 9), a *portion* that the dead no longer have (v. 6). That is the difference between the living and the dead: the living still have a portion (the possibility of enjoyment), the dead do not." Seow, *Ecclesiastes*, 306.

37. Cf. Proverbs 5:18, "Rejoice in the wife of your youth."

38. Provan, *Ecclesiastes*, 185-86. In the early church the apostle Paul vehemently opposed those who "forbid marriage and demand abstinence from foods, which God created to be received with thanksgiving. . . . For everything created by God is good, and nothing is to be rejected, provided it is received with thanksgiving" (1 Tim 4:3-4).

39. "The play on the impossibility of 'finding' any large-scale explanation of the universe throughout the preceding chapters is obvious. If the reality of death is to set the context for the living of life (7:1-12), then 'finding' should best be directed at the business of living in itself." Ibid., 182.

40. Longman, *Book of Ecclesiastes*, 231, with credit to Hengstenberg, *Commentary on Ecclesiastes*, 216. For the same idiom, see Judges 9:33 and 1 Samuel 10:7.

Teacher, it turns out, hard work is part of the joy of living.[41] God created us to work (Gen 2:15). So purposeful work should give us satisfaction and joy.

In view of the certainty of our death, therefore, the Teacher urges us to seize the day: "Eat your bread with enjoyment!" "Drink your wine with a merry heart!" "Enjoy life with the wife whom you love!" And, "Whatever your hand finds to do, do with your might!"

In verses 11 and 12 the Teacher moves on to the unpredictability of our lives and the unexpectedness of our death. "Again I saw that under the sun the race is not to the swift, nor the battle to the strong, nor bread to the wise, nor riches to the intelligent, nor favor to the skillful; but time and chance happen to them all."

Human life, he observes, is unpredictable. We would expect a race to be won by the swift. But the Teacher writes, "The race is *not* to the swift." Unexpected things happen in a race. The fastest people in a footrace may trip; they may pull a muscle; they may be boxed in.[42] In the recent Olympic Games, an American woman, Lola Jones, was expected to win gold in the hurdles. She was known to be the fastest in the world. But she tripped on the ninth hurdle and came in, not first but seventh. "The race is not to the swift." Life is unpredictable.

The Teacher offers a second example: "Nor is the battle to the strong." Goliath was big and strong as an ox. He had won many battles for the Philistines. He taunted Israel to send its strongest soldier. Out came little David, the shepherd boy, without any armor — only a slingshot and a few stones. He struck Goliath in the forehead. The mighty Goliath died. The battle is not always to the strong. There are exceptions. Life is unpredictable.

From these examples of physical prowess, the Teacher moves to three examples of intellectual superiority: "nor bread to the wise, nor riches to the intelligent, nor favor to the skillful." The wise could be either artisans or teachers.[43] One would think that teachers would have bread, that is, a good livelihood. Proverbs 3:16 comments on wisdom: "Long life is in her right hand; in her left hand are *riches* and honor." But there are exceptions. Life is unpredictable.

41. "For the biblical sage, work is just as integral to joy as it is a part of humanity's limiting lot (see also 2:24a; 3:13a, 22; 5:18 [Heb v. 17]; 8:15b). . . . As Qohelet has consistently claimed, the value of work is not derived from the gain that one's labors may yield but, rather, is found in the very doing of work, in the challenge of formidable toil." Brown, *Ecclesiastes*, 95. See also Brown, "Whatever Your Hand Finds to Do," *Int* 55/3 (2001) 282.

42. Commentators caution that the Teacher may have had in mind not an athlete but a courier since Greek contests were introduced into Palestine at a late date. But Crenshaw, *Ecclesiastes*, 164, observes that the Teacher "may have heard about such races before their entrance into Jewish life." Certainly for a contemporary audience, the image of a contemporary (Olympic) race will make the point more vividly.

43. Murphy, *Ecclesiastes*, 93.

"Nor riches to the intelligent." One would expect that the intelligent, that is, the clever financiers and entrepreneurs,[44] would be rich. But again there are exceptions. "Nor favor to the skillful." The skillful are, "literally, those who know how to do or make something."[45] One would think that people would always appreciate the skillful. But there are exceptions.

Why is it that there are so many exceptions to our expectations? We expect the swift to win the race; the strong to win the battle; wise teachers to have a good salary; intelligent entrepreneurs to be rich; and the skillful to be appreciated. Why is it that there are so many exceptions to our expectations?

The Teacher answers at the end of verse 11, "but time and chance happen to them all." The problem is "time and chance."[46] Literally he says that the problem is "a time and an incident," or "a timely incident." Today we would call this "an accident."[47] We have already seen that we cannot control the times: "a time to be born, and a time to die," etc. (3:1-15). But we cannot control accidents either. Accidents happen: runners can trip, the strong can be outsmarted, wise teachers can lose their jobs, intelligent entrepreneurs can go bankrupt, the skillful can fall out of favor. The point is: we are not in complete control of our destiny. Accidents can cause us to fall far short of our goal. Life is unpredictable.

"For," the Teacher continues in verse 12, "no one can anticipate the time of *disaster*. Like fish taken in a cruel net, and like birds caught in a snare, so mortals are snared at a time of *calamity*, when it suddenly falls upon them." Not only is life unpredictable; the time of death is also unpredictable. The Teacher likens this time of disaster to "fish taken in a cruel net." In the East, fishermen often use a round net. From their boats, or even standing in the water close to shore, they will cast a round net into the air. The net seems to hover in the air for a moment; then suddenly it plummets into the water on unwary fish. A time of disaster for the unsuspecting fish.

The time of disaster is also "like birds caught in a snare." A simple snare consists of a noose staked into the ground or tied to a tree. The birds go about their business, feeding on seeds on the ground. They are at ease because there

---

44. Whybray, *Ecclesiastes*, 146.

45. Ibid.

46. "Chance" for *pega'* "is an unhappy choice of translation, since this word connotes an impersonal and random force, whereas Qohelet is clear throughout the book that human fate lies ultimately in God's hands, no matter how random and impersonal what befalls us may appear. The verbal form *pg'* means 'to meet, encounter.' A *pega'* is simply something we encounter on the path of life — a circumstance or situation over which we have no control." Provan, *Ecclesiastes*, 183, n. 2.

47. Seow, *Ecclesiastes*, 321. The technical term for two words expressing one idea is "heniadys."

are no predators around. A bird sticks its head through the noose and it tightens around its neck. A time of disaster. Caught in a snare!

"Like fish taken in a cruel net, and like birds caught in a snare, so mortals are snared at a time of calamity, when it suddenly falls upon them." All of a sudden, death can overtake us. We may not suspect a thing; we are just going about our business. Suddenly the net can fall on us; we are caught in the snare — and life is over.

With not only the certainty of death in view but now also its suddenness and unexpectedness, the Teacher urges us all the more to enjoy the life God gives us. Because we will all die, and death can snare us suddenly and unexpectedly, enjoy to the fullest the days God gives you!

The New Testament, of course, teaches us that death is not the end but a new beginning — our entrance into eternal life. But that does not alter the message that we ought to enjoy the days God gives us on this earth. Jesus himself enjoyed "eating and drinking" (see Matt 11:18-19). On several occasions Jesus provided bread for the masses to enjoy (Matt 14:13-21; 15:32-39). He even turned plain water into "good wine" for people to enjoy at a wedding (John 2:9-11).

Jesus also teaches us not to worry about food and drink. Worry about where the next meal will come from kills any enjoyment. Jesus urges us not to worry: "Do not worry, saying, 'What will we eat?' or 'What will we drink?' . . . Indeed your heavenly Father knows that you need all these things. But strive first for the kingdom of God and his righteousness, and all these things will be *given* to you as well" (Matt 6:31-33).

Since food and drink are *gifts* from our heavenly Father, we should enjoy them. If we do not enjoy God's gifts, we dishonor the Giver. Then we are like children who receive gifts at Christmas, take off the wrapping, and simply toss the gifts aside. Our enjoyment of God's gifts is an expression of our gratitude to him. The early Christians understood this well. We read in Acts 2:46, "Day by day, as they spent much time together in the temple, they broke bread at home and ate their food with *glad* and generous hearts."

Not only are we to enjoy our food and drink, but we must also make a point of enjoying life with our spouse. Jesus honored marriage by being present at the wedding in Cana (John 2:1-11). And Paul enjoins us, "Husbands, love your wives, just as Christ loved the church and gave himself up for her" (Eph 5:25).

And finally, we must also enjoy our work and do it with all our might. The Teacher motivated us to work heartily because, he wrote, "there is no work or thought . . . in Sheol," that is, in the abode of the dead. Jesus says something similar. He says, "We must work the works of him who sent me while it is day; night is coming when no one can work" (John 9:4). Jesus has in mind the night, the darkness of death, that will soon overtake him as well as his disciples. Unless the Lord returns first, each one of us will die. Before that hour strikes, Jesus says, we must work the works God has assigned us. Paul adds, "Whatever your task, put yourselves into it, as done *for the Lord* and not for your masters, since you know that from the Lord you will receive the inheritance as your reward; you serve the Lord Christ" (Col 3:23-24).

Because Jesus died and rose to save us from our enslavement to sin and to reconcile us to God, we can begin to live as God intended in the beginning: enjoying our food and drink, enjoying life with our spouse, and enjoying our work. Paul enjoins us, "Whether you eat or drink, or whatever you do, do everything for the glory of God" (1 Cor 10:31).

Unfortunately, we so often fritter away our days with meaningless pursuits: grudges, petty arguments, frustrations, anger, worries, you name it. We waste our days as if there were an unlimited supply. You may have heard of people who were told by their doctor that they had only a few months to live. Suddenly their outlook on life changed. They lived each day as if it could be their last. They tried to live each day to the full.[48]

When White House secretary Tony Snow returned to work after five weeks of cancer treatment, he said, "Not everybody will survive cancer. But on the other hand, you have got to realize you've got the gift of life, so make the most of it."[49] Tony died a year later at the age of 53. Each day *could* be our last. Therefore, we ought to enjoy each day to the full. We should remind ourselves every morning when we wake up: "This is the day that the LORD has made; let us rejoice and be glad in it" (Ps 118:24).[50]

48. From almost forty years ago, I remember distinctly the story of Dr. Tony Brouwer (1917-1971) of Calvin College. After he was diagnosed with incurable cancer, he changed his way of living and allowed a film to be made of his last days on earth as well as of his funeral. Preachers who can include in their sermon such a story of a person known in the community will have a powerful confirmation of the message of the Teacher.

49. Quoted in *Time,* July 28, 2008.

50. My sermon based on this research is found in Appendix 4.

CHAPTER 13

Because of the Harm Inflicted by Folly, Use Wisdom!

Ecclesiastes 9:13–10:20

Wisdom is better than weapons of war,
  but one bungler destroys much good. . . .
Wisdom helps one to succeed. . . .
Words spoken by the wise bring them favor,
  but the lips of fools consume them.

(Eccl 9:18; 10:10, 12)

Of all the passages in Ecclesiastes, this one is probably the most difficult to interpret and preach. But that should not stop preachers who believe that "all scripture is inspired by God and is useful for teaching, for reproof, for correction, and for training in righteousness" (2 Tim 3:16). This preaching text teaches, reproves, corrects, and trains in righteousness by urging us not to be foolish but to use wisdom not only in politics but also in our daily lives.

Still, it is a difficult text. Commentators are not at all agreed on what constitutes the literary unit and what are the subunits within it.[1] This problem is related to the fact that the passage seems to lack coherence. Roland Murphy states, "Most commentators agree that this section contains relatively disparate units, and hence it is difficult to bring them under one overarching title."[2] If it is difficult to formulate "one overarching *title*," it will be even more difficult to formulate an overarching *theme*. Michael Fox writes, "The topics of rulers and speech, wise and foolish, recur throughout 9:13–10:20, but there is no overall design or movement of thought, and the topical clusterings seem merely asso-

---

1. See Ogden, "Qoheleth 9:17–10:20," *VT* 30 (1980) 27-29, for an overview of the positions taken by various commentators.

2. Murphy, *Ecclesiastes,* 103. Cf. p. 99, "A conceptual unity is lacking to 9:13–10:15."

ciative."[3] If there is "no overall design or movement of thought," it is impossible not only to formulate a textual theme but also to devise a coherent expository sermon. We shall begin with the issue of what constitutes the literary unit.

Text and Context

Since we concluded the last preaching text with 9:12, a logical place to begin this one would be 9:13. Although some would begin this literary unit with 9:11 because of its "Again I saw," in the foregoing chapter we demonstrated that this transitional unit (9:11-12) fits well with 9:1-10. Since 9:13 clearly begins a new section with its "I have also seen," we can begin our preaching text with 9:13. But its ending is not so clear.

Murphy, following A. Wright (see p. 19 above), determines the length of this unit "by the occurrence of the key phrase 'not know' in 10:14-15."[4] He also suggests that "possibly 'city' can be taken as an inclusion (9:14; 10:15)."[5] But choosing 9:13–10:15 leaves 10:16-20 as an orphan,[6] since 11:1 begins a new unit on economics. In terms of the contents, 10:16-20, dealing as it does with the king and princes, fits very well with the foregoing, which also deals with kings, rulers, and princes (see 9:14, 17; 10:4, 5, 6). In fact, 10:4 and 10:20 offer similar advice in dealing with the king: calmness and self-control. Moreover, as Ogden points out, there is a rhetorical feature that ties this unit together, namely, "the small animal or insect representing a potential source of danger": the fly in verse 1, the snake in verses 8 and 11, and the bird in verse 20.[7]

In addition, because of repetition of "key terms, such as 'city' (9:14; 10:15), 'king' (9:14; 10:16, 20), 'strength' (9:16; 10:10, 17), 'words' and 'wisdom' (9:15-18; 10:10-14), 'quietness/abandon/allay' (Heb. *nûaḥ*, 9:17; 10:4), 'ruler' (9:17; 10:4), 'fool/folly' (9:17; 10:6), 'sinner/offence' (Heb. *ḥaṭṭā'*, 9:18; 10:4), 'weapons/axe' (9:18; 10:10)," Stephen Brown suggests an overall chiastic structure:[8]

---

3. Fox, *A Time to Tear Down*, 298. Cf. Whybray, *Ecclesiastes*, 150, "It is not possible, despite various attempts which have been made, to find any overall structure in the section [10:1–11:6] as a whole."

4. Murphy, *Ecclesiastes*, 99.

5. Ibid.

6. Seow, *Ecclesiastes*, 338, argues that 10:16–11:6 constitutes the next unit under the heading, "Living with Risks." But he also acknowledges that the Teacher presents two kinds of risks: "Risks in the Political Realm" (10:16-20) and "Risks in the Economic Realm" (11:1-6). Although preachers could consider selecting as their preaching text 10:16–11:6, I think that 10:16-20 has more in common with 9:13–10:15 than with 11:1-6.

7. Ogden, "Qoheleth 9:17–10:20," *VT* 30 (1980) 35.

8. Stephen Brown, "The Structure of Ecclesiastes," *EvRT* 14/3 (1990) 204.

9:13	A	Introduction
9:14-16	B	Wisdom is better than much folly
9:17–10:1	C	Wisdom is vulnerable to a little folly
10:2-3	D	The contrast of wise and foolish men
10:4-9	C′	Wisdom is vulnerable to a little folly
10:10-15	B′	Wisdom is better than much folly
10:16-20	A′	Conclusion

This suggested chiasm seems rather strained because it disregards literary units such as 10:5-7 ("I have seen" inclusio) and 10:8-11 ("snake" inclusio). The repetition of key terms, however, is further evidence for the unity of this passage. Therefore we can select as our preaching text Ecclesiastes 9:13–10:20.

As to the context, although the theme of death is dropped after 9:12, the notion that we are subject to accidents (9:11, "The race is not to the swift," etc.) is repeated in our passage in 10:8-11 ("Whoever digs a pit will fall into it," etc.). The story of the poor wise man delivering a city by his wisdom is an elaboration of the earlier proverb, "Wisdom gives strength to the wise more than ten rulers that are in a city" (7:19). The Teacher's advice not to leave your post when confronted by an angry ruler (10:4) contrasts with his earlier advice to "go from his presence" (8:3). The observation that "fools talk on and on" (10:14a) reflects the earlier admonition, "Never be rash with your mouth" (5:2), as well as the proverb, "The more words, the more vanity" (6:11). And the idea that "No one knows what is to happen" (10:14b) repeats similar sayings in 3:11; 6:12; 7:14; and 8:7.

Literary Features

Again, for discerning the structure of the text, it will be helpful to note the various literary forms.[9] The passage begins with a reflection (9:13, "I have seen under the sun") on wisdom's strength and vulnerability (9:13-18). The reflection contains an anecdote of a poor wise man delivering a city (9:14-15), followed by a "better than" proverb (9:16a) and the Teacher's observation that "the poor man's wisdom is despised" (9:16b). This is followed by two more "better than" proverbs, the first consisting of antithetic parallelism (wise versus fool; 9:17) and the second consisting of synthetic parallelism (9:18).[10] This section is con-

---

9. Murphy's *Wisdom Literature*, 146-47, and *Ecclesiastes*, 99, are somewhat helpful, but his presuppositions lead to different divisions and interpretations from mine.

10. For this pattern from a traditional proverb on the wise and fools to the Teacher's subsequent comments concentrating on fools, see Whybray, "The Identification and Use of Quotations in Ecclesiastes," *VTSup* 32 (1981) 435-51.

cluded by a proverb (synonymous parallelism) about dead flies spoiling the ointment (10:1).

Chapter 10:2 begins a new section with a traditional proverb cast in antithetic parallelism (wise/right versus fool/left) and continues with the Teacher's vivid description of fools (10:3). This is followed by a command about conduct before an angry king and motivation for this advice (10:4).

10:5 ("I have seen under the sun") begins a new reflection on the evil of overturning the political order in society (10:5-7; note the inclusio "I have seen" in vv. 5 and 7). It consists of an observation of an evil stemming from an error committed by the ruler (10:5) followed by an "illustrative anecdote."[11] The anecdote presents two examples of the evil, with synonymous parallelism between verses 6 and 7 and antithetic parallelism within each verse:

> folly is set in many high places,
>> and the rich sit in a low place (10:6).
> I have seen slaves on horseback,
>> and princes walking on foot like slaves (10:7).

This reflection is followed by a series of connected proverbs about accidents that can happen if one does not use wisdom (10:8-11; note the inclusio "snake" in vv. 8 and 11). This series of proverbs is followed by another series of proverbs on fools (10:12-15). It begins with a proverb cast in antithetic parallelism (wise/favor versus fools/consume; 10:12), and continues with proverbs tracing the downhill journey of fools (10:13-15; similar to 10:2-3).

In the conclusion, 10:16-20 comes back to the subject of the king (cf. 10:16, 20 and 9:14), the evil of overturning the political order (cf. 10:16 and 10:5-7), and how to deal with the ruler (cf. 10:20 and 10:4). It begins with two oracles that are antithetic (curse versus blessing) to each other (10:16, "Alas for you, O land, when your king is a servant," and 10:17, "Happy are you, O land, when your king is a nobleman"). This is followed by a proverb on the results of sloth and indolence (synonymous parallelism; 10:18) and a proverb on feasts, wine, and money (10:19). The conclusion is the command not to curse the king, not even in your thoughts, with the motivation that a little bird may tell him (10:20).

In seeking to determine the textual unit above, we noted the repetition of many terms in this passage. Here we will just highlight the repetition of a few key terms. The focus on the contrast between the wise and fools is brought out in the elevenfold repetition of "wisdom/wise" (9:13, 15 [2x], 16 [2x], 17, 18; 10:1, 2, 10, 12) and the ninefold repetition of "fool/folly/foolishness" (9:17; 10:1, 2, 3 [2x], 12, 13, 14, 15). The focus on politics is brought out in the repetition of words like

---

11. Longman, *Book of Ecclesiastes*, 242.

"king" (9:14; 10:16, 20), "ruler" (9:17; 10:4), "city" (9:14, 15; 10:15), and "land" (10:16, 17).

This passage also contains several metaphors. Hearts inclining "to the right" and "to the left" (10:2) are metaphors. The saying that fools "do not even know the way to town" (10:15) is probably "a metaphor for being foolish."[12] The little bird that tells the king your thoughts (10:20) is also a metaphor. But one must be careful not to identify as metaphors words that make good sense when taken literally. Is the "blunt ax" (10:10) indeed "a metaphor here for the wise man who is not having great success"?[13] If that is a possibility, what is to stop preachers from understanding the poor wise man who is despised (9:16) as a metaphor for Israel, which has "great resources by virtue of her wisdom" but is despised? And of construing "the ruler" of 10:5 as a metaphor for "God Himself"? And of interpreting the snake of 10:11 as a metaphor for "the wicked rulers [who] will bite Israel"?[14] The point is, unless one handles metaphors with care, one is on the slippery slope that leads from extended metaphor straight into arbitrary allegorical interpretation.

Textual Structure

Although it is difficult to detect a coherent development in this passage, the literary forms will help us discern a somewhat logical arrangement.

I. Reflection on wisdom's strength in politics and its vulnerability[15] to a little folly (9:13–10:1)
   A. Observation: I have also seen this example of wisdom (9:13)
   B. Anecdote: a poor wise man delivers a city and is not remembered (9:14-15)
   C. Proverb: wisdom is better than might (9:16a)
      1. yet the poor man's wisdom is despised (9:16b)
         and his words are not heeded (9:16c)

---

12. Ogden, *Qoheleth*, 175. Cf. Fox, *A Time to Tear Down*, 308, "As an idiom it may signify incompetence."

13. Provan, *Ecclesiastes*, 196. See ibid., n. 4, where Provan suggests that we should perhaps consider the terms "rich" and "princes" as metaphors "for those who are 'wealthy' in wisdom and possess leadership skills," and "slaves" as a metaphor for those lacking these skills.

14. Leupold, *Exposition of Ecclesiastes*, respectively 224-25, 235, and 243. On p. 261 Leupold seeks to defend this "allegorizing." Understanding "the ruler" of 10:5 as God himself goes back to Jerome and is supported by Hengstenberg, *Commentary on Ecclesiastes*, 225.

15. See the subtitle of Ogden's article, "Qoheleth 9:17–10:20: Variations on the Theme of Wisdom's Strength and Vulnerability," *VT* 30/1 (1980) 27.

    D. Proverb: The quiet words of the wise are more to be heeded (9:17)
                than the shouting of a ruler among fools

    E. Proverb: Wisdom is better than weapons of war (9:18)
                but one bungler destroys much good

    F. Proverb: Dead flies make the ointment give off a foul odor (10:1)
                so a little folly outweighs wisdom and honor

II. Opposite inclinations of the wise and fools with a command to use wisdom in politics (10:2-4)

    A. Proverb: The heart of the wise inclines to the right (10:2)
                but the heart of a fool to the left

    B. Proverb: Even when fools walk on the road, they lack sense (10:3)
                and show to everyone that they are fools

    C. Command: Do not leave your post before the angry king (10:4)
        1. Reason: for calmness (wisdom) will undo great offenses

III. Reflection on the political order being overturned by the ruler's error (10:5-7)

    A. Observation: There is an evil that I have seen under the sun (10:5)
        1. as great an error as if it proceeded from the ruler

    B. Anecdote consisting of two examples:
        1. Proverb: Folly is set in many high places (10:6)
                 and the rich (wise) sit in a low place
        2. Proverb: I have seen slaves on horseback (10:7)
                 and princes walking on foot like slaves

IV. Use wisdom in your daily work to avoid getting hurt (10:8-11)

    A. Proverb: Whoever digs a pit will fall into it (10:8)
                and whoever breaks through a wall
                will be bitten by a snake

    B. Proverb: Whoever quarries stones will be hurt by them (10:9)
                and whoever splits logs will be endangered by them

    C. Proverb: If the iron is blunt, and one does not whet the edge (10:10)
                then more strength must be exerted
        1. but wisdom helps one to succeed

    D. Proverb: If the snake bites before it is charmed (10:11)
                there is no advantage in a charmer

V. Proverbs contrasting the words of the wise with the babble of fools (10:12-15)

    A. Proverb: Words spoken by the wise bring them favor (10:12)
                but the lips of fools consume them
        The words of their mouths begin in foolishness (10:13)
                and their talk ends in wicked madness
        1. Observation: yet fools talk on and on (10:14a)

    B. Proverb: No one knows what is to happen (10:14b)

            and no one can tell anyone what the future holds

    C. Proverb: The toil of fools wears them out (10:15)

            for they do not even know the way to town

VI. Opposite political orders with a final command to use wisdom in speaking (10:16-20)

    A. Two oracles (curse and blessing):

        1. Alas for you, O land, when your king is a servant (10:16)

            and your princes feast in the morning

        2. Happy are you, O land, when your king is a nobleman (10:17)

            and your princes feast at the proper time

          a. for strength, and not for drunkenness

    B. Proverb: Through sloth the roof sinks in (10:18)

            and through indolence the house leaks

    C. Proverb: Feasts are made for laughter (10:19)

            wine gladdens life

            and money meets every need

    D. Command: Do not curse the king, even in your thoughts (10:20)

            or curse the rich, even in your bedroom

        1. Reason: for a bird of the air may carry your voice

            or some winged creature tell the matter

Theocentric Interpretation

This passage does not mention God at all. In speaking of the strength of wisdom, however, the Teacher assumes, along with other Old Testament wisdom literature, that "the fear of the LORD is the beginning of wisdom" (cf. Prov 1:7; 9:10; and Eccl 3:14; 5:7; 8:12; and 12:13).

Textual Theme and Goal

It is difficult to discern a single theme that covers all the topics in this passage. What is often helpful is to list the main points, that is, the topics covered in the subunits, and see if there is a constant that ties them together. In analyzing the structure of this text, we arrived at the following main points. To sharpen the focus even more, it is helpful to highlight key words and phrases:

I. Reflection on *wisdom's strength in politics and vulnerability to a little folly* (9:13–10:1)

II. Opposite inclinations of the wise and fools with a command to *use wisdom in politics*
(10:2-4)

III. Reflection on the *political order* being overturned by the *ruler's error* (10:5-7)

IV. *Use wisdom* in your work to avoid getting hurt
(10:8-11)

V. Proverbs contrasting the *words of the wise with the babble of fools* (10:12-15)

VI. Opposite *political orders* with a final command to *use wisdom* in speaking (10:16-20)

This listing of topics confirms our earlier result in listing key words: the focus in this passage is on the contrast between wise and foolish inclinations, words, and actions, particularly in the arena of politics.[16] The first reflection on wisdom's strength in the political arena and its vulnerability to a little folly seems to set the stage for, and is supported by, the following subunits.[17] These considerations lead to the following theme formulation: "Especially in the political arena, a little folly easily ruins the strength of wisdom." But this formulation fails to include the Teacher's hints (e.g., 9:18; 10:10, 12), and even commands (10:4, 20), that we are to use wisdom. Adding this idea results in the following theme: *Since a little folly can ruin the strength of wisdom, especially in the political arena, use wisdom to navigate your way through life.*

Along with hints to use wisdom, the Teacher gives two commands that imply as much. In 10:4 he commands his readers not to leave their post to dodge the anger of the ruler but to use "calmness" to smooth things over. And in 10:20 he commands his readers not to curse the king, for a bird may carry their voice and tell the king. We can therefore formulate the Teacher's goal as, *to urge his readers to use wisdom, especially in the political arena, to navigate their way through life.*

---

16. "This collection of proverbs, anecdotes, and observations all center on a common theme: the impulsive nature of political power." Garrett, *Proverbs, Ecclesiastes, Song of Songs,* 333.

17. According to Ogden, *Qoheleth,* 161, "the two 'Better'-proverbs in 9:17-18 function as introductory devices for the unit. . . . Within the illustrative material of 10:1-20 the theme of wisdom's vulnerability in 10:1, 8-11, 20 has the effect of binding together all the material in the chapter, as does the reference to small insects or animals as the source of danger. This theme is woven closely into the material which argues for wisdom's power, indicating that Qohelet believes both to be a truthful reflection of reality." Cf. ibid., 163, and his article, "Qoheleth 9:17–10:20," *VT* 30/1 (1980) 31-32, 37.

Ways to Preach Christ

In moving from this message to Jesus Christ in the New Testament, the ways of redemptive-historical progression, promise-fulfilment, and typology will be nonproductive. That leaves four possible ways to explore: analogy, longitudinal themes, New Testament references, and contrast.

Analogy

There are several analogies between the teachings in this passage and the teachings of Jesus in the New Testament. In 10:2 the Teacher contrasts the heart of the wise (inclining to the right) with the heart of a fool (inclining to the left). In 10:12-14a he contrasts the words of the wise with those of fools ("their talk ends in wicked madness"). Jesus points out the same contrast when he says, "For out of the abundance of the heart the mouth speaks. The good person brings good things out of a good treasure, and the evil person brings evil things out of an evil treasure" (Matt 12:34-35).

In 10:10 the Teacher encourages his readers to use wisdom to survive in a dangerous world (see 10:8-9). Jesus similarly encourages his followers to use wisdom in a dangerous world: "See, I am sending you out like sheep into the midst of wolves; so be wise as serpents and innocent as doves" (Matt 10:16).

In 10:20 the Teacher warns his readers not to curse the king, for he will hear about it. In a different context, Jesus says to his disciples, "Nothing is covered up that will not be uncovered, and nothing secret that will not become known. Therefore whatever you have said in the dark will be heard in the light, and what you have whispered behind closed doors will be proclaimed from the housetops" (Luke 12:2-3).

Longitudinal Themes

In our preaching text the Teacher urges his readers to use wisdom to navigate their way through life. One can trace this theme from the Old Testament to Jesus in the New Testament. Negatively, in the context of the coming desolation, Jeremiah speaks the word of the LORD, "My people are foolish, they do not know me; they are stupid children, for they have no understanding" (Jer 4:22). Hosea proclaims a similar word of the LORD: "My people are destroyed for lack of knowledge" (Hos 4:6). Positively, the Psalmist prays, "So teach us to number our days that we may gain a heart of wisdom" (Ps 90:12). Proverbs describes wisdom as "a tree of life to those who lay hold of her; those who hold her fast are called happy" (Prov 3:18; cf. 8:34).

In the New Testament Jesus tells his followers: "See, I am sending you out like sheep into the midst of wolves; so be wise as serpents and innocent as doves" (Matt 10:16; also used as an analogy above). For the coming persecution, Jesus promises his followers, "I will give you words and wisdom that none of your opponents will be able to withstand or contradict" (Luke 21:15). Paul tells the Ephesian Christians, "Be careful then how you live, not as unwise people but as wise, making the most of the time, because the days are evil" (Eph 5:15-16). To the Colossians he writes, "Let the word of Christ dwell in you richly; teach and admonish one another in all wisdom" (Col 3:16). Concerning outsiders, he adds, "Conduct yourselves wisely toward outsiders, making the most of the time. Let your speech always be gracious, seasoned with salt, so that you may know how you ought to answer everyone" (Col 4:5-6).

In the Bible one can also find many illustrations of the theme that a little folly ruins the strength of wisdom. For example, in the Old Testament we read about the folly of King David in taking the wife of Uriah (2 Sam 11), the foolishness of the wise king Solomon in loving many foreign women (1 Kings 11), and the folly of King Rehoboam in taking the foolish advice of the younger counselors, thus splitting the kingdom (1 Kings 12). In the New Testament, one can think of the foolishness of the rich fool in Jesus' parable (Luke 12:19-20), of the folly of Judas's betraying Jesus (Matt 26:48; 27:3-5), and of the needless lie of Ananias and Sapphira (Acts 5:4).

New Testament References

There are no direct quotations of or allusions to this passage in the New Testament.

Contrast

In 10:14, in connection with fools talking on and on, the Teacher states, "No one knows what is to happen, and who can tell anyone what the future holds?" In connection with our speaking, Jesus reveals part of what the future holds: "I tell you, on the day of judgment you will have to give an account for every careless word you utter; for by your words you will be justified, and by your words you will be condemned" (Matt 12:36-37).

Sermon Theme and Goal

We formulated the textual theme as, "Since a little folly can ruin the strength of wisdom, especially in the political arena, use wisdom to navigate your way through life." Because the New Testament does not change this message, we can make the textual theme the sermon theme: *Since a little folly can ruin the strength of wisdom, especially in the political arena, use wisdom to navigate your way through life.*

The Teacher's goal was "to urge his readers to use wisdom, especially in the political arena, to navigate their way through life." With a slight change, we can make this the sermon goal: *to urge our hearers to use wisdom, especially in the political arena, to navigate their way through life.* This goal points to the need addressed in this sermon: people fail to use their God-given wisdom in life; they undercut the strength of wisdom with folly.

Sermon Form

Because of the large number of seemingly unrelated items in this passage, the clearest sermon form is deductive development: that is, we state the theme at the beginning of the sermon and then show how each section supports the theme. With this preaching text deductive development is natural since the opening anecdote is an illustration of the theme.

Since the textual structure reveals six main points in this passage, we should check if we can combine some points so as to make it easier for the hearers to remember the points. Checking back to the "Textual Structure" above, it looks like we may be able to combine points I and II, III and IV, and V and VI. This would give us three main points for the sermon:

I. Since a little folly ruins the strength of wisdom in politics, use wisdom in your political dealings (9:13–10:4).
II. Since a little folly can overturn the political order as well as daily life, use wisdom in your daily walk (10:5-11).
III. Since a little folly can get you into deep trouble, use wisdom in your daily talk (10:12-20).

Seeing that the text contains many Hebrew proverbs, it would be consistent to give this flavor to the sermon by spicing it with appropriate English proverbs.

Sermon Exposition

In the sermon introduction, one can show the relevance of this sermon for contemporary life by relating a current story of a politician who destroyed his or her career with a foolish act or statement (unfortunately, we need not look far). Then bring it home by raising the questions: Do we always use our God-given wisdom? Or do we hurt ourselves and our neighbors at times with foolish outbursts and/or behavior?

In this passage, the Teacher shows that, especially in politics, a little folly easily ruins the strength of wisdom. So he urges us to use wisdom, practical wisdom, insight, skill, to navigate our way through life. His first point is this: Since a little folly ruins the strength of wisdom in politics, we ought to use wisdom in our political dealings.

He begins in 9:13, "I have also seen this example of wisdom under the sun, and it seemed great to me." Then he tells the story: "There was a little city with few people in it. A great king came against it and besieged it, building great siegeworks against it." Note the contrasts: "a little city with few people" and "a great king . . . building great siegeworks." That little city with few people didn't have a chance. This great king built great siegeworks around the little city. They may have been movable assault towers,[18] allowing the troops to catapult their projectiles over the walls directly into the city. Humanly speaking, this little city didn't have a chance. But as the Teacher has just reminded us in 9:11, "the race is not to the swift, nor the battle to the strong." So we may be in for a surprise.

Verse 15, "Now there was found in it [the city] a poor wise man, and he by his wisdom delivered the city." In this verse we are told twice that the man was poor. He did not have any financial resources to help the city in its hour of need. He was dirt poor. But he did have wisdom, and "he by his wisdom delivered the city."[19] We are not told what he did to deliver the city, just that he did it "by his wisdom." The Teacher retells this story to illustrate the tremendous strength of wisdom in the political arena. As he wrote in chapter 7:19, "Wisdom gives strength to the wise more than ten rulers that are in a city." By his *wisdom* this poor wise man delivered the city.

But then follows the sad conclusion of this story, "Yet no one remembered

---

18. See Seow, *Ecclesiastes*, 309.

19. Several commentators, e.g., Seow, ibid., 310, argue for the translation that "he *might have* delivered the city" if the people had only listened to him (9:16b). But Fox, *Ecclesiastes*, 66, argues that verse 15 is not hypothetical: "If the wise man had not actually saved the city, how could anyone know that he *could* have done so? Moreover, the first part of Qohelet's conclusion in verse 16 ['So I said, "Wisdom is better than might"'] would be unjustified." In any event, since the options make no difference to the point illustrated, I would not make an issue of this in the sermon but simply follow the translation/interpretation of the pew Bibles.

that poor man." Proverbs 10:7 says, "The memory of the righteous is a blessing." But in reality the righteous are not always remembered. In this case, no one remembered the poor wise man. "Even though he had proved himself wise, he found himself disregarded once the danger passed — as unvalued as he had been beforehand."[20]

The Teacher draws his conclusion from this story in verse 16: "So I said, 'Wisdom is better than might; yet the poor man's wisdom is despised, and his words are not heeded.'" The Teacher is probably quoting a familiar proverb: "Wisdom is better than might." That's like our proverb, "Brains are better than brawn." Wisdom is indeed stronger than might, and yet it is extremely vulnerable: "the poor man's wisdom is despised, and his words are *not heeded*."

But even so the Teacher insists in verse 17: "The quiet words of the wise are *more to be heeded* than the shouting of a ruler among fools." The "shouting" of a foolish[21] ruler draws more attention in our society than "the quiet words of the wise." Some of us still remember Nikita Khrushchev of Russia at the United Nations shouting and pounding his shoe on the table. If one wishes to draw a crowd, if one wishes to be on the evening news, try shouting ludicrous slogans. But, says the Teacher, "the *quiet* words of the wise are more to be heeded." The quiet words of the wise can deliver a city. The quiet words of the wise are "better than might"; they ought to be heeded.

In verse 18 the Teacher reiterates, "Wisdom is better than weapons of war." Indeed it is! Wisdom can deliver a city even when it is surrounded by siegeworks and weapons of war. "But," the Teacher adds, "one bungler destroys much good." Note the contrast between "one" and "much." It takes only one foolish bungler, only one person who "misses the mark," to destroy the many good things accomplished by wisdom. "Wisdom is indeed powerful and beneficial, but may be rendered impotent by even a minor indiscretion. Wisdom is vulnerable."[22]

Think of King Rehoboam when he succeeded his father Solomon. His older counselors advised him to "lighten the hard service" Solomon had placed on the people. But he disregarded their wise counsel and turned to his younger counselors. They advised him: "Thus you should say to this people. . . , 'Whereas my father laid on you a heavy yoke, I will add to your yoke. My father disciplined you with whips, but I will discipline you with scorpions'" (1 Kings 12:10-11). Rehoboam followed this foolish advice, and as a result he lost ten of the twelve tribes of Israel. It takes only one bungler to destroy much good.

20. Provan, *Ecclesiastes*, 192.

21. "'Ruler of fools' is not just a ruler surrounded by fools but a ruler who is himself foolish." Garrett, *Proverbs, Ecclesiastes, Song of Songs*, 334.

22. Ogden, *Qoheleth*, 163.

In chapter 10:1 the Teacher summarizes this point with a proverb: "Dead flies make the perfumer's ointment give off a foul odor." In English we would say: "One rotten apple spoils the whole bushel." The contrast again is between one and many, between little and much. You can hardly see the little dead flies. But when they fall into the perfumer's fragrant ointment, the whole batch gives off a foul odor. A few dead flies can spoil a large, expensive batch of perfume. "So," the Teacher says, "a little folly outweighs wisdom and honor."[23] We would say, "An ounce of folly outweighs a pound of wisdom."[24] In the political arena, a little folly often has greater impact than wisdom and honor. The point, then, is that especially in politics, a little folly can easily ruin the strength of wisdom.

Why is wisdom so vulnerable to folly? It is because wisdom and folly are diametrically opposed to each other. The Teacher writes in verse 2, "The heart of the wise inclines to the right, but the heart of a fool to the left." He does not mean "right" and "left" in the American political sense of conservative and liberal, or Republican and Democrat. "In ancient Israel the right hand connoted power and deliverance [see, e.g., Ps 89:13]; the right side, moral goodness and favor. Hence the place of honor was on the right side. The left hand usually symbolized ineptness and perversity."[25] In Jesus' parable of the judgment of the nations we also read that the Son of Man "will put the sheep at his right hand and the goats at the left" (Matt 25:33). So here, the Teacher says, "The heart of the wise inclines to the right, but the heart of a fool to the left." From the heart "flow the springs of life" (Prov 4:23), and the heart of the fool inclines toward stupidity and perversity.

In fact, the Teacher continues in verse 3, "Even when fools walk on the road, they lack sense, and show to everyone that they are fools." Fools cannot hide that they are fools, that they lack sense. Even when they walk on the road, even in public places, they show everyone that they are fools. Proverbs 12:23 states, "The heart of fools broadcasts folly." Today we would say, "You can see one coming from a mile away."

In chapter 9:17 the Teacher said, "The quiet words of the wise are *more to be heeded* than the shouting of a ruler among fools." In chapter 10:4 he comes back to this foolish ruler. What should you do when this ruler starts shouting in anger at you? What should you do when your boss lashes out in anger at you? In different circumstances the Teacher had counseled in chapter 8:3: "Go from his presence!" But that is not always the wisest course of action. Walking away from an angry superior might make him or her even more furious. In this case, the

---

23. "The use of the Hebrew words for 'outweighs' and 'honor' is another interesting wordplay, for both words are used for weight or value and social esteem." Donald Glenn, "Mankind's Ignorance," in Zuck, *Reflecting with Solomon*, 328.

24. Crenshaw, *Ecclesiastes*, 169.

25. Ibid.

Teacher counsels: "If the anger of the ruler rises against you, do not leave your post, for calmness will undo great offenses."[26] A fool might respond to anger with his own anger. But "anger met by anger only ensures needless conflict and destruction from the . . . 'ruler.'"[27] Proverbs 15:1 states, "A soft answer turns away wrath, but a harsh word stirs up anger" (cf. Prov 16:14; 25:15). That's wisdom: responding to anger with "a soft answer," that is, with "calmness."

So the first point the Teacher makes is this: Since a little folly easily ruins the strength of wisdom in politics, we ought to use wisdom in our political dealings. His second point is similar but broader by extending it to our daily life: Since a little folly can overturn the political order as well as our daily life, we ought to use wisdom in our daily walk. He begins again with the political arena. He writes in verse 5, "There is an evil that I have seen under the sun, as great an error as if it proceeded from the ruler." The evil turns out to be the overturning of the political order. Verse 6, "Folly is set in many high places, and the rich sit in a low place." Can you imagine: incompetent fools have been promoted to places of leadership. The very people who, according to verse 3, "lack sense" have become rulers. And the rich, that is, the wealthy upperclass who are well educated and who normally rule,[28] are sitting in a low place. It has become an upside-down world.[29]

Verse 7 adds to this picture of political upheaval: "I have seen slaves on horseback, and princes walking on foot like slaves." Proverbs 19:10 says, "It is not fitting for a fool to live in luxury, much less for a slave to rule over princes." But here what is "not fitting" has taken place: fools are ruling from palaces and servants are riding on horseback. Meanwhile the ruling class finds itself in low places and princes walk on foot. How did this upside-down world come about? According to verse 5, through the foolish error of the ruler.[30] In the political arena, the benefits of wisdom are easily lost to a foolish error.

But this is true in other areas of life as well. The Teacher gives four illustrations of what may happen in our lives when we don't use wisdom. Verse 8, "Whoever digs a pit will fall into it; and whoever breaks through a wall will be bitten by a snake." The pit refers to a trap for animals. In those days hunters would dig a pit and camouflage it with a net,[31] probably covering it with leaves

---

26. "The sinking of the passions conveyed by *marpē'* and *yanniaḥ* provides a sharp contrast with the rising fury of the ruler (*rûaḥ* plus the verb *'ālâ*, to ascend)." Crenshaw, *Ecclesiastes*, 170.

27. Brown, *Ecclesiastes*, 98.

28. Seow, *Ecclesiastes*, 315. See the synonymous parallelism in Ecclesiastes 10:20, equating "the king" and "the rich." Cf. Proverbs 22:7.

29. See Raymond C. Van Leeuwen, "Proverbs 30:21-23 and the Biblical World Upside Down," *JBL* 105 (1986) 599-610.

30. "When social chaos comes as a result of the action of a despot, wisdom is helpless." Loader, *Ecclesiastes*, 117.

31. See Seow, *Ecclesiastes*, 316, 326.

or brush. But if the hunter did not pay careful attention to where he had dug his pits, he could easily fall into one himself and get hurt.

"And whoever breaks through a wall will be bitten by a snake." Even today in Israel we see low stone fences built around orchards and vineyards. When the farmer wishes to move such a wall, he has to be very careful, for small poisonous snakes often nest in the cracks between these rocks.[32] If the farmer is in a hurry and not careful, he can easily be bitten and die. A little folly can result in death.

Verse 9, "Whoever quarries stones will be hurt by them; and whoever splits logs will be endangered by them." Israel has an abundance of stones. People would dig these stones from the ground and use them for building their homes. But especially on the hillsides this could be dangerous work. One could easily be hurt by a rolling stone or by dropping it on one's toes. The log splitter also had to be careful. The log could roll on him, or a splinter of wood could hit and damage his eye. A little folly can result in serious injuries.[33]

In the next two verses the Teacher encourages us to use our God-given wisdom in our daily task. Verse 10, "If the iron is blunt, and one does not whet the edge, then more strength must be exerted; but wisdom helps one to succeed."[34] Woodcutters know that it is hard to cut through wood with a dull ax. Besides being dangerous, it takes more strength to get the job done. "But wisdom helps one to succeed." Wisdom will tell the woodcutter to "whet the edge," to sharpen the ax, before he starts work. Thus the use of wisdom will help him to succeed.[35]

The Teacher continues in verse 11, "If the snake bites before it is charmed, there is no advantage in a charmer." Snake charming is still an occupation in the Eastern world. If the snake charmer is in a hurry and starts handling the snake before it is charmed, he will get bitten and probably die. But if he uses wisdom, he will make sure the snake is charmed before he handles it. The use of wisdom will help him survive handling even such a deadly animal as a poisonous snake.

---

32. Ibid. According to Fox, *Ecclesiastes*, 69, there are currently some twenty species of poisonous snakes in Israel.

33. With these four examples, the Teacher suggests "that people face dangers in their daily occupations. Most often such accidents are caused by momentary lapses of concentration, or small hazards not guarded against. . . . Each is illustrative of the thesis in 9:18 that a small amount of folly can undo much wisdom." Ogden, *Qoheleth*, 169.

34. "This verse has been described as linguistically the most difficult in the book, and both ancient and modern translations have rendered it very differently. . . . The last part . . . has been described as 'untranslatable,' and its meaning is conjectural." Whybray, *Ecclesiastes*, 153.

35. "One must use his skill and good sense in a timely fashion, before it becomes necessary to apply force — just as the 'possessor of the tongue' in the next verse must use his magical competence in a timely fashion." Fox, *A Time to Mourn*, 306.

Thus, not only in the political arena but in other areas of life as well, we ought to use wisdom to navigate our way through life.[36]

So far the Teacher has made two main points: First, since a little folly ruins the strength of wisdom in politics, we ought to use wisdom in our political dealings. And second, since a little folly can overturn the political order as well as daily life, we ought to use wisdom in our daily *walk*. His final point is: Since a little folly can get us into deep trouble, we ought to use wisdom in our daily *talk*.

The Teacher begins by contrasting the talk of the wise and the babble of fools. Verse 12, "Words spoken by the wise bring them favor, but the lips of fools consume them." "Words spoken by the wise bring them favor." When Jesus preached in the synagogue of his hometown Nazareth, the people's first reaction was favorable. We read, "All spoke well of him and were amazed at the gracious words that came from his mouth" (Luke 4:22). "Words spoken by the wise bring them favor," that is, they bring the favor of other people upon the wise.

By contrast, "the lips of fools consume them." The lips of fools "swallow up" the fools themselves. The talk of fools does not bring favor to the fools but ruin. Proverbs 18:7 says, "The mouths of fools are their ruin, and their lips a snare to themselves." Fools get caught in their own words. Think of the many people whose talk gets them into trouble even today.

The Teacher continues his description of fools in verse 13, "The words of their mouths begin in foolishness, and their talk ends in wicked madness; yet fools talk on and on." That's amazing, isn't it? Even though their words ruin them, fools "talk on and on." Even though their words "begin in foolishness" and descend from there to "wicked madness," they don't shut their mouths. They "talk on and on." They must be blind to their own folly.

In their madness, they even talk about the future. They think that they know what the future holds. But, as he has done before,[37] the Teacher reminds us in verse 14, "No one knows what is to happen, and who can tell anyone what the future holds?" No one! God has set the times, and we don't know what the future holds. So what makes fools think that they can talk about the future? They must be mad.

In verse 15 the Teacher adds, "The toil of fools wears them out, for they do not even know the way to town." Not knowing "the way to town" is an idiomatic expression for incompetence.[38] Fools don't know the most elementary thing. We would say, "They don't know enough to come in out of the rain."[39]

36. "Both of these verses call for the exercise of wisdom." Murphy, *Ecclesiastes,* 102.
37. Ecclesiastes 3:22; 6:12; 7:14; 8:7.
38. See Fox, *A Time to Mourn,* 308.
39. Crenshaw, *Ecclesiastes,* 175.

They are so stupid, they don't even know "the way to town." And so their toil "wears them out" because they keep talking about things they know nothing about. As the Teacher said in verse 12, "the lips of fools consume them."

This vivid description of fools and their babbling is a major incentive not to be counted among their number. Instead we ought to use wisdom in our daily talk. For, as the Teacher said in 10:12, "Words spoken by the wise bring them favor."

The Teacher concludes this passage by returning to the political arena and contrasting two opposite political orders. The first political order is the upside-down order where fools reign. He spoke of this order earlier in verse 6: "folly is set in many high places, and the rich sit in a low place." Now he concludes in verse 16: "Alas for you, O land, when your king is a servant [or a child], and your princes feast in the morning!" It is not good for a land when the king is a servant or a child.

When Solomon succeeded his father David, he asked the LORD for wisdom to rule wisely. He prayed, "Now, O LORD my God, you have made your servant king in place of my father David, although I am only a little child; I do not know how to go out or come in ["the way to town"?]. . . . Give your servant therefore an understanding mind to govern your people" (1 Kings 3:7, 9). A child does not have the maturity to govern wisely. Neither does a servant who, without any training, is cast into the role of king of the nation.

The lack of wisdom of this king shows up in the behavior of the princes. Instead of working conscientiously for the good of the nation, the princes, like fools, live only for themselves. They begin their feasting in the morning already.[40] "Alas for you, O land." "Woe to you!"

By contrast, the Teacher proclaims in verse 17, "Happy are you, O land, when your king is a nobleman, and your princes feast at the proper time — for strength, and not for drunkenness!" "Blessed are you, O land, when your king is a nobleman" — a free, independent,[41] wise person who is able to provide good leadership in the nation. His solid leadership shows up in the responsible actions of the princes. They feast not in the morning but at the proper time, and not for drunkenness but for strength. Blessed are you when your leaders in government work responsibly for the nation.

As the Teacher earlier (vv. 13-15) expanded on the words of fools, so now he expands on the foolishness of an upside-down political order. The princes described in verse 16 as feasting already in the morning are not only foolish but

40. "Drinking at an early hour is a sign of debauchery (Isa 5:11) and a breakdown in leadership (cf. Isa 5:22-23)." Murphy, *Ecclesiastes*, 105. See also Acts 2:15.
41. "The 'son of free men' is one whose position in society enables him to act with an independent spirit. The contrast, therefore, is not so much between young and old as between a mature, bold approach to life and an immature, servile manner." Eaton, *Ecclesiastes*, 137.

lazy: they spend their days partying instead of working. In verse 18 the Teacher quotes an appropriate proverb about laziness: "Through sloth the roof sinks in, and through indolence the house leaks." In the Middle East the flat roofs of houses required regular maintenance. The roofs "were covered with lime, which eventually cracked and allowed rain to seep in . . . , since no run-off was provided."[42] So the owner would have to apply fresh plastering from time to time. If the owner was too lazy to do this, the house would begin to sag and leak.

The nation with its upside-down political order is like a house[43] that is not maintained. The king is incompetent and the princes are off partying. Who is looking after the welfare of the nation and its citizens? The princes[44] say, verse 19, "Feasts are made for laughter; wine gladdens life, and money meets every need." This may have been a drinking song they would sing at their feasts.[45] They are totally focused on the good times they can have for themselves. They like their feasts, their wine, and use the public purse for their partying:[46] "Money meets every need."[47] "Let the good times roll!"

Meanwhile, no one is looking after the nation. People suffer. People become more and more frustrated with the king and his cronies. They are tempted to curse the king.[48] But the Teacher warns in verse 20, "Do not curse the king, even in your thoughts." "Don't even *think* about it!"[49] And do not "curse the rich, even in your bedroom; for a bird of the air may carry your voice, or some winged creature tell the matter." It would be extremely foolish to curse the king.[50] Careless talk can get you into deep trouble. For the king can do

---

42. Murphy, *Ecclesiastes*, 105.

43. "The word 'house' may not refer just to the literal house of the lazy fool, but also to the royal 'house.'" Seow, *Ecclesiastes*, 331; cf. ibid., 340.

44. Whybray, *Ecclesiastes*, 157, suggests that this "may be a cynical comment of Qohelet, who elsewhere appears to despise 'laughter' (2:2; 7:3, 6) and warns his readers against thinking that wealth can provide happiness (4:7-8; 5:10-17 [MT 9-16])." Instead of reading this verse as a cynical comment, I think the Teacher is putting words into the mouths of the feasting princes of verse 16 — an expansion on their foolish partying similar to the expansion in verses 13-15.

45. "Perhaps it was originally a drinking song, as some have suggested (Galling, Lauha)." Seow, *Ecclesiastes*, 332.

46. "'Money is the answer for everything' is probably a reference to corruption in the affairs of the state." Loader, *Ecclesiastes*, 123.

47. "The failure of the slothful life is seen here: bread . . . wine . . . money is the limit of its horizon." Eaton, *Ecclesiastes*, 138.

48. "The king or the rich who act as if 'money answers everything' may deserve to be cursed." Farmer, *Who Knows What Is Good?* 189. Cf. Loader, *Ecclesiastes*, 124, "It makes complete sense that an oppressed and exploited people will curse the prospering upper crust in their hearts and that they will want to vent their hostility in an inner room."

49. Fox, *A Time to Tear Down*, 310.

50. "In ancient treaties, the vassal was always cautioned against critical language because this was an expression of rebellion." Ogden, *Qoheleth*, 180.

"whatever he pleases" (8:3). And you never know how he may hear about it. Perhaps a little bird of the air may carry your voice.[51] We still have the expression, "A little bird told me." We also have another expression, "The walls have ears." And if the king hears about you cursing him, you will receive harsh punishment. A little folly in your talk can mean your death. The message is: Do not curse the king! Be wise and survive! Watch your talk!

We have seen that in this passage the Teacher stresses how easily a little folly ruins the strength of wisdom, especially in the political arena. He began[52] with the story of the poor wise man who by his wisdom delivered a city — the strength of wisdom! But the foolish citizens soon forgot the wise man and did not want to listen to him. With a series of proverbs the Teacher next showed that it takes only a little folly to destroy the good built up by wisdom: "one bungler destroys much good"; dead flies spoil the perfumer's ointment; "a little folly outweighs wisdom." He illustrated this point again with the story of the upside-down kingdom: fools reign in high places while the wise sit in low places. This political mess was the result of an error by the ruler. Next he showed that a little folly can harm us in other areas of life as well: a hunter may fall into his own pit; a farmer may be killed by a snake; a stone digger may be hurt by a stone; and a woodcutter may be injured by the wood. The point was, in our daily task, too, we must use wisdom to avoid getting injured or killed. The Teacher concludes by referring again to the upside-down kingdom where fools reign. The situation in such a kingdom can become so bad that people feel like cursing the king. The Teacher warns us not to do such a foolish thing, for it can cost us our life.

The easiest way to remember the message of the Teacher is to think of the three kinds of animals he has mentioned in this passage: flies, snakes, and birds. "All are small and apparently insignificant creatures, but each has a potential for harm."[53] Dead flies spoil a lot of precious ointment; little snakes can kill a big person; and a little bird can tell the king your secret thoughts and get you into trouble. Just like these little animals, a little folly can do a lot of harm.

This, the Teacher claims, is all the more reason for you to use your God-given wisdom, your insight, your skill, to navigate your way through life. He repeats this point in various ways. Chapter 10:4, "If the anger of the ruler rises against you, do not leave your post, for calmness will undo great offenses." In other words, use wisdom in *political dealings*. Verse 10, "If the iron is blunt, . . .

---

51. "The allusion may be to the ubiquitous presence of spies. . . . Various government informants during the Persian period [were] known as 'the eyes and ears of the king.'" Seow, *Ecclesiastes*, 341.

52. Because of the many ideas in this passage, a short summary at the end of the sermon may be helpful for your hearers.

53. Ogden, *Qoheleth*, 181.

wisdom helps one to succeed" by sharpening it. In other words, use wisdom in *your daily walk.* Verse 20, "Do not curse the king, even in your thoughts, . . . for a bird of the air may carry your voice." In other words, use wisdom in *your talk.* Use your God-given wisdom to navigate your way through life.

We also find this theme elsewhere in the Bible. The Psalmist prays, "So teach us to number our days that we may gain a heart of *wisdom*" (Ps 90:12). Proverbs describes wisdom as "a tree of *life* to those who lay hold of her; those who hold her fast are called happy" (Prov 3:18). Jesus used wisdom when he refused to go to Judea because the religious leaders conspired to kill him before his time (John 7:1, 8). Jesus also tells his followers: "See, I am sending you out like sheep into the midst of wolves; so be *wise* as serpents and innocent as doves" (Matt 10:16). Jesus also warns his followers about the dangers of the coming persecutions but promises, "I will give you words and *wisdom* that none of your opponents will be able to withstand or contradict" (Luke 21:15).[54] Paul writes, "Be careful then how you walk, not as unwise people but as *wise,* making the most of the time, because the days are evil. So do not be *foolish,* but understand what the will of the Lord is" (Eph 5:15-17). As followers of Jesus Christ, use your God-given wisdom to navigate your way through life!

---

54. Paul likewise tells the Christians in Colossae, "Conduct yourselves wisely toward outsiders, making the most of the time. Let your speech always be gracious, seasoned with salt, so that you may know how you ought to answer everyone" (Col 4:5-6).

CHAPTER 14

Take Risks Boldly but Wisely!

Ecclesiastes 11:1-6

Send out your bread upon the waters,
for after many days you will get it back.
Divide your means seven ways, or even eight,
for you do not know what disaster may happen on earth.

(Eccl 11:1-2)

This is an excellent preaching text for hard economic times. Though the text is short, it still presents some peculiar challenges. The first is to establish the boundaries of the literary unit, for commentators offer a great variety of opinions on this issue. A second challenge is to arrive at a correct interpretation. For example, verse 1 reads, "Send out your bread upon the waters, for after many days you will get it back." At least three different interpretations are offered for this familiar verse: Give alms, and you will eventually be rewarded; Send your goods across the seas, and after many days you will profit from your trading; and, Do something senseless, and it can lead, paradoxically, to a good result.[1] We shall begin with establishing the textual unit.

---

1. See Murphy, *Ecclesiastes*, 106-7. Fox, *A Time to Tear Down*, 311-12, lists four different interpretations. The latest and strangest interpretation is offered by Michael M. Homan, "Beer Production by Throwing Bread into Water: A New Interpretation of Qoh. xi 1-2," *VT* 52/2 (2002) 275-78: "A more likely interpretation, given the process by which beer was brewed in the ancient Near East, is that Qohelet is recommending both beer production and consumption in perilous times" (p. 275).

Text and Context

As mentioned, commentators are not agreed on the boundaries of this text. Some see this passage as part of the foregoing section: either chapters 9:13–11:6, 10:1–11:6, or 10:16–11:6.[2] Others see it as part of the sequel: either 11:1-8[3] or 11:1–12:8.[4] Still others see it as an independent unit with no connection to what precedes or follows.[5]

In terms of contents, 11:1 clearly begins a new unit: it moves from the topic of politics (land, king, princes in 10:16-20) to the topic of economics ("Send out your bread upon the waters," "divide your means," sowing and reaping in 11:1-6). This unit ends at 11:6, for 11:7-8 changes the topic from economics to rejoicing. Moreover, 11:6 also concludes this section with the section marker "you do not know."[6] Therefore we can select as our preaching text Ecclesiastes 11:1-6.

This is not to say that this text is isolated from its context. The Teacher's earlier observation, that "the race is not to the swift, nor the battle to the strong" because accidents happen (9:11), might give readers the idea that there's no point in trying to accomplish something. The Teacher reiterates in this passage that accidents do indeed happen; we are not in control; "you do not know what disaster may happen on earth" (11:2). And he reiterates again that we do not know what God has in store: "Just as you do not know how the breath comes to the bones in the mother's womb, so you do not know the work of God, who makes everything" (11:5; cf. 3:11; 7:13-14, 24; 8:17). But this does not mean that we should fatalistically give up. In concluding his book, the Teacher offers more concrete advice on how we can live in the midst of the uncertainty we face in this world. His major admonitions in this passage are: "Send out your bread upon the waters. . . . In the morning sow your seed, and at evening do not let your hands be idle" (11:1, 6 [inclusio]; cf. 9:10).

---

2. Ogden, "Qoheleth 11:1-6," *VT* 33/2 (1983) 222, mentions R. Gordis, G. R. Castelino, and A. G. Wright. See also Murphy, *Ecclesiastes*, 104; Seow, *Ecclesiastes*, 328; and Whybray, *Ecclesiastes*, 150.

3. See Leupold, *Exposition of Ecclesiastes*, 254; and Provan, *Ecclesiastes*, 204.

4. Ogden, "Qoheleth 11:1-6," *VT* 33/2 (1983) 222, mentions W. Zimmerli, G. A. Barton, and O. S. Rankin. See also Daniel Fredericks, "Life's Storms and Structural Unity in Qoheleth 11:1–12:8," *JSOT* 52 (1991) esp. 97-99.

5. Ogden, ibid., mentions K. Galling.

6. Note that this marker is also found in 11:2, so that A. G. Wright suggests two units: 10:16–11:2 and 11:3-6 (see p. 21 above). Murphy, *Wisdom Literature*, 147, regards the "not know" of verse 2 "as more or less parenthetical" and extends the unit to verse 6. A stronger argument for the unity of 11:1-6 is its content and tone. "11:1, 2, and 6 contain verbs mostly in the imperative mood. These provide the general ethos of the section. Such verb forms do not extend beyond 11:6." Ogden, "Qoheleth 11:1-6," *VT* 33/2 (1983) 223.

Literary Features

Noting the literary features will help us discern the structure of the text and the meaning of this passage. The imperatives of verses 1, 2, and 6 show that the form of this passage is instruction. The parallelisms in verses 1-4 indicate that these verses are poetry (see the NRSV printing). The Teacher either used existing proverbs or composed these himself. Verses 5 and 6 may also be poetry (see the TNIV printing), though the NRSV prints these verses as prose.

Ogden observes, "In verses 1-4 there are three sets of paired sentences [1-2, 3, and 4] each in parallel form, while verse 5 could be described as exhibiting 'ascending parallelism.' Verse 6 follows a sentence form similar to verses 1-2 with its imperatives and motive clause."[7] Verse 6 also uses synthetic parallelism in the first two lines:

> In the morning sow your seed,
>> and at evening do not let your hands be idle;
> for you do not know which will prosper. . . .

Further, verse 2, "Divide your means seven ways, or even eight," employs "numerical heightening" — well known from the book of Proverbs (6:16-19; 30:15, 18, 21) and Amos (1:3, 6, 9, 11, 13; 2:1, 4, 6).

Possible metaphors are found in verse 1, "bread," and "waters," in verse 2, "divide your means/give a portion," and in verse 6, "sow your seed." Understanding these words and phrases as metaphors largely accounts for the many different interpretations.

The most important repetition is the fourfold refrain, "you do not know" (vv. 2, 5a, 5b, and 6). This repetition sets the Teacher's message against the background of human ignorance. Other repetitions linking the verses in this passage are "for" (*kî*; vv. 1, 2, 6), "clouds" (vv. 3, 4), "full/pregnant" (vv. 3, 5), "wind/ breath" (vv. 4, 5), and "sow" (vv. 4, 6).

Textual Structure

The literary features reveal that this short passage makes five related points:

  I. Admonition: Be bold, but wise (vv. 1-2)
    A. Send out your bread upon the waters (v. 1a)
      1. Reason: for after many days you will get it back (v. 1b)

---

7. Ogden, "Qoheleth 11:1-6," *VT* 33/2 (1983) 223.

    B. Divide your means seven ways (v. 2a)

        1. Reason: for *you do not know* what disaster may happen on earth (v. 2b)

  II. We do know certain laws of nature (v. 3)

    A. When clouds are full (v. 3a)

        1. they empty rain on the earth

    B. Whether a tree falls to the south or to the north (v. 3b)

        1. in the place where the tree falls, there it will lie

 III. Waiting for ideal conditions leads to doing nothing (v. 4)

    A. Whoever observes the wind (v. 4a)

        1. will *not sow*

    B. Whoever regards the clouds (v. 4b)

        1. will *not reap*

 IV. We do not know the plan of God, who controls everything (v. 5)

    A. As *you do not know* how the life-breath comes to a fetus (v. 5a)

        1. so *you do not know* the work of God (v. 5b)

           a. who makes everything

  V. Since *you do not know* what will prosper use every opportunity to work (v. 6)

    A. In the morning *sow* your seed (v. 6a) and at evening do not let your hands be idle

        1. Reason: for *you do not know* which will prosper (v. 6b)

           a. this or that

           b. or whether both alike will be good

Theocentric Interpretation

This passage mentions God only once, but with far-reaching implications. In verse 5 the Teacher states, "You do not know the work of God, who makes everything." On the one hand he highlights again human ignorance of the work, the "doings," of God. On the other hand he confesses that God "makes everything." In other words, God is sovereign; he governs everything; he controls everything in this world. We may be ignorant of the plan of God, but we do know that he has the final say and everything is in his hands.

Textual Theme and Goal

The textual structure with its admonitions and its repetition of "you do not know" helps us discern the theme of this passage. The Teacher begins with the mandate, "Send out your bread upon the waters, for after many days you will get it back" (v. 1). He is urging his readers to be bold, to do something unheard of, to take a risk, for eventually it will pay off. But he does not want his readers to go overboard and take foolish risks, for he adds: "Divide your means seven ways . . . , for you do not know what disaster may happen on earth" (v. 2). Be bold, but wise!

Next the Teacher notes that by observation we can get to know a certain regularity in nature (v. 3), but waiting for ideal weather conditions paralyzes us and leads to doing nothing (v. 4). Moreover, we do not know the plan of the sovereign God, who controls everything (v. 5). This leads to the final mandate in verse 6, which in structure (imperative followed by a motive clause) and contents is similar to the opening mandate (inclusio):[8] "In the morning sow your seed, and at evening do not let your hands be idle; for you do not know what will prosper, this or that, or whether both alike will be good."

The inclusio reveals the point of this passage: in view of our ignorance of what will prosper we ought to work boldly but wisely by covering all our bases. We can therefore formulate the textual theme as follows: *Since we do not know what God will prosper, use every opportunity to work boldly but wisely.*

As to the goal, Seow observes that the Teacher's "audience lived in a world where they longed to have control and desired to predict what might happen. Many no doubt lived like the poor miser who hoarded his wealth only to lose it all. They lived in fear of what might happen in their fragile world."[9] Given the imperatives, the Teacher's goal with this message was *to urge his readers not to be paralyzed by their lack of knowledge but to use every opportunity to work boldly but wisely.*

Ways to Preach Christ

How shall we move from the Teacher's message to Jesus Christ in the New Testament? Since this passage contains neither a promise of the coming Messiah nor a type of Christ,[10] we shall check the other five ways. Because redemptive-

---

8. Cf. Fox, *A Time to Tear Down,* 315, "In structure and message, 11:6 recapitulates 11:1f. and thereby rounds out the unit with its central teaching: compensate for ignorance by preparing for multiple eventualities."

9. Seow, "The Socioeconomic Context of 'The Preacher's' Hermeneutic," *PSBul* 17/2 (1996) 193.

10. Percy P. Stoute, "Bread upon the Waters," *BSac* 107 (1950) 222-26, suggests typology in verse 1: The "bread" refers to Jesus, the "Bread of Life" (John 6), and the "waters" signify "the nations or Gentiles" (Rev 17:5). This method is a form of typologizing which degenerates into allegorical interpretation.

historical progression and longitudinal themes are again intertwined, we shall combine them in this presentation.

Redemptive-Historical Progression/Longitudinal Themes

The theme focuses on human work. According to the opening chapters of Genesis, God created human beings in his image to have dominion over all of God's creatures (1:26-28). Genesis 2 zeroes in on a garden: "The LORD God took the man and put him in the garden of Eden to till it and keep it" (2:15). In other words, responsible human work is part of God's good creation, part of God's plan for humanity.

Unfortunately, human sin spoiled God's good creation: God "cursed the ground"; it brought forth "thorns and thistles," and satisfying human work became "toil" (Gen 3:17-18). "Thorns and thistles" not only increased the workload but made the fruit of work uncertain. Yet in his grace God promised that human toil would still result in sufficient food: "By the sweat of your face you shall eat bread" (Gen 3:19).

Later God brought his people Israel into the Promised Land. In this land "flowing with milk and honey" (Exod 3:8) there was more certainty that their toil would result in sufficient bread to eat — but no guarantees (see the covenant curses in Deut 28). Through Isaiah God promised a new earth (65:17) where "they shall plant vineyards and eat their fruit" (65:21). Still, the uncertainties of making a living increased for Israel when they became involved in risky international trade. In that setting the Teacher urged Israel to use every opportunity to work boldly, "for you do not know which will prosper."

Jesus came to earth to pay the penalty for human sin and restore the creation to what God had intended it to be. He viewed work in the context of the coming kingdom of God. He called fishermen to follow him and said, "I will make you fish for people" (Mark 1:17). He urged his followers to do the work of God: "We must work the works of him who sent me . . ." (John 9:4). Jesus linked our work with inheriting the kingdom of God: "The king [Jesus] will say to those at his right hand, 'Come, you that are blessed by my Father, inherit the kingdom prepared for you from the foundation of the world; for I was hungry and you gave me food, I was thirsty and you gave me something to drink . . .'" (Matt 25:34-35).

Paul also related our work to the coming kingdom and specifically to Jesus Christ: "Whatever you do, in word or deed, do everything in the name of the Lord Jesus, giving thanks to God the Father through him" (Col 3:17; cf. 1 Cor 15:58). When Jesus returns he will make all things new — also work (Rev 21:1-7; 22:12-14).

Analogy

Although Jesus sees work at a deeper level than the Old Testament Teacher does, there are still analogies between the Teacher's instructions and Jesus' teachings. As the Teacher urged his readers to use every opportunity to work, so Jesus urged his hearers to work diligently. Jesus said, "We must work the works of him who sent me while it is day; night is coming when no one can work" (John 9:4). Jesus also tells the parable of the talents, in which the hardworking servants were rewarded while the lazy servant was punished (Matt 25:14-30). Moreover, Paul speaks for "the Lord" when he tells the Ephesians: "Thieves must give up stealing; rather let them labor and work honestly with their own hands, so as to have something to share with the needy" (Eph 4:17, 21, 28).[11]

We may also be able to use an analogy that focuses specifically on verse 6: as the Teacher urged his readers to sow their seed both morning and evening, "for you do not know which will prosper," so Jesus tells his hearers the parable of the sower who sowed the seed liberally (on the path, on rocky ground, among thorns, and on good soil), not knowing which would prosper (Matt 13:3-9, 18-23).

New Testament References

The appendix of the Greek New Testament lists only one New Testament reference to this passage. For verse 5, "As you do not know the path of the wind, or how the body is formed in a mother's womb" (TNIV), it lists John 3:8, where Jesus says to Nicodemus, "The wind blows where it chooses, and you hear the sound of it, but you do not know where it comes from or where it goes. So it is with everyone who is born of the Spirit." This reference is not helpful, however, since not knowing the path of the wind is not the point of either passage.

Contrast

Although there is a deepening of the concept of work in the New Testament (see "Redemptive-Historical Progression" above), there is no contrast between the message of the Teacher and that of the New Testament.

---

11. Cf. 1 Thessalonians 4:11, "We urge you, beloved . . . to work with your hands, as we directed you." Paul reinforced this command in a follow-up letter: "Anyone unwilling to work should not eat" (2 Thess 3:10).

Sermon Theme and Goal

We formulated the textual theme as follows, "Since we do not know what God will prosper, use every opportunity to work boldly but wisely." Seeing that the New Testament does not contradict this idea, we can use the textual theme as the sermon theme: *Since we do not know what God will prosper, use every opportunity to work boldly but wisely.*

The goal of the Teacher was "to urge his readers not to be paralyzed by their lack of knowledge but to use every opportunity to work boldly but wisely." With a slight change we can make this the goal of the sermon: *to urge our hearers not to be paralyzed by their lack of knowledge but to use every opportunity to work boldly but wisely.* This goal indicates the need addressed by this sermon: people are often paralyzed by their lack of knowledge and other uncertainties and let opportunities to work fruitfully slip by.

Sermon Exposition

The sermon introduction can illustrate how easily we fail to act because of our lack of knowledge and other uncertainties. For example, when farmers are not sure that they can sell their crop that year, they may let the land lie fallow. When business people are not certain they can turn a profit, they may back out of a deal. When we do not know that our work will be successful, we tend to do nothing.

The Israelites whom the Teacher addressed found themselves in the same predicament. The nation had undergone major upheavals. The small agricultural country had become the bridge for international trade between Egypt and Asia/Europe. Some Israelites had tried their hand at the trading business and lost. In chapter 5 the Teacher describes people who lost their riches in what he calls "a bad venture." He writes, "As they came from their mother's womb, so they shall go again, naked as they came; they shall take nothing for their toil, which they may carry away with their hands" (5:14-15). Seeing some people lose everything in a bad venture was enough for others not to risk anything at all. One never knows what might happen. So they hoarded their possessions. But that was neither safe nor wise. In concluding his book, the Teacher offers two major admonitions on how to live in a world with many uncertainties. The first admonition is found in our text and has to do with our work and possessions.

Verse 1, "Send out your bread upon the waters, for after many days you will get it back." That seems like a risky thing to do. Take a loaf of Aunt Millie's Multi-Grain Bread and send it out upon the waters. What would happen? It would soon become waterlogged and sink. You'd never see that loaf of bread again!

But, of course, we should not think of Aunt Millie's bread but of the bread they baked back then. "What is envisioned is a *pita,* a thin, flat and probably hard disc that will float at least briefly on the current, until it is carried out of sight."[12] "Send out your bread upon the waters"; put it in the river and let it float around the bend. But as with Aunt Millie's bread, you will never see it again!

Yet the Teacher says, "Send out your bread upon the waters, for after many days you *will get it back.*" He cannot possibly mean that you will literally get your bread back. What he is saying is, Do something risky, like sending out your bread upon the waters. Do something so risky that a return seems impossible. The bread will be carried downstream. It will sink. You'll never see it again. But be bold! Step out in faith! Do something risky, "for after many days you will get it back."

What does the Teacher have in mind? Today there are two different interpretations, and both may be right.[13] Many commentators now think of the sea trade. That was a risky business, especially in those days. The journeys were long and hazardous. And the owners had no idea how their ships and goods were faring. Many shipwrecks dot the bottom of the Mediterranean Sea. The Bible tells us that King Solomon had a fleet of ships that would return with their gold, silver, and ivory once *every three years* (1 Kings 10:22). With the maritime trade in mind, the TNIV translates verse 1 as follows: "Ship your grain across the sea; after many days you may receive a return." Dare to take a risk! Be bold! We would say, "Nothing ventured, nothing gained."

The Teacher wants us to take risks but not foolish ones. So he cautions in verse 2, "Divide your means seven ways, or even eight, for you do not know what disaster may happen on earth." Don't put all your goods on a single ship, "for you do not know what disaster may happen." If that ship should sink in a storm, you would be bankrupt. "Divide your means seven ways, or even eight."[14] That

---

12. Davis, *Proverbs, Ecclesiastes, Song of Songs,* 219.

13. As indicated in the introduction to this chapter, commentators are divided on the meaning of verses 1-2. Many argue that sending out your bread upon the waters refers to sending out your goods across the seas in maritime trade. Verse 2, "divide your means [portion] seven ways," would then mean to divide your goods over several ships in case of disaster. Because of the parallelism with verse 6, this seems like the right interpretation. But others (e.g., Brown, Fox, Ogden, Seow) argue quite convincingly that verse 1 refers to giving bread, alms, to the poor, in which case verse 2 calls for generosity before disaster strikes: literally, "give a portion to seven and even to eight." I wonder if we need to choose between one or the other interpretation. As we are intended to hear both sides in synonymous parallelism, could the Teacher here use deliberate ambiguity that allows us to hear one side as well as the other? The challenge will be to move in the sermon from one interpretation to the other in a natural way.

14. "Seven" is the biblical number for fullness, completeness. "Seven, or even eight" means going even one better than completeness.

means, divide your goods over a large number of ships. If one ship sinks, you will still have most of your possessions. Today we would say, "Don't put all your eggs in one basket!"[15] Diversify your investments. But do dare to take risks. Be bold!

In the parable of the talents Jesus offers similar advice. The rich owner went on a journey. Before he left, he gave one of his servants five talents of money, another two talents, and a third one talent. The first servant immediately started to trade with his money and before long made five more talents. The second also worked hard with his money and made another two talents. But the third was afraid. He was afraid to risk his master's money. With so many unknowns, he could easily lose it. So he dug a hole in the ground and hid the money. His master's money was safe. Now he could not lose it. It seemed like a prudent thing to do. When the master returned home, he rewarded the first two servants for their hard work. But he rebuked the third one. He called him a "wicked and lazy servant" and "worthless." And he punished him severely (Matt 25:14-30). Jesus' point is that we must work diligently in and for the kingdom of God. And in doing so, we must dare to take a risk with what God has entrusted to us. We must dare to step out in faith.

Daring to take a risk does not apply only to sea trade, of course. We need to take risks in many areas of life. Students spend many years in college and university preparing for their life's work. They take the risk that there may not be a job opening in their chosen field when they are ready. Writers spend many years working on a book. They take the risk that their work may not be published or that it may not be well received. We take risks when we buy a house, when we travel, when we try different foods, when we select a surgeon. We take a risk even when we give money to the poor.

In chapter 4:1 the Teacher observed "all the oppressions that are practiced under the sun. Look, the tears of the oppressed — with no one to comfort them!" Is there no one to comfort the oppressed? Is there no one to help the poor? Could the Teacher imply in our text that we ought to take a risk also in giving money to the poor?

In the Middle Ages, commentators often understood the words, "Send out your bread upon the waters" as, Give bread to the oppressed![16] Give alms to the poor! That's taking a real risk. From a secular perspective giving to the poor looks like money down the drain. We don't know what the poor will do with the money. Moreover, we'll never see that money again. But the Teacher assures

---

15. Jacob practiced this principle when he saw his brother Esau approaching with 400 men (Gen 33:1-3).

16. Seow, *Ecclesiastes*, 343, mentions the Targum *Qoheleth Rabbah*, b. *Yebamot* 121a, Gregory Thaumaturgus, and the medieval Jewish commentators Rashi and Rashbaum, as well as the Reformer Martin Luther.

us, "For after many days you will get it back." It will bear fruit. It will come back to you.

Scholars have found a similar proverb in Egyptian wisdom literature. It reads like this: "Do a good deed and throw it in the water; when it dries you will find it."[17] It may look like the good deed has disappeared in the water, but when the water dries up you will find it again.

One commentator calls the imagery of "sending out your bread upon the waters" "an image of liberality."[18] This demand for liberality would be confirmed in verse 2, which says literally, "Give a portion to seven, or even eight." Give a portion of your possessions to seven or even to eight people. Seven is the number of perfection, of completeness. In giving money to the poor, go completeness one better! Liberally spread your wealth around! "Give a portion to seven, or even eight, for you do not know what disaster may happen on earth."

Given the possibility of a disaster, our instincts are "to hoard in anticipation of scarcity."[19] But verse 2 encourages us not to hang on to our possessions so tightly. The Teacher earlier exclaimed, "The lover of money will not be satisfied with money, nor the lover of wealth, with gain" (5:10; cf. 4:7-8; 5:13-17). Jesus also said, "One's life does not consist in the abundance of possessions" (Luke 12:15). Possessions cannot buy happiness. Possessions are to be used to help those in need. So verse 2 suggests that we ought to give liberally to the poor while we have possessions to give, "for you do not know what disaster may happen." That's taking a big risk. It requires stepping out in faith with the assurance of verse 1 that "after many days you will get it back."

How will we get back what we give to the poor? Proverbs 22:9 says, "Those who are generous are *blessed*, for they share their bread with the poor." Proverbs 19:17 puts it this way, "Whoever is kind to the poor lends to the LORD, and will be *repaid in full*." In Deuteronomy God says, "Give liberally and be ungrudging when you do so, for on this account the LORD your God will *bless you* in all your work and in all that you undertake" (Deut 15:10). Jesus says similarly, "Give, and it will be given to you. A good measure, pressed down, shaken together, running over, will be put into your lap; for the measure you give will be the measure you *get back*" (Luke 6:38).[20]

17. Seow, "Theology When Everything Is Out of Control," *Int* 55/3 (2001) 247, with a reference to Lichtheim, *Ancient Egyptian Literature*, 3:174.

18. Seow, ibid. Cf. Seow, *Ecclesiastes*, 343, "To release the bread on the waters is to take the risk of a spontaneous good deed. . . . [It] is a metaphor for doing good without expecting rewards: one should throw away a good deed, as it were — just let it go — without expecting a return."

19. Davis, *Proverbs, Ecclesiastes, Song of Songs*, 220.

20. See also Jesus' parable of the dishonest manager, Luke 16:1-9, and Jesus' conclusion, "I tell you, make friends for yourselves by means of dishonest wealth so that when it is gone, they may welcome you into the eternal homes."

Jesus even urges us to give liberally when there is no chance that people can repay us. He says, "When you give a luncheon or a dinner, do not invite your friends or your brothers or your relatives or rich neighbors, in case they may invite you in return, and you would be repaid. But when you give a banquet, invite the poor, the crippled, the lame, and the blind. And you will be blessed, because they cannot repay you, for you will be *repaid* at the resurrection of the righteous" (Luke 14:12-14).

"Send out your bread upon the waters, for after many days you *will* get it back." Dare to take a risk!

In verses 3 and 4 the Teacher expands on this theme. He has just said in verse 2 that we "do *not* know what disaster may happen on earth." But there are some things we do know. He points us to some of the regularities, the certainties, we can observe in nature. Verse 3, "When clouds are full, they empty rain on the earth; whether a tree falls to the south or to the north, in the place where the tree falls, there it will lie."

"When clouds are full, they empty rain on the earth." Clouds were meaningful signals, especially in Palestine. When the heavy clouds blew in from the Mediterranean, people knew that the rainy season was upon them. "When clouds are full, they empty rain on the earth." We observe this all the time; there are no exceptions. It's a law of nature we can observe and count on.

A second example, "Whether a tree falls to the south or to the north, in the place where the tree falls, there it will lie." Picture a forest. A tree falls in that forest. The tree could fall to the south or to the north, or to the east or to the west — it doesn't matter.[21] The point is: "In the place where the tree falls, there it will lie." It's another law of nature. A fallen tree is not going to get up. A fallen tree is not going to move into a different direction from where it fell. This happens all the time; there are no exceptions. It's a law of nature we can count on. So there are some things we can *know* by observing nature.[22] There are some certainties.

But we can demand more certainty than is good for us. The Teacher states in verse 4, "Whoever observes the wind will not sow; and whoever regards the clouds will not reap." Farmers prefer ideal weather for sowing and for reaping. Even today farmers carefully study the clouds and watch the weather channel. In ancient Palestine the best time to sow was when there was little or no wind. This allowed farmers to scatter the seed evenly over their fields. But if they

---

21. "South-north is a merism signifying 'everywhere.'" Fox, *A Time to Tear Down*, 314.

22. Some commentators, e.g., Longman, *Book of Ecclesiastes*, 257, state that the point of verse 3 is "that humans do not control what is happening around them." But Ogden, *Qoheleth*, 186-87, looking at this verse in the context of verse 1, contends against "those who would argue that the theme of v. 3 is what humankind is unable to accomplish, that we cannot alter the laws of nature to prevent it raining," and instead focuses on what we can *know*.

waited and waited for perfect weather, they might never sow. At some point they needed to take the risk.

When it came time to harvest, the perfect weather would be sunny — not a cloud in the sky. Rain would spoil the harvest. So farmers would study the clouds and weigh the chances of rain. But if they waited for perfect weather, they might never reap. At some point they needed to take the risk.

This principle of risk taking applies not only to farmers, of course. Merchants have to take risks; homemakers have to take risks; students have to take risks. We all have to take risks. "The overly cautious individual is destined to fail, for optimal conditions may not materialize."[23] Therefore, even though we can never be certain that our timing is perfect, we ought not to let the unknown paralyze us. Rather, we ought to use every opportunity to do our work boldly. "Those who don't try, never succeed."

In verse 5 the Teacher comes back to what we don't know: "Just as you do not know how the breath comes to the bones in the mother's womb, so you do not know the work of God, who makes everything."[24] In ancient times they didn't have a clue how life develops in a mother's womb. The Psalmist exclaims, "My frame was not hidden from you, when I was being made in secret, intricately woven in the depths of the earth" (Ps 139:15). Even with great advances in medical knowledge, we today do not really know how life comes into being.

"So," and this is the point, "so you do not know the work of God, who makes everything." We don't know the work of God.[25] We don't know what God will do next. We don't know his plans for the future. We live with a great deal of uncertainty.

But there is one thing that we do know, and that is that God "makes *everything.*" Nothing in this world is outside his control. The storms that sink ships on the sea, the clouds that rain on the earth, the trees that fall in the forest, the winds that blow, the crops that grow, the life-breath for babies — God makes everything! That knowledge provides us with stability in an uncertain world. The fact that God makes everything can give us the courage to do our work faithfully. The fact that God makes everything can give us the boldness to take

23. Crenshaw, *Ecclesiastes*, 180. Cf. Fox, *Ecclesiastes*, 73, "Forethought and timely action are important, but planning too meticulously for the incalculable can paralyze initiative."

24. The TNIV translates, "As you do not know the path of the wind, or how the body is formed in a mother's womb. . . ." Whether one uses two illustrations or combines them into one (as in the NRSV), the point remains the same: ". . . so you cannot understand [or, 'do not know'] the work of God, the Maker of all things."

25. "The 'work of God' . . . is not creation, which is not relevant here, but God's ongoing governance of the world, manifest in his causation of processes, such as a misfortune, the clouds emptying, a tree falling, a particular planting succeeding, and the life-spirit animating the fetus." Fox, *A Time to Mourn*, 315,

some risks. We need not wait for absolute certainty before we act. We need not be so uptight. God makes everything. So we can send out our bread upon the waters, knowing that after many days we will get it back.

In verse 6 the Teacher again urges us to use every opportunity to work boldly but wisely. "In the morning sow your seed, and at evening do not let your hands be idle; for you do not know which will prosper, this or that, or whether both alike will be good." Think of the risk farmers take when they sow their seed. They could eat this seed to satisfy their hunger. That would be a sure bet. But instead of eating the seed they bury it in the ground. Now they have nothing — unless they get a good harvest. So they sow in hope, but they cannot be certain of getting a good crop. There may be too much rain, or too little. There may be hail or a plague of locusts. What should people do when they don't know the odds of success?

Some people do not sow, as we saw in verse 4, and therefore will not reap. Others wait too long to reap, and therefore waste a crop. These people are not willing to take the risk necessary for successful sowing and reaping. But the Teacher advises: Precisely because of the uncertainty, precisely because you do not know, you ought to use every opportunity to work. "You do not know which will prosper, this or that." Perhaps the seed you sow in the morning will prosper. Perhaps what you sow in the evening will lead to a good crop. Perhaps both sowings will prosper. Precisely because you do not know, you ought to cover all your bases. Sow your seed both in the morning *and* in the evening.[26] Use every opportunity to work boldly!

Four times in six verses the Teacher says that we do not know: verse 2, "you do not know what disaster may happen"; verse 5, "you do not know how the breath comes to the bones in the mother's womb," and "you do not know the work of God," and verse 6, "you do not know which will prosper, this or that." We live in a world with many uncertainties because we "do not know." How should we live in such a precarious world? The Teacher admonishes: Since we do not know what God will prosper, use every opportunity to work boldly but wisely!

Jesus offers similar advice. He tells his hearers the parable of the sower. "A sower went out to sow. And as he sowed, some seeds fell on the path, and the birds came and ate them up . . ." (Matt 13:3-9). The sower knew, of course, that some of the seed might be eaten by birds, but he risked it anyway. He sowed the seed liberally, not knowing which seed would prosper. Some seed was indeed

---

26. In verse 6 the Teacher "gives the reason why one should work hard: it is precisely because the result is uncertain that one should work hopefully and without anxiety." Whybray, *Ecclesiastes*, 160. Cf. Fox, *Ecclesiastes*, 74, "We should respond to ignorance not by inaction or passivity but by being flexible and diversifying our efforts and investments."

eaten by birds; some sprouted quickly but was scorched by the hot sun; some young plants were choked by thorns. A lot of uncertainty and failure. But the sower sowed anyway. In the midst of much uncertainty, he knew that some of the seed would prosper. So he sowed liberally and boldly.

Jesus intended his parable to be understood at a deeper level than the literal sowing of seed. He explained that the seed is "the word of the kingdom" (Matt 13:19). We are to sow the word of the kingdom liberally because we don't know when or where God will prosper it. So Jesus commands his disciples to be his "witnesses in Jerusalem, in all Judea and Samaria [Samaria of all places], and to the ends of the earth" (Acts 1:8).

Sometimes we may be discouraged by all the uncertainties. Sometimes we may be discouraged by our lack of success. It is not easy to live with uncertainties. Especially in our culture, it is not easy to live with our "not knowing." It seems better to play it safe. As a result we may miss God-given opportunities. This passage urges us: precisely because of the uncertainties, precisely because you don't know what God will prosper, use every opportunity to work boldly but wisely. And entrust the results to the hands of almighty God, who through Jesus Christ is our Father in heaven. He'll take care of us.

CHAPTER 15

Remember Your Creator!

Ecclesiastes 11:7–12:8

Rejoice, young man, while you are young,
*   and let your heart cheer you in the days of your youth. . . .*
Remember your creator in the days of your youth,
*   before the days of trouble come. . . .*

(Eccl 11:9; 12:1)

Since this passage addresses especially the young, it is an ideal text for a youth service. The major challenge in preaching this text will be to interpret it correctly. For example, what does the Teacher mean in verse 9 when he recommends youths to "follow the inclination of your heart and the desire of your eyes"? This advice seems to contradict God's law: Do "not follow the lust of your own heart and your own eyes" (Num 15:39). The Teacher continues by reminding youths that "for all these things God will bring you into judgment." Is this reminder intended to curb their joy, or is there another explanation?

There are also many questions about the interpretation of the final poem. Michael Fox calls Ecclesiastes 12:1-8 "the most difficult passage in a difficult book."[1] Long ago Jerome observed that on this text there are "almost as many opinions as there are people."[2] Today there are more people and more "opinions" than there were in Jerome's time. The options are to interpret the poem literally, metaphorically, allegorically, or a mixture of these three. This results in a variety of understandings: the poem is about old age and death, or a funeral, or a storm with people cowering inside a house, or the end times with the death

---

1. Fox, "Aging and Death in Qoheleth 12," *JSOT* 42 (1988) 55.
2. Seow, "Qohelet's Eschatological Poem," *JBL* 118/2 (1999) 209.

of all people.[3] Even when some commentators agree on the big picture, say, old age and death, they may still disagree on the details because of some inherent arbitrariness in allegorical interpretation. For example, "when the doors on the street are shut" (12:4) has been understood as "feet" (Targum), "lips" (e.g., Ewald), "eyes" (e.g., Hengstenberg), and "ears" (e.g., Wildeboer).[4] And "the grasshopper drags itself along" (12:5) "has been taken to refer to either bad joints, swollen ankles, a halting walk, or impotence."[5]

Although preachers have to make up their minds on the interpretation of these images, fortunately these details do not affect the main thrust of the passage, which the Teacher states very clearly: "Rejoice!" (11:9) and "Remember your creator!" (12:1). But these two commands raise further questions about the theme of this passage: How are these two commands related? Which is the dominant command? How can we formulate a *single* theme that does justice to both? In the course of our study we shall have to come to clarity on these and other issues, but we shall begin with the parameters of the text and its context.

Text and Context

In the previous chapter we noted that some commentators include 11:7-8 with the foregoing section and thus would start this one with 11:9.[6] But we concluded the last section with 11:6 because it has the section marker, "you do not know," and 11:7-8 changes the topic from economics to rejoicing — a theme that will be further expounded in 11:9-10. Similarly, 11:8 introduces the topic of "remember" — a theme that will be further expounded in 12:1-8.[7] Also, the word "vanity" in 11:8, 10, and 12:8 ties this section together into a cohesive unit. "Moreover, the themes of light and darkness link 11:7-8 with the rest of the passage: the mention of the sun and the light in 11:7 is matched by the reference to the darkening of the sun and the light in 12:2. One notes, too, the recurrence of certain expressions for time: 'years' (11:8a; 12:1c), 'days' (11:8b; 11:9; 12:1a, 1b), 'before' (12:1b, 2,

---

3. Seow, ibid., 210, lists many interpreters who understand the poem to be describing either "actual conditions and experiences of old age, [or] a house or estate in disrepair, [or] a gloomy winter day, [or] the approach and experience of a thunderstorm, or a funeral." On p. 212, Seow grants that "although traditional sayings — perhaps even an old poem — about old age may lie in the background, the poet now portrays the demise of human life in entirely eschatological terms. All the images in vv. 2-7 are consistent with the author's intent to depict a permanent end of human existence."

4. Ogden, *Qoheleth*, 203.

5. Garrett, *Proverbs, Ecclesiastes, Song of Songs*, 342.

6. See, e.g., Leupold, *Exposition of Ecclesiastes*, 267, and Provan, *Ecclesiastes*, 211.

7. See Ogden, *Qoheleth*, 193-94.

6). . . . Indeed, 11:7-8 may be seen as the 'overture' (so Ravasi) to Qohelet's grand finale."[8] We can therefore begin this text at 11:7.

The question remains where to end this section, at 12:7 or 12:8? 12:8 switches from the first-person speech of the foregoing to the third person: "Vanity of vanities, says the Teacher; all is vanity." This statement may be the conclusion of an editor, which raises the question whether it should be included with the teaching of the Teacher in 11:7–12:7 or left for the following editorial section (12:9-14).[9] Fox states, "This verse [12:8] is the pivot between the poem on dying and the epilogue; it belongs to both units."[10] Although this statement is true, it does not solve the problem whether to include 12:8 with the present unit or the following one or both. Of course, 12:8 forms an inclusio with 1:2, thus bracketing the whole book. But it also sums up this section very well as it repeats the exclamations of vanity in 11:8 and 10. Moreover, the Teacher himself could very well sum up his message in the third person.[11] In any event, in terms of contents, 12:9 begins a new section. Therefore we shall select as our text Ecclesiastes 11:7–12:8.

This text has numerous connections with its context. The Teacher earlier urged people to rejoice (2:24-26; 3:12-13, 22; 5:18-20; 8:15; and 9:7-9). In this passage he does so again for the seventh and final time (11:7-10). Earlier he motivated people to rejoice by reminding them that they are all going to Sheol (9:10b). Here he uses the same motivation but much more elaborately: "the days of darkness will be many" (11:8), and the darkness of old age and death awaits all (12:1-7).[12] Earlier he asked, "Who knows whether the human spirit goes upward and the spirit of animals goes downward to the earth?" (3:21). Here he states that the human spirit "returns to God who gave it" (12:7). Earlier he spoke of God's judgment (3:17; 5:6); here he repeats that notion (11:9), as will also the final editor in the Epilogue (12:14).

Structurally the most striking feature is that the Teacher began his book with a poem about the unending cycles in nature and now he concludes his book with a poem about the ending of human life. The opening poem made the point that "a generation goes *(hōlēk)*, and a generation comes, but the earth

---

8. Seow, *Ecclesiastes,* 368. Seow also mentions "eyes" in 11:7 and 9 as well as "delight" ("pleasant" and "cheer").

9. Longman, *Book of Ecclesiastes,* 274, argues for the unity of 12:8-14: "The NIV and NRSV use a rubric to divide vv. 8 and 9, but it is clear from the shift in narrative voice that vv. 8-14 must be treated as the final unit of the book."

10. Fox, *Ecclesiastes,* 82.

11. Even if 12:8 is the work of a later editor, this does not mean that it should necessarily be excluded from our text. Content decides this issue. Moreover, in our first text we of necessity included the same third-person words (1:2).

12. The subject of death has come up many times. See 2:14-16; 3:19-20; 9:3, 10-12.

('*ereṣ*) remains forever *(lĕ'ôlām)*" (1:4). The closing poem states that "all must go *(hōlēk)* to their eternal *('ôlām)* home" (12:5) and "the dust returns to the earth *('ereṣ)* as it was" (12:7).[13]

Literary Features

The commands in this passage indicate that the overall form is instruction.[14] The Teacher opens this passage with a metaphorical proverb, "Light is sweet, and it is pleasant for the eyes to see the sun" (11:7). In other words, Life is good. He follows this up in verse 8 with two jussives: "should rejoice" and "let them remember." Then he singles out the first jussive and turns it into the imperative, "Rejoice!" He elaborates on this important command with four more imperatives: "Follow!" "Know!" "Banish!" and "Put away!" (vv. 9-10). Next he selects the second jussive, "let them remember," and turns this also into an imperative: "Remember your creator!" He elaborates on this command in a lengthy sentence that runs from 12:1-7. The sentence is divided into three parts by the repetition of "before," which has the effect of repeating "remember your creator": "Remember your creator before the days of trouble come" (v. 1). Remember your Creator "before the sun and the light . . . are darkened" (v. 2). Remember your Creator "before the silver cord is snapped" (v. 6).

The use of metaphors is prominent especially in the concluding poem. This makes interpretation difficult. It also raises the question whether some of the metaphors are connected in a direct way to form an allegory (see 12:3-4a). Von Rad writes, "The occasional confusion of image and object did not trouble the ancient listener. Fully worked-out allegories are, of course, rare. Often an image is allegorical only in parts, only to move away from that particular style again. Above all, the transitions between what is simply metaphorical and what is allegorical are fluid."[15]

Several keywords are highlighted by repetition. "Rejoice" *(śimḥâ)* is mentioned twice (11:8, 9) and reinforced with other words and phrases: "let your

13. Dorsey, *Literary Structure*, 197, mentions these and many other Hebrew words that are used in both the opening poem and this concluding poem.

14. "Because of the commands, this section should be read as an instruction, although the description of old age taken by itself might be viewed as a reflection." Murphy, *Wisdom Literature*, 148.

15. Von Rad, *Wisdom in Israel*, 45. Cf. p. 46, n. 33, "One must speak of an allegory where we have a passage containing two or more metaphors belonging to the same context of meaning and mutually interpreting one another." In contrast, Krüger writes, "Because of the erratic and irregular change in form and content, 12:1b-7 has more the effect of a 'collage' than that of a regular 'poem.' . . . The text evokes a series of images for 'bad times' that in the future await the 'young man' addressed in 11:9–12:1." *Qoheleth*, 201.

heart cheer you," "follow the desire of your eyes," and "banish anxiety and pain" (11:9, 10). "Remember" *(zēker)* is also mentioned twice (11:8; 12:1) and implied another three times: remember "before" (12:1, 2, 6). Further we note a threefold repetition of "vanity" *(hebel)* to conclude the introduction (11:8) and each of the two main sections (11:10 and 12:8).[16] Moreover, the emphasis on youth is brought out in various ways: "young man," "young," "days of your youth" (11:9), "youth and dawn of life" (11:10), "days of your youth" (12:1). In addition to God's judgment (11:9), God is mentioned twice, once as Creator (12:1) and once as "God who gave breath" (12:7), thus forming an inclusio for the poem.[17] And finally we should note the juxtaposition between light and darkness: "light" and "sun" in 11:7 followed by "days of darkness" in 11:8, and "the sun and the light and the moon and the stars are darkened" in 12:2. There are also many parallel constructions, which we shall note in the textual structure below.

Textual Structure

The literary features help us in outlining the structure of the text, which in turn will help us in discerning the theme and designing an expository sermon outline.

   I. Rejoice in the goodness of life (11:7)
        but remember that days of darkness are coming
     A. Light is sweet (11:7)
         and it is pleasant for the eyes to see the sun
     B. Those who live many years should rejoice in them all (11:8)
         1. Yet remember that the days of darkness will be many
            a. All that comes is vanity
  II. Command: Rejoice in the days of your youth
     A. Rejoice, young man, while you are young (11:9)
         and let your heart cheer you in the days of your youth.
     B. Follow the inclination of your heart
         and the desire of your eyes
         1. but know that for all these things God will bring you into judgment.
     C. Banish anxiety from your mind (11:10)
         and put away pain from your body
         1. for youth and the dawn of life are vanity
 III. Command: Remember your creator in the days of your youth (12:1)
     A. Remember your creator *before* the days of trouble come
         and the years when you will say, "I have no pleasure in them"

---

16. Ogden, *Qoheleth*, 193.
17. Huwiler, "Ecclesiastes," 216.

   B. Remember your creator *before* the darkness of old age overtakes you
       1. before the sun, the light, the moon, and the stars are darkened (12:2)
           and the clouds return with the rain
       2. in the day when (12:3)
          a. the guards of the house tremble
          b. and the strong men are bent
          c. and the women who grind cease working because they are few
          d. and those who look through the windows see dimly
          e. when the doors on the street are shut (12:4)
          f. and the sound of the grinding is low
          g. and one rises up at the sound of a bird
          h. and all the daughters of song are brought low
          i. when one is afraid of heights (12:5a-e)
          j. and terrors are in the road
          k. the almond tree blossoms
          l. the grasshopper drags itself along
          m. and desire fails
       3. because all must go to their eternal home (12:5f)
           and the mourners will go about the streets
   C. Remember your creator *before* death overtakes you
       1. before the silver cord is snapped (12:6)
           and the golden bowl is broken
       2. and the pitcher is broken at the fountain
           and the wheel broken at the cistern
       3. and the dust returns to the earth as it was (12:7)
           and the breath returns to God who gave it
   D. Vanity of vanities, says the Teacher (12:8)
       all is vanity

Theocentric Interpretation

The Teacher urges people of all ages (11:8) but especially the young to rejoice in the life God has given. He encourages boundless joy but reminds them that God will judge their behavior (11:9). In order to really rejoice, they are urged to remember their Creator in the days of their youth (12:1). Their Creator has given them their life-breath (12:7); he has given them "the days of life" (8:15); he has determined their time to be born, and their time to die (3:2); he has given them "wisdom and knowledge and joy" (2:26); "he has made everything suitable for its time" (3:11); he has given them "wealth and possessions," and enables them "to enjoy them" and even find "enjoyment" in their "toil" (5:19). They are to rejoice in God's good gifts as long as they can — until God takes back his gift of life (12:7). The poem begins and ends with God the Creator, God the Giver. Thus the Teacher counsels youth "to commence early and develop a life-style in which God as creator and sustainer is central."[18]

Textual Theme and Goal

The focus of this passage is on two commands: "Rejoice while you are young!" (11:9) and "Remember your creator in the days of your youth!" (12:1). The question is, What is the relationship between these two commands? It seems clear that, reinforced with four more imperatives, the dominant command is to rejoice. But the command to remember also receives much weight because it is part of a seven-verse sentence with three ominous "before's." It appears that the command to remember your Creator is given to lend support to the command to rejoice. In other words, people ought to remember their Creator in order to rejoice.[19]

The Teacher has recommended many times that we ought to rejoice. What is unique about his command in this passage is that it is aimed primarily at young people and that it is linked to remembering their Creator before the darkness of old age and death overtakes them. Therefore we can formulate the theme of this text as follows: *Before it is too late, remember your Creator in order to truly enjoy life.*

Given the imperatives, the Teacher's goal is *to urge especially young people to remember their Creator before it is too late in order that they may truly enjoy life.*[20]

Ways to Preach Christ

Earlier we traced through the Old Testament to Jesus Christ in the New the theme of rejoicing (see above, pp. 54-56, 225-26). With this passage we should focus on the specific combination of remembering your Creator in order to re-

18. Ogden, *Qoheleth,* 199.

19. Cf. Hengstenberg, *Commentary on Ecclesiastes,* 244: "*In order* that thou mayest be able to rejoice, and to put away discontent, remember thy Creator" (his emphasis). Cf. Leupold, *Exposition of Ecclesiastes,* 273, "12:1a gives the absolute essential foundation for true joy." It is telling that most contemporary commentators fail to deal with this crucial issue and instead concentrate on the details of the poem.

20. Cf. Seow, "Qohelet's Eschatological Poem," *JBL* 118/2 (1999) 209: "There is substantial agreement on the unity of the passage, and even on its purpose; scholars in general concur that the author means to exhort people to enjoy life while there is still time."

joice. Since this passage has neither a promise nor a type of Christ, we shall explore the remaining five ways to Christ in the New Testament. For the sake of efficiency we shall again combine redemptive-historical progression and longitudinal themes.

Redemptive-Historical Progression/Longitudinal Themes

In Paradise people walked with God, or, rather, God walked with them, and they rejoiced because of God's presence and his gifts of life, companionship, and the beautiful garden they were to manage. When they disobeyed God, they no longer rejoiced but hid from him in fear.

Later, when God saved his people from slavery in Egypt, he instituted the Passover feast so that Israel would remember God's salvation and rejoice. The LORD said, "This day shall be a day of remembrance for you. You shall celebrate it as a festival to the LORD" (Exod 12:14). At Sinai the LORD gave Israel his law so that the people would know how to live joyfully before the LORD. God wanted them to remember his law: "Keep these words that I am commanding you today in your heart. Recite them to your children and talk about them when you are at home and when you are away, when you lie down and when you rise. Bind them as a sign on your hand, fix them as an emblem on your forehead, and write them on the doorposts of your house and on your gates" (Deut 6:6-9). To help Israel remember his law, God even instructed them to make fringes on the corners of their garments: "You have the fringe so that, when you see it, you will remember all the commandments of the LORD and do them, and not follow the lust of your own heart and your own eyes. So you shall remember and do all my commandments, and you shall be holy to your God" (Num 15:39-40).

When the LORD brought Israel into Canaan, he warned them not to forget the LORD in their prosperity: "If you do forget the LORD your God and follow other gods to serve and worship them, I solemnly warn you today that you shall surely perish" (Deut 8:19). The LORD also instituted more signs so the people would remember his salvation. He instructed Joshua to take twelve stones from the middle of the Jordan and place them in their first camp; "When your children ask in time to come, 'What do those stones mean to you?' then you shall tell them that the waters of the Jordan were cut off in front of the ark of the covenant of the LORD. . . . So these stones shall be to the Israelites a memorial forever" (Josh 4:6-7). Later when the LORD saved Israel from the Philistines, "Samuel took a stone and set it up between Mizpah and Jeshanah, and named it Ebenezer; for he said, 'Thus far the LORD has helped us'" (1 Sam 7:12). These were memorials to help Israel remember their Creator and Redeemer so that they might rejoice in him.

But the LORD would do still more for his people. Zechariah (9:9) prophesied:

Rejoice greatly, O daughter Zion!
  Shout aloud, O daughter Jerusalem!
Lo, your king comes to you;
  triumphant and victorious is he,
humble and riding on a donkey,
  on a colt, the foal of a donkey.

In the fullness of time God sent his own Son to redeem his creation. "God so loved the world that he gave his only Son, so that everyone who believes in him may not perish but may have eternal life" (John 3:16). Paul proclaimed, "In Christ God was reconciling the world to himself, not counting their trespasses against them" (2 Cor 5:19). Jesus urged his followers to remember him. He said, "I am the vine, you are the branches. Those who abide in me and I in them bear much fruit, because apart from me you can do nothing. . . . If you keep my commandments, you will abide in my love. . . . I have said these things to you so that my joy may be in you, and that your joy may be complete" (John 15:5, 10, 11). By remembering Jesus in keeping his commandments our joy will be complete.

Jesus also commanded his followers to remember his saving work. When he celebrated with his disciples the Passover, the Old Testament feast of remembrance, Jesus "took a loaf of bread, and when he had given thanks, he broke it and gave it to them, saying, 'This is my body, which is given for you. Do this in remembrance of me'" (Luke 22:19). Paul explained the future dimension of this remembrance: "As often as you eat this bread and drink the cup, you proclaim the Lord's death until he comes" (1 Cor 11:26).[21] John writes about the future marriage supper of the Lamb. He heard "what seemed to be the voice of a great multitude . . . crying out, 'Hallelujah! For the Lord our God the Almighty reigns. Let us *rejoice* and exult and give him the glory, for the marriage of the Lamb has come . . .'" (Rev 19:6-7).

Until Jesus comes again, he wants us to remember him not only by keeping his commandments and by celebrating the Lord's Supper but also by remembering that he is always with us. As Jesus sent his disciples out to make disciples of all nations, he said, "Remember, I am with you always, to the end of the age" (Matt 28:20). When Jesus returns at the end of the age, his people will greatly rejoice. "Blessed are those who wash their robes [other manuscripts have "do

---

21. Jesus himself speaks of this future in John 16:22 when he prepares his disciples for his departure: "So you have pain now; but I will see you again, and your hearts will rejoice, and no one will take your joy from you."

his commandments"], so that they will have the right to the tree of life and may enter the city by the gates" (Rev 22:14).

Analogy

We can draw an analogy between the Teacher's message and that of Jesus: As the Teacher urged us to rejoice by remembering our Creator, so does Jesus. In the Beatitudes, Jesus calls us "blessed" and urges us to "rejoice and be glad" (Matt 5:12). He teaches us to remember our Father in heaven by praying to him daily that his name may be hallowed, his kingdom may come, his will may be done, and that he will "give us this day our daily bread" (Matt 6:9-11). Jesus also insists that we remember God by obeying his law: "Not everyone who says to me, 'Lord, Lord,' will enter the kingdom of heaven, but only the one who does the will of my Father in heaven" (Matt 7:21).

We can also draw an analogy between the Teacher's message and that of Paul: As the Teacher urged us to rejoice by remembering our Creator, so Paul urges us, "Rejoice in the Lord always; again I will say, Rejoice. . . . Do not worry about anything, but in everything by prayer and supplication with thanksgiving let your requests be made known to God. And the peace of God, which surpasses all understanding, will guard your hearts and your minds in Christ Jesus" (Phil 4:4-7).

New Testament References

There are no New Testament references or allusions to this passage.

Contrast

There is no contrast between the message (theme) of the Teacher and that of the New Testament. There are, however, some important contrasts in the details. In contrast to the Old Testament Teacher who offers no hope for life beyond death (12:6-8), the New Testament Gospels were written because of the astounding news that Jesus rose from the dead (all four Gospels end with Jesus' resurrection). Paul adds, "In fact Christ has been raised from the dead, the first fruits of those who have died. For since death came through a human being, the resurrection of the dead has also come through a human being; for as all die in Adam, so all will be made alive in Christ. But each in his own order: Christ the first fruits, then at his coming those who belong to Christ" (1 Cor 15:20-23).

Moreover, according to the Teacher, when people die they go to their "eternal home" (12:5), that is, the grave. "The dust returns to the earth as it was, and the breath returns to God who gave it" (12:7). The "breath" or "spirit" is the life-breath. In the Teacher's conception, when God takes back the life-breath, human life ends. Progressive revelation, however, indicates that the soul survives death. Hence Jesus can promise the criminal dying on a cross next to him, "Truly, I tell you, *today* you will be with me in Paradise" (Luke 23:43). And Jesus can say to his followers, "In my Father's house there are many dwelling places. . . . If I go and prepare a place for you, I will come again and will take you to myself, so that where I am, there you may be also" (John 14:2-3). In this connection Paul also writes, "For we know that if the earthly tent we live in is destroyed, we have a building from God, a house not made with hands, eternal in the heavens" (2 Cor 5:1; cf. Phil 1:21-24).

Sermon Theme and Goal

Since the New Testament affirms the theme of the Old Testament Teacher, we can use his theme as our sermon theme: *Before it is too late, remember your Creator in order to truly enjoy life.*

The Teacher's goal was "to urge especially young people to remember their Creator before it is too late in order that they may truly enjoy life." We can also adopt the Teacher's goal as our goal for this sermon: *to urge especially young people to remember their Creator before it is too late in order that they may truly enjoy life.* This goal points to the need addressed: people fail to find true joy because they do not (sufficiently) remember their Creator.

Sermon Exposition

One can introduce the sermon with an illustration of a contemporary person who forgot God. Prosperity can make us forget God. When our freezer is filled with food and we have a good nest egg for a rainy day, it is easy to forget God.

When God brought Israel into the prosperity of the Promised Land, he warned them specifically not to forget him. God said, "*Remember* the long way that the LORD your God has led you these forty years in the wilderness . . . , testing you to know what was in your heart, whether or not you would keep his commandments. . . . For the LORD your God is bringing you into a good land, a land with flowing streams . . . , a land of wheat and barley . . . , a land where you may eat bread without scarcity, where you will lack nothing. . . . You shall eat your fill and *bless the LORD* your God for the good land that he has given you.

Take care that you do not *forget* the LORD your God, by failing to keep his commandments. . . . When you have eaten your fill and have built fine houses and live in them, and when your herds and flocks have multiplied, and your silver and gold is multiplied, and all that you have is multiplied, then do not exalt yourself, *forgetting* the LORD your God. . . . But *remember* the LORD your God, for it is he who gives you power to get wealth. . . . If you do *forget* the LORD your God and follow other gods to serve and worship them, I solemnly warn you today that you shall surely perish" (Deut 8:2-19).[22]

Israel often forgot God, and so do we. That's why this message of the Old Testament Teacher is so important. He urges people to remember their Creator in order to truly enjoy life.

The Teacher begins in chapter 11:7, "Light is sweet, and it is pleasant for the eyes to see the sun." You may not have expected this statement from a person who is often considered a pessimist. He is basically saying: Life is good! It is sweet! You want to enjoy it the way you enjoy the sweetness of honey. "It is *pleasant* for the eyes to see the sun." Life is good! You want to enjoy it to the utmost.

The Teacher continues in verse 8, "Even those who live many years should rejoice in them all; yet let them remember that the days of darkness will be many." Even when we live many years, he says, we should *rejoice* in every one of those years. Sometimes we take life for granted. We don't enjoy the present. We would just as soon skip over certain days. We look forward to the weekend; or we look forward to our vacation; or we look forward to retirement. The Teacher urges us not to waste any time: "Even those who live many years should rejoice in them *all;* yet let them remember that the days of darkness will be many." He spurs us on to rejoice each day because we know that some day the sweet light will dim and "the days of darkness will be many."[23] So don't waste any time. Instead, make a conscious effort to rejoice every day, and all the more by remembering that "the days of darkness will be many."

In verse 8 we find two important verbs. They are, "rejoice" and "remember." We are to rejoice all the more by remembering. We are motivated to rejoice every day when we remember that "the days of darkness will be many."[24] Once

---

22. This passage could also be read before the sermon and briefly referenced in the sermon.

23. The Teacher "seems to argue that an acute sense of life's brevity should increase the degree to which we cherish life while we have it." Farmer, *Who Knows What Is Good?*, 191.

24. Some commentators claim that "the days of darkness" refers to death. E.g., Whybray, *Ecclesiastes*, 161, says that "darkness is a metaphor for death." But it does not make sense to say that "the days of death will be many." In this context "the days of darkness" must refer to "the days of trouble" and the years "when you will say, 'I have no pleasure in them,'" because all is darkness (12:1-2). "The days of darkness" refers to the darkness (suffering) of old age (12:1-5), which ends in death (12:6-7).

the days of darkness come, we cannot rejoice in retrospect. The time to rejoice is now! For, the Teacher concludes, "All that comes is vanity." Literally he says, "All that comes is a vapor." Life is like vapor, a puff of smoke. It is fleeting. You will be in the days of darkness before you know it. Therefore don't waste any time. Rejoice every day!

When we are young we don't count the days. It looks like we have countless days ahead of us. So the Teacher next turns specifically to young people in verse 9: "Rejoice, young man, while you are young, and let your heart cheer you in the days of your youth." There is that word "rejoice" again, but for emphasis it is now stated as a command.[25] And to make his point even more forcefully, the Teacher adds another command: "Follow the inclination of your heart and the desire of your eyes." That is, follow your desire! Enjoy what is present before your eyes![26] Don't postpone enjoyment to a future time when, say, you have your own car, or when you finish college, or when you have landed a good job. Enjoy the present moment!

The Teacher adds, "but know that for all these things God will bring you into judgment." Having commanded full enjoyment, does the Teacher now temper it? Does his reminder of God's judgment put a damper on our rejoicing? The answer is, No. But he does not want us to seek joy in directions that can only lead to pain and sorrow.[27] He does not want us to seek joy in being promiscuous, in doing drugs, in watching harmful movies. What may seem like fun can be a disaster. So the Teacher reminds us, as he did before,[28] that God will judge us for our actions. We are accountable to God for what we do. In other words, the Teacher commands "*responsible* pleasure, not license to exploit others or squander our own bodies and abilities."[29] At the same time, "this theme of judgment is designed not to *temper* . . . [his] command to enjoy life but to *underscore* and *direct* it."[30] For, according to the Teacher, enjoyment is a gift of God.[31] "Human be-

25. "The young man should enjoy his life already in his youth, not because he can no longer do so in old age [see 11:8], but because in old age he can never make up for the pleasures missed in his youth — and because it is by no means certain that he will get old at all." Krüger, *Qoheleth*, 198.

26. See Seow, *Ecclesiastes*, 349-50. See Ecclesiastes 6:9, "Better is the sight of the eyes than the wandering of desire."

27. "The following of the heart and the eyes is to be carried out in the sure knowledge that there is moral accountability in the universe." Provan, *Ecclesiastes*, 212.

28. Ecclesiastes 3:17 and 5:6. See also the editor's final comment in 12:14.

29. Davis, *Proverbs, Ecclesiastes, Song of Songs*, 222. Note Paul's advice in 2 Timothy 2:22, "Shun youthful passions and pursue righteousness, faith, love, and peace, along with those who call on the Lord from a pure heart."

30. Brown, *Ecclesiastes*, 105 (his emphases). See Davis, *Proverbs, Ecclesiastes, Songs of Songs*, 222, "Judgment does not cancel out rejoicing but on the contrary makes it imperative."

31. See Ecclesiastes 2:24-26; 3:12-13, 22; 5:18-20; 8:15; and 9:7-9.

ings are supposed to enjoy life to the full because that is their divinely assigned portion, and God calls one into account for failure to enjoy."[32] The Teacher is saying that God will judge us also to see whether or not we have sufficiently enjoyed his gifts.

He continues in verse 10 by commanding young people, "Banish anxiety from your mind, and put away pain from your body; for youth and the dawn of life are vanity." Youth is fleeting like a vapor. It's here one moment and the next it's gone. Before you know it, the dawn of life turns into the dusk of life. Therefore, while you can still do so, "banish anxiety from your mind." Anxiety is "that which angers, grieves or irritates."[33] Anxiety is that which undermines and prevents joyful living. For joyful living we have to banish anxiety from our *mind.* Physical pain can also prevent joyful living. So the Teacher commands, "Put away pain from your body." The TNIV translates, "Cast off the troubles of your body." In the next verse, the Teacher will mention "the days of trouble" when you can no longer get rid of the pain and suffering.[34] So while you are young, you should as much as possible banish anxiety from your mind and put away pain from your body. Let nothing diminish your joy. "Rejoice, young man, while you are young!"

To enable us to truly rejoice, the Teacher adds another command in chapter 12:1, "Remember your creator in the days of your youth." There is that word "remember" again. In 11:8 he wrote, "Even those who live many years should *rejoice* in them all, yet let them *remember* that the days of darkness will be many." Rejoice all the more by remembering that "the days of darkness will be many." In verse 9 he switched specifically to addressing young people, "Rejoice, young man, while you are young." And now in 12:1 he adds, "Remember your creator in the days of your youth."[35] Remember your Creator so that you may really rejoice when you are young.

The Teacher does not say, Remember *God,* but remember your *Creator.* The word "Creator" reminds us of the one who gave us everything we have. Our Creator is the one who made us and gave us life. Our Creator created the family and friends that surround and support us. Our Creator made this marvelous creation for us to live in and manage. Our Creator, the Teacher said earlier, gives us "wisdom and knowledge and joy" (2:26). He gives us "wealth and possessions," and enables us "to enjoy them" (5:19). Remember your Creator in order to truly enjoy life!

---

32. Seow, *Ecclesiastes,* 371. Seow, ibid., quotes a passage from the Talmud, "Everyone must give an account before God of all good things one saw in life and did not enjoy (*y. Qidd.* 4:12)."

33. Eaton, *Ecclesiastes,* 146.

34. "One should try to avoid pain and misery, for there will come a time when it will no longer be possible to avoid such unpleasantness." Seow, *Ecclesiastes,* 350.

35. "The expression 'the days of your youth' in 12:1a stands in contrast with 'the days of unpleasantness [trouble]' in 12:1b." Seow, ibid., 375.

The Teacher commands, "Remember your Creator *in the days of your youth.*" Especially when we are young it is so easy to forget the one who made us. It is so easy simply to think about ourselves. There are so many things to experience and learn and do. Well, here is the most important thing we can learn and do: "*Remember* your Creator in the days of your youth." To remember your Creator is more than to recall that there is a Creator, more also than to think about him from time to time. To remember your Creator means to bring to mind daily what your Creator has done for you and to act on this knowledge.[36] To remember your Creator is to make God central in your life[37] and to focus your life on doing his will.

In the remainder of this passage, the Teacher hammers home that we have to remember our Creator before it is too late. Notice how he repeats the word "before" in verses 1, 2, and 6. This has the effect of repeating three times, "Remember your creator." Notice verse 1, "Remember your creator in the days of your youth, *before* the days of trouble come, and the years draw near when you will say, 'I have no pleasure in them.'" Verse 2, Remember your Creator "*before* the sun and the light and the moon and the stars are darkened and the clouds return with the rain." Verse 6, Remember your Creator "*before* the silver cord is snapped."

The Teacher implies that days are coming when it will be difficult if not impossible to remember your Creator. He uses an imposing number of images to sketch those days. He begins in verse 1 with, "Remember your creator in the days of your youth, before the days of trouble come, and the years draw near when you will say, 'I have no pleasure in them.'" The days of trouble are the days of pain and suffering. They are the days when you can no longer "put away pain from your body" (11:10). They are the years when you will say, "I have no pleasure in them."

From this rather general statement the Teacher moves to a more specific picture in verse 2: Remember your Creator "before the sun and the light and the moon and the stars are darkened and the clouds return with the rain." Whereas he began in 11:7 with "*Light* is sweet, and it is pleasant for the eyes to see the *sun,*" now "the sun and the light"[38] are dimmed. The "dawn of life" (11:10) has

---

36. "When God 'remembered' Hannah (1 Sam 1:19), he did more than say, 'Oh yes, Hannah; I almost forgot you.' When he remembered her, he *acted* decisively on her behalf, and she who was barren conceived the child Samuel." Kaiser, *Ecclesiastes,* 118. For an extensive exposition of the word "remember," see H. Eising, "*Zākhar*," in *TDOT,* Vol. IV (1980), pp. 64-82.

37. Young people are "to commence early and develop a life-style in which God as creator and sustainer is central." Ogden, *Qoheleth,* 199.

38. "The light refers to the light of day. In the Hebrew Bible, the light of day is not equated with the sun. . . . The distinction between 'light' and 'sun' is made in Genesis 1, where light is called 'day' (Gen 1:4) and it existed before the luminaries of the sky were made (Gen 1:14-18)."

flown by. Dusk has come and gone. And now life can be described only as dark and gloomy. He pictures old age as a winter storm in Palestine.[39] The clouds roll in from the Mediterranean. Even in daytime it is dark: "The sun[40] and the light are darkened." And the night is pitch black: "The moon and the stars are darkened." Old age can be a season of darkness. There is no break in the clouds to let some sunlight through: "the clouds return with the rain." Elderly people receive one setback after another: they fall and break a hip; they get pneumonia; one of their children gets into trouble with the law; another has marital problems; a good friend dies. It is one depressing thing after another: "The clouds return with the rain." Remember your Creator in the days of your youth, before those days of gloom and darkness overtake you. It will be very difficult to remember your Creator in those days of darkness.

And things will get worse. The Teacher paints a depressing picture of the decline that takes place in old age.[41] Beginning with verse 3, he likens the body of an old man to a decaying old house. "In the day when the guards of the house tremble." What has guarded the old man's body all these years? His hands. His hands defended his body; his hands provided food for his body. Now, in old age, his hands tremble; they shake. They cannot work for the old man any more, let alone defend him.

"And the strong men are bent." The strong men that have carried the old man's body are his legs. In old age they can barely carry the weight any more. They bend. The old man becomes bowlegged.

"And the women who grind cease working because they are few." These

---

Seow, *Ecclesiastes*, 353. Cf. Leupold, *Exposition of Ecclesiastes*, 276, "In the Scriptures 'light' is quite generally a symbol of joy."

39. Seow, "Qohelet's Eschatological Poem," *JBL* 118/2 (1999), 209-34, and other commentators interpret these verses as "eschatological images" with "cosmic signs" of the Day of the LORD (see also Seow's *Ecclesiastes*, 353-82). But this is not convincing. Wisdom literature cannot be read as apocalyptic literature. The poem ends with the death of an individual, a man, *hā'ādām* (not "all," as the NRSV translates), with "mourners going about the streets" (12:5), and "the dust returning to the earth . . . and the breath to God" (12:7). To interpret this as "humanity proceeding to an 'eternal house'" and "the permanence of the end of human existence" (Seow, *JBL* 118/2 [1999] 234) is implausible. Moreover, it is hard to see how the possibly distant Day of the LORD would motivate a young man to remember his Creator in the days of his youth. Cf. Collins, *Proverbs, Ecclesiastes*, 107, "Ecclesiastes did not in fact expect the end of the world (Eccl 1:4 . . . 'the earth remains forever'). Eschatology, in the sense of matters relating to the end of the world or the messianic age, has no place in either Proverbs or Ecclesiastes."

40. In Ecclesiastes "the sun is mentioned thirty-five times [5 x 7], but now, in its final appearance, the sun is darkened." Seow, "Qohelet's Eschatological Poem," *JBL* 118/2 (1999) 213.

41. Cf. the description of old age in 2 Samuel 19:35, "Today I am eighty years old; can I discern what is pleasant and what is not? Can your servant taste what he eats or what he drinks? Can I still listen to the voice of singing men and singing women?"

"grinders" represent the old man's teeth, his molars.[42] Without modern dental care, the teeth would easily decay. The old man has but a few teeth left — not enough to chew the food properly.

"And those who look through the windows see dimly." Those who look through the windows are the eyes.[43] In the time before eyeglasses, the old man would see but dimly.

Verse 4, "When the doors on the street are shut." Shutting the doors on the street mutes the noise coming into the house. The doors on the street represent the ears.[44] The old man becomes hard of hearing.

"And the sound of the grinding is low." Having lost most of his teeth, the old man can eat only soft foods. "Thus no noise is made, for no hard bread or parched corn is being chewed."[45]

"And one rises up at the sound of a bird." The old man sleeps lightly. He rises early in the morning when the birds begin to sing.[46]

"And all the daughters of song are brought low." The old man cannot sing anymore. "The aging voice rasps or loses pitch or becomes weak."[47]

Verse 5, "when one is afraid of heights." The old man does not like to climb stairs anymore or sit on the cool roof of his home. His limbs are stiff, and he easily loses his balance. A fall can kill him.

"And terrors are in the road." Many roads in Jerusalem are extremely steep and rutted. The old man may trip and fall or he may be knocked off balance by a passing donkey. It is safer for him to stay in his home.

"The almond tree blossoms." The almond tree is one of the first to blossom in Palestine. From a distance it looks a like a human head with white hair.[48] The old man's hair turns snow white.

---

42. See Seow, *Ecclesiastes,* 355, for the linguistic connection in Arabic between "grinders" and "molar teeth." Leupold, *Exposition of Ecclesiastes,* 278, refers to this connection with the Greek word *mylai.* And Webster's dictionary mentions the same connection in English and Latin between grinders at the mill and molar teeth: "Molar . . . [L. *molaris,* fr. *mola* mill.] 1. Having power to grind; grinding."

43. "Elsewhere in the Hebrew Bible, the feminine participle *rō'ôt* always refers to the eyes . . ." Seow, *Ecclesiastes,* 356.

44. Most houses in Palestine had only one door to the street. "Significantly, *doors* is in the dual *(dĕlātayim),* encouraging an identification with some body part that has two parts." Longman, *Book of Ecclesiastes,* 271.

45. Kaiser, *Ecclesiastes,* 120. Another possible interpretation is that "the voice weakens with age" (Murphy, *Ecclesiastes,* 118), but this will be covered in the following phrase, "the daughters of song are brought low."

46. "The MT can be interpreted to mean that one rises from bed when the birds sing." Murphy, *Ecclesiastes,* 119; cf. p. 113, n. 4a.

47. Fox, *Ecclesiastes,* 80.

48. Leupold, *Ecclesiastes,* 281.

"The grasshopper drags itself along." The grasshopper is the "embodiment of lightness and agility."[49] Now it "drags itself along." The old man who was so agile in his younger days now has slowed to a crawl. He painfully moves with great difficulty.

"And desire fails." The Hebrew reads literally, "the caperberry fails." The caperberry was thought to stimulate the appetite.[50] But it does not work anymore for the old man. His appetite, his desire for food, fails. He eats but little. He begins to lose weight.

"Because all must go to their eternal home [i.e., the grave], and the mourners will go about the streets." Death is coming closer. The professional mourners are about to go out on the street to start their wailing.[51] The old man is dying.

The Teacher urges young people to remember their Creator before these days of darkness set in, days when they can feel their body deteriorate until they are close to death.

In verse 6 the Teacher lists a final "before." Remember your Creator "before the silver cord is snapped, and the golden bowl is broken." He compares human life to a precious lamp: the golden bowl is hanging from a silver cord. Silver and gold: life is precious. The golden bowl contains the oil that keeps the lamp burning. Suddenly one day "the silver cord is snapped," and the golden bowl crashes to the floor and is broken.[52] The oil flows out and the light is extinguished. Suddenly life is snuffed out.[53]

Another picture, this one about life-giving water. Especially in Israel with its long, dry summer, people were aware of the necessity of water. They would get this water from a fountain or from a cistern. But one day "the pitcher is broken at the fountain."[54] One cannot get life-giving water anymore. "And the

---

49. Kidner, *Time to Mourn*, 103.

50. See Seow, *Ecclesiastes*, 363. Seow also mentions its use as an aphrodisiac, but Whybray, *Ecclesiastes*, 167, cautions, "The idea that the caper has aphrodisiac qualities does not appear in extant literature earlier than the mediaeval Jewish commentaries (see Ginsburg, pp. 463-64). It is probably best, therefore, to take the phrase simply as referring to lack of appetite (Gilbert, pp. 105-6)."

51. "This may mean that they gather and walk up and down in front of the house of the dying man in the hope of employment." Whybray, *Ecclesiastes*, 167.

52. "These objects symbolize the awful impact of death as a state from which there is no repair, and so serve to dramatize the call to 'remember' before death comes." Ogden, *Qoheleth*, 206.

53. Cf. Proverbs 13:9, "the lamp of the wicked goes out."

54. "Broken pots have been found in Jewish tombs from the second temple period. . . . Since mortals were viewed as earthen vessels made by the divine potter (cf. Isa 29:16; 64:8; Jer 18:6; Gen 2:4b-7), it is likely that the shattering of earthen vessels during a funeral represented the end of life." Seow, *Ecclesiastes*, 366.

wheel [is] broken at the cistern." People would turn the wheel, the pulley, at the cistern to raise the water. But the wheel is broken. There is no water to be had. Life ebbs away.[55]

Note the repetition in verse 6: "broken," "broken," "broken." Life is broken beyond repair. Death is final and irreversible. Remember your Creator before you die!

The English pastor/poet John Donne (1572-1631) bought a coffin and placed it in his bedroom. Occasionally he would sleep in his coffin "as a reminder of his mortality and of the life of sin he had renounced."[56] We need not go to that extreme to know that we will all die, unless the Lord comes back before that time. We should honestly face the prospect of our death.

At some seminaries, students for the ministry have to prepare their own funeral service. It is a good way to have them face their own mortality. One day we will die. Then there is no more time to remember our Creator. Therefore it is urgent that we remember our Creator before we die.

Verse 7, "and the dust returns to the earth as it was, and the breath returns to God who gave it." According to Genesis 2:7-8, "The LORD God formed man from the dust of the ground, and breathed into his nostrils the breath of life; and the man became a living being." Here the Teacher pictures death as the reversal of creation. The dust from which God made us returns to the earth: dust to dust. And the breath of life which God breathed into us "returns to God who gave it." Our life is a gift from God. At death God takes it back again.[57]

The Teacher has sketched the reality of human deterioration and death so graphically for only one reason: to urge young people to remember their Creator before it is too late. Young people often think that they are immortal, that they have eternal life on earth. Not so, says the Teacher. Verse 8, "Vanity of vanities, says the Teacher; all is vanity." Literally he says, "vapor of vapors; all is vapor." A vapor exists only for a moment and then it's gone. Human life is like a vapor. Your life on earth is fleeting. It goes by in a flash. "Fleeting, fleeting, says the Teacher, everything is fleeting."[58] So don't waste any time. Savor the moment! Rejoice every day. Remember your Creator and all he has given you in order to rejoice each day. Establish this pattern in your life when you are young and certainly before old age and death.

The Old Testament Teacher thought that death was the end. From the New

---

55. "The picture of a fountain in disrepair suggests that the water of life can no longer be drawn, and the end has come." Crenshaw, *Ecclesiastes*, 188.

56. Paul S. Wilson, *A Concise History of Preaching* (Nashville: Abingdon, 1992), 113.

57. "God temporarily united body and spirit, and now the process is undone. We have in this verse no affirmation of immortality. According to Qohelet, death is the end." Longman, *Book of Ecclesiastes*, 273.

58. This translation is suggested by Provan, *Ecclesiastes*, 218. Cf. Psalm 103:15-16.

Testament we know that Jesus conquered death and that through him there is life beyond death. But the fact that there is life beyond death should not lead us to waste this present life on earth. On the contrary, we should concentrate all the more on rejoicing every day by remembering our Creator. For our Creator has given us much more than the Teacher knew in the Old Testament. In the fullness of time God sent his own Son to redeem his creation. "God so loved the world that he gave his only Son, so that everyone who believes in him may not perish but may have eternal life" (John 3:16). Jesus died for our salvation. And Jesus commanded us to remember his saving work. The night before he died, Jesus celebrated the Passover with his disciples. Jesus "took a loaf of bread, and when he had given thanks, he broke it and gave it to them, saying, 'This is my body, which is given for you. Do this in *remembrance* of me'" (Luke 22:19).

After his resurrection, Jesus sent his followers out to make disciples of all nations. He said to them, "Remember, I am with you always, to the end of the age" (Matt 28:20). "*Remember,* I am with you always." Jesus is with us each day, also in the days of darkness. Also when we get old and suffer from pain, isolation, and depression. Jesus is with us always, so there is always reason to rejoice. In fact, Jesus commands us to "rejoice and be glad," even when people revile us and persecute us: "Rejoice and be glad!" (Matt 5:12).[59]

Especially when we are young we ought to form the habit of truly rejoicing every day by remembering our Creator and what he has done for us. He has given us life; he has given us family and friends to support us; he has given us our daily bread and many things to enjoy; he has given his Son for our salvation; and when we die, Jesus has promised to receive us into his Father's house. Remember your Creator, and you cannot help but rejoice.

---

59. Cf. 1 Pet. 4:13, "Rejoice insofar as you are sharing Christ's sufferings, so that you may also be glad and shout for joy when his glory is revealed."

CHAPTER 16

Fear God, and Keep His Commandments!

Ecclesiastes 12:9-14

The end of the matter; all has been heard.
Fear God, and keep his commandments;
for that is the whole duty of everyone.

(Eccl 12:13)

In this final passage of Ecclesiastes an editor offers a compact conclusion to the writings of the Teacher.[1] Its focus on our obligation to "fear God and keep his commandments" makes this an excellent text for countering our culture's emphasis on human autonomy. The main challenge will be to interpret correctly the figures of speech in this passage. For example, verse 11 reads, "The sayings of the wise are like goads, and like nails firmly fixed are the collected sayings that are given by one shepherd." Are the nails fixed in the tips of the goads so that the intent is a single image or are there two images, goads and nails (tent pegs), each relating a different concept? Moreover, these "collected sayings . . . are given by one shepherd." Should the "one shepherd" be understood literally or metaphorically, that is, does the editor refer here to a literal shepherd, or does he have in mind Moses, Solomon, the Davidic Messiah, or God? A further challenge is to formulate a single theme, for, as in the previous passage, we again have two parallel imperatives: "Fear God, and keep his commandments" (12:13).

1. Commentators disagree whether it was one editor, or two — the first praising the Teacher (12:9-12) and the second correcting the Teacher (12:13-14), or even three editors. The position one holds on this issue has serious repercussions for one's interpretation of this passage. See pp. 8-9 above. For a listing of the proponents of the various positions, see Murphy, *Ecclesiastes*, 127-28, and Seow, "'Beyond Them, My Son, Be Warned,'" in *Wisdom, You Are My Sister*, 125-26, nn. 1-3.

Text and Context

As we saw in the last chapter, there is no consensus regarding the beginning of this passage. Although a few commentators begin this passage with verse 8,[2] there are good reasons to begin this text with verse 9. We have seen that 12:8 forms an inclusio with 1:2, thus marking the boundaries of the writings of the Teacher. A change in contents to the Teacher's person and work indicates that verse 9 begins a new unit. Moreover, 12:9-10 "refer to Qohelet in the past tense. . . . This appendix appears to look back at the book and to reflect on the work of the sage in whose name the book is written; it talks *about* Qohelet."[3] Therefore we can select as our preaching text Ecclesiastes 12:9-14.

In this epilogue the editor accentuates several thoughts in the Teacher's writings. He writes that the Teacher was "wise" (12:9), a claim confirmed by the Teacher himself (see, e.g., 1:13, 16; 2:15, 19; 7:23; 8:16). He also speaks of "the sayings of the wise" (12:11), as the Teacher did earlier in 9:17 (cf. Prov 22:17; 24:23). He likens the sayings of the wise to stinging "goads" (12:11), while the Teacher wrote earlier about "the rebuke of the wise" (7:5). The editor sums up the end of the matter as the command to "fear God" (12:13). The Teacher also commanded this in 5:7, "With many dreams come vanities and a multitude of words; but fear God." The Teacher further referred to the fear of God in 3:14, "all should stand in awe before him" (literally, "should fear him"); 7:18, "the one who fears God shall succeed with both," and in 8:12-13, "I know that it will be well with those who fear God, because they stand in fear before him, but it will not be well with the wicked . . . because they do not stand in fear before God." And finally, the editor speaks of God's judgment (12:14), as did the Teacher in 3:17, "God will judge the righteous and the wicked"; and especially in 11:9, "Follow the inclination of your heart and the desire of your eyes, but know that for all these things God will bring you into judgment" (cf. 8:12-13).

Literary Features

The editor begins verse 9 with "besides" *(wĕyōtēr)* — a word he will repeat in verse 12, "beyond this," thus dividing the epilogue into two subsections, verses 9-11 and 12-14.[4] In verses 9 and 10 the editor first describes the Teacher's per-

2. See, e.g., Leupold, *Exposition of Ecclesiastes,* 291, and Longman, *Book of Ecclesiastes,* 274.

3. Seow, "'Beyond Them, My Son, Be Warned,'" 125. Cf. Murphy, *Ecclesiastes,* 124, "The tone of these verses suggests a backward view, looking back at the work of Qohelet (including this book)."

4. See Murphy, *Ecclesiastes,* 124. Ogden, *Qoheleth,* 208, adds the following reasons for two subsections: "Verses 9-11 speak about Qohelet in the third person, and respect his learning and

son and work: the Teacher was wise and "taught the people knowledge": "weighing and studying and arranging many proverbs," searching for "pleasing words," and writing "words of truth plainly." He follows up in verse 11 with a proverb:

> The sayings of the wise are like goads,
>> and like nails firmly fixed are the collected sayings.

In addition to the inverted parallelism, we note two similes ("like goads" and "like nails"). The editor adds, "that are given by one shepherd," which is a metaphor.

The editor opens the second subsection with another *wĕyōtēr* (v. 12), which begins an instruction (imperative "beware"): "Of anything beyond these, my child, beware." He follows this up with another proverb as indicated by the parallelism:

> Of making many books there is no end,
>> and much study is a weariness of the flesh.

Finally he sums up in verse 13, "The end of the matter; all has been heard," followed by two imperatives: "Fear God, and keep his commandments." For obeying these commands he offers two motivations. The first is literally, "for that is the whole of everyone" ("duty" is not in the Hebrew text). The second motivation is a reminder of God's judgment: "For God will bring every deed into judgment, including every secret thing, whether good or evil."

With respect to repetition two items stand out. God is mentioned four times, twice explicitly and twice implicitly (see "Theocentric Interpretation" below). Further we note the cluster of three imperatives in the second half of the epilogue.

Textual Structure

This literary analysis enables us to sketch the structure of the text:

I. Description of the Teacher's person and works (vv. 9-10)
  A. The Teacher was wise (v. 9a)

---

role in the wisdom community. Verses 12-14 are imperatival. . . . . *Dibrê'* in vv. 9-11, used three times, refers to wisdom material including that of Qohelet, while *dābār* in v. 13 carries the general meaning, 'matter.' Qohelet and his contribution are the theme of vv. 9-11; vv. 12-14 address the faithful."

B. The Teacher's activities
  1. He taught the people knowledge (v. 9b)
  2. His work with existing proverbs (v. 9c)
    a. He weighed
    b. studied, and
    c. arranged many proverbs
  3. His work composing his own proverbs (v. 10)
    a. He sought to find pleasing words
    b. He wrote words of truth plainly
C. Proverb: The sayings of the wise are like goads (v. 11)
              and like nails firmly fixed are the collected sayings
          that are given by one shepherd

II. Instruction: three commands (vv. 12-14)
  A. Of anything beyond these, my child, beware! (v. 12)
    1. Motivational proverb:
        Of making many books there is no end
          and much study is a weariness of the flesh
  B. Two concluding commands (v. 13)
    1. Summation: The end of the matter
                all has been heard
    2. Fear God, and keep his commandments!
    3. Two motivations
      a. for that is the whole (duty) of everyone
      b. for God will bring every deed into judgment (v. 14)
        i. including every secret thing
        ii. whether good or evil

Theocentric Interpretation

In this short epilogue, the editor mentions God twice explicitly and twice implicitly ("one shepherd," v. 11, and his commandments, v. 13). At the conclusion of the first subsection, he speaks of "the collected sayings that are given by one shepherd." Since ordinary shepherds do not give collected sayings of wisdom, the word "shepherd" must be a metaphor for some other person. It could be Solomon, who, according to Proverbs 1:1 ("The proverbs of Solomon son of David, king of Israel"), gave Israel a collection of proverbs. But this would exclude the work of the Teacher, who, we have seen, is not Solomon. In verses 9-10 the editor has been speaking specifically of the work of the Teacher in collecting and composing proverbs, so these would certainly be included in "the collected sayings" of verse 11. Since the shepherd who gave "the collected sayings" is neither Moses nor Solomon, most commentators identify the shepherd with God. Accordingly, both the RSV and the NIV capitalize "Shepherd."[5] God was known as the "Shepherd of Israel" (Ps 80:1).[6] The Teacher also said that "*God* gives wisdom and knowledge and joy" (2:26; cf. Prov 2:6). In giving his people these collected sayings God is guiding them like a shepherd guides his sheep to green pastures.[7]

In the second subsection the last two imperatives refer to God twice: "Fear God, and keep his [i.e., God's] commandments" (v. 13). The editor highlights the importance of obeying this dual command with his first motivation, "for that is the whole (duty) of everyone." His second motivation mentions God again, "For God will bring every deed into judgment" (v. 14).

Textual Theme and Goal

The central message of the editor is found not in his description of the person and work of the Teacher — which was customary at that time[8] — but in his commands to "his son": "Beware!" "Fear!" and "Keep!" (vv. 12-13). With his reference to "the end of the matter" in verse 13, the editor seems to place the most weight on the latter two: "Fear God, and keep his commandments." This is also borne out by the following clause, "for that is the whole (duty) of everyone" (v. 13b). The singular "that" in this clause indicates that these two commands are "a single value."[9]

For the sake of formulating a single theme, the question for us is how these two imperatives are related. It seems clear that "fear God!" is the dominant command, for not only does the editor mention it first, but the Teacher himself has mentioned fearing God no fewer than six times.[10] Moreover, fearing God is the broader category; it describes one's attitude before God. Like Deuteronomy,[11] the editor links fearing God to keeping his commandments. In other words, the *attitude* of fearing God should result in the *action* of keeping his commandments. Further, the editor motivates obedience to these commands by pointing out that this is the whole (duty) of everyone and that God will bring every deed into judgment. We can capture the highlights of his message in the following theme: *Fear God, demonstrating it by keeping his commandments!*

5. The TNIV has "shepherd," with a footnote, "Or Shepherd." The NRSV has "shepherd," but dropping the capital may be due to a change in policy since, in 12:1, it also dropped the RSV capital in "Creator."

6. Cf. Psalm 23:1, "The Lord is my shepherd"; Genesis 49:24, "Shepherd, the Rock of Israel"; Isaiah 40:10-11, "The Lord God . . . will feed his flock like a shepherd."

7. See further "Typology" on pp. 301-2 below.

8. Loader, *Ecclesiastes*, 133.

9. Fox, *A Time to Tear Down*, 373.

10. Ecclesiastes 3:14; 5:7; 7:18; and 8:12-13 (3x).

11. See, e.g., Deuteronomy 6:1-2; 8:6; 10:12; 13:4; 31:12.

In order to determine the editor's goal, we need to ask the questions, Who wrote this text? To whom? And why? Concerning the author who wrote this text, Fox argues that it was the author/narrator of the Teacher's words himself.[12] However, there is some evidence to the contrary. Like the author of Proverbs, this editor addresses his reader(s) as "my son" (*běnî,* 12:12) — a form of address never used by the Teacher. This editor also links fearing God with keeping God's commandments (12:13) — a connection the Teacher never makes.[13] Moreover, the editor goes beyond the Teacher in clarifying God's judgment: "God will bring every deed into judgment, including every secret thing, whether good or evil" (12:14; cf. the Teacher's rather indefinite view about the judgment in 3:17; 8:12-13; and 11:9). The majority of commentators, therefore, opt for at least one editor as the author of this passage.

Source critics, as we have seen above, claim that they can discern the hands of one, two, three, and even more than eight editors.[14] Much of this digging behind the text is pure speculation and interferes with sound interpretation when one assumes that one of these editors is critical of the Teacher. As we noted in Chapter 1 (pp. 8-9), it makes little sense for an editor to pass on twelve chapters of the Teacher's reflections only to turn against them in a short epilogue. A better assumption is that the Teacher and the editor(s) speak with one voice.

As to the number of editors, since the presupposition of a single editor enables us to understand the entire passage coherently, there is no reason for presupposing more than one. This editor, who also introduced this book in 1:1, has added his epilogue not only to recommend the writings of the Teacher to his readers but also to summarize them and to drive home the main thrust of this difficult book. The editor's goals, then, are basically two: *to recommend the Teacher's writings to his readers and to urge them to fear God, demonstrating this attitude by keeping God's commandments.*

Ways to Preach Christ

Since this passage does not contain a promise of Christ, we shall check the remaining six ways for possibilities of moving from this particular theme to Jesus Christ in the New Testament.

---

12. See Fox, *A Time to Tear Down,* 363-77.

13. The Teacher uses the word "commandment" (*miṣwôt*) only once, referring to the king's command (8:5).

14. For defenders of one, two, and three editors, see n. 1 on p. 295 above. Krüger, *Qoheleth,* 208, mentions that "according to Jastrow [there are] more than eight editors who are different from the editor of the corpus of the book."

Redemptive-Historical Progression

The obligation that we fear God and demonstrate it by keeping his commandments changes only a little as we move from the Old Testament to the New (see "Longitudinal Themes" below), but the *reason* why we ought to do so changes dramatically. The editor motivated his readers to fear God and keep his commandments because "that is the whole (duty) of everyone, and God will bring every deed into judgment, including every secret thing, whether good or evil" (12:14). The editor motivated his readers to fear God with the threat of God's judgment.

The New Testament reveals that in the fullness of time God sent his Son Jesus to bear God's judgment for us with his suffering and death. Since the penalty has been paid, those who believe in Jesus need no longer dread God's judgment. Moreover, Jesus will be the judge in the final judgment. As Jesus himself said, "The Father judges no one but has given all judgment to the Son. . . . Very truly, I tell you, anyone who hears my word and believes him who sent me has eternal life, and *does not come under judgment*, but has passed from death to life" (John 5:22, 24).[15] After Jesus' death and resurrection we seek to revere God and keep his commandments not because we dread the coming judgment but because we are grateful for God's grace in providing salvation for us through his Son Jesus Christ.

Typology

This is one of only two passages in Ecclesiastes that may contain a type of Christ (the other passage is 1:12–2:26 with the figure of Solomon). This passage speaks of "one shepherd": "The sayings of the wise are like goads, and like nails firmly fixed are the collected sayings that are given by one shepherd." Nicholas Perrin[16] notes that the phrase "one shepherd" is used only three times in the Hebrew Bible, once here in Ecclesiastes and twice in Ezekiel. In Ezekiel the LORD promises Israel a glorious future under "one shepherd," another king like David:

> "I will set up over them *one shepherd (rʿh ʾḥd)*, my servant David, and he shall feed them: he shall feed them and be their shepherd. And I, the LORD, will be

---

15. Paul also links the final judgment with Jesus Christ, calling it "the day when, according to my gospel, God, through Jesus Christ, will judge the secret thoughts of all" (Rom 2:16). Cf. 2 Corinthians 5:10, "For all of us must appear before the judgment seat of Christ, so that each may receive recompense for what has been done in the body, whether good or evil."

16. Perrin, "Messianism in the Narrative Frame of Ecclesiastes?" *RB* 108 (2001) 51-57.

their God, and my servant David shall be prince among them; I, the LORD, have spoken." (Ezek 34:23-24)

"My servant David shall be king over them; and they shall all have *one shepherd (wr'h 'hd)*. They shall follow my ordinances and be careful to observe my statutes. They shall live in the land that I gave to my servant Jacob, in which your ancestors lived; they and their children and their children's children shall live there forever; and my servant David shall be their prince forever." (Ezek 37:24-25)

Assuming that the editor of Ecclesiastes had these passages in mind, his reference to "one shepherd" would function as a type of the coming Davidic shepherd king.[17]

The New Testament identifies Jesus not only as another King David ("Jesus the Messiah, the son of David," another number fourteen = *dvd* [Matt 1:1, 17]) but also as the shepherd king. Jesus himself said, "I am the good shepherd. The good shepherd lays down his life for the sheep. . . . I am the good shepherd. I know my own and my own know me, just as the Father knows me and I know the Father. And I lay down my life for the sheep. I have other sheep that do not belong to this fold. I must bring them also, and they will listen to my voice. So there will be one flock, *one shepherd*" (John 10:11-16; cf. Heb 13:20).

Analogy

Analogy offers the opportunity to link several aspects of the editor's theme to the teachings of Jesus. As the editor of Ecclesiastes urged his readers to keep God's commandments, so did Jesus. When the rich young man asked Jesus what he had to do to inherit eternal life, Jesus answered, "If you wish to enter into life, *keep* the commandments" (Matt 19:17). Jesus also said, "If you love me, you will *keep* my commandments" (John 14:15).

Moreover, as the Old Testament editor spoke of God bringing every deed into judgment, so did Jesus. Jesus said, "I tell you, on the day of judgment you will have to give an account for every careless word you utter; for by your words you will be justified, and by your words you will be condemned" (Matt 12:36-37).

17. "At the time of the writing of Ecclesiastes, when sapiential and apocalyptic genres come to overlap, the phrase 'one shepherd' would have been instantly recognized as a reference to the Davidic Messiah." Perrin, ibid., 57.

Longitudinal Themes

One can trace the theme "Fear God, demonstrating it by keeping his commandments!" from the Old Testament to Jesus Christ in the New Testament. Deuteronomy especially connected fearing God with keeping his commandments. Moses said, "Now this is the commandment . . . that the LORD your God charged me to teach you . . . so that you and your children and your children's children may *fear* the LORD your God all the days of your life, and *keep* all his decrees and his commandments that I am commanding you, so that your days may be long" (Deut 6:1-2; cf. 8:6). Later, he again emphasized the connection between fearing God and keeping his commandments: "So now, O Israel, what does the LORD your God require of you? Only to *fear* the LORD your God, to walk in all his ways, *to love him*, to serve the LORD your God with all your heart and with all your soul, and to *keep* the commandments of the LORD your God and his decrees that I am commanding you today, for your own well-being" (Deut 10:12-13; cf. 13:4; 31:12).[18] As we see in this passage, as well as others (e.g., Deut 6:5; 11:1), "to fear the LORD your God" includes "to love him."

In the New Testament Jesus also emphasizes that the fear, awe, of God includes love for God. In summarizing God's commandments Jesus places first our love for God: "'You shall love the Lord your God. . . .' This is the greatest and first commandment. And a second is like it: 'You shall love your neighbor as yourself'" (Matt 22:37-39). Later, John will make the same connection: "For the love of God is this, that we obey his commandments" (1 John 5:3).

Jesus also links our love for him with keeping his commandments: "If you *love* me, you will keep my commandments" (John 14:15). And again, "They who have my commandments and keep them are those who *love* me" (John 14:21).

New Testament References

The appendix of the Greek New Testament lists 2 Corinthians 5:10 as a reference to Ecclesiastes 12:14. The latter states that "God will bring every deed into judgment, . . . whether good or evil." Paul writes, "For all of us must appear before the judgment seat of Christ, so that each may receive recompense for what has been done in the body, whether good or evil."

---

18. Psalm 112:1 makes this connection with synonymous parallelism:

> Happy are those who fear the LORD,
>> who greatly delight in his commandments.

Contrast

Aside from the contrasts observed under redemptive-historical progression and longitudinal themes, there is no contrast between the message of this editor and that of the New Testament.

Sermon Theme and Goal

Since the New Testament does not change the basic message of the editor of Ecclesiastes, we can make the textual theme the sermon theme: *Fear God, demonstrating it by keeping his commandments!*

The editor's goals were "to recommend the Teacher's writings to his readers and to urge them to fear God, demonstrating this attitude by keeping God's commandments." Since Ecclesiastes is now part of the Bible, we should not have to recommend this book to our hearers, especially not at the end of a series of sermons on this book. We can, therefore, concentrate on the editor's second goal and make this our goal for the sermon: *to urge our hearers to fear God and to demonstrate this attitude by keeping his commandments.* This goal discloses the need targeted by this sermon: people do not fear God and disobey his commandments.

Sermon Exposition

The sermon introduction can reveal the target of this sermon by telling the story of a contemporary person, perhaps an atheist or agnostic, who thinks he is autonomous (a law unto himself) and therefore does not fear God and disobeys his commandments. Then raise the question if in our secular society we might be tempted to see ourselves as autonomous and not all that concerned about our relationship with God and obeying his commandments. Or, depending on the congregation, one can tell the story of a person who worshiped other gods than the true God and therefore neither feared God nor kept his commandments. Then raise the question if we might be tempted to serve other gods (family, money, possessions, sex, drugs), which interferes with our adoration of the true God and keeping his commandments.

Israel certainly failed in that respect. At Mount Sinai they heard God's law, "You shall not make for yourself an idol. . . . You shall not . . . worship them." A few weeks later, while still at Mount Sinai, they made a golden calf and worshiped it. Throughout its history Israel was tempted to disobey God and worship other gods. Ecclesiastes was written at a critical time in Israel's history. Israel was at the crossroads of a booming international trade. Fortunes could be made and lost overnight. People focused on making money and storing up wealth. The temptation was great to forget the God who had saved them from slavery in Egypt and to ignore his commandments.

In this final passage in Ecclesiastes an editor recommends the Teacher's reflections and summarizes his central message. Six times the Teacher mentioned the crucial importance of fearing God, standing in awe of God. The editor selects this basic idea but amplifies it by writing that we ought to "fear God *and keep his commandments.*"

But before he gets to this central point, he first, according to the customs of that time, praises the Teacher and his work. In our day we place endorsements on the cover of a book or in a foreword. In those days the recommendation was given at the end of the scroll in a postscript — an afterword. So the editor writes in verse 9, "Besides being wise, the Teacher also taught the people knowledge, weighing and studying and arranging many proverbs."

The Teacher, he says, was "wise." Wisdom in the Old Testament is not theoretical wisdom but practical wisdom; it is insight into how to make the most of each day. Psalm 111:10 claims, "The fear of the LORD is the beginning of wisdom; all those who practice it have a good understanding." The wisdom book of Proverbs likewise states: "The fear of the LORD is the beginning of wisdom. And the knowledge of the Holy One is insight" (Prov 9:10; cf. 1:7). The source of true wisdom is the fear of the LORD. That is where it begins, and from there it impacts all areas of life.

This wise Teacher did not keep his wisdom to himself, for the editor tells us in verse 9 that he "taught the people knowledge." How did he teach the people knowledge? In two ways. First by "weighing and studying and arranging many proverbs." "Proverbs" is a broad term. It included not only what we think of as proverbs but also parables, riddles, and sayings.[19] When the Teacher wrote his book, much wisdom literature existed in and around Israel. So he would *weigh* these existing wisdom sayings; he would put them in the balance scales and evaluate whether they reflected true wisdom. Next he would *study* them, examining them carefully. And finally he would *arrange* them, that is, set them in a certain order. Thus he would compose larger literary units.

Verse 10 tells us the second way in which the Teacher taught the people knowledge: "The Teacher sought to find pleasing words, and he wrote words of

19. "The 'proverb' *(māšāl)* had a wide range of meaning. It could include such things as Jotham's fable (Judg 9:7-15), the riddle of Samson (Judg 14:12ff.), the witticisms concerning Saul and David (1 Sam 10:12; 18:7), the 'proverb of the ancients' (1 Sam 24:13) and Nathan's parable (2 Sam 12:1ff.)." Eaton, *Ecclesiastes*, 153. The wide range of meaning of *māšāl* is also evident from the New Testament, where Jesus is described as teaching the people "many things in parables" (Mark 4:2). The Greek word *parabolē* is the equivalent of the Hebrew *māšāl*.

truth plainly." The "pleasing words" refers to words that were aesthetically pleasing. Think of the opening poem about the cycles of nature: "The sun rises and the sun goes down. . . ." And the central poem about the times: "a time to be born, and a time to die. . . ." And the closing poem about old age and death: "in the day when the guards of the house tremble. . . ." Think also of the picture language: human life is "a breath," "a vapor." It has very little substance. It's here one moment and gone the next. "The silver cord is snapped, and the golden bowl is broken." Think of the crisp proverbs and their parallelism. "The Teacher sought to find pleasing words."

But he was after more than just aesthetically "pleasing words." He was after more than entertainment. He had a serious message to convey. So his words also were "words of truth." And he wrote them "plainly," that is, honestly, correctly.[20]

Like the Teacher before him, the editor supports his statement with a fitting proverb. Verse 11, "The sayings of the wise are like goads, and like nails firmly fixed are the collected sayings that are given by one shepherd."

The shepherd who gave these collected sayings could be God himself. The Teacher also said, "*God* gives wisdom and knowledge" (2:26; cf. Prov 2:6). God was known in Israel as the "Shepherd of Israel" (Ps 80:1). Isaiah proclaims that God "will feed his flock like a shepherd" (40:11). David declares in Psalm 23:1, "The Lord is my shepherd." In giving his people these collected sayings God is guiding his people to green pastures. But while David declares, "Your rod and your staff — they comfort me," the editor has in mind a more painful tool of the trade.

He writes, "The sayings of the wise[21] are like *goads*." Goads were ancient cattle prods. They were large pointed sticks which the shepherd would poke into an animal to get it moving and turning in the right direction. Goads work because they can cause pain. The sayings of the wise likewise can be painful.[22] It was painful to hear the Teacher say, "Vanity of vanities . . . all is vanity" (1:2). It was shocking to hear him say that "the fate of humans and the fate of animals is the same; as one dies, so dies the other" (3:19). It was devastating to hear him proclaim, "Surely there is no one so righteous as to do good without ever sinning" (7:20). These goads sought to spur Israel to action and guide them in the right direction.[23]

---

20. "The point in our text . . . is the legitimacy and correctness of Qohelet's words." Seow, *Ecclesiastes*, 386.

21. "With rare exceptions, a *ḥākām* in the Bible is any person possessing special expertise or the virtue of wisdom, not a member of a professional class or one who subscribes to a particular school of thought." Fox, *A Time to Tear Down*, 353.

22. See Fox, *Qohelet and His Contradictions*, 325. Cf. Seow, *Ecclesiastes*, 393. The Teacher himself alludes to the pain when he speaks of "the rebuke of the wise" (7:5).

23. Some Jewish communities read Ecclesiastes on the Feast of Tabernacles while reliving

Parents sometimes use biblical sayings as goads to push their children in the right direction. When I was a youngster and would lose my temper, my mother would quote Proverbs 16:32b, "One whose temper is controlled [is better] than one who captures a city." When I would lip off, she would paraphrase Psalm 141:3, "Set a guard . . . , O LORD, . . . over . . . my lips."

The "one shepherd" of verse 11 could also refer to the Messiah. This phrase "one shepherd" is used only two other times in the Old Testament and there, in Ezekiel, it refers to the promised son of David, the shepherd king. In the New Testament Jesus calls himself "the good shepherd" (John 10:11). The good shepherd also used his words as goads. Jesus warned, "Beware of false prophets, who come to you in sheep's clothing but inwardly are ravenous wolves" (Matt 7:15). When Peter tried to keep Jesus from his road of suffering, Jesus rebuked him, "Get behind me, Satan!" (Mark 8:33). When Saul was on the way to Damascus to persecute the church, the risen Lord confronted him. Paul later described this experience: "I saw a light from heaven, brighter than the sun, shining around me and my companions. When we had all fallen to the ground, I heard a voice saying to me in the Hebrew language, 'Saul, Saul, why are you persecuting me? It hurts you to kick against the goads'" (Acts 26:13-14). Jesus' words, "Why are you persecuting *me*," hurt Paul like goads hurt cattle. And they made Saul reverse direction. The goads turned Saul the persecutor into Paul the missionary. "The sayings of the wise are like goads."

Verse 11 continues, "and like nails firmly fixed are the collected sayings that are given by one shepherd." With the word "nails" we can think of tent pegs.[24] Tent pegs or stakes are firmly planted into the ground to keep the shepherd's tent stable — to keep it from blowing away in a storm. So "the collected sayings" give stability and security to one's life. Think of the stability and focus for our lives provided by the Teacher's repeated pleading that we "fear God" — that we stand in awe of the almighty creator God (3:14; 5:7; 7:18; 8:12). Think of the comfort provided by his teaching that "it will be *well* with those who fear God" (8:12). Think of the security provided by his teaching that God is in control; he has set the times: "a time to be born, and a time to die" (3:2). Think of the focus provided for our lives by his constant exhortations that we seize the day and en-

---

the journey through the desert (see n. 4 on pp. 1-2 above). They may have recalled the painful goads God used on the long journey to bring his people into the Promised Land.

24. "While *nt'* regularly applies to 'planting,' it may also describe the driving of tent pegs into the ground (Dan 11:45)." Ogden, *Qoheleth*, 210. Some commentators understand the nails as fixed in the goads, so that verse 11 makes one point: painful correction. See, e.g., Fox, *Qohelet and His Contradictions*, 324-25. But the verse has two similes, "goads" and "nails," matched by two referents, "the sayings of the wise" and "the collected sayings." Therefore I think it better to understand this verse as making two points: painful correction and stable security.

joy God's good gifts.[25] The Teacher himself called the stability and security provided by "the collected sayings" *protection* and *life*. He wrote in 7:12, "For the *protection* of wisdom is like the protection of money, and the advantage of knowledge is that wisdom gives *life* to the one who possesses it." The goads prod us to movement in the right direction; the nails firmly fixed provide stability and security.[26]

Having highly recommended the Teacher's writings, the editor continues in verse 12, "Of anything beyond these, my child, beware." Beware of anything beyond these "collected sayings that are given by one shepherd."[27] In those days — and today — there were many writings that were passed off as wisdom. But the editor warns his readers to be careful with those other books. Beware of anything beyond "the collected sayings" that God provided. "The point of the warning is the sufficiency of the text. The sages have adequately given their instructions and there is, therefore, no need to go beyond them."[28]

Verse 12 next refers to these other books. "Of making many books there is no end, and much study is a weariness of the flesh." How well we know that there is no end to making many books. Our bookstores are filled to overflowing. Most people earning a Ph.D. have to write a book (a dissertation). And after that it is "publish or perish." But the editor has more in mind than that there is no end to the making of many books. He *evaluates* the activity itself. "Making many books is endless in the sense of leading nowhere."[29] It is pointless. "And much study is weariness of the flesh." Like making many books, much study is pointless. Much book-learning leads only to "weariness of the flesh." As the Teacher wrote earlier, "The toil of fools wears them out" (10:15). Like the Teacher before him,[30] the editor seeks balance. Wisdom is good, but it can be overdone.[31]

After his commendation of the Teacher's writings and his warning not to

---

25. Ecclesiastes 2:24-26; 3:12-13, 22; 5:18-20; 8:15; 9:7-10, and 11:7-10.

26. "This second simile complements the first: the teaching of the wise . . . may be said both to spur its recipients to action and to constitute a reliable basis for life." Whybray, *Ecclesiastes*, 172. Cf. Eaton, *Ecclesiastes*, 154, "The two words speak of the twofold effect of the Preacher's words, which stimulate to action and establish teaching in the memory."

27. "Instead of being a criticism of Qohelet, this verse is in fact praising his work; there is no need of more wisdom writings! In this view one should not postulate a second redactor responsible for vv. 12-14." Murphy, *Ecclesiastes*, 126.

28. Seow, *Ecclesiastes*, 388. See ibid. and pp. 393-94 for evidence that this warning was a standard formula, "an affirmation of the completeness and sufficiency of the text." Cf. Deuteronomy 4:2; 12:32 and Revelation 22:18-19.

29. Fox, *A Time to Tear Down*, 357.

30. "Do not be too righteous, and do not act too wise" (Eccl 7:16).

31. "Wisdom is to be embraced and employed wisely rather than used for one's own foolish ends." Provan, *Ecclesiastes*, 228, with references to 1:12-18 and esp. 10:15.

go beyond "the collected sayings," the editor is ready to conclude. Verse 13 "The end of the matter;[32] all has been heard. Fear God, and keep his commandments."

The Teacher had earlier urged us to "fear God." In chapter 3:14 he wrote, "I know that whatever God does endures forever . . . ; God has done this, so that all should stand in awe before him [literally, should fear him]." In chapter 5:7 he commanded, "With many dreams come vanities and a multitude of words; but fear God." In chapter 7:18 he encouraged, "the one who fears God shall succeed with both." And in chapter 8:12 he comforted, "I know that it will be well with those who fear God, because they stand in fear before him." To fear God is not to be terrified of God[33] but to stand in awe of him. God is the almighty Creator; we are mere creatures. God is eternal; we are a finite vapor. God is sovereign; we are dependent. God is holy; we are sinners. It is only fitting that we stand in awe of the eternal, almighty, creator God.

To fear God is to take God seriously, to acknowledge him in our lives as the highest good, to revere him, to honor and worship him, to center our lives on him. As Paul said to the philosophers in Athens, "In him we live and move and have our being" (Acts 17:28).

The editor explains how we can show in our lives that we fear God: "Fear God, and keep his commandments." The one leads to the other.[34] The attitude of fearing God leads to the action of keeping his commandments. We demonstrate that we fear God by keeping his commandments. If we really stand in awe of God, we will seek to keep his commandments. If we acknowledge God as our King, we will naturally seek to do what he says. Jesus also said, "If you love me, you will *keep* my commandments" (John 14:15).

Moses already linked fearing God with keeping his commandments. He asked Israel, "So now, O Israel, what does the LORD your God require of you?" And he responded, "Only to *fear the LORD your God*, to walk in all his ways, to love him, to serve the LORD your God with all your heart and with all your soul, and to *keep the commandments* of the LORD your God and his decrees that I am commanding you today, for your own well-being" (Deut 10:12-13).[35]

The editor next gives two reasons why we should fear God and keep his commandments. At the end of verse 13 he writes, "for that is the whole duty of everyone." The Hebrew does not have the word "duty," so it reads literally that fearing God and keeping his commandments "is the *whole* of everyone." It's not

---

32. "The use of this and similar phrases elsewhere (see esp. Dan 7:28) shows that it marks the end of the book or other major textual unit." Fox, *Ecclesiastes*, 85.

33. On fearing God see pp. 17, 22, and 126-27, esp. nn. 17 and 18.

34. "A knowledge of God leads to obedience; not vice versa." Eaton, *Ecclesiastes*, 156.

35. Cf. Deuteronomy 5:29; 6:2; 8:6; 13:4; 31:12. See also Psalm 112:1, "Happy are those who fear the LORD, who greatly delight in his commandments." Cf. Psalms 119:63 and 128:1.

just our duty, it's our *essence.* God created us to stand in awe of him and keep his commandments. That's God's design for us. We ought to fear God and keep his commandments because that's the way to fulfill God's plan for us. That's "the very best and fullest way of being human."[36]

In verse 14 the editor gives a second reason for fearing God and keeping his commandments: "For God will bring every deed into judgment, including every secret thing, whether good or evil." God will bring *every* deed into judgment, including *every* secret thing. Nothing will be excluded. God will judge our every deed, our every word, even our every thought.[37]

In the New Testament, Jesus also says, "I tell you, on the day of judgment you will have to give an account for every careless word you utter; for by your words you will be justified, and by your words you will be condemned" (Matt 12:36-37). And yet, things have changed for New Testament Christians. We should keep God's commandments not because we dread his judgment. "God so loved the world that he gave his only Son, so that everyone who believes in him *may not perish* but may have eternal life" (John 3:16). On the cross Jesus took upon himself God's judgment for sin. The penalty for sin has been paid. So dread of God's judgment is no longer a motivation to keep God's commandments. Moreover, the Judge is also our Savior. Jesus said, "The Father judges no one but has given all judgment to the Son. . . . Very truly, I tell you, anyone who hears my word and believes him who sent me has eternal life, and does *not come under judgment,* but has passed from death to life" (John 5:22, 24).

God's judgment is no longer a threat for Christians. So we do not seek to keep God's commandments because we dread the coming judgment. Rather, we seek to keep God's commandments because we are grateful for his grace, for saving us from that judgment.

This is "the end of the matter": After all God has done for us through his Son Jesus Christ, we love God. And when we love God, we will naturally seek to obey his commandments. John writes, "For the *love* of God is this, that we obey his commandments" (1 John 5:3). And Jesus declares, "If you *love* me, you will keep my commandments" (John 14:15).[38] We ought to show our reverence and love for God and for his Son Jesus by keeping his commandments.

---

36. "To fear God and keep his commandments is the whole man, the very best and fullest way of being human." Kugel, *The Great Poems of the Bible,* 323.

37. Cf. Paul in Romans 2:6, "God, through Jesus Christ, will judge the secret thoughts of all."

38. Cf. John 14:21, "They who have my commandments and keep them are those who love me."

Ten Steps from Text to Sermon

1. Select the preaching-text.
Select the preaching-text with an eye to congregational needs. The text must be a literary unit and contain a vital theme.

2. Read the text in its literary context.
Read and reread the text in its context and jot down initial questions.

3. Outline the structure of the text.
In the Hebrew or Greek text, note the major affirmations, clausal flow, plot line, scenes, or literary structures. Mark major units with headings and verse references.

4. Interpret the text in its own historical setting.
  a. Literary interpretation;
  b. Historical interpretation;[1]
  c. Theocentric interpretation.
Review your results with the help of some good commentaries.

5. Formulate the text's theme, goal, and need addressed.
  a. State the textual **theme** in a brief sentence that summarizes the *message* of the text for its original hearers: subject and predicate. What is the text saying?
  b. State the **goal** of the author for his original hearers. What is the text doing? Does the author aim to persuade, to motivate, to urge, to warn, to comfort? Be specific.
  c. State the need the author addressed — the question behind the text.

1. In order to avoid repetition, in the essays I combine historical interpretation with determining the author's goal in Step 5b.

6. Understand the message in the contexts of canon and redemptive history.
   a. Canonical interpretation: interpret the message in the context of the whole canon;
   b. Redemptive-historical interpretation: understand the message in the context of God's redemptive history from creation to new creation;
   c. Christocentric interpretation: explore the ways of (1) redemptive-historical progression, (2) promise-fulfillment, (3) typology, (4) analogy, (5) longitudinal themes, (6) New Testament references, and (7) contrast.

7. Formulate the sermon theme, goal, and need addressed.
   a. Ideally, your **sermon theme** will be the same as your textual theme (Step 5a). If Step 6 forces a change, stay as close as possible to the textual theme. Your theme will guide especially the development of the body of the sermon.
   b. Your **goal** must be in harmony with the author's goal (Step 5b) and match the sermon theme. Your goal will guide the style of the sermon as well as the content of its conclusion.
   c. State the **need** you are addressing. This need should be similar to the need addressed by the author. The need will inform the content of your introduction.

8. Select a suitable sermon form.
Select a sermon form that respects the form of the text (didactic or narrative, deductive or inductive) and that achieves the goal of the sermon.

9. Prepare the sermon outline.
If possible, follow the flow of the text (Step 3) in the body of the sermon. Main points, derived from the text, support the theme. The introduction should expose the need. The conclusion should clinch your goal.

10. Write the sermon in oral style.
Say it out loud as you write it. Write in oral style, using short sentences, vivid words, strong nouns and verbs, active voice, present tense, images, and illustrations.

An Expository Sermon Model

A. **Introduction** (usually no more than 10 percent of the sermon)
   1. Normally, begin with an illustration of the **need** addressed (Step 7c).
   2. Connect this illustration to the need of the present hearers.
   3. **Transition:** Show that this need or a similar issue was also the question behind the biblical text.
   4. State the **theme** of the text/sermon (Step 7a). For the sake of maintaining suspense, you may postpone disclosing the theme at the beginning (inductive development), but by statement and restatement, you must make sure that the hearers catch the point of the sermon.
B. **The Sermon Body**
   1. Expose the **structure of the text**. The main points, affirmations, moves, and scenes of the text (Step 3) normally become your main points in the sermon.
   2. The **main points** should usually support the theme and be of the same rank.
   3. Follow the **textual sequence** of the points unless there is good reason to change it, such as climactic arrangement (Step 9).
   4. Use simple, **clear transitions** that enable the hearers to sense the structure of and movement in the sermon.
      E.g., "Not only . . . but also. . . ."
      Or, "Let's first see. . . . Now we see secondly. . . ."
      Or, "Let's look at verse 8." "Now please look with me at verse 12."
   5. Use **verse references** before quoting the text so that the hearers can read along. Visual learning is nine times more effective than aural.
   6. Use some personal observations to **illustrate** difficult concepts or to make the point. Personal illustrations are more natural and powerful than canned illustrations about Bishop Whately. Personal experiences may also be used but be careful not to preach yourself but Christ.

C. **Conclusion**
  1. Be brief.
  2. Don't introduce new material. Narrow the focus; don't expand it.
  3. Clinch **the goal** (Step 7b).
  4. Be concrete. Can you offer some concrete suggestions of what the hearers can do in response to the Word preached?

"God Set the Times"

A Meditation on Ecclesiastes 3:1-15[1]

Ecclesiastes 3:1-15 is the familiar passage about God setting the times: "For everything there is a season, and a time for every matter under heaven: a time to be born, and a time to die; a time to plant, and a time to pluck up what is planted. . . ." The Teacher says that God "has made everything suitable for its time" (v. 11). The key question is, Why did God set the times?

The Teacher answers in verse 14, "God has done this, so that all should stand in awe before him." The sovereign God set the times "so that all should stand in awe before him." We all live through these different times: spring, summer, fall, winter, 2006, 2007, 2008. The seasons and the years fly by, and we hardly give it a thought. Do these fixed times really make us stand in awe before God?

I had just finished writing a chapter on this passage, when our son, Nathan, called from Winnipeg inviting us to come over to babysit. Well, he was really inviting Marie — she is good at that sort of thing — but I was the designated driver. Nathan and Heather, his wife, had just moved to Winnipeg and were expecting their third child. Since both of their children were born five days before the due date, they encouraged us to arrive before that date. So we drove the 1100 miles from Grand Rapids to Winnipeg and arrived nicely on time — five days before the due date. But no baby came that day, or the next, or the next. Then the due date came and went, and still no baby. The other children encouraged the baby to come out, but the baby did not control the date of her birth. Heather, understandably, became rather anxious to deliver the baby, but she also could not control the time. Finally, after fifteen days of waiting together, she went to the hospital to see if the doctor needed to induce labor. But the doc-

---

1. This meditation was published in *The Emmaus Walk: Meditations between Easter and Pentecost.* Grand Rapids: First Christian Reformed Church, 2008.

tor declined because, she said, inducement often leads to complications — similar complications, I suspect, as we experience when we plant our annual flowers too early in the spring. As with planting our flowers, we simply had to wait for God's time.

God often works his time by natural means. For the "time to plant" God uses the tilt of the earth and the earth's rotation around the sun. For the "time to be born," I learned, God uses a hormone that needs to be released in the mother's body. On the sixteenth day, at three o'clock in the morning, Nathan poked his head into our bedroom and whispered, "It's time!" Within two hours a healthy daughter/granddaughter was born. We often have to wait for God's time. "God has done this, so that all should stand in awe before him."

God also set the time when Jesus would be born. Paul calls this "the fullness of *time*" (Gal 4:4). Jesus began his ministry by preaching, "*The time* is fulfilled, and the kingdom of God has come near; repent, and believe in the good news" (Mark 1:15). Jesus was very much aware that God had set a time for his death ("my time is near"; Matt 26:18) as well as for his resurrection ("after three days"; Mark 8:31). Before Jesus ascended into heaven, his disciples asked him, "Lord, is this *the time* when you will restore the kingdom to Israel?" Jesus replied, "It is not for you to know *the times* or periods that the Father has set by his own authority" (Acts 1:6-7). God has sovereignly set the times. It is not for mere creatures to know these times. In God's time, Jesus will come again to establish God's kingdom on earth in perfection.

Given our failure to stand in awe before God, the Teacher encourages us to consider the hand of God in creation around us. God set the times to which we are subject. God set the time for our birth and the time for our death and every appropriate time in between. God also set the time for our resurrection, when Jesus returns to renew his creation (Matt 24:30-31). In other words, God is in control, and we are completely dependent on him. Awareness of our total dependence on God can help us "stand in awe before him."

"Have a Good Day!"

A Sermon on Ecclesiastes 9:1-12[1]

I prepared this sermon at the invitation of Dr. David Mosser for publication in his forthcoming book[2] on the topic of "helping pastors preach congregations/individuals through change." In preparing a sermon for a specific occasion or need, as we often do, the danger is that the need addressed will drive and skew the interpretation instead of the interpretation leading to the need addressed. Fortunately Ecclesiastes 9:1-12 is a good fit for "helping pastors preach congregations/individuals through change." For the Teacher who wrote Ecclesiastes sought to guide Israel when it had undergone major changes from a rather isolated, agricultural nation to a people caught up in international trade and intrigue in the third century B.C.

The sermon is designed as an expository sermon with inductive development from verses 1-6 to the theme revealed in verses 7-10, then again inductive development from the verses 11-12 to the theme revealed in the New Testament.

Text: Ecclesiastes 9:1-12

Theme: In view of the certainty of death and the unpredictability of life, enjoy to the fullest the days God gives you!

Goal: To urge the hearers, in view of the certainty of death and the unpredictability of life, to enjoy to the fullest the days God gives them.

---

1. The sermon quotes the NRSV.

2. The provisional title for the book is *Preaching Today in a World of Change: Preaching Change Strategies in the Modern Church.*

Dear Brothers and Sisters,

Our society and culture are undergoing changes at an ever-increasing pace. The changes are coming so fast that Beloit College began to produce an annual "Mindset List." The list reminds professors that references familiar to them may mean nothing to their students. The list notes that students entering college this year "have lived their whole lives in a digital world — where GPS has always been available, phones always have had caller ID, and tax returns always could be filed on line." These students have not used dial phones or IBM typewriters; they have not bought milk and cokes in glass bottles; they have not asked the gas station attendant to check the oil and add some air to the tires. They don't know Viet Nam, Watergate, and Johnny Carson. "Every time the list comes out, the school hears from people around the world who say it makes them feel as though life is passing them by."[3] Life is passing them by!

The rapid changes rob people of the joy of living. Changes in our society, in our churches, in our workplaces, in our families are often upsetting and difficult to handle. They can rob us of the joy of living.

But we are not the first ones to go through rapid changes. The Teacher who wrote Ecclesiastes addressed this book to Israel when it had undergone major changes. For centuries they had been a rather isolated, agricultural people. But all this changed in the third century b.c. Then they became caught up in international trade between Egypt and the rest of the world. People left their pastoral way of life and began to pursue riches. This led to fierce competition ("envy," 4:4), the loss of riches "in a bad venture" (5:14), corruption in high places and bribery (7:7), "the oppression of the poor and the violation of justice and right" (5:8). The Teacher writes about "the tears of the oppressed — with no one to comfort them!" (4:1). People began to complain that the former days were better than the present days (7:10). They wished they were back in the good old days. The changes had killed the joy of living.

In this particular passage the Teacher deals with changes that are beyond our control. He deals with the certainty of death and the unpredictability of life. In chapters 7 and 8 he has been struggling with the question why bad things happen to some good people. Why is it that some good people die young while some evil people live to a ripe old age? Why did John F. Kennedy die at such a young age? And Martin Luther King Jr.? How can a just God allow this to happen?

The Teacher ended chapter 8 with the conclusion that *no one* can find out all the work of God; "even though those who are wise claim to know, they cannot find it out." Then he begins chapter 9, "All this" — that is, that the righteous sometimes suffer while the wicked prosper and that we don't know the ways of

3. *The Grand Rapids Press*, August 25, 2008. See www.beloit.edu/publicaffairs/mindset

God — "All this I laid to heart, examining it all, how the righteous and the wise and their deeds are in the hand of God; whether it is love or hate one does not know."

No matter how much they suffer on earth, "the righteous and the wise and their deeds are in the hand of *God*." They are in God's care. Even the evil that befalls good people is not outside God's control. God is sovereign. God set the times: "a time to be born, and a time to die" (3:2). God is in control. So when good people suffer, it is a perplexing yet consoling thought that "the righteous and the wise and their deeds are in the hand of God." They are in God's care.

This is the problem, the Teacher continues: "whether it is love or hate one does not know." The righteous and the wise do not know whether their experience is an expression of God's love, God's favor, or of God's hate, God's anger. For example, when we become sick, is that a result of God's love or God's anger? When we are involved in an accident, is that a result of God's love or God's anger? We don't know, says the Teacher.

So he concludes at the end of verse 1, "Everything that confronts them is vanity [it doesn't make sense] since the same fate comes to all, to the righteous and the wicked, to the good and the evil, to the clean and the unclean, to those who sacrifice and those who do not sacrifice. As are the good, so are the sinners; those who swear are like those who shun an oath."

The same fate, that is, death, comes to all: "to the righteous and the wicked, to the good and the evil." Death comes to all. Whether we have been good or bad, in the end we all die. When the mass murderer Saddam Hussein was executed in 2006, we probably thought that he received his just deserts. But nine years earlier mother Teresa died. The person who had offered her life for the poor in Calcutta also died. Does this sound just? The same fate that comes to the wicked also comes to the righteous.

In verse 3 the Teacher bursts out, "This is an *evil* in all that happens under the sun, that the *same* fate comes to everyone." It is an evil, isn't it, that good people as well as bad people suffer the tragedy of death? We can sense his outrage.

But the Teacher adds, "Moreover, the hearts of all are full of evil; madness is in their hearts while they live, and after that they go to the dead." When he writes, "the *hearts of all are full of evil*," he may be thinking of God's observation before he sent the great flood: "The LORD saw that the wickedness of humankind was great in the earth, and that every inclination of the thoughts of their *hearts was only evil continually*" (Gen 6:5). Because the LORD saw that human hearts were full of evil, he said, "I will blot out from the earth the human beings I have created" (Gen 6:7).

Perhaps the Teacher is thinking back even further, to Paradise, where God gave but one commandment: "Of the tree of the knowledge of good and evil you shall not eat, for in the day that you eat of it you shall *die*" (Gen 2:17). Adam and Eve disobeyed God's commandment, and God's judgment followed: "You are dust, and to dust you shall return" (Gen 3:19). Since we have all inherited this evil disposition of disobeying God, we all deserve to die. As Paul puts it in Romans, "Death spread to all because all have sinned" (Rom 5:12). The so-called righteous as well as the wicked deserve to die.

The Teacher says, "madness is in their hearts while they live." It is madness to defy our Creator God. "And after that they go to the dead." The life of all persons will suddenly be cut off, and they go to the abode of the dead — to the grave we would say. It's a somber picture of the destiny of every person.

Still, there are advantages to being alive. The Teacher writes in verse 4, "But whoever is joined with all the living has hope, for a living dog is better than a dead lion." The living have hope that they may still experience some of the joy that the Teacher repeatedly advocates. Today we express this hope in a proverb, "Where there's life, there's hope." The Teacher also uses a proverb to support his point that the living have hope. He writes, "For a living dog is better than a dead lion." In the ancient Near East a dog was not a beloved pet but a despised scavenger. Today we might think of a rat — a loathsome creature. By contrast, the lion, just like today, was admired as king of the animal world. Now the Teacher says that the living have hope, for a living scavenger dog is better than a dead lion. In other words, even a dog's life is better than death, for the living still have hope.

Moreover, he says in verse 5, "The living know that they will die, but the dead know nothing." The living have "consciousness"; "the living are self-aware";[4] they "*know* that they will die, but the dead know *nothing*." In addition, the dead "have no more reward": they have nothing to look forward to; they have no future. "And even the memory of them is lost": their past accomplishments are forgotten by those who live later. The dead, as the Teacher pictures it, have no future and no past. They have nothing at all. It's as if they had never lived.

Verse 6, "Their love and their hate and their envy have already perished. Never again will they have any share in all that happens under the sun." This is probably the starkest biblical description of the dead: they are gone; no more rewards; soon forgotten; their passions perished; no more share in life.

Against this dark background of death that awaits us all, the Teacher has some important advice for the living. Verse 7, "Go, eat your bread with enjoyment, and drink your wine with a merry heart; for God has long ago approved what you do." In this book the Teacher includes seven passages[5] where he encourages us to enjoy the life God gives us, but here he is most urgent. We cannot

---

4. Longman, *Book of Ecclesiastes*, 228.
5. Ecclesiastes 2:24-26; 3:12-13; 3:22; 5:18-20; 8:15; 9:7-10; and 11:7-9.

waste a day! So the Teacher here puts his advice in the most urgent form. He casts his advice in the form of commands: Go! Eat! Drink! Enjoy! Do!

The first command is, "Go!" It's a wakeup call. Stop complaining about the changes! Stop nursing your anger! Stop brooding about your problems! Get past your anxiety and frustrations! "Go!"

The Teacher's second command is, "Eat your bread with enjoyment!" Enjoyment! Don't rush through your meals to get to the next task. Don't gulp down your food like a pig. God made us so that we not only need food in order to live but so that we can enjoy it. He has provided us with a rich variety of delicious foods. "Eat your bread with enjoyment!"

"And drink your wine with a merry heart." God has also provided a rich variety of drinks for us to enjoy. In Israel wine was a favorite. In other countries it may be coffee or tea. Whatever we drink, we should enjoy it. "Drink your wine with a merry heart!"

Some people think that this advice is the same as the pagan slogan, "Let us eat and drink, for tomorrow we die" (Isa 22:13; 1 Cor 15:32). But that slogan is shallow and selfish. The Teacher's advice is much more profound. He writes in verse 7, "Go, eat your bread with enjoyment, and drink your wine with a merry heart; *for* [because] God has *long ago* approved what you do." Long ago God approved our enjoyment of food and drink. The Teacher is probably thinking of the creation story. God placed the first human creatures in a beautiful garden and gave them many plants and fruit for food (Gen 1:29; 2:16). In other words, God not only created us with the need for food but he provided food with great variety so that we can enjoy it. Psalm 104 proclaims, "The LORD gives wine to gladden the human heart, oil to make the face shine, and bread to strengthen the human heart" (Ps 104:15). So if we enjoy our meals, God approves. He is pleased, because our enjoyment was his intent from the beginning. Our enjoyment was God's design. Our enjoyment is an expression of our gratitude to God for his provisions.

The Teacher continues in verse 8, "Let your garments always be white; do not let oil be lacking on your head." In a hot climate, white garments would reflect the heat of the sun, and oil would keep the skin from drying out. Here the white garments and oil are symbols of joy. When people were distraught and in mourning, they showed their sadness by wearing sackcloth and putting ashes on their head (see 2 Sam 13:19). By contrast, when people were joyful they showed it by wearing white clothes and putting oil on their head. In our culture we might show our joy by wearing colorful clothes and having a neat hairdo and a smile on our face.

In verse 9 the Teacher becomes more specific: "Enjoy life with the wife whom you love, all the days of your vain [your brief] life that are given you under the sun, because that is your portion in life and in your toil at which you toil under the sun." "Enjoy life with the wife whom you love!" Again, the Teacher may well be thinking of Paradise, where God made the woman as a partner for the man. We read in Genesis, "Therefore a man leaves his father and his mother and clings to his wife, and they become one flesh" (Gen 2:24).

Unfortunately, there have always been ascetic tendencies in the Christian tradition. In his day already, Paul found it necessary to oppose false teachers who, he writes, "forbid *marriage* and demand abstinence from *foods,* which God created to be received with thanksgiving by those who believe and know the truth." Paul adds, "For *everything* created by God [food, wine, marriage, sex] is good, and *nothing* is to be rejected, provided it is received with thanksgiving" (1 Tim 4:3-4). Enjoying God's good gifts is "true spirituality."[6]

In verse 10 the Teacher adds one more command, "Whatever your hand finds to do, do with your might; for there is no work or thought or knowledge or wisdom in Sheol, to which you are going." Sheol is the abode of the dead. So the Teacher reminds his readers again of death that awaits. "There is no work . . . in Sheol." All the more reason to "do with your might" "whatever your hand finds to do." For the Teacher, it turns out, hard work is part of the joy of living. Again he may be thinking of Paradise, where God put the man "in the garden of Eden to till it and keep it" (Gen 2:15). God created us to work. So purposeful work should give us satisfaction and joy.

In view of the certainty of our death, therefore, the Teacher urges us to seize the day: "Eat your bread with enjoyment!" "Drink your wine with a merry heart!" "Enjoy life with the wife whom you love!" And, "Whatever your hand finds to do, do with your might!"

In verse 11 the Teacher moves on to the unpredictability of our lives. "Again I saw that under the sun the race is not to the swift, nor the battle to the strong, nor bread to the wise, nor riches to the intelligent, nor favor to the skillful; but time and chance happen to them all."

Human life, he observes, is unpredictable. We would expect a race to be won by the swift. But the Teacher writes, "The race is *not* to the swift." Unexpected things happen in a race: the swift may trip; they may pull a muscle; they may be boxed in. In the recent Olympic Games, an American woman, Lola Jones, was expected to win gold in the hurdles. She was known to be the fastest in the world. But she tripped on the ninth hurdle and came in, not first but seventh. "The race is not to the swift." Life is unpredictable.

The Teacher offers a second example: "Nor is the battle to the strong." At the Olympic Games we also noticed that the strong did not always win gold. Sometimes they had to settle for silver, or bronze, or nothing. The battle is not always to the strong. There are exceptions. Life is unpredictable.

6. Provan, *Ecclesiastes,* 185-86.

From these examples of physical abilities, the Teacher moves to three examples of intellectual superiority: "nor bread to the wise, nor riches to the intelligent, nor favor to the skillful." The wise could be either teachers or artists. You would think that teachers would have bread, that is, a good livelihood. But there are exceptions. Life is unpredictable.

"Nor riches to the intelligent." You would expect that the intelligent, that is, the clever financiers and entrepreneurs, would be rich. But again there are exceptions.

"Nor favor to the skillful." The skillful are those who know how to make things. You would think that people would appreciate the skillful. But there are exceptions.

Why is it that there are so many exceptions to our expectations? We expect the swift to win the race; the strong to win the battle; wise teachers to have a good salary; intelligent entrepreneurs to be rich; and the skillful to be appreciated. Why is it that there are so many exceptions to our expectations? Why is life so unpredictable?

The Teacher answers at the end of verse 11, "but time and chance happen to them all." The problem is "time and chance," that is, "timely incidents." We would say, the problem is "accidents." We cannot control accidents. Accidents happen: runners can fall; the strong can get a cramp; wise teachers can lose their jobs; intelligent entrepreneurs can go bankrupt; the skillful can fall out of favor. The point is: we are not in complete control of our destiny. Accidents can cause us to fall far short of our goals.

In verse 12 the Teacher ends with the most tragic accident of all: "For no one can anticipate the time of *disaster*. Like fish taken in a cruel net, and like birds caught in a snare, so mortals are snared at a time of *calamity*, when it suddenly falls upon them." He likens this time of disaster to "fish taken in a cruel net." You may have seen pictures of how they fish in the East. From their boats or even standing in the sea close to the shore, fishermen will cast a round net into the air. The net seems to hover in the air for a moment; then suddenly it plummets into the water on unwary fish. A time of disaster for the unsuspecting fish.

The time of disaster is also "like birds caught in a snare." You have probably seen pictures of simple snares: a noose staked into the ground or tied to a tree. The birds go about their business, feeding on seeds on the ground. Since there are no predators around, the birds are at ease. A bird casually sticks its head through the noose and it tightens around its neck until it chokes him. A time of disaster. Caught in a snare!

"Like fish taken in a cruel net, and like birds caught in a snare, so mortals are snared at a time of calamity, when it suddenly falls upon them." All of a sudden, death can overtake us. We may not suspect a thing; we are just going about our business. Suddenly the net falls on us; we are caught in the snare — and life is over.

With not only the certainty of death in view but now also its suddenness and unexpectedness, the Teacher urges us all the more to enjoy the life God gives us. Enjoy to the fullest the days God gives you!

The New Testament, of course, teaches us that death is not the end but a new beginning: our entrance into eternal life. But that does not change the message that we ought to make every effort to enjoy the days God gives us on this earth. Jesus himself enjoyed "eating and drinking" (see Matt 11:18-19). On several occasions he provided bread for the masses to enjoy (Matt 14:13-21; 15:32-39). He even turned plain water into "good wine" for people to enjoy at a wedding (John 2:9-11).

Jesus also teaches us not to worry about food and drink. Worry about where the next meal will come from kills any enjoyment. Jesus urges us: "Do not worry, saying, 'What will we eat?' or 'What will we drink?' . . . Indeed your heavenly Father knows that you need all these things. But strive first for the kingdom of God and his righteousness, and all these things will be given to you as well" (Matt 6:31-33). Food and drink will be *given* us.

Since food and drink are *gifts* from our heavenly Father, we should enjoy them. If we do not enjoy God's gifts, we dishonor the Giver. Then we are like children who receive gifts at Christmas, rip the wrapping off one and toss it aside in order to grab the next gift. Our enjoyment of God's gifts is an expression of our gratitude to him. The early Christians understood this well. We read in Acts 2:46, "Day by day, as they spent much time together in the temple, they broke bread at home and ate their food with *glad* and generous hearts."

Not only are we to enjoy our food and drink; if we are married, we must also make a point of enjoying life with our spouse. Jesus honored marriage by being present at the wedding in Cana (John 2:1-11). And Paul enjoins us, "Husbands, love your wives, just as Christ loved the church and gave himself up for her" (Eph 5:25).

And finally, we must also enjoy our work and do it with all our might. The Teacher motivated us to work with all our might because, he wrote, "there is no work . . . in Sheol," that is, in the abode of the dead. Jesus says something similar. He says, "We must work the works of him who sent me while it is day; night is coming when no one can work" (John 9:4). Jesus has in mind the night, the darkness of death, that will soon overtake him as well as his disciples. Unless the Lord returns first, each one of us will die. Before that hour strikes, Jesus says, we must work the works God has assigned us. Paul adds, "Whatever your task, put yourselves into it, as done *for the Lord* and not for your masters, since you know that from the Lord you will receive the inheritance as your reward; you serve the Lord Christ" (Col 3:23-24).

Because Jesus died and rose to save us from our enslavement to sin and to reconcile us to God, we can begin to live as God intended at the beginning: enjoying our food and drink, enjoying life with our spouse, and enjoying our work.

Unfortunately, we so often fritter away our days with meaningless pursuits: frustrations about all the changes we encounter, worries about losing our homes to foreclosure or losing our jobs, anger, grudges, petty arguments — you name it. We waste our days as if there were an unlimited supply. You may have heard of people who were told by their doctor that they had only a few months to live. Suddenly their outlook on life changed. They lived each day as if it could be their last. They tried to live each day to the full.

When White House secretary Tony Snow returned to work after five weeks of cancer treatment, he said, "Not everybody will survive cancer. But on the other hand, you have got to realize you've got the gift of life, so make the most of it."[7] Tony died a year later at the age of 53. "You've got the gift of life, so make the most of it." Each day *could* be our last. Therefore, enjoy each day to the full. We ought to remind ourselves every morning when we wake up: "This is the day that the LORD has made; let us rejoice and be glad in it" (Ps 118:24).

---

7. Quoted in *Time*, July 28, 2008.

Select Bibliography

Bartholomew, Craig G. *Reading Ecclesiastes: Old Testament Exegesis and Hermeneutical Theory.* Rome: Pontificio Istituto Biblico, 1998.

Blenkinsopp, Joseph. "Ecclesiastes 3:1-15: Another Interpretation." *JSOT* 66 (1995) 55-64.

Brown, Stephen. "The Structure of Ecclesiastes." *EvRT* 14/3 (1990) 195-208.

Brown, William P. *Ecclesiastes.* Louisville: John Knox, 2000.

———. "'Whatever Your Hand Finds to Do': Qoheleth's Work Ethic." *Int* 55/3 (2001) 271-84.

Collins, John J. *Proverbs and Ecclesiastes.* Atlanta: John Knox, 1980.

Crenshaw, James L. "The Wisdom Literature." In *The Hebrew Bible and Its Modern Interpreters.* Eds. Douglas A. Knight and Gene M. Tucker. Philadephia: Fortress, 1985. Pp. 369-407.

———. *Ecclesiastes: A Commentary.* Philadelphia: Westminster, 1987.

Davis, Ellen F. *Proverbs, Ecclesiastes, and the Song of Songs.* Louisville: Westminster John Knox, 2000.

Delitzsch, Franz. *Commentary on the Song of Songs and Ecclesiastes.* Trans. M. G. Easton. Grand Rapids: Eerdmans, n.d.

Dillard, Raymond B., and Tremper Longman III. *An Introduction to the Old Testament.* Grand Rapids: Zondervan, 1994.

Dorsey, David A. *The Literary Structure of the Old Testament: A Commentary on Genesis–Malachi.* Grand Rapids: Baker, 1999.

Eaton, Michael A. *Ecclesiastes: An Introduction and Commentary.* Downers Grove: InterVarsity Press, 1983.

Farmer, Kathleen Anne. *Who Knows What Is Good?: A Commentary on the Books of Proverbs and Ecclesiastes.* Grand Rapids: Eerdmans, 1991.

Fletcher, Douglas K. "Ecclesiastes 5:1-7." *Int* 55/3 (2001) 296-98.

Fox, Michael V. "The Meaning of *Hebel* for Qohelet." *JBL* 105/3 (1986) 409-27.

———. "Qohelet 1:4." *JSOT* 40 (1988) 109.

———. "Aging and Death in Qohelet 12." *JSOT* 42 (1988) 55-77. Reprinted in *Reflecting with Solomon: Selected Studies on the Book of Ecclesiastes.* Ed. Roy B. Zuck. Grand Rapids: Baker, 1994. Pp. 381-99.

————. *Qohelet and His Contradictions.* Sheffield: Almond, 1989.

————. "What Happens in Qohelet 4:13-16." *Journal of Hebrew Scriptures* (1996-97) 5 pages in E Journal.

————. "The Inner Structure of Qohelet's Thought." In *Qohelet in the Context of Wisdom.* Ed. Antoon Schoors. Leuven: Peeters, Leuven University, 1998. Pp. 225-38.

————. *A Time to Tear Down and a Time to Build Up: A Rereading of Ecclesiastes.* Grand Rapids: Eerdmans, 1999.

————. *Ecclesiastes: The Traditional Hebrew Text with the New JPS Translation.* Philadelphia: Jewish Publication Society, 2004.

Fredericks, Daniel C. "Chiasm and Parallel Structure in Qoheleth 5:9–6:9." *JBL* 108/1 (1989) 17-35.

————. "Life's Storms and Structural Unity in Qoheleth 11:1–12:8." *JSOT* 52 (1991) 95-114.

Garrett, Duane A. "Preaching Wisdom." In *Reclaiming the Prophetic Mantle: Preaching the Old Testament Faithfully.* Ed. George L. Klein. Nashville: Broadman, 1992. Pp. 107-26.

————. *Proverbs, Ecclesiastes, Song of Songs.* Nashville: Broadman, 1993.

Glenn, Donald R. "Mankind's Ignorance: Ecclesiastes 8:1–10:11." In *Reflecting with Solomon: Selected Studies on the Book of Ecclesiastes.* Ed. Roy B. Zuck. Grand Rapids: Baker, 1994. Pp. 321-29.

Goldberg, Louis. *Ecclesiastes.* Grand Rapids: Zondervan, 1983.

Goldsworthy, Graeme. *Gospel and Kingdom: A Christian Interpretation of the Old Testament.* Exeter: Paternoster, 1983.

————. *Gospel and Wisdom: Israel's Wisdom Literature in the Christian Life.* Exeter: Paternoster, 1987.

Gordis, Robert. *Koheleth — The Man and His World.* New York: Jewish Theological Seminary of America, 1951.

Gowan, Donald E. *Reclaiming the Old Testament for the Christian Pulpit.* Atlanta: John Knox, 1980.

Greidanus, Sidney. *The Modern Preacher and the Ancient Text: Interpreting and Preaching Biblical Literature.* Grand Rapids: Eerdmans, 1988.

————. *Preaching Christ from the Old Testament: A Contemporary Hermeneutical Method.* Grand Rapids: Eerdmans, 1999.

————. *Preaching Christ from Genesis: Foundations for Expository Sermons.* Grand Rapids: Eerdmans, 2007.

Hendry, G. S. "Ecclesiastes." In *New Bible Commentary Revised.* Eds. D. Guthrie and J. A. Motyer. Grand Rapids: Eerdmans, 1970. Pp. 570-78.

Hengstenberg, E. W. *Commentary on Ecclesiastes.* Trans. D. W. Simon. Philadelphia: Smith, English, 1860.

Holm-Nielsen, Svend. "On the Interpretation of Qoheleth in Early Christianity." *VT* 24/2 (1974) 168-77.

Huwiler, Elizabeth. "Ecclesiastes." In *Proverbs, Ecclesiastes, Song of Songs.* Eds. Roland E. Murphy and Elizabeth Huwiler. Peabody: Hendrickson, 1999. Pp. 159-218.

Johnson, Robert K. "Confessions of a Workaholic: A Reappraisal of Qoheleth." *CBQ* 38 (1976) 14-28.

Jones, Scott C. "Qohelet's Courtly Wisdom: Ecclesiastes 8:1-9." *CBQ* 68 (2006) 211-28.

Kaiser, Walter C., Jr. *Ecclesiastes: Total Life.* Chicago: Moody, 1979.

————. "Integrating Wisdom Theology into Old Testament Theology: Ecclesiastes 3:10-

15." In *A Tribute to Gleason Archer*. Eds. Walter C. Kaiser and Ronald F. Youngblood. Chicago: Moody, 1986. Pp. 197-209.

Kidner, Derek. *A Time to Mourn, and a Time to Dance: Ecclesiastes and the Way of the World*. Downers Grove: InterVarsity Press, 1976.

―――. *The Wisdom of Proverbs, Job, and Ecclesiastes: An Introduction to Wisdom Literature*. Downers Grove: InterVarsity Press, 1985.

Krüger, Thomas. *Qoheleth: A Commentary*. Trans. O. C. Dean Jr. Minneapolis: Fortress, 2004.

Kugel, James. *Great Poems of the Bible*. New York: Free Press, 1999.

Leupold, Herbert Carl. *Exposition of Ecclesiastes*. Grand Rapids: Baker, 1952.

Limburg, James. *Encountering Ecclesiastes: A Book for Our Time*. Grand Rapids: Eerdmans, 2006.

Loader, J. A. *Ecclesiastes: A Practical Commentary*. Trans. John Vriend. Grand Rapids: Eerdmans, 1986.

Lohfink, Norbert. "Qoheleth 5:17-19 — Revelation by Joy." *CBQ* 52 (1990) 625-35.

Longman, Tremper, III. *The Book of Ecclesiastes*. Grand Rapids: Eerdmans, 1998.

Murphy, Roland Edmund. *Wisdom Literature: Job, Proverbs, Ruth, Canticles, Ecclesiastes, and Esther*. Grand Rapids: Eerdmans, 1981.

―――. *Ecclesiastes*. Dallas: Word, 1992.

Ogden, Graham S. "Qoheleth's Use of the 'Nothing Is Better' Form." *JBL* 98/3 (1979) 339-50.

―――. "Qoheleth 9:17–10:20: Variations on the Theme of Wisdom's Strength and Vulnerability." *VT* 30/1 (1980) 27-37.

―――. "Qoheleth 11:1-6." *VT* 33/2 (1983) 222-30.

―――. "The Mathematics of Wisdom: Qoheleth 4:1-12." *VT* 34/4 (1984) 446-53.

―――. *Qoheleth*. Sheffield: JSOT Press, 1987.

―――, and Lynell Zogbo. *A Handbook on Ecclesiastes:* New York: United Bible Societies, 1998.

Parsons, Greg W. "Guidelines for Understanding and Proclaiming the Book of Ecclesiastes." *BSac* 160 (2003) 159-73 and 283-304.

Perdue, Leo G. *Wisdom Literature: A Theological History*. Louisville: Westminster John Knox, 2007.

Perrin, Nicholas. "Messianism in the Narrative Frame of Ecclesiastes?" *RB* 108 (2001) 51-57.

Provan, Iain W. *Ecclesiastes, Song of Songs* (The NIV Application Commentary). Grand Rapids: Zondervan, 2001.

Rad, Gerhard von. *Old Testament Theology*. Vol. 1. Edinburgh: Oliver and Boyd, 1962.

―――. *Wisdom in Israel*. Nashville: Abingdon, 1972.

Reitman, James S. "The Structure and Unity of Ecclesiastes." *BSac* 154 (1997) 297-319.

Ricker, Bob, and Ron Pitkin. *A Time for Every Purpose*. Nashville: Nelson, 1983.

Ryken, Leland, "Ecclesiastes." In *A Complete Literary Guide to the Bible*. Eds. Leland Ryken and Tremper Longman III. Grand Rapids: Zondervan, 1993. Pp. 268-80.

Salyer, Gary D. *Vain Rhetoric: Private Insight and Public Debate in Ecclesiastes*. JSOT Sup 327. Sheffield: Sheffield Academic, 2001.

Schoors, Antoon. "Koheleth: A Perspective of Life after Death?" *ETL* 61/4 (1985) 295-303.

Seow, Choon Leong. "The Socioeconomic Context of 'The Preacher's' Hermeneutic." *PSBul* 17/2 (1996) 168-95.

————. *Ecclesiastes: A New Translation with Introduction and Commentary.* New York: Doubleday, 1997.

————. "'Beyond Them, My Son, Be Warned': The Epilogue of Qohelet Revisited." In *Wisdom, You Are My Sister.* Ed. Michael L. Barre. Washington: Catholic Biblical Association, 1997. Pp. 125-41.

————. "Qohelet's Eschatological Poem." *JBL* 118/2 (1999) 209-34.

————. "Theology When Everything Is out of Control." *Int* 55/3 (2001) 237-49.

Shepherd, Jerry. "Ecclesiastes." In *The Expositor's Bible Commentary,* Vol. 6. Eds. Tremper Longman III and David E. Garland. Grand Rapids: Zondervan, 2008. Pp. 253-365.

Towner, W. Sibley. "The Book of Ecclesiastes." In *The New Interpreter's Bible,* Vol. 5. Nashville: Abingdon, 1997. Pp. 265-360.

Van Leeuwen, Raymond C. Notes for "Ecclesiastes." In *The Harper Collins Study Bible.* New York: Harper Collins, 1993.

Verheij, Arian. "Paradise Retried: On Qohelet 2:4-6." *JSOT* 50 (1991) 113-15.

Whybray, Roger Norman. "The Identification and Use of Quotations in Ecclesiastes." *VTSup* 32 (1981) 435-51. Reprinted in *Reflecting with Solomon: Selected Studies on the Book of Ecclesiastes.* Ed. Roy B. Zuck. Grand Rapids: Baker, 1994. Pp. 185-99.

————. "Qoheleth, Preacher of Joy." *JSOT* 23 (1982) 87-98.

————. "Ecclesiastes 1:5-7 and the Wonders of Nature." *JSOT* 41 (1988) 105-12.

————. *Ecclesiastes.* Grand Rapids: Eerdmans, 1989.

————. "Qoheleth as a Theologian." In *Qohelet in the Context of Wisdom.* Ed. Antoon Schoors. Leuven: Peeters, Leuven University, 1998. Pp. 239-65.

Wright, Addison G. "The Riddle of the Sphinx: The Structure of the Book of Qohelet." *CBQ* 30 (1968) 313-34.

————. "The Riddle of the Sphinx Revisited: Numerical Patterns in the Book of Qohelet," *CBQ* 42 (1980) 38-51.

————. "The Poor but Wise Youth and the Old but Foolish King (Qoh 4:13-16)." In *Wisdom, You Are My Sister.* Ed. Michael L. Barre. Washington, DC: Catholic Biblical Association, 1997. Pp. 142-54.

Wright, J. Robert. *Proverbs, Ecclesiastes, Song of Solomon.* Downers Grove: InterVarsity Press, 2005.

Wright J. Stafford. "The Interpretation of Ecclesiastes." *EvQ* 18/1 (1946) 18-34.

Young, Edward J. *Introduction to the Old Testament.* Grand Rapids: Eerdmans, 1964.

Scripture Index

Bold page numbers indicate detailed analysis and exposition of the passage.

Subject Index

Bold page numbers indicate key definition, description,
or explanation, sometimes in the footnotes.

Targets for Sermons

For the primary target addressed in each identified preaching text, see the Subject Index above, Sermon: need addressed. Bold page numbers indicate key description, explanation, or extended exposition of the topic.

Topics for Sermons

Bold page numbers indicate extensive exposition of the topic.